Semantic Web Standards

This figure illustrates the Semantic Web layered technology architecture of Web standards, which are described in the table below.

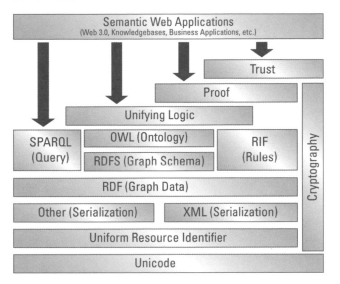

Standard	Description
RDF	Resource Description Framework is the core Semantic Web language for defining data. Data is linked as a data graph using triples. Triples consist of a subject, a predicate, and an object and are uniquely identified by a URI.
RDFS	RDF Schema is the data modeling language for RDF.
OWL	Web Ontology Language is an advanced data modeling language for RDF.
SPARQL	The Simple Protocol and RDF Query Language.
RIF	Rule Interchange Format defines business rule languages for RDF and OWL (not standardized as of Jan 2009).
GRDDL	Gleaning Resource Descriptions from Dialects of Languages — for transforming XML and XHTML to RDF.
SAWSDL	Semantic Annotations for Web service definitions (WSDL) — typically used with RDF or OWL models.
RDFa	RDF Attributes is for inserting structured RDF data inside XHTML pages.

Semantic Web For Dummies®

Important RDF and OWL Keywords

Keyword	What It Does
rdfs:Resource	Top-level class for everything modeled in RDF.
rdfs:Class	The classification of resources in RDF. (For example, rdfs:Class is an instance of rdfs:Class.)
rdfs:Literal	Class of literal values such as strings and integers.
rdf:Property	Class of RDF properties. All RDF properties are instances of rdfs:Class. Properties define RDF relationships.
rdf:type	An instance of rdf:Property identifying a resource as a class.
rdfs:subClassOf	An instance of rdf:Property identifying all instances of a class are instances of another class (for example, C1 rdfs:CubClass C2).
rdfs:subPropertyOf	Used to state that all resources related by one property are related by another.
owl:Thing	Top-level class for everything modeled in OWL.
owl:Class	The classification, or sets, of things modeled in OWL.
owl:equivalentClass	Denotes that two classes have precisely the same instances.
owl:imports	Used to import the namespace and data from another model.
owl:intersectionOf	Class constructor set definition to find the intersecting instances of two or more classes.
owl:unionOf	Class constructor set definition to find the union of instances among two or more classes.
owl:inverseOf	Relationship between two properties that one implies the other. (For example, in Jeff Produces Box, Produces implies hasMaker, and therefore Box hasMaker Jeff — Produces is inverse of hasMaker.)
owl:sameAs	Used to specify that an instance is exactly the same as another.
owl:TransitiveProperty	Defines transitive properties/relationships (for example, if A then B, and B then C, then also A then C).

For Dummies: Bestselling Book Series for Beginners

Semantic Web

FOR

DUMMIES®

by Jeffrey T. Pollock

WILEY

Wiley Publishing, Inc.

Semantic Web For Dummies®

Published by
Wiley Publishing, Inc.
111 River Street
Hoboken, NJ 07030-5774
www.wiley.com

Copyright © 2009 by Wiley Publishing, Inc., Indianapolis, Indiana

Published by Wiley Publishing, Inc., Indianapolis, Indiana

Published simultaneously in Canada

For general information on our other products and services, please contact our Customer Care Department within the U.S. at 877-762-2974, outside the U.S. at 317-572-3993, or fax 317-572-4002.

For technical support, please visit www.wiley.com/techsupport.

Wiley also publishes its books in a variety of electronic formats. Some content that appears in print may not be available in electronic books.

Library of Congress Control Number: 2009922582

ISBN: 978-0-470-39679-7

Manufactured in the United States of America

10 9 8 7 6 5 4 3 2 1

WILEY

About the Author

Jeffrey T. Pollock is a technology visionary and author of the enterprise software books *Semantic Web For Dummies* and *Adaptive Information* (both published by Wiley). Currently a Senior Director with Oracle's Fusion Middleware group, responsible for management of Oracle's data integration product portfolio, Mr. Pollock was formerly an independent systems architect for the Defense Department and Vice President of Technology at Cerebra and Chief Technology Officer of Modulant, developing semantic middleware platforms and inference-driven SOA platforms since 2001. Throughout his career, he has architected, designed, and built application server/middleware solutions for Fortune 500 and U.S. Government clients. Previously, Mr. Pollock was a Principal Engineer with Modem Media and Senior Architect with Ernst & Young's Center for Technology Enablement. He is a frequent speaker at industry conferences, author for industry journals, active member of W3C and OASIS, and formerly an engineering instructor with UC Berkeley's Extension for object-oriented systems, software development process, and enterprise systems architecture.

Dedication

For my family: Kathryn, Carson, Sienna, and Sirus. Especially for my wife, who as a former ontologist is more understanding and patient than most people could ever be with a semantics-obsessed husband. Without her love and support, this book would not have been possible.

Author's Acknowledgments

Semantic Web is a passion for me. Without the inspiration of Tim Berners-Lee, Jim Hendler, Ora Lassila, Deb McGuinness, Ian Horrocks, and others like them, I would not have ever embraced this vision for the future. Without people like Nova Spivack, Mark Greaves, Eric Miller, and Dean Allemang constantly evangelizing and refining the way we all talk about the Semantic Web vision, I would not have been able to simplify and distill my own thoughts into a coherent whole. Finally, I owe very special thanks to Samir A. Batla and David Provost, whose contributions to several chapters in this book have made it a better work, more practical and more encompassing of the full scope of the Semantic Web.

Publisher's Acknowledgments

We're proud of this book; please send us your comments through our online registration form located at `http://dummies.custhelp.com`. For other comments, please contact our Customer Care Department within the U.S. at 877-762-2974, outside the U.S. at 317-572-3993, or fax 317-572-4002.

Some of the people who helped bring this book to market include the following:

Acquisitions and Editorial

Project Editor: Kim Darosett

Acquisitions Editor: Katie Mohr

Copy Editor: Virginia Sanders

Technical Editor: Samir A. Batla

Editorial Manager: Leah Cameron

Editorial Assistant: Amanda Foxworth

Sr. Editorial Assistant: Cherie Case

Cartoons: Rich Tennant
(`www.the5thwave.com`)

Composition Services

Project Coordinator: Erin Smith

Layout and Graphics: Samantha K. Allen, Reuben W. Davis, Cheryl Grubbs, Christine Williams

Proofreaders: Jessica Kramer, Toni Settle

Indexer: Potomac Indexing, LLC

Special Help
Linda Morris

Publishing and Editorial for Technology Dummies

    Richard Swadley, Vice President and Executive Group Publisher

    Andy Cummings, Vice President and Publisher

    Mary Bednarek, Executive Acquisitions Director

    Mary C. Corder, Editorial Director

Publishing for Consumer Dummies

    Diane Graves Steele, Vice President and Publisher

Composition Services

    Gerry Fahey, Vice President of Production Services

    Debbie Stailey, Director of Composition Services

Contents at a Glance

Table of Contents

Introduction

· ·

*T*he Semantic Web community has a distinct feeling of manifest destiny. Here in the early part of the 21st century, the Web is still in its infancy (less than 20 years old), and the scope of unsolved digital data challenges is simply enormous. To many in the software industry, myself included, it seems inevitable that the next great Web revolution must address these universally acknowledged data problems.

In the face of exponentially rising volumes of digital data, the existing software solutions simply fail to provide any meaning or understanding among all that digital noise. Today, many thousands of Semantic Web developers, architects, and visionaries are working to bring meaning to a very messy world of digital data.

Semantic Web is not only a vision, but also a technology, a social phenomenon, and a Web-scale architecture. This book aims to describe all these aspects of the Semantic Web.

About This Book

This book is an unintimidating yet thorough introduction to the Semantic Web. It isn't intended to be a programmer's desk reference or an exhaustive how-to book. This book is written for savvy technologists and forward-thinking businesspeople who want to see the whole Semantic Web picture, while still being firmly grounded in the fundamentals and reality of an emerging technology.

Because the Semantic Web is a revolutionary path forward for data processing and metadata specifications, it will have an exceptionally broad impact on every aspect of all types of software.

This book explores the social, consumer, business, and purely technical impacts of the Semantic Web. Unlike many programming language books that you may have read before, this book covers the visionary and architectural aspects of the Semantic Web in addition to the specific technology languages and programming specifications.

Conventions Used in This Book

Just about every technical book starts with a little typeface legend, and *Semantic Web For Dummies* is no exception. What follows is a brief explanation of the typographical conventions used in this book:

- New terms are set in *italics*.

- When I want you to type something or perform a step, I use **bold.**

- You will also see this `monospaced` font, which I use for code, filenames, Web page addresses (URLs), on-screen messages, and other such things. Also, if something you need to type is really long, it appears in `monospaced` font on its own line or lines.

- For many code examples used in this book, some verbose and unimportant syntax items may be omitted or shortened. For example, in an RDF header, an http namespace may appear as *xx:*SomeName, in this case, the *xx* is referring to "any namespace," and no particular namespace is important for the example.

Foolish Assumptions

When I wrote this book, I made a few assumptions about you, the reader. If one of these assumptions is incorrect, you should be fine. If all of these assumptions are incorrect . . . well, you should buy this book anyway and give it to someone who fits the profile! (Hey, I need the money for my kids' college fund!)

- **I assume that you know little or nothing about the Semantic Web.** This book isn't an "all things to all people" book: It's squarely aimed at the technically savvy, curious individual who is a novice to the Semantic Web. If you're brand-new to the world of semantic computing, this is the book for you.

- **I assume that you can think logically.** You don't have to be a developer for this book to be worthwhile for you, but you have to have some semblance of structured thinking. So much of the Semantic Web is based on formal logic, that although I don't teach math in this book, you better be ready to think in a highly organized manner to keep up with the examples!

- **I assume that you have some knowledge of the Web, business software systems, or ideally both.** Just because this book is aimed at the Semantic Web novice doesn't mean it's a good book for the average technology-hating Luddite. To get the most out of this book, you should already be pretty familiar with the basic technical aspects of the Web (HTML, HTTP, and so on) and be familiar with the business software systems (databases, XML, transaction systems, and so on). Understanding why the Semantic Web is cool depends on having some of that basic knowledge for why the existing technology isn't perfect.

How to Use This Book

I wish I could say that you can open this book up to any page and immediately begin to be productive coding the Semantic Web. In one sense this is true — the code examples in each chapter allow you to write your own little corner of the Semantic Web — but a significant portion of this book is dedicated to explaining the bigger picture about the Semantic Web. To understand why the code you're writing is different and better than the code you could have written with Java or XML, the bigger picture of how things fit together is very important.

In this book, I've divided the content into manageable chunks. You can jump straight to the programming parts of the book, or read about the social implications of the Semantic Web in business and on the Web. This book is designed as a modular reference, meaning that you can skip around to the chapters that interest you, or you can read the book from front to back. When I need to refer to content from another chapter, I include a note for you to reference where you can find more details.

How This Book Is Organized

Writing a book about the Semantic Web in 2008 is like writing a book about the Internet in 1995 — in addition to the details about technology at a moment in time, a substantial part of the book needs to explain how vastly different the future will be and how to prepare for that future.

The impact of the Semantic Web will be felt for decades to come. This book is organized in such a way to help the reader understand just how much the world of data will soon change, why the technology enables these changes, and exactly how to use the programming languages to make those changes.

This book is divided into the following parts:

Part I: Welcome to the Future of Data and the Web

The chapters in Part I introduce you to the full scope and potential of the Semantic Web. Chapter 1 is an introduction to the vastness of the Semantic Web focusing on the differences between consumer and business adoption styles. Chapter 2 explores how the typical Internet user will feel the effects of the Semantic Web, and Chapter 3 stresses the variety of ways businesses will change when Semantic Web data becomes more pervasive.

Part II: Catch the Wave of Smart Data Today

This part shows you today's Semantic Web technology with some easy examples and then explains why the new languages are so powerful for Web sites and businesses. Chapter 4 is a quick primer on Semantic Web technology specifications. Chapter 5 provides detailed examples of how the technology is different than anything that came before, and Chapter 6 describes in detail why Semantic Web metadata is the key enabler for massive software benefits.

Part III: Building the Semantic Web

Sometimes the Semantic Web can seem very complicated. In this part of the book, I simplify the Semantic Web by breaking it down into manageable steps that are easy to follow. Chapters 7 and 8 help you understand how to program RDF and OWL, and Chapter 9 describes how business rules fit into the picture.

Part IV: Putting the Semantic Web to Work

The effects of the Semantic Web will be felt in the workplace in a myriad of ways. New kinds of jobs will appear, and new business processes, technology architectures, and procurement strategies will evolve as a consequence of Semantic Web adoption. Part IV looks at some of the managerial, architectural, and lifecycle challenges to prepare yourself for in the coming years. I also introduce some of the definitive case studies of early Semantic Web success.

Part V: The Part of Tens

The Part of Tens is where you can easily find answers to common questions about the Semantic Web. Chapter 16 clarifies some of the most prevalent misconceptions about the Semantic Web. Chapters 17 and 18 provide guideposts for finding today's state of the art Semantic Web examples and also for gauging where the future advances will lead us.

Icons Used in This Book

A big part of writing a *For Dummies* book is the style and simplicity of how the content is presented. As such, I use some elemental icons to help you scan and dissect the key parts of the book. Here's a list of the icons used in this book:

A tip is an extra piece of information — something helpful that the other books may forget to tell you.

Everyone makes mistakes. Goodness knows that the Semantic Web is easy to make mistakes with. When I think of a mistake that people are especially prone to make, I mark it with a Warning icon.

I'm as forgetful as anybody. Keys, names, addresses — I forget them all. There are lots of details in the Semantic Web that you ought to remember, especially compared with other technologies. When I want to stress a point to be remembered, I use the Remember icon.

Sometimes it's easy to dive too deep into the technical stuff, especially in an introductory book like this. For the more advanced readers, these may be the most interesting parts, but if you're a novice or you're simply in a hurry, you might want to skip on by. In either case, the technical commentary is labeled with the Technical Stuff icon.

Where to Go from Here

If you've gotten this far, it's time to start reading about the Semantic Web. Think of me as your personal guide through this complex topic. I do everything I can to simplify your experience, keep you interested and entertained, and still give you the useful information that you want. (If you didn't want that info, I presume you wouldn't be reading this book!) If you like what you read and want to send me a note, please e-mail me at `jeff@semanticwebfordummies.com`.

Part I

Welcome to the Future of Data and the Web

In this part . . .

In the beginning there was the Web, and people liked to surf Web sites, check e-mail, and create new software programs for their companies. Life was good.

But soon people came to like the Web too much, and all the data on the Web was a tantalizing resource for them to use in new ways. But the Web was made for sharing documents, not for sharing the data inside those pages. And people were sad.

Then the Semantic Web was created to extend the Web and make data easy to reuse everywhere.

In this part of the book, you begin to understand why people will soon be happy again, and why life will be good when information is free.

Chapter 1

Getting the Gist of the Semantic Web

In This Chapter

▶ Understanding why the Semantic Web is just another way of saying Web 3.0

▶ Looking past the hype for real solutions to real problems

▶ Discovering how the Semantic Web may change the world

▶ Figuring out how to make smart data work for you

Congratulations on your curiosity: It takes courage and open-mindedness to even open the pages of a book with the word *semantic* in the title. Of course, the title also contains the word *Dummies,* which lessens the intimidation factor just a bit! The intent of this book is to give you a gentle and complete introduction to the Semantic Web. For many people, this is just the first step. Only a few chapters in this book have code examples — just enough to whet your appetite in case you decide that the next step is to fire up your trusty text editor and bang out some code. More often, I'll be giving you a guided tour of how the Semantic Web changes the Web as you know it, as well as business software applications, open-source software, social networking, and even everyday search engines that you're already using.

In this chapter, I give you a general introduction to what the Semantic Web is, how it may benefit you in your daily life, and how your job might change because of these important developments. The Semantic Web is much more than just a new technology; like any important subject, the Semantic Web is a multi-faceted and sometimes controversial topic. First and foremost, it is a Web technology platform, but it is also one of the newest incarnates of the artificial intelligence legacy, it will become a key enabler for enterprise software, and as a social movement, it just might change the world. But most importantly, this chapter explains how the Semantic Web will make your life easier.

Exploring Different Ways of Looking at the Semantic Web

One of the most frustrating things about the Semantic Web for newcomers is that it means so many different things to different people and communities. I've taken special care in this book to carefully distinguish a few elemental, but differing views of the Semantic Web. Here are some of the different ways of looking at Semantic Web:

- ✓ As an upgrade to the current Web/Internet
- ✓ As a metadata technology for business software
- ✓ As a social movement favoring open-source data
- ✓ As a new generation of artificial intelligence

In fact, each of these views is quite true, but they each appeal to different audiences and focus on different facets of the Semantic Web itself. The Web community is mainly concerned with making Web sites more interesting and easier to use. Starting in 2004, a special focus on group and social collaboration on the Web has produced a wave of new Web sites that call themselves Web 2.0. *Web 2.0* is a term used to distinguish Web sites (such as Amazon.com, Facebook.com, YouTube.com, Digg.com, Wikipedia.org, Twitter.com, and so on) that harness the collective inputs from hundreds or thousands of people in order to make their features and content more interesting than could ever be developed by just one company. But now with the availability of Semantic Web technology, many people are gearing up for what's now called *Web 3.0*.

Finding the Connection to Web 3.0

Most people agree that the first Web (Web 1.0, if you please) has profoundly changed the world. It has connected people in faraway places and ushered in a new era of learning opportunities for folks of any race, creed, culture, or religion to become exposed to fresh ideas with the click of a mouse. The Web hasn't solved world hunger, but it has leveled the educational playing field for millions of souls who would have otherwise been denied fair access to the amassed knowledge of humanity.

The second wave of the Web, Web 2.0, as it is known in pop culture, is no less profound, but perhaps more subtle in reach. Web sites that are part of the Web 2.0 phenomenon have already altered the political landscape of America, helped to elect the first African-American president of the United

States, cracked major news stories before the networks, impacted an entire generation of kids under the age of 18, and collected the largest cache of human knowledge in the world — not too shabby.

Web 3.0 — the Semantic Web — is what folks are calling the third major wave of the Web. Interestingly, the principal inventor of the Web itself, Tim Berners-Lee, doesn't much favor the idea of versioning the Web, and he views the Semantic Web as more aligned with his original vision anyway — which means that we're actually just now seeing the evolution of a Web he was thinking about almost 20 years ago.

Nova Spivak, an entrepreneur and Web visionary, has a compelling chart, similar to the one shown in Figure 1-1, that he uses to describe the Web 3.0 phenomenon. This chart compares the technical power of the way people connect data inside technology and the social richness of the connections people can make using that same technology. In this way, you can see the clear progression of technology from the Personal Computing era, to the first Web 1.0 of pages and documents, to the Web 2.0 era of social networking, and to the Web 3.0 era of the Semantic Web and data networking. In Nova's conception of Web 4.0, he envisions the Web as an operating system for applications with global reach and data systems that exist entirely in the network.

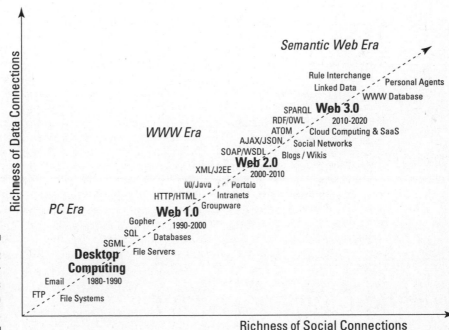

Figure 1-1: Four major waves of Web evolution.

It's still much too early to foretell what profound changes to humanity the Semantic Web and Web 3.0 evolution will bring, but there are indeed some early indications that the changes will be every bit as cataclysmic as Web 1.0 and Web 2.0 were. For example, this book shows you how the Semantic Web may well lead to a "giant database in the sky" containing data, not just pages, about anything you can think of. In this book, I explain how medical researchers from every corner of the globe are using Semantic Web formats to exchange and mash up data that might lead to the next great scientific breakthroughs. I also share with you how the Linked Data Initiative is organizing the publication of terabytes of information into the public domain, and how it's using the Semantic Web formats so that you can freely remix and publish your own Web sites with open-source data. You also discover how businesses large and small are aiming to change the rules of their industries by using Semantic Web data and technology to create new business models. Who knows, maybe this book will give you the spark for a new idea that changes the world that your children will live in!

Exploring the Business Side of Semantics

If you're interested in core technology and money-making, the business side of the Semantic Web will hold a lot of appeal for you. Each year, companies all over the globe spend trillions of dollars buying and installing software that will help them run their businesses. A significant portion of that money spent on software is spent on getting the software to talk to other kinds of software. The Semantic Web technology represents a fundamentally new way of formatting data — a way that can potentially save businesses billions of dollars and help software vendors spur a new growth wave of business software.

Semantic Web data formats were designed from the ground up as purpose-built languages for metadata — providing a way to accurately describe and define data by using more data. In business software systems, these new formats provide a way to more easily connect and exchange data with many systems, and the Semantic Web also provides new ways to model complex data environments that can be more simply maintained over time. Business software created between 2010 and 2020 will be built substantially on the Semantic Web formats of today. I go into much more explanation about these business software topics in Chapters 3, 5, and 10.

Setting Information Free

"Information wants to be free." That has become the unofficial motto for the free content movements that are often associated with Creative Commons copyright licenses and open-source software. The legal foundations for free content and free software have been inexorably moving forward on the principle that people can collectively help to make humanity wealthier by allowing others to copy, remix, and reuse all sorts of content and software. Very much in this same spirit, Tim Berners-Lee and the Linking Open Data Community Project are working hard to leverage Semantic Web data formats as a means to share databases of content, link them to one another, and effectively build a Web of linked data that spans the globe.

Unlike the current Web of linked documents, the Web of linked data will allow publishers to describe data models, data concepts, and data records in such a way that they can be linked, described, and queried as if they were part of a single database.

Much of this vision is already materializing: The current state of Linking Open Data is described in Chapters 2, 15, and 17. Already available to you are the entire contents of Wikipedia, CIA World Factbook, WordNet, and many commercial data models for music, restaurant reviews, and social networks defined and accessible in the Linking Open Data project (which is described in Chapter 2). Practically speaking, you could build your own application on open data in the Semantic Web formats today. This book can help you get started.

Rebirthing Artificial Intelligence

The science of artificial intelligence (AI) goes through ups-and-downs in the academic community. In times past, artificial intelligence research has seemed to hold the promise of radical new computers and the keys to new forms of life, but after years of failed promises, the research funding for AI inevitably dries up. This boom-and-bust cycle for AI has repeated itself many times throughout the 1960s, '70s, '80s, and '90s. Now, the boom cycle has come again, largely due to the Semantic Web excitement.

New research funding since the late 1990s into the areas of knowledge representation (KR) and AI for the Web has grown substantially worldwide, with particular growth in Europe and Asia. The Semantic Web has been yet another source of rebirth for AI, and most of the Semantic Web roots go deep into KR and AI problems that originally emerged several decades ago. For academics and researchers, these AI foundations of the Semantic Web are the most interesting and fruitful.

Checking Out the Semantic Web's Origin

The modern origins of the Semantic Web can be traced to Netscape and the Defense Departments of the United States and Europe. In 1998, Tim Bray and Ramanathan Guha built a metadata language called MCF (Meta Content Framework) for XML to help Netscape describe content ratings of Web pages.

Soon thereafter, the World Wide Web Consortium (W3C) looked to create a general-purpose metadata language called RDF (Resource Description Framework). This new language was largely based on the original MCF specification by Guha and Bray.

Also in 1999, the Defense Departments of the United States and the European Union (EU) Commission independently opened research topics in the area of intelligent agents. Both the United States and the EU had recognized that in order for software to act more autonomously — without the constant updating by human engineers — the software needed a better data format than XML, relational databases, or the Unified Modeling Language (UML) could provide. So the U.S. Defense Advanced Research Projects Agency (DARPA) created DAML (DARPA Agent Markup Language), and the EU created OIL (Ontology Inference Layer). These two formats were remarkably similar and were eventually combined to form DAML+OIL, and that finally turned into OWL (Web Ontology Language).

Today, RDF and OWL are the backbone of the Semantic Web and are recommended standards maintained by the W3C. (See Chapters 5 and 6 for more on RDF and OWL.)

Unpacking Semantic Web Baggage

Inevitably, profound ideas generate profound resistance, and the Semantic Web is no exception. The seminal article announcing the arrival of the Semantic Web was published in May 2001 in *Scientific American* magazine. But years later, the Semantic Web hasn't really changed much of anything. Critics are rightfully disappointed with the lack of real change wrought by Semantic Web formats in the years since they were announced by Tim Berners-Lee, Jim Hendler, and Ora Lassila. There's still a lot of baggage left over (missed expectations, pointed critiques, and unfulfilled capabilities) from these early and grand proclamations, so what gives?

Inflated hype and expectations

Early writings about the Semantic Web made it seem like a computer would soon be able to read your mind, to know what you mean without you really saying much to the computer at all. Promises about linguistic parsing and expert analysis of your queries gave way to the reality that data semantics are hard. Those early ideas about having software that automatically knew what you were searching for or programs that could automatically connect your datebook to travel plans made in other programs seem naive and simplistic

today. And despite the fact that many of those early promises are now finally
finding business models, the time that it took to go from idea to prototype
makes the whole thing seem improbable and not worthwhile. In fact, the early
hyperbole directed at the Semantic Web has prompted many pundits and skep-
tics to ignore the impressive breakthroughs that the community *has* yielded
and effectively throw the baby out with the bathwater by dismissing the whole
notion as a failed fad.

The legacy of artificial intelligence

Some folks are savvy enough about the roots of the Semantic Web to trace
back core ideas and concepts to their artificial intelligence (AI) legacy. For
some, the AI origin of the Semantic Web alone is enough to dismiss the whole
thing as an ivory-tower exercise in futility. Originally based in the logical
foundations of Semantic Networks and Description Logics (each well-known
domains of AI research), most mathematicians and AI researchers see those
AI foundations as anachronisms from the 1970s that don't have a place in
modern computing. It's true that the Semantic Web formats are grounded
in these mathematical foundations that are almost 40 years old, but it's also
true that the Semantic Web fundamentally alters these older AI concepts
and catapults them into the Web age by making them dependent on URIs
(Universal Resource Indicators) and compatible with XML. In fact, this combination of AI roots with Web foundations is what makes the Semantic Web so
compelling and so different from other modern software languages.

Politics of standards movements

Professional software engineers accept that committee-based designs are
often the worst of all worlds. Although the W3C does a phenomenal job of
avoiding "groupthink" and *anti-patterns* (common patterns of incorrect solutions) in their specifications, the Semantic Web is often rightly criticized as
accepting design trade-offs intended to appeal to small minorities. In general,
it's difficult to do anything when you depend upon consensus from a large
and diverse committee. That's why it can take many years to design and
approve even simple specifications. RDF, OWL, and other Semantic Web
technology standards are not perfect by any means. But neither are any
standards. In the software industry, consumers (like you and me) accept the
slow and sometimes painful process of the standards groups because the
outcomes are generally good for us in the end. By having a reference implementation and specification, you can go out and build your own part of the
Semantic Web and have the confidence that it will work well with others —
and that's worthwhile in my book.

Instilling Simplicity in Complex Data

Simply put, the Semantic Web helps to simplify a very complex world of data. Semantic Web data formats are a way of leveling the field for data of any type and origin. Out of necessity, the Semantic Web itself can be viewed as complex, but it can also be incredibly simple.

The real world of data is complex — exceedingly complex. Humanity has generated more new data in the last few years than previously generated in all the preceding years of human history combined. This newly generated data comes in all kinds of formats, structures, styles, and languages. The Semantic Web offers a common baseline for these many complex kinds of data. It's powerful enough to capture the computational semantics of most other kinds of data formats, and it's simple enough to then allow modelers to begin connecting all the data.

There's no magic in the Semantic Web. You can't push a button and see all your data cleaned up or all your Web pages linked together. But whereas the problem was at one time insurmountable, there's now hope for more automated, routine, and predictable ways to bring data together, share it, and make it useful for newer software applications.

In this age, this time, people all over the world are looking to recombine data from the Web in new ways. New inventions, Web sites, and businesses in the future will work on Web data directly, and the Semantic Web will be a substantial means of empowerment for the young entrepreneurs of today.

Seeing the Semantic Web's Starring Role in Web 3.0 Showcase Applications

Any good technology should be more than just vision; in fact, most good technologies start from an underground hacker ethos that encourages the continuous tweaking and refinement of code. So what's available today? What can you go out and see today that's substantially built upon the ideas and technology of the Semantic Web?

First, that crazy vision of the "giant database in the sky" is actually happening. Second, without too much fanfare, a whole host of new business applications are being built using the Semantic Web formats and standards. Third, the entire set of global standards is already being aligned with Semantic Web underpinnings, promising some hope for data interoperability in the coming decades. Finally, don't look now, but your tax dollars have been funding Semantic Web government projects since 1998, and some government agencies depend on the Semantic Web data for some pretty serious projects. In the next few sections, I take a closer look.

Linked open data in the cloud

A controversial dream of many is to enable the Web itself to evolve into a global federated database. This idea of massive technology virtualization is the kind of science fiction that used to make serious people laugh. But today more than 30 organizations publish their libraries of data into Semantic Web formats and make them queryable from the Web itself. The leap of understanding that you need to absorb is that, unlike a regular database, the Semantic Web data and data models can be directly and precisely linked together over the Web itself. Instead of having to go through proprietary software APIs and query listening services, the data and data models are fully accessible from the Web itself. I can publish some data in a model from Australia, and you can include it directly in your data and data model published from New York. As long as we both have an Internet connection and use the Semantic Web, a lot of magic happens for free.

The organizations that are participating in this movement aren't fly-by-night companies or mom-and-pop shops with a small amount of data. The U.S. Central Intelligence Agency's World Factbook, containing detailed data about every country in the world, is accessible in Semantic Web formats. All the data from Wikipedia containing data about practically everything is accessible in Semantic Web formats. Every data item in Freebase, a Web database for anybody to use, is accessible in the Semantic Web formats. And you and I can build any software application we want that will remix and mash up data from any of those sources for free!

But taking this vision even further, media giant Thomson Reuters offers a free service — cloud-based Software as a Service (SaaS) — that can automatically semantically parse any unstructured text you send it, and give you back a Semantic Web–compatible list of people, places, things, and so on that are automatically linked to any of those open-source data models available in that giant database in the sky. Now you can start from any document, any time, from anywhere and automatically get structured data about the concepts and data from your raw text. Welcome to the Semantic Web!

Now imagine what the next few years will yield.

Active metadata in business systems

Once upon a time, business software systems were islands of information that couldn't easily be connected. In fact, most business systems are still just that: disconnected applications that largely work in a self-contained manner. Over the years, a specialized kind of software called *middleware* has evolved to connect business software together, but it's still quite hard, laborious, and expensive to do that. You might have even heard of a new family of standards that was created to solve that problem; service-oriented architecture (SOA) standards aim to solve this with standardized XML frameworks.

The truth is that all this middleware and SOA software depend entirely on metadata formats for data, processes, and APIs, but those formats are exceedingly brittle and don't respond well to change.

Major business software vendors like IBM, Microsoft, and Oracle (to name just a few) are already investing in the Semantic Web as a way to expand their business software systems. Oracle has released functionality that brings the Semantic Web into its database systems, into the governance and risk applications, and even its SOA systems. IBM has built its software registry and repository business software using the Semantic Web foundations, and Microsoft has several business solutions that use Semantic Web languages for media management and user-profile management in the telecommunications environment.

New businesses and online properties are trending toward the Semantic Web as well. Commercial and non-commercial sites like Digg.com, Yahoo!, and BBC online are using the Semantic Web metadata in very interesting ways to improve their visitor experiences. Garlik is a very successful startup using Semantic Web data aimed at protecting the privacy of its customers and preventing identity theft.

At its core, the Semantic Web is more than just a social movement or a big database in the sky: It offers tangible benefits for technologists interested in finding powerful solutions to very fine-grained problems with traditional metadata formats and languages. The Semantic Web is more than just a pretty face, a neat vision, or a trendy idea: It's a legitimately different technology that's purposefully built to make metadata active, dynamic, and change resilient. No other data technology is comparable in its flexibility and power.

Bridges across global standards

One powerful testament to the impact the Semantic Web has already made can be found in the adoption rate of its technology among the ranks of standards bodies. In the world of software, a few key global organizations are entrusted with the reference standards for the data formats and protocols that drive the electronic economies of every nation on earth.

Every single one of the major standard organizations is in the process of adopting Semantic Web formats for the implementation of some of their newest standards, or as a central framework for unifying their standards into a common cannon of specifications.

 The World Wide Web Consortium (W3C) is the main standards body for the Web, XML, and Web services. The W3C holds the reference standards for the Semantic Web and is actively mapping the Semantic Web to other technical areas inside its organization — including to XML and Web services. The International Standards Organization (ISO) maintains thousands of standards including key metadata and data exchange standards for numerous industries. Many of the newest ISO standards leverage the Semantic Web as a way to unify a family of standards and to provide a common reference language for the standards themselves.

Object Management Group (OMG) is the global standards organization that maintains the Unified Modeling Language and other software modeling formats that apply to databases, online analytical processing (OLAP), and data warehousing. OMG is also incorporating the Semantic Web into its core specifications as a metamodel for many of its core reference models. Finally, OASIS (Organization for the Advancement of Structured Information Standards) is also leveraging the Semantic Web formats in its community for a host of standards that aim to improve data processing for security, data centers, and Web service process definitions.

The Semantic Web is becoming a common bridge across silos of disconnected standards in a way that no other technology could. The Semantic Web isn't just a fancy software vocabulary like so many others: It's a foundational data language upon which any other data language can be built. And by building with the Semantic Web, you can all go a long way toward making software easier to connect in the future.

Cutting-edge research and development for nation states

Despite all the cool new things that the Semantic Web allows you to do with your most frequently visited Web sites, business software systems, and global standards, there are actually some much more serious reasons for the Semantic Web, too.

The origin of the Semantic Web came from government funding into research and development on serious problems that countries face in several key areas:

- **National security:** What is the best way to link the entities and records among enormous volumes of data the government collects every day? By linking that data together more effectively, experts can see national security threats forming before they become reality. In that regard, the Semantic Web is like a more powerful telescope that lets people see deeper into the masses of data on the networks.

- **Disaster preparedness:** How do you create computer systems that can be mashed up and remixed on the fly in times of emergency? Disasters rarely happen exactly as you've planned for them. Aiding first-responders and government officials to quickly assess all the data they can, to best organize a response to the changing ground situation, is critical for limiting casualties in those precious first hours of any large-scale disaster.

- **Military operations:** How do you enable a network-centric software architecture that can dynamically connect to your friends' and allies' data? Within one country, and among allies of different countries, huge, complex command structures need to work together seamlessly to be efficient and fight in a coordinated way. Software systems, data, and networks must be capable of that dynamic interoperability in order for those future combat systems to work properly.

The Semantic Web was originally conceived to help solve these gigantic serious challenges at the national level. Today, there are Semantic Web–based systems in production that solve parts of those challenges. Hundreds of more projects are underway that use the Semantic Web in key ways that help government officials communicate more effectively and more quickly than ever before.

Many of these national-level research programs (in the United States and also abroad, especially throughout Europe) are funded through university grants for special programs. Thousands of schools worldwide are teaching classes and funding active research into the use of Semantic Web languages, formats, and technical components to help push forward the various industrial uses of the technology. These special programs are sometimes very focused on the logical and mathematical foundations of the Semantic Web, whereas other research programs are more high-level and seek to find more of a systemic use of the technology in applied settings.

Likewise, much of the Semantic Web research and development happening in the university system, from government funding or private funding, is being applied in other areas. A particularly popular area of applied research in the Semantic Web domain is life sciences: drug discovery, clinical healthcare, and biological research. Semantic Web research in these domains is particularly strong because these areas have suffered for years from an inability to effectively share complex research and clinical data sets with other researchers who might be able to use them for new discoveries. As a consequence of this historical deficiency, the life sciences area is now one of the fastest-growing domains for adopting Semantic Web data formats — it helps the whole community exchange data easier and with better accuracy.

Core research and development may not be the most compelling case to convince pragmatic businesspeople or casual Web surfers to embrace the Semantic Web, but no one can deny the impact these researchers are having on society and governments as a consequence of their investment in Semantic Web.

Recognizing Compelling Reasons for the Semantic Web

By now, you've already heard about a lot of compelling things that the Semantic Web can do or is already doing for you:

- Making your country safer
- Making your country more prepared for disasters
- Improving the speed with which researchers create new medications
- Unifying disconnected software standards
- Making business software more change-resilient and less expensive
- Building a giant database in the sky from open-source data
- Giving humanity the gift of open knowledge

But all of those reasons might seem a little altruistic, esoteric, or even farfetched for most people. What about some pragmatic, down-to-earth ways that the Semantic Web can be good for you today? The following sections preview what I tell you about what Semantic Web can do for you in the rest of the book:

- ✔ Make your life simpler
- ✔ Save you money and time
- ✔ Help do new projects faster

Make your life simpler

The whole purpose of using a computer in the first place is to have it handle the routine and repetitive tasks for you. Doing the hard work, the boring work, and the insanely complex work is precisely what a well-designed Semantic Web application should do for you. Here are a few examples of how the Semantic Web can make your life simpler today:

- ✔ **Use fewer mouse clicks to find the data you need.** Try searching with Yahoo! Search, which uses the Semantic Web inside SearchMonkey.

- ✔ **Stay organized on the Web and in your Web browser.** Try the Adaptive Blue Glue toolbar, which uses Semantic Web metadata to better link your actions and predict what you might want to do next.

- ✔ **Collect your interests more intuitively and share them with others.** Try Twine's Semantic Web–enabled interest networking site, where you can put the ideas you're interested in and share them with like-minded people who share their interests with you too.

- ✔ **Organize your disconnected travel plans better.** Try TripIt's travel service, which lets you combine itineraries and bookings made from different Web sites into a single compact Semantic Web–enabled itinerary that summarizes just what you need to know.

- ✔ **Pinpoint the *exact* news you want to see.** Try the Thomson Reuters Calais Web Service, which lets you automatically scan news stories for ideas and concepts (not just keywords) and then link them to any other Semantic Web resource on the Web (like Wikipedia, Freebase, or the World Factbook) for more data.

Save money and time

You might be one of those very practical folks who isn't really interested in improving your Web surfing; instead, you'd rather invest your time and money in solving big business problems for your company. Here are some ways you might be able to help your company save money on the operational tasks that it already does:

✔ **Finding business resources more quickly and easily:** How much time do people spend every day trying to find people or documents that they need? Try thinking about how the Semantic Web could help with locating business resources and read on to find out how IBM and NASA are doing just that. (See Chapters 11 and 15.)

✔ **Diagnosing remote technical problems:** How often can complex mechanical problems be diagnosed and cross-referenced to technical data in real time? Try thinking about how the Semantic Web might help decipher complex data for root-cause analysis and read on to hear how the French automaker Renault and the U.S. Defense Department are aiming at that challenge. (See Chapters 11 and 15.)

✔ **Preserving corporate knowledge:** The embedded corporate knowledge that goes home when the lights go out is astounding. How can businesses preserve and encourage a corporate knowledge center? Think about how the Semantic Web can help build a better knowledge base and read on to find out more about what the oil company Chevron and pharmaceutical giant Pfizer are thinking about that problem. (See Chapters 10 and 11.)

✔ **Integrating information:** Most companies have severe cost overruns associated with the need to integrate information and metadata, but there has to be a better way. Think about how the Semantic Web data formats will make it easier to bring together complex data and then read on to find out more about how companies like Oracle, British Telecom, Metatomix, and BBC are headed that way. (See Chapters 3, 11, and 15.)

Do new projects faster

Sometimes you might have a tactical necessity to improve a process or just help a business project move along more quickly. Semantic Web vendors, and many companies using the Semantic Web, are looking to make completing projects easier and faster:

✔ **Finding and linking Web services:** In complex and large IT systems, finding services can be tricky. IBM is leveraging the Semantic Web to make that job faster and more effective.

✔ **Building application mashups faster:** For millions of Web entrepreneurs, the speed with which they can build a new application and place it in the clouds is crucial. The Thomson Reuters Calais service helps those businesses reduce their time to market with impressive Semantic Web data scanning.

✔ **More targeted and effective advertising:** How do you quickly boost click-throughs and get more people to look at your business's offer? Dapper has an advertising program that can help you place the ads more effectively with Semantic Web metadata and analysis.

✔ **Empowered information workers:** Every modern business is powered by information workers that build, use, and depend on software applications in their daily lives. Making this infrastructure work are armies of information workers who maintain metadata, data files, and master records in all sorts of applications. Try the Dow Jones Synaptica Taxonomy Management Tool for a Semantic Web–driven approach to making information workers more effective at managing the lifecycle of corporate data and metadata.

Chapter 2

The Semantic Web in Your Life

*I*n 2009, more than 1.5 billion people will use the Internet. One out of every five people in the world is a Web user. The Web has broken down political, social, and cultural barriers: It's a modern-day printing press bringing advancement and change to the farthest reaches of the globe.

In an amazingly brief span of time, the Web has become part of the fabric of humanity; the Web weaves a rich tapestry of information that connects people, enriches lives, and shrinks the greatest of distances by bringing the world's knowledge to the farthest places. The Semantic Web is an evolutionary step in the Web itself.

This chapter introduces you to how the Semantic Web will change the way you use the Web. I explain why the Semantic Web helps to accelerate the newest Web 2.0 trends for collective intelligence on the Web, and I share some practical examples of semantic wikis, semantic search, semantic mashup applications, semantic news feeds, semantic blogs, and other ways that Web entrepreneurs and hackers are looking to redefine how the Web works.

As of 2009, Semantic Web is still in its earliest days, but if you start to pay attention now, you'll find plenty of opportunities to simplify the way you use the Web, and maybe even a new idea worth millions!

Taking a Look at How the Web Is Used Daily

People use the Web for all sorts of different things. But in spite of the great diversity, you can find remarkable similarities in what people actually do on the Web. For example, here are some of the most popular activities on the Web:

- **E-mail:** Send electronic correspondence to friends and family from Web-based or regular e-mail systems.

- **Searching:** Use a search engine to find more information about anything that you might be interested in.

- **Shopping:** The convenience of shopping from home was first discovered by the catalog companies of decades past, but the Web brings a whole new level of bargain hunting and simplicity to every kind of shopping trip.

- **Checking the weather:** Find up-to-the-minute weather forecasts, view webcam video of a location, or even check the surf at your favorite beach.

- **Booking travel:** Arrange air travel, hotels, and rental cars. Does anybody really remember what it was like to buy a plane ticket before the Web? Yikes!

- **Writing a blog:** For many people, the process of writing in a journal has been completely supplanted by *blogging,* which is putting the story of your life and/or interests into the public domain for anybody to read and comment on.

- **Organizing a work or family calendar:** Keeping track of family, friends, and your busy schedule is much easier on the Web.

- **Reading the news:** The dramatic decline of print newspaper circulation is one strong indicator of how much news Web sites have changed the way people find and consume their news.

- **Connecting with friends:** The rise of social networking sites and the huge numbers of young people with online identities hints at an even more Web-dependant future.

- **Professional networking:** Even older professionals can't resist the temptation to network online. Hundreds of millions of adults put their professional stories online and aim to connect, network, and build new relationships with others.

Using the Internet for daily tasks is a part of everyday culture. For many people, the Web is as commonplace as television and as natural as eating breakfast in the morning. But the true beauty of the Web is that it is an evolving and dynamic place to be. The Web of 2009 is vastly different than the Web of 1999, and so too will the Web of 2019 make the Web today seem simple and quaint.

Exploring the Web 2.0 Movement and What It Means

The first generation of the Web, from roughly 1990 to 2000, was mostly about publishing HTML (Hypertext Markup Language) pages onto a server. These pages were static documents that could only be updated in rudimentary ways.

The second generation of the Web, which started in 2000 and continues today, is still pretty much driven by pages of documents, but the source of content within these documents is much more dynamic and interactive than anything before it.

Nowadays people expect to get more from their interactions with the Web. People want to *interact* with the thoughts and ideas of others. The Web weaves a rich tapestry of diverse opinions and new connections. This richness is about helping people benefit from the actions and input of others. Whether it's the personal review of a book on Amazon.com, the political opinion piece from that blog in Iowa, or the music recommendation from a friend of a friend in Facebook, people are putting more trust in what they find on the Web than they have in any media that came before.

With Web 2.0, people surf the Web for answers to complex problems, to find new ideas that challenge their beliefs, and to find friendship and community among others who share their values. The Web has moved beyond a place for publishing and entertainment; it's now very much a behavioral and humanistic part of the very fabric of society.

An Internet microbubble

The behavioral shift from Web 1.0 to Web 2.0 and the acceptance of the Web by the masses have generated new business opportunities for entrepreneurs everywhere. Many new business models that would have been impossible just a few years ago make much more sense today.

The Web is a way to influence millions of people through all kinds of direct and indirect methods. The advertising business has been turned upside down by the Web as it becomes ever more possible to reach consumer audiences that rival the size of those on television. In turn, this creates new economies of funding, venture capital, corporate ventures, and other kinds of business exploitation and risk-taking.

Understandably, the corresponding hype about this new phenomenon has produced inflated expectations for Web 2.0 businesses that result in high-profile, high-value acquisitions of iconic Web 2.0 companies like YouTube, Flickr, and

MySpace. Others, like Facebook, are still independent despite billion-dollar takeover offers from traditional media companies that would benefit from access to their databases of information about their millions of users.

Web 2.0 has certainly created a microbubble of sorts — an economic boom for businesses taking advantage of this new wave of social interaction with the Web. This microbubble has even generated new slang terms like *Google-bait* for new startup companies founded on the idea of offering a small but important feature for Google, hoping to be bought out early (like YouTube) for huge profits.

Web 2.0: Technological or social?

Unlike the first wave of Web 1.0, which was grounded in the wide accessibility of new networking protocols, document formats, and client/server technology, the Web 2.0 bubble is not a technology boom. Web 2.0 is an advertising boom.

The top-ten social networking sites reach more than 500 million people worldwide; usually, these are the very desirable younger demographics that advertisers crave. Web 2.0 social networks are connected directly to a tremendous amount of purchasing power accessible through those communities. Access to that purchasing power, to those demographics, is where the dollar value of Web 2.0 lies.

Advertising budgets and speculation might be fueling the Web 2.0 boom, but the engine of Web 2.0 growth is the people themselves. That is exactly what marks the difference between Web 1.0 of disconnected people reading static pages in contrast to the intensely connected people interacting and building communities on the Web. Clearly, the Web 2.0 phenomenon is social, humanistic, and not technical in nature.

Defining the Features of Web 3.0 — the Semantic Web

Web 3.0, the Semantic Web, is about improvements in the technology of the Web. New Web sites with new features and capabilities are becoming available now. In some ways, these new technologies are about improving the connectedness of the Web, but in other ways, the technology is helping to do new things that could not be done before.

Perhaps the simplest way to think about Web 3.0 is to imagine that the words and pictures you see inside your Web browser have been pieced together from many different places, just for you, at this moment in time. Imagine that few of the words or pictures you see have actually come from the Web site you're looking at. The words have been written by different people at different times, but they all go together to make a consistent story and give you the information you want. Imagine that you could write a blog whose words and pictures appeared in my Web browser, mixed up with words and pictures from other people with similar interests and ideas. Imagine that any idea, concept, or data point could be reorganized in a moment and printed to a page just for you. That's the remix nature of Web 3.0.

Web 3.0 is fundamentally about using new technology that helps remix, reuse, and repurpose data on the Web in new ways. One way to understand the nature of Web 3.0, building upon a series of attributes originally conceived by Nova Spivak, is to think about Web 3.0 as having the following key defining characteristics:

- **Ubiquitous networking:** Web 3.0 requires that data can be connected and intertwined without concern for its physical location. Devices and access points are assumed to have Web access, or protocols that gracefully accommodate low bandwidth or downtime periods. Broadband rollout and adoption are vital for Web 3.0 because data should always be available. Mobile Internet access and mobile devices are a Web 3.0 foundation point for both data generation (sensors) and data access (screens).

- **Open everything:** Web 3.0 depends on unprecedented levels of automation and smarts. As a consequence, the many parts of the network must remain open and not closed. Open data, open services, and open identity are all parts of the bigger Web 3.0 vision.

  Already, the Linking Open Data project (see Figure 2-1) is bringing together databases and data models published from all corners of the globe into a giant virtual data resource for Web 3.0. Open technologies, open APIs and protocols, open data formats, open-source software platforms, and open data (for example, Creative Commons, Open Data License) all contribute to the remix, reuse, and repurpose ability of Web 3.0 infrastructures. Open identity (OpenID), open reputation (like how user reputations are rated at Amazon.com), roaming portable identity, and open personal data (FOAF) set the stage for intelligent software to act on your behalf while you're busy with other things.

- **Adaptive information:** Web 3.0 has been described as the "data Web" and also as the "executable Web." Both labels are accurate. Using the analogy of word processing, the Web 1.0 is a single person editing a document, the Web 2.0 is a group of people editing a document, and Web 3.0 is a group of people creating bits of data outside of documents altogether. That is the *data Web*. To use an analogy of file system permissions, Web 1.0 was read-only, Web 2.0 is read-write, and Web 3.0 is read-write-execute. That is the *executable Web*. In both cases, the core idea is that information on the Web is becoming more connected, more fine-grained, and more dynamic. Information isn't just about pages; it's about data that's connected and capable of being reassembled on demand. This reassembly of data, the reorganization of data pieces, is a key central element of the Web 3.0 and Semantic Web movements — that is the *executable data Web*.

✔ **Adaptive service clouds:** With Web 3.0, data is a service. Instead of software services becoming simply about behavior and programming interfaces, the Web 3.0 and Semantic Web movement are enabling the publication and consumption of the data and data models as services inside *cloud computing systems* (software applications that are hosted entirely via Web protocols and services). Software for reasoning with this data and these data models, based on inference engines and intelligent agents, can enable applications that use sets of rules to express relationships between concepts and data from anywhere on the Web. Network computing, Software as a Service (SaaS) business models, distributed computing applications, and grid computing are all part of this Web 3.0 movement — the data, applications, and processing of software are all becoming virtual, shared, and open as services hosted within clusters of adaptive service clouds.

Project Description

The ● Open Data Movement aims at making data freely available to everyone. There are already various interesting open data sets available on the Web. Examples include ● Wikipedia, ● Wikibooks, ● Geonames, ● MusicBrainz, ● WordNet, the ● DBLP bibliography and many more which are published under ● Creative Commons or ● Talis licenses.

The goal of the W3C SWEO Linking Open Data community project is to extend the Web with a data commons by publishing various open data sets as RDF on the Web and by setting RDF links between data items from different data sources.

RDF links enable you to navigate from a data item within one data source to related data items within other sources using a Semantic Web browser. RDF links can also be followed by the crawlers of Semantic Web search engines, which may provide sophisticated search and query capabilities over crawled data. As query results are structured data and not just links to HTML pages, they can be used within other applications.

The figure below shows the data sets that have been published and interlinked by the project so far. Collectively, the data sets consist of over two billion RDF triples, which are interlinked by around 3 million RDF links (October 2007).

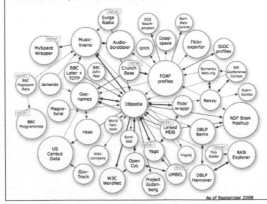

Figure 2-1:
A pictorial representation of the Linking Open Data project.

✔ **Federated data:** Web 3.0 is first and foremost about the emergence of a data Web. The data Web consists of structured data records that are published to the Web in reusable and remotely queryable Semantic Web formats. The construction of the data Web, underway since 2001, is being accomplished via both *top-down* (formal and costly development) and *bottoms-up* (informal and inexpensive) approaches. Both approaches can be published from any Web server and remixed using standards-based query languages like SPARQL for searching across distributed RDF databases on the Web. This new *federated* (when data is stored and retrieved from different locations during a single query) data Web enables new levels of data integration, portability, and application interoperability, thereby making data as openly accessible and linkable as Web pages.

As Web 3.0 and the Semantic Web continue to mature, both structured data and unstructured/semi-structured content will become widely accessible in these newer federated data formats. After a critical mass is achieved, the Semantic Web will yield to a future where data can be easily reused and remixed from anywhere on the Web.

✔ **Simulated intelligence:** Web 3.0 will know what you want and understand what you mean! A crucial new feature of Semantic Web and Web 3.0 is the introduction of better algorithms for working with data. Building upon decades of research into Semantic networks and description logics, some aspects of the Semantic Web can use powerful algorithms as a way to inject some smarts into the behavior of your data on the Web. The driving force for Web 3.0 might well be the rise of intelligent Web-based systems. Although the Semantic Web algorithms are not magic, they're substantially more powerful than existing commonplace algorithms used to process data on the Web.

Some people think that machine intelligence will emerge in an organic fashion, as an outgrowth of communities of intelligent people putting data on the Web (such as with Web 2.0 applications like del.icio.us, Flickr, and Digg) and Semantic Web applications that extract meaning and order from that same data to automate the way people interact with it. Automation and intelligence in the data are key promises that the Semantic Web has yet to fulfill. If that vision comes to fruition in the next ten years, it will be with the aid of other technology areas like natural language processing, machine learning, machine reasoning, and autonomous software agents.

These characteristics of the Web 3.0 and Semantic Web may seem downright preposterous, with a healthy dose of wishful thinking thrown in for good measure, but I can assure you that each idea mentioned is more than just speculation. Yes, the Web of 2010 to 2020 will grow faster, become more dynamic, and be smarter than anything you might have thought about the Web before.

Checking Out Some Ahead-of-the-Curve Semantic Web Sites

Remember: The decade of Web 3.0 and the Semantic Web hasn't yet arrived. Early adopter Web sites that use the Semantic Web today are still experimenting with new uses of the technology. However, the working timeline for Web 3.0 and Semantic Web to reach maturity is much more likely to be between 2010 and 2020. This will be the third full decade of the Web's existence. So, although some beta applications of the Semantic Web are here today, you can look forward to many more in the coming years.

Yahoo! Search with SearchMonkey

Fire up your favorite Web browser and go to `http://gallery.search.yahoo.com`. Here, you can find an awesome set of Semantic Web extensions that you can add to your Yahoo! search results. I have extensions installed that let me view content on the main search results page that typically I would have to click a link to see. I use extensions for local restaurant reviews, LinkedIn profiles, and business reviews from CitySearch. This kind of Web 3.0 functionality is a good example of how Yahoo! is enabling site owners to make their content reusable by others. By annotating its own Web pages, Yahoo! can display data on a search result, helping people like you find what you need to with fewer clicks.

Twine: Interest networking

Go ahead and sign up for Twine at `www.twine.com`. You won't regret using this Semantic Web–based interest networking service. Twine is a Web site that helps you stay connected and organize your many interests. The main benefit from Twine is twofold: You have better ways to organize the stuff you're interested in, *and* you get the benefit of having input from others in discovering new stuff that you'll like. If you've ever used the "Customers Who Bought This Item Also Bought" feature on Amazon to look for new stuff to buy, Twine is like that but for your ideas, interests, and hobbies. Twine gives you a way of discovering new ideas from its Web site and also via e-mail, and it can be non-intrusive and low effort if you want it to be.

TripIt: Travel aggregator

If you travel, and you probably do, you should go take a peek at TripIt now: www.tripit.com. This Semantic Web–enabled application can aggregate your airline travel, car rentals, hotel information, and most other travel data from any Web site you might have booked it from. Just send a copy of your confirmation e-mail to TripIt, and it has the smarts to put everything together in one itinerary. It's even intuitive enough to know what activities are part of one trip and what activities aren't. This is a great example of how Web 3.0 technology helps you make the most of all the data you normally would have scattered about in different places on Web 2.0 Web sites!

ZoomInfo: People finder

Have you googled yourself? If so, put this book down and immediately go to www.zoominfo.com. ZoomInfo is a Web 3.0 site that is always crawling the Internet looking for data about people and businesses. It has the semantic smarts to associate data from different places and build a profile of you from that data. If you were excited by a few page hits the first time you googled yourself, the experience with ZoomInfo could be a little scary, so beware! ZoomInfo isn't always accurate and can be fooled by some common names, but if you've led a life that has been documented on the Internet in any way, ZoomInfo is very likely to know who you are.

Dapper: Mashups and semantics

If you're at all interested in advanced data feeds or the next generation of Web-based advertising, go directly to the Dapper demo at www.dapper.net/dapperDemo. Dapper is a core technology for capturing content from any Web site and making that content useful to any other application. A number of Semantic Web applications use the power of Dapper for bringing semantics to the masses (try Semantify: www.dapper.net/semantify) and building a better mashup ad network (try MashupAds: www.dapper.net/mashupads). A Web site mashup blends data from other locations into a single feature. Dapper is a building block technology for mashups that can help extract useful data from otherwise difficult-to-use unstructured Web 2.0 Web sites. Although this kind of screen-scraping technology can be brittle in highly dynamic environments, it's often the only way to repurpose data from Web sites that don't supply any Semantic Web annotations themselves. Dapper applications are powerful examples of Web 3.0 applications that attempt to build bridges between Web 2.0 data silos.

Peering into the Crystal Ball of the Semantic Web

There are many ideas for how to make your regular Internet sites more semantically rich — in other words, Web 3.0–enabled. The general idea for adding semantics is to make sites more intuitive, more responsive, and easier to use. Because most of the ideas for how to bring the Semantic Web to your favorite Internet site are still in the incubation phase, I make no claims about having perfect foresight into the future, and my ideas about how the Semantic Web will improve a particular application are no doubt incomplete. But with that caveat, the following Web applications are very likely suspects for Semantic Web technology to revolutionize their core foundations. So if you agree with me that there's a Semantic Web opportunity in one of these applications, maybe you'll be the one who does it best!

Semantic Web desktop applications

Most people view the Web from a software application called the Web browser. It's the main application through which you see Web pages and use the features that the Web publishers make available. The Web browser has toolbars for browsing activities, a browsing history section for tracking sites you've browsed, and bookmarks for you to save the location of pages you want to see again in the future. But browsers don't really have much smarts about the data you see on the Web. In fact, browsers are lousy at understanding what you're looking at.

One way that the Web 3.0 and the Semantic Web will be different is that the browsers will start to understand more about the content of what you're browsing and begin to make recommendations or help organize the content for you. Having more smarts in the Web browser means that you'll have a partner in your Web surfing that can read what you're reading and use that information to save you time later. A company called Adaptive Blue is exploring this path with a product called Glue (www.getglue.com). Glue is a browser toolbar (see Figure 2-2) that tells you when you're looking at Web content that your friends have looked at and lets you know what they thought about it. Glue also gives you recommendations about other topics that you might want to check out. You don't have to belong to a social network or go to a Web page to get this kind of interaction: It's right there in your browser application. Using such browser smarts is one way that the Web of tomorrow seems smarter than what you use today.

Other areas for Web 3.0 applications include the emergence of semantic e-mail applications. The Mangrove Project is looking at ways to use semantic annotations and Natural Language Processing (NLP) to automate e-mail processes such as taking RSVPs, coordinating meeting logistics, organizing subgroups on a list, and handling processes that would otherwise require humans to read and parse the messages. Semantic calendars are a related area for future developments. A semantic calendar application would be capable of organizing and displaying events based on the content of the event, and it could automatically provide cross-references to other events, e-mail, or Web sites with similar content. One notable early implementation here is the semantic calendar extension to Semantic MediaWiki (`http:// semantic-mediawiki.org/wiki/Help:Calendar_format`), a semantics-driven wiki application.

Finally, the desktop itself may one day be the Semantic Web application you've been waiting for. KDE (K Desktop Environment) is a desktop system that can run on many different operating systems like Linux, BSD, Solaris, Windows, and Mac OS X. The K Desktop Environment (`www.kde.org`) is a platform that provides a window manager, file manager, desktop search, and other group-ware suites. KDE 4.0 includes a desktop semantic search application called Soprano that was contributed by the NEPOMUK (Networked Environment for Personal Ontology-based Management of Unified Knowledge) EU (European Union) project. This semantic search application works by creating a Semantic Web–based index of all your desktop files and making them instantly available for you to search more intelligently. Additionally, anybody can annotate any file on your computer with Web 3.0 tags that become part of a local ontology describing the contents of your computer.

Figure 2-2:
The Adaptive Blue Glue toolbar for commenting on Web content.

Over time, your local desktop files can be connected to any data on the Semantic Web and remixed with anybody else's data that you have access to. Semantic desktops are starting with search, but eventually the operating system and any application running on your computer might be a Web 3.0 application. Whether it's just a browser, your e-mail client, your calendar, or the desktop itself, the Semantic Web will be changing the way you look at the Web.

Semantic blogging

Semantic blogging takes blogging, already one of the most popular and controversial aspects of Web 2.0, to an even more interconnected level. Some existing semantic blogs can integrate with blogging platforms like Wordpress, Blogger, and Typepad to suggest pictures, links, articles, and tags related to your blog postings.

One such semantic blog is from a startup company called Zemanta (`www.zemanta.com`). Zemanta uses proprietary natural language processing and semantic algorithms to compare the words in a blog post to its preindexed database of other content in order to suggest related items that will display next to your blog post. The articles Zemanta suggests come from 300 different media sources as well as the other blogs of Zemanta users. The images come from Wikimedia Commons, Flickr, and stock photo providers like Shutterstock and Fotolia.

If you're an existing blogger who wants to get started with a semantic blog, you'll very likely need to install an extension to your Web browser. After your extension is installed, visit your favorite blog Web site with that browser and then begin to write your post.

Zemanta's semantic blog is interactive and dynamic. While you're writing your blog, Zemanta places a sidebar to your post filled with related, automatically generated content as you type. Because of the way Zemanta's index and NLP algorithms work, each blog entry should be at least 300 words for Zemanta to generate accurate sidebar links and other recommended content.

The jury is still out on whether semantic blogging is its own application or more appropriately a new feature on existing blog engines. Regardless of whether Zemanta changes the rules of blogging, you can be assured that more and more smart technology will be injected into the blogging software you're already using. A great deal of those new smarts will be thanks to the Semantic Web.

Semantic wikis

Wikis are in some ways the defining application of the Web 2.0 movement —
they were the first widespread application of technology that allowed groups
to work on the same Web content. But regular Wikis are pretty basic technology by today's standards: They generally consist of some places for people
to type unstructured text and insert uncategorized hyperlinks into a Web
page. Although Wikis are pretty good at version control on Web pages, they
don't really have a whole lot of smarts built in to them in other ways.

In contrast, a *semantic wiki* is a wiki that has an underlying model of the information described in its pages. Semantic wikis give users the ability to capture
or identify additional data/metadata about the wiki pages and their relations
to other Web content. For example, imagine a semantic wiki devoted solely
to cars. The page for BMW would contain, in addition to standard human-
readable text information, some machine-readable or machine-generated
semantic data.

One basic example of semantic data about a car wiki might be that a BMW is
a kind of car manufacturer — the relation between "BMW" and "car manufacturer" is known as an inheritance relationship. The semantic wiki might be
capable of automatically generating a list of car manufacturers simply by listing all pages that are tagged as (or inferred to be) a type "Car Manufacturer."
Other semantic tags in the BMW page might indicate more data about BMWs,
including their history, models, repair data, driving characteristics, and any
other data that was considered notable. These tags could be derived (perhaps using NLP) from the text, but with some chance of error from the automatic tagging: accordingly, the tags could be presented alongside the Wiki
data so that they can be easily corrected.

Another good reason for semantic wikis is that they can then export their
data in a standard Semantic Web format. This means that the wiki data can
then be queried in the same ways that a regular database might so that external Web sites or power users could submit queries to your wiki data and use
that data on their own Web sites.

Here are a few examples of semantic wikis:

- **Metaweb:** The software that powers Freebase (www.metaweb.com)
- **IkeWiki:** Developed by Salzburg Research (http://ikewiki.salzburg research.at)
- **Semantic MediaWiki:** An extension for the popular MediaWiki software that turns it into a semantic wiki (http://semantic-mediawiki.org)

- ✔ **OntoWiki:** A semantic wiki developed by AKSW Research (`http://ontowiki.net`)

- ✔ **SweetWiki:** A Semantic Web Enabled Technology Wiki (`http://sweetwiki.inria.fr/wiki`)

It remains to be seen whether any semantic wiki will stand on its own or whether the features will simply be folded into other more popular conventional wikis. But the trends seem to point to a future where wikis move beyond simple pages with simple links and become more capable of understanding the content they contain, generating new links and organizing themselves based on the raw content keyed in by humans. This capability will be part of the path to a smarter and more automated Web.

Semantic search engines

Due in no small part to the incredible story of Google's rise to Internet dominance, the area of Web search has been a booming place to find Semantic Web innovations. Whereas traditional search engines mainly operate on keyword indices and simple results pages, the semantic search engines attempt to give smarter results by first searching for concepts and then making the results more navigable for people who want to drill around in the data results. In general, semantic search attempts to augment and improve traditional searches by leveraging Semantic Web–formatted data to add more meaning to search queries and Web text in order to increase the accuracy of results, as well as to make it easier to navigate to the best answer.

In practice, there are two major types of search behavior:

- ✔ **With a navigational search,** the user is using the search engine as a navigation tool to navigate to a particular document of interest. For navigational-style searches, the Semantic Web can provide a rich category framework for filing and retrieving specific documents of interest. The KDE 4.0 Semantic Desktop search system gives a good example of how documents can be organized and annotated for navigational searches to find items more simply.

- ✔ **With a research search,** the user queries the search engine with a phrase that signifies an object or idea about which the user is trying to gather information. The user isn't trying to get to any particular document she knows of. Rather, she's trying to locate a number of documents that together will give her the information she's trying to find.

  In the research-style of searching, the search engine can augment ranking algorithms, such as Google's PageRank, to predict relevancy, with semantic annotations and inference engines to further improve the accuracy of wide-scale searching. (See Figure 2-3, a Powerset example of a Research query.) The goal of a semantic search engine is to deliver exactly the information queried by a user rather than returning a list of loosely related keyword results that the user has to click through.

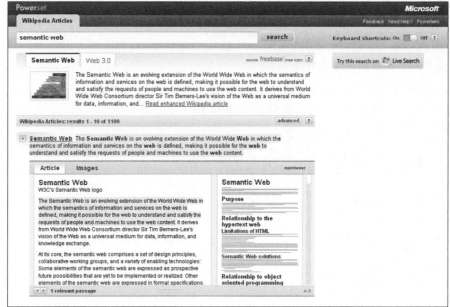

Figure 2-3:
Microsoft
Powerset
with a
research-
style query.

Although semantic search gets a lot of attention in the media and could truly be a game-changing technology if a company could rival Google's ongoing dominance of the search space, I personally don't feel that the Semantic Web will adequately solve the remaining problems in the search space until there is more Semantic Web data to index. Until that point, my belief is that the Web 3.0 and Semantic Web search engines will find success in narrow niches that they can optimize for and generate their own semantic data models within.

Here are a few search engines using Web 3.0 technology:

- ✔ **Yahoo!:** Using semantics for remixing content in search results (www.yahoo.com)

- ✔ **Hakia:** Using semantics for better search accuracy (www.hakia.com)

- ✔ **Swoogle:** Using semantics to search public ontologies (http://swoogle.umbc.edu)

- ✔ **Microsoft Powerset:** Using semantics to catalog Wikipedia and Freebase (www.powerset.com)

- ✔ **Zitgist:** A Semantic Web browser for linked data (www.zitgist.com)

Go ahead and try a few of these search engines yourself. You're likely to be both impressed and underwhelmed. These semantic search applications excel in certain situations, but they still fall short of being a perfect solution for everyday use. That's where the advancements in the next ten years will have to come — in the scale and simplicity to solve search problems for everyday Web users.

Semantic news feeds and publishing

Keeping track of events happening in the world becomes more difficult year after year. Ironically, the more information that becomes available, the more difficult it becomes to parse it, understand it, and place it in context with other data that you already know about. For some folks, this process of information gathering is merely a hobby, but for others, it's big business and a way of life. The news industry and the publishing industry live and die on the basis of information access, discovery, and reuse: Obviously, they're big parts of the Web, and major investors in the rise of Web 3.0 technology.

Semantic news feeds are an idea that is still in its infancy, but much more than simply a dream. Thomson Reuters is placing a big bet that companies and people will want a better way to get their news more accurately and with more precision than ever before. The new service provided by Thomson Reuters is called Calais, and it gives you the ability to subscribe to news based upon concepts and ideas — not just keywords or news feeds. The Calais service (`http://opencalais.com`) can scan news content from anywhere and automatically categorize it according to an ontology of concepts like people, places, events, and things. You can use this service to subscribe to topics of your choice, such as, "legal events in the U.S. Congress." The Calais service helps you find news content that matches that concept regardless of whether those keywords appear in the article.

In the publishing domain, *semantic publishing* generally refers to publishing documents and information as data objects using a Semantic Web format. Semantic publication is intended for computers to understand the structure and meaning of the information, making information search and data integration more efficient. Semantic publishing has been developed and exploited internally by major publishers for several years, using ontology as a way to categorize and search content of all types, but it's only now starting to break into mainstream publishing applications that are usable by consumers.

Some pundits expect the Semantic Web and Web 3.0 to change the publishing industry as a whole — enabling companies to mix, reuse, and repurpose their copyrighted content with open content in ways that were unimaginable a few years ago. In particular, the area of scientific publishing is ripe for major changes. Tim Berners-Lee predicted in 2001 that the Semantic Web, "will likely profoundly change the very nature of how scientific knowledge is produced and shared, in ways that we can now barely imagine." One area of scientific publishing being invested in today is to enable researchers to self-publish their experiment data in Semantic Web formats directly onto the Web. Imagine a future where a scientist in Berlin could design and run an experiment and then post the research data immediately for a researcher in Tokyo to begin reusing that data in her own experiments. This kind of collaboration is impossible with conventional data formats and requires too tight of coupling between researchers to be pragmatic at huge scales. Interest groups at the W3C (World Wide Web Consortium) are exploring this idea of self-publishing scientific data, and early prototypes have been considered a strong success.

At a very high level, there are at least two different approaches for semantic publishing:

- **Publish information as data objects encoded in Semantic Web languages and formats.** These ontologies and data graphs are usually developed for specific data domains. Often, this more formal approach is expensive and performed only by profit-minded corporations or organizations with a charter for the public good (like government agencies or publicly funded media groups).

- **Use the Web 3.0 technology to annotate existing documents or databases with Semantic Web metadata formats.** This approach can be simpler and more automated when you already have lots of existing non-semantic data to publish. Both approaches already have been deployed into product settings and are in use by major publishing organizations worldwide.

Regardless of whether you're a casual reader of news who wants more targeted suggestions or you represent a high-powered publishing company looking for ways to reach your audience more efficiently, the Semantic Web and Web 3.0 transition that's due to happen between 2010 and 2020 will very likely change your way of thinking about how you subscribe and receive information on the Web.

Semantic social networks

By any measure, the rise of Web-based social networks has defined the age of Web 2.0. By some accounts, more than 40 percent of all Internet traffic (page requests) is going to a social network. The extreme proliferation of social networks has even resulted in a mildly derogatory acronym — YASNS (Yet Another Social Networking Service) — used to deride the emergence of the latest and greatest new social network. The Semantic Web and Web 3.0 are not YASNS! But these newer semantic technologies can bring a lot of value to the existing social network platforms in many ways.

Here are a few major problems with social networking sites and examples of how Semantic Web can help:

- ✓ **Social networking sites don't work with each other.** There's little incentive from a business standpoint to interoperate among social networks, but the people using social networks are frequently frustrated with the fact that they cannot own their own profiles (descriptions about themselves, their interests, the people they know, where they work, and so on) and reuse them in different networks. Instead, the social network users have to retype data from one Web site to the next in a repetitive way just to get the benefits of using some particular social network.

  The Semantic Web can enable social network data portability with a format called FOAF (Friend of a Friend). The FOAF format is already widely used by millions of people, and some social networks already allow import and export of FOAF data so that their users can keep and reuse all that data that they upload to their services. If you think about it, this is really quite a leap from the social network literally owning your personal data to taking back control and ownership of your own data on your own terms. This is one small example of how the Semantic Web can help you regain control over your data.

- ✓ **Social networks predominantly focus on building communities around a particular social object.** Facebook is oriented around friends, and Flickr focuses on social networking around photos. Del.ico.us focuses social networking around bookmarks. VOX focuses on social networking with blogs. LinkedIn focuses on social networking around your job. The challenge comes when people want to engage in networks that span multiple types of social objects. Why do we have to keep our Facebook profiles, LinkedIn profiles, and VOX profiles all separate? The rest of our lives aren't partitioned this way!

  Web 3.0 and Semantic Web technologies can help you engage in a diverse range of social objects without becoming partitioned into only one interest area. For example, Twine is an "interest networking" Web site built on Web 3.0 technology that allows the community members to create social objects around their interests themselves. The Web site is continuously mining user entries and other Web content to recommend new topics to the people who belong to a particular interest group. The system can be browsed from the Web or set up to e-mail interests to the network on a regular basis.

Chapter 3

The Data Web at Work for Business

I've been building and selling semantic technology for businesses since 2001. I know first-hand how difficult it is to sell the Semantic Web vision to profit-minded businesses keyed into bottom-line results. This chapter is a comprehensive examination of top business and chief information officer (CIO) issues with a focus on how the Semantic Web can help. Asset-minded professionals should want to know they can preserve and protect their most valuable capital investments — data.

What's the big deal about the Semantic Web for businesses? The Semantic Web enables businesses to start creating their own webs of universal data connections throughout all their corporate data, content, and documents. This chapter describes the capability of Semantic Web technologies. You find out how businesses currently manage their data-handling needs and how Semantic Web technologies can work with the systems already in place to offer IT solutions that are cheaper to implement and easier to expand and maintain.

Getting a Handle on Enterprise Data Challenges and Opportunities

Data is an asset to any business. In fact, modern businesses are dependent on electronic data. Businesses use electronic data to evaluate past performance and also to guide future investments worth trillions of dollars to the global economy. Large businesses already have access to a lot of data and have made substantial investments in systems to store, manipulate, and report on that data.

Any right-minded businessperson wants perfect visibility into all the highest-quality business data at just the right time for the lowest possible cost. But despite the fact that businesses have tons of existing data (and are creating unprecedented amounts of new data daily), they're still incapable of linking it all together in any sort of timely and cost-efficient way. They're trying to take a drink from the fire hose of data gushing in their businesses.

If the problem were simply about collecting all that data fast enough, the solution would involve engineering existing databases and other content management systems to catch it all. But the real problem is *not* the large quantity of data items (the amount of water gushing out of the fire hose); the problem is capturing the business connections that exist between them (getting a drink of water).

Businesses don't need faster ways to collect data, nor do they need more ways to store or report on data. If anything, they have too many different ways to do all those tasks already. Likewise, businesses don't need more metadata for metadata's sake, nor do they need more integration tools to integrate data from one place into another. Some businesses end up paying to integrate the integration tools!

One technical pain point that Semantic Web solves for businesses is that it provides a universal and powerful way to link data from anywhere to anything. The Semantic Web enables a business to start creating its own web of universal data connections throughout all its corporate data, content, and business documents. These links become the physical web of data — and data definitions — for business.

In the 1990s, the common benchmarks for huge enterprise computing technologies were the global businesses of the United States. But in the 21st century, the new benchmarks for massive corporate software infrastructure have gone global. Some emerging market banks in India and China have data warehouse systems that already rival even the largest retail chains like Wal-Mart.

In global mega-industries like oil and gas, pharmaceuticals, banking, and consumer packaged goods, electronic data is routinely used to generate goods and services worth trillions of dollars to the global economy. Decisions about where to drill for oil, which drugs to produce, and how much money to invest in targeted marketing campaigns are all dependent on access to accurate and comprehensive data.

With continued globalization, the amount of business data, as well as its geographic distribution, is reaching a scale that has never been seen before in the software industry. Here's a glimpse of what most businesses have already made substantial investments in:

- **Databases:** Every business has databases large and small. The database is typically the centerpiece technology infrastructure for nearly every kind of business software application.

- **Data warehouses:** High-end databases typically come configured specifically as data warehouses that are optimized for very fast read times with lots of data.

- **Business intelligence:** Business intelligence refers to the software applications that manipulate data inside data warehouses and run reports for finance, sales, and most other parts of any large business.

- **Information Lifecycle Management (ILM):** Most mature businesses use ILM tools to archive older data yet still make sure it's accessible in case of audits.

- **Content Management Systems (CMS):** These systems are the central repositories for business documents that need to be version controlled and shared from a common storage system. Large businesses typically have several.

- **Enterprise Resource Planning (ERP):** Central business functions like financial ledgers, human resources, and supply chain and logistics software systems are usually categorized as ERP systems.

- **Integration:** Data integration, process integration, and message integration technologies are typically used to help the rest of these software systems work together.

- **Enterprise search:** A search engine can create a large index of content and keywords that can be easily searched — thereby allowing people to search for text matches in the data.

And those are just the data management systems! Clearly there are many existing challenges, and therefore opportunities, in the enterprise software environment. No opportunities stand out more than the chance to help businesses turn data into information.

Understanding the Difference between Information and Data

All businesses have data to manage. Any business large enough to have its own accounting software also has applications, databases, spreadsheets, and other desktop documents full of business data. Much of this data is *logically connected* — it relates to the same business elements — but is *physically disconnected* in ways that prevent any search engine, database, or other content management system from linking up the separate bits of data.

Savvy IT professionals are aware of these implicit, undocumented *logical connections* among business data. They also recognize the problems that can arise when critical business applications don't "talk" to each other over physical connections. For example, financial risk metrics for global banking systems cannot be calculated if the brokerage systems don't exchange risk coefficient data with ledger applications. IT professionals may know of many ways to fix these kinds of problems. But if you've been involved with trying to resolve logical data problems in real enterprise software, you know that the effort can take massive amounts of manual labor, and the success rate of projects that tackle these problems is dismally low.

For example, whenever a person in one department of your organization updates a spreadsheet saved on his or her personal computer, that person creates a new business event and new business data that is untraceable and completely disconnected from your corporate system. Although you may have a proprietary solution that allows the integration of desktop documents into other corporate applications, these are probably *point solutions* (solutions that work for a limited and prearranged set of situations).

In practice, businesses bring together their various systems on an "as needed" basis, and the data tends to be shared in a "need to know" manner. For example, suppose your business needs to create a special report that requires a one-off integration between the facilities database and the financial systems for the purpose of a regulatory audit. The result? Only the data that absolutely must be shared actually is shared when the project is delivered.

This "sharing as needed" practice has an unfortunate consequence of creating a rigid and fragile data ecosystem with the following characteristics:

  ✔ **Difficult data tracking:** Tracing backwards to the original source data can be difficult. For example, in corporate banking environments, it's often necessary to perform an analysis of the data lineage to accurately state how the financial data came to be — this is a requirement both for auditing and risk management.

✔ **Data isolation:** Finding out about associated data that might be related to the original source data is not straightforward. Because so many copies are made of the data, into new silos or other applications, the data may become irreconcilable with other similar data that should match.

✔ **Irregular updating:** All too often, data from separate sources is merged into the department *data mart* (departmental database) intermittently, often weeks apart. At a different interval, that same data might then make its way into the corporate enterprise data warehouse (EDW). Such irregular updating can cause duplicate, erroneous, or incomplete data.

In the abstract, these ideas about data visibility seem somewhat esoteric, but imagine for a minute how these fragile data ecosystems impact your own life. The subprime mortgage crisis everyone felt in 2008 was due in no small part to the inability of the financial institutions to easily assess the actual risk of the loans that they were buying and selling for hundreds of billions of dollars. In actuality, many very large loan bundles were miscategorized to be lower risk than they really were and sold to buyers who thought they were better protected. Then the loan interest rates rose, and homeowners started defaulting. Each financial institution holding large collections of subprime loans had very imprecise ways to assess how risky their loans actually were — before or after the fact. At its essence, this subprime mortgage crisis may have been a larger institutional problem, but it had very real and very painful data issues at its core.

To have reliable information about business performance, the separate data items that your business collects must bridge the gaps between systems and come together to form a complete picture. What your business needs — and what the Semantic Web can provide — is a universal solution for linking disassociated business content into a larger web of cohesive corporate data concepts and business data values. In other words, the Semantic Web can help provide you with easily accessible business information.

Evaluating the Web in Your Current Systems

Somewhat ironically, a semantic web (lowercase *s*) already exists within every large business. This web results from the logical, implied, and undocumented relationships between data in different software systems, and its existence is simply a fact of life for enterprise software. The same IT pragmatists who might say that the Semantic Web vision is unachievable fluff are very likely fighting fires with their own undocumented semantic web.

Each software application has its own domain of data with data objects and values. For example, suppose that one application has a database column attribute called CST_ID, and a data value of 12-34567-GH. But another application has a software class called Customer that has an attribute called SSN with a value of 987654321. A third XML data file uses a tag called <CUID>. In these three data locations, one customer — say, "John Smith" — is represented by three completely different Unique Identifier values, but the logical associations that link this one customer to three different physical data representations are an undeniable part of this undocumented semantic web, as shown in Figure 3-1.

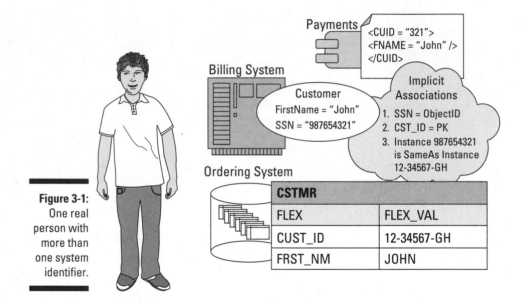

Figure 3-1:
One real person with more than one system identifier.

As a result, businesses tend to tackle the job of turning complex implicit relationships among data into explicit relationships only when they are under extreme pressure to do so. The challenges for taking on these problems are varied and include

- **Technical challenges:** From the software standpoint, it can be an exceptionally difficult manual task to perform the mappings and create the system-level integrations.

- **Scope challenges:** The extreme scale of enterprise computing requires that scope be constantly managed, and usually only the minimal level of duplicative work is funded.

- **Operational challenges:** Businesses need to stay on an even keel to continue operations at (at least) the current performance level. Often, having a poorly working system of operations is better than having none at all due to a failed attempt at improvement, which could halt business operations and result in huge amounts of lost revenue.

So, although all those logical data connections may be there to start, the technical and organizational challenges required to make them actionable may be too high of a financial burden for most organizations. In the following sections, I describe the importance of maintaining existing legacy systems and how the average CIO (Chief Information Officer) prioritizes his or her projects.

Maintaining existing business applications

Most large businesses operate with several enterprise resource planning (ERP) applications. These ERP systems are the lifeblood of business operations. Everything — from how financial books are reconciled to how orders are fulfilled — is driven by these enterprise software applications.

A small mom-and-pop business may use desktop programs like QuickBooks or package shipment software applications from shipping companies like FedEx. The typical large company has several ERP applications for its operations, such as the General Ledger, Shipping and Logistics, Supply Chain Management, and Inventory Management. The same large company probably also has dedicated Reporting systems for each of those ERP applications.

The reasons that large businesses have many ERP systems are as numerous as businesses themselves. Sometimes this complexity is a result of merger and acquisition (M&A) activity, and sometimes the business simply chooses a decentralized IT strategy. In either case, when you have a diversified ERP environment, the costs to consolidate are massive.

In addition to ERP applications, every large IT organization manages thousands of infrastructure software systems that run alongside those operational systems. This infrastructure includes technologies such as

- **Online transaction processing (OLTP)** databases for transactional data such as purchase orders, general ledger activity, and other high-volume transactional data

- **Transaction processing systems (TPS)** such as TPS Monitors that guarantee transaction success as well as enterprise application integration (EAI) and service oriented architecture (SOA) solutions that provide message bus services and enable system integration

- **Enterprise data warehouse (EDW)** appliances and business intelligence systems that perform data aggregations, make calculations, and allow for an intelligent synthesis of many facts

The point is this: Your business already has a significant investment of time and money in software systems to run the operations and manage the related data. Simply maintaining these systems requires continued investment of resources. Instead of spending on innovation and process improvement, your IT department on average spends approximately 80 percent of its budget simply maintaining basic functions.

 As the demand for more information increases, the importance of connecting the data in all your separate systems increases, too. What you need is a solution that enables your existing applications and infrastructure to work together to supply information without having to make another major investment of time and money.

CIO priorities and decision making

Businesses have plenty of data, but they always need people and well-run organizations to turn it into *useful* information. CIOs are faced with enormous pressure: The weight of a modern business rests on the data and software that processes its financial transactions and customer relationships.

Executive leaders in any company need to stay on an even keel that maintains the status quo for operations to continue at their current performance levels. Oftentimes, a poorly working operational system is better than a failed attempt to improve it because the unanticipated failures are the ones that bring business operations to a standstill and result in huge amounts of lost revenue. Most IT executives are inherently risk averse and take a very measured and conservative approach to modernizing software systems. Rarely do you find a cavalier CIO who is embarking on too much change too quickly.

So what is on the global 2000 CIO's mind? Firms like Gartner, CIO Magazine, and CIO Insight regularly survey IT leaders to determine their priorities and areas of focus. A summary of 2008 findings shows that the top-ten concerns are

1. Improving business processes

2. Better customer service

3. Investing in business intelligence

4. Managing server and storage technology

5. Innovating — new products and services

6. Legacy modernization

7. Improving worker productivity

8. Securing the enterprise IT environment

9. Regulatory compliance and corporate governance

10. More flexible and cheaper systems integration

Because 80 percent of a CIO's budget typically is spent maintaining existing functions, only 20 percent is left for innovation and new initiatives. If 80 cents of every dollar you could spend was already spoken for, you too would be cautious about how you used the remaining 20 cents.

Existing investments and infrastructure are the basis for all IT spending patterns in any large business. It is the CIO's job to protect and maintain those investments.

The typical CIO of a Global 2000 enterprise will be faced with data management challenges that may include

- Hundreds of terabytes of warehouse data
- Petabytes of information in a managed lifecycle
- Hundreds of millions of documents and other content under management
- Dozens of departmental data warehouses
- Several enterprise data warehouses
- Dozens of possibly overlapping operational systems that are mission critical for the day-to-day business
- Several transaction processing systems, including multiple integration platforms for integrating applications
- Capital expenditures for both hardware and software on a global basis and in several geographical regions

Navigating huge amounts of data under CIO pressures can be daunting indeed! Enterprise data challenges are numerous and exceptionally complex. After 30 years of infrastructure build-out, large businesses and governments are awash in legacy systems and very inflexible data. The Semantic Web is not a silver bullet for all data ills, but it can offer a dramatically improved way to move forward for strategic-minded managers.

Grasping the Vision of the Semantic Web at Work

What if enterprises could invest in a technology that made data cheap and abundantly easy to find, change, and distribute anywhere? What if your business could seamlessly combine open-source data from the Web with organizational data from your data warehouses and ERP applications? What if your corporate decisions were made with 100 percent visibility into your institutional data and the best of the free data from the Web?

If these "what if" questions sound like the direction you'd like your business to take, I suggest you take a look in the direction of the Semantic Web for some innovative solutions.

People use terms like *semantic web, Web 3.0,* and the *data web* interchangeably to describe the vision behind recently approved standards created by the World Wide Web Consortium (W3C). Although catchy, none of these buzz words supply any hint about this new technology's ability to transform the foundation of enterprise software; empower radical new business capabilities; and throttle back IT spending in the notoriously expensive areas of data integration, master data management, and enterprise information management.

Semantic Web technology doesn't require monolithic software infrastructure to be effective, nor does it require that businesses scrap their existing investments. The technology doesn't require massive software projects to design the perfect global single data model for your enterprise. It is also much more effective than simple search tools for finding what you need.

This technology makes all your business data look like a high-powered database — regardless of whether that data is a document on an employee's hard drive, an existing database, or a repository of many documents in any format — without having to centralize any of that original data into one place.

The Semantic Web of tomorrow is technically more similar to today — and more pragmatic — than you might think. In tomorrow's Semantic Web, there are ERP applications, databases, integration tools, corporate directories, and security systems just like today. There are business process analysis tools, legacy systems, and business intelligence reporting systems. There are even old and new technologies comingled in the same infrastructure. So what's different?

The single largest feature of this future utopia that's different than today is this: Every source of data, every master software system and application, and every platform integration and database provide an interface to its data and business rules in an RDF (Resource Description Framework)–compatible graph data language. When this ubiquity of Web-addressable graph data is achieved, you'll see a dramatic and sustainable cost reduction around data sharing.

RDF will do for data what the Web did for documents. Do you remember what computing was like before the Web? Do you remember how you found documents before the search engine? Do you remember what it cost to share documents before the Internet? Those are the days that gray-haired IT guys and pencil-sharpening finance gals would like to forget.

The transformative power of making minute data pieces addressable at Web scale, on Web protocols, and with powerful artificial intelligence search, reasoning and learning capabilities cannot be overestimated. This utopian vision is probably an inevitability — how else could the future unfold? Some may argue that we've reached the height of IT data capabilities — that all the future may hold is more eXtensible Mark up Language (XML), more Java, and more proprietary vendor solutions. I contend, however, that software will significantly improve, becoming easier, cheaper, and more automatic.

Flourishing in a Semantic Web Utopia

In the future utopia of easily accessible and distributable data, business will have many new capabilities at hand. Consider the following effects on some major industries:

- ✔ **Manufacturers** would be able to easily and simply identify all data, documents, and other electronic content about any product they make. This new accessibility would take place without the manufacturer having to move all that data into the same place. But the ability to answer highly complex queries would make product-recall investigations or other compliance-related needs go much more smoothly than they do today.

- ✔ **International banks** could drill into accounts, transactions, and financial histories without requiring many months of expensive IT projects to do so. Financial institutions could assess risk with greater accuracy because more of the relevant data would be available without large IT investments. Perhaps even a major capital markets crisis (subprime mortgage lending, perhaps?) might be averted in the future when data is more transparent and auditable.

- ✔ **Mega-pharmaceutical companies** could slash the costs of drug development. When these companies can easily combine open-source Web data with their own proprietary data, they can have a much higher success ratio with their investments and waste fewer dollars in unsuccessful drug targets.

- ✔ **Communications systems** would be radically different. American and European markets would enjoy a preponderance of choices for new phone and media plans. Released from the rigid provisioning and billing systems of yesteryear, telecommunications data would be more fluid and dynamic than ever before.

- ✔ **Clinical health providers and consumers** would have access to leading research. Different standards and regulations could be better aligned with more flexible and secure data exchange. Insurance regulations and

> guidance would be applied easily at the electronic data level without creating a conflict of interest from primary care providers. Costly and inefficient data governance problems, like defining which treatments are valid treatments for a given health condition, could be reconciled and financed at the community level without forcing a central membership committee to all adopt the same rules.

This utopian picture would also include a means for protecting the civil liberties and privacy rights of citizens while allowing for a sensible way of monitoring data that can help law enforcement catch the bad guys. It will be possible to search through data records and seek nefarious activity while avoiding any data-level infringements on citizen privacy. These systems will be open, flexible, transparent, and easily configurable to match the policy direction of the government who controls them.

When and if this utopian vision becomes a reality, productivity and efficiency in all industries will skyrocket. Manufacturers will waste no time with inefficient supply chains, and retail chains will be able to better assess customer buying patterns across multiple points of contact. All businesses will benefit from faster merger and acquisition abilities, tighter IT integration, and low-cost modernization efforts with their legacy systems.

Newer Semantic Web–based business systems, applications, databases, and directories, as described in the following sections, will transform how businesses respond to change.

Semantic Web applications

Semantic Web applications — designed using RDF, OWL, and SPARQL — will be the next major evolution in how application-specific software is written. Much like the CASE (computer-aided software engineering) vision of the 1980s, semantic applications will be capable of round-trip engineering lifecycles based entirely on the metadata models describing the application. Unlike Java programming of today or UML (Unified Modeling Language) modeling features, the applications of the future will actually have executable domain models at the heart of their applications.

For the technically astute, think "ontology-based plain old Java objects (POJO) layer without compiled code." In simpler terms, the semantic application will be capable of substantial evolution without requiring a programmer to rigidly encode the program's execution path in advance. Likewise, because each of these semantic applications will make all their data Web-addressable in an open graph data format, the costs of reusing that data in other systems will be trivial.

Semantic Web databases

The heart of semantic applications is a semantic database. Unlike a relational database, whose main purpose in life is static data storage, the semantic database will contain highly adaptive, dynamic data records that respond to changing conditions. This level of data adaptability is required because when traditional applications work with *data in-memory* (the code that is executing in the computer's random access memory [RAM]), they always have to apply additional rules, transaction logic, and other programming features to enrich the statically stored data beyond what is simply saved on the hard drive. This adaptive, dynamic, fully instantiated data must be exposed and available at Web scale, as executable models that don't require brittle compiled code to find the implications of data rules and data logic. (Compiled code is brittle because to change program logic, the code must be recompiled.) Semantic databases will use — but not replace the need for — relational databases. Likewise, they may also take the form of *in-memory databases* (databases where the data is held in RAM). But each and every semantic database, regardless of implementation, will enable a Web-addressable standard graph data format that can go a long way toward supplying businesses with easy and low-cost data integration options.

Semantic Web integration

Because the costs of data integration can't be completely free, there must be a kind of infrastructure that provides integration for very low cost. This same semantic integration infrastructure will provide "wrapper services" for applications and databases that aren't semantics-aware so that they can participate in the semantic integration scenarios as well (by wrapping the non-semantic applications with semantic interfaces). These semantic integration tools will look a lot like today's service-oriented architecture (SOA) systems, but with additional low-cost semantic capabilities built in to their process orchestration and data integration subsystems. Therefore, the existing SOA and data integration subsystems can be fully leveraged from within a semantic integration super-process. The combination of old and new integration patterns will supply a universal and standards-based way of making data from anywhere at any time at any scale available to businesspeople.

Semantic Web directories

A semantic directory will be where you go to find something in the business. It will include the regular text search capabilities that you've become used to. It will also include a way to read all those LDAP (Lightweight Directory

Access Protocol) and Active Directory registries that are strewn about within a typical large global enterprise. A semantic directory will also supply a super-set indexing service for the many content management systems your business likely owns. And, of course, for those EAI (enterprise application integration) and SOA infrastructure services, the semantic directory will provide UDDI (Universal Description, Discovery, and Integration) registry type capabilities for registering and finding services. What makes the semantic registry unique is that it will be capable of automatically finding associations among all the aforementioned indexes and directories so that you can actually have a one-stop place to go for finding electronic business stuff.

Semantic Web policies and data security

One predominant feature that will be common across all semantic applications, databases, and directories will be a trustworthy security layer. This semantic policy layer will reliably encapsulate the trust and proof languages of today — like JAAS (Java Authentication and Authorization Service), WS-Policy (Web Service Policy), SAML (Security Access Markup Language), and XACML (eXtensible Access Control Markup Language). The semantic policy layer will also being able to reconcile differences between them and apply them to a wide set of resources.

A central problem in the security and access technology standards area is that there is no shared baseline for expressing the many kinds of complex rules and logic that must be expressed in order to adequately secure complex software applications. Therefore it's still possible to end up in situations where JAAS permissions conflict with WS-Policy rights (or XACML, or SAML) and the security of an entire system is compromised. This newly envisioned Semantic Web–based policy layer will supply that logical baseline for other policy languages and provide a guaranteed way of encoding policies that can be enforced from one application to the next. Far from being simply a vehicle for technical wizardry, the semantic policy infrastructure will ensure that different software security products and applications can have a shared and correct interpretation of important business policies.

Discovering Why Semantics Are for Everyday Businesspeople

Sometimes lost in the jumble of technology acronyms and high-minded scenarios about future IT abilities is the basic reality that normal, nontechnical people are the vast majority of the global workforce. Despite the proliferation of enterprise software, most businesses require their employees to work with only the most basic of computer skills. Perhaps a little bit of word-processing and Web-browser software experience is the minimum required to perform basic data operations for the average employer.

Whatever the semantic future of software may be, you can be sure that it has to be at least as easy as today's applications to have any hope of success. Everyday people are involved in manufacturing automobiles and farm equipment and making decisions about retail products, inventory, and marketing programs. Everyday people open banking accounts and use the health care system. These folks would benefit from less wasted time finding corporate policies and regulations, from easier access to headquarter business systems and data, and from a clearer picture of what metrics matter most to executive leadership. These everyday people find themselves in extraordinary jobs of all sorts, as discussed in the following sections.

Commercial trading alliances

From Wal-Mart to Toyota, from British Airways to Pepsi, the world's largest businesses participate in economically staggering trade alliances. Often moving transactions that total in the billions or trillions of dollars annually, these businesses are the true lifeblood of the global economy. Everyday people who work at these businesses will key in data that eventually might be aggregated, recalculated, and sent electronically all over the globe. These sorts of data-intensive jobs are everyday jobs — the kind of jobs that will be impacted most by semantic applications, databases, and integration technologies within their businesses.

National security programs

The U.S. armed services, federal agencies, and state and local services employ millions of everyday people whose jobs involve making every citizen more safe and secure. These everyday people include firemen, police officers, case workers, and civil servants who consume and supply data to the government about their particular area of responsibility. As a whole, these databases, alert systems, and public reporting tools are the basis from which citizens take action in a time of emergency. These everyday jobs can be made easier and more effective with smarter data made available from semantic applications, databases, and integration technologies.

Business operations

Everyday jobs for most businesses require exceptional data needs. People who take orders at cash registers or who send business e-mails and sign up for their employee benefits are all creating and manipulating business data that is used operationally for running the business. Each operational data point is later aggregated and recalculated for future analysis within some sort of software analytic program. Retail sales for clothing, food items, and even utilities are scrutinized within analytic software applications as a way to improve operational efficiency. The everyday people who use business software can be more efficient and more effective if they begin to use semantic applications, databases, and integration technologies.

Making the Semantic Web Choice Now

The Semantic Web is a fundamentally unique way of specifying data and data relationships. It's more declarative, more expressive, and more consistently repeatable than Java/C++, relational databases, and XML documents. It builds on and preserves the conventional data model's respective strengths. The following sections explain why the Semantic Web will

- Empower, directly and indirectly, new business capabilities
- Throttle back IT expenditures within medium and large businesses
- Transform the foundation of enterprise software, and data integration in particular

Your call to action is to do the following now:

- Invest in training and skills development
- Prototype a solution and explore the new tools
- Ask your software vendors about their semantic technology roadmap
- Compel your enterprise architects to formulate a multi-year metadata strategy

The following sections give you an understanding of the overall superiority of Semantic Web technologies, why they'll be embedded in the fabric of nearly all data-intensive software within several years, and why you should start investing in them now.

Understanding why people buy enterprise business software

The businesspeople who buy enterprise software and approve technology investments make decisions that involve spending about $150 billion each year. These expenditures primarily come from medium and large businesses with annual revenues greater than $50 million. Your business may be looking to upgrade or add new systems for any of the following business reasons:

- ✓ **Competitive pressures:** To keep up with overall industry improvements
- ✓ **Executive mandates:** To fulfill new business initiatives mandated by sponsoring executives
- ✓ **Cost controls:** To streamline outdated processes and generate new efficiencies
- ✓ **Regulatory demands:** To meet the requirements of corporate, local, state, and federal governance
- ✓ **Strategic advantages:** To gain business advantage through use of information, for example, in collaboration

But what factors impact a buying decision for enterprise software? Contrary to popular belief, the relative quality or technical superiority of the software is rarely a decision-making advantage for the vendors. Likewise, the long-term strategic fit of the technology is usually not enough of a reason for a substantial enterprise software buy. Instead, the following selection drivers are most frequently the factors that explain why large sums of money for enterprise software change hands:

- ✓ **Lowest risk option:** Where risk is calculated on the basis of overall fit and vendor reputation
- ✓ **Tactical fit:** Where the short-term requirements trump any long-term disadvantages
- ✓ **Partner/vendor choices:** Where the important ties between customer and vendor matter

Although it may be a straightforward task to promote the Semantic Web technology stack on the basis of its technical and strategic superiority for enterprise software, I suggest first building a business case that speaks toward the real buying pressures in the market: lowest risk, tactical fit, and vendor relationships. Only then can I explain why Semantic Web is a superior technical choice for many hard data problems.

Low-risk choice

Your first look may tell you that the Semantic Web technology seems like a riskier alternative to conventional database technologies, basic XML, and software development using UML and Java. For starters, the Semantic Web technology faces these challenges:

- ✓ Minimal large vendor support for development tools
- ✓ Required skill sets that are hard to find and expensive to hire
- ✓ Few proven reference implementations in the public domain
- ✓ Required and very real paradigm shift in modeling, design, and declarative programming techniques

But I challenge you to change your mindset and shift the risk horizon to five years from now. When you do, the status quo technologies begin to look like the riskier option. Software professionals know that when they develop new software on the basis of purely tactical decisions, the chaotic result includes incomprehensible data silos that are much more costly — and risky — to handle in the long run.

Examples of the chaos include the following:

- ✓ **Data proliferation:** Data breeds like bunnies, resulting in incompatible formats, multiple naming conventions, and different applications, all using different metadata.

- ✓ **Sensor (instrument) proliferation:** Sensors and other devices are creating more and more silos of data, faster, and with more expectations.

- ✓ **Complexity explosion:** The work gets more complicated as you acquire more data models, transformation rules, business rules, XML, UML, Java, and so on.

- ✓ **Executive mandates:** Expectations of IT are higher than ever and becoming more demanding.

New thinking about innovation shows how the discounted cash flow (DCF) trap can distort conventional business risk assessments by incorrectly favoring do-nothing strategies. By shifting time horizons, you can begin to see that the limits of plain old Java, XML, and RDBMS simply can't adapt quickly enough to the new world of enterprise software.

Try asking a Fortune 500 CIO whose company is working under the strain of thousands of systems to change a core business data definition; or ask the CIO to produce a report that shows which enterprise software systems handle purchase order data. Seemingly simple tasks for a computer become unsolvable situations when the data is disconnected, inconsistently formatted, and invisible to any sort of cohesive view.

Old technology itself is not the problem. The uncoordinated proliferation of old technology is the actual problem. And the *uncoordinated* part is a nonnegotiable reality of 21st century big business.

Thus, although choosing the traditional technology that appears to be low-risk today seems like a smart idea, it takes only a little foresight to stretch your risk horizon, avoid the DCF trap, and realize that the current path of data management status quo is unsustainable at current rates of data proliferation and complexity.

The DCF trap

The *Harvard Business Review* has a great explanation of the DCF trap: "Most executives compare the cash flows from innovation against the default scenario of doing nothing, assuming — incorrectly — that the present health of the company will persist indefinitely if the investment is not made. For a better assessment of the innovation's value, the comparison should be between its projected discounted cash flow and the more likely scenario of a decline in performance in the absence of innovation investment."

The following figure is a visual representation of how the DCF trap can lead to false strategy conclusions.

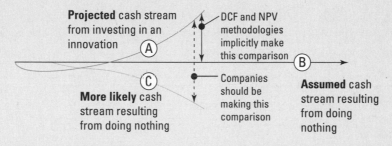

Projected cash stream from investing in an innovation Ⓐ

DCF and NPV methodologies implicitly make this comparison

Ⓒ Companies should be making this comparison

More likely cash stream resulting from doing nothing

Ⓑ **Assumed** cash stream resulting from doing nothing

Semantic Web technologies are lower risk in the medium-term timeframe; in the short term, they're also most likely to become the roadmap for traditional data technologies — based on technical merits alone.

In terms of absolute risk, accounting for a long horizon, and the DCF Trap, the low-risk choice for an info-centric organization is to begin investing in Semantic Web technology as a common metadata foundation for adaptive data and as a common control point for information held in various repositories, applications, and physical structures.

Tactical choice

By definition, most enterprise software projects will have a simple tactical software solution available to them — the enterprise software industry itself has evolved to a sufficiently mature state that most software problems in most industries will have a specific vendor with a specific solution as at least one option. But now more than ever, these tactical solutions are seen for what they are — often a stop-gap series of temporary fixes that usually create new silos of disconnected data and rarely fit within an organization's strategic direction. Nonetheless, there is usually compelling business and financial motivation to choose a strong tactical enterprise software solution, where a top-priority business problem can be temporarily fixed, even if the bigger technical problem remains unresolved.

In contrast, a Semantic Web–based solution almost never looks like a tactical fit from the surface. But dig a little deeper, and more narrowly define the meaning of a "tactical fit," and Semantic Web technologies will look a lot more down-to-earth.

For instance, many enterprise software projects revolve around the notion of information-centric operations. *Information-centric operations* are what most large global businesses and modern defense organizations use as a guiding strategy for their operations. Information is increasingly viewed as a high-value asset from which other strategies are built and executed. When the tactical fit of enterprise software depends on information-centricity, it's hard to beat the power of Semantic Web data specifications. Tactical projects for a large, information-centric organization might include:

- Data integration, at the XML, RDBMS, and object software tiers
- Data warehousing and business intelligence
- Service-oriented architecture (SOA) data services
- IT maintenance and IT infrastructure management
- Portal applications and data mashups
- Data replication, migration, and transformation

Each of these tactical areas has both large and small vendor solutions servicing demand by using Semantic Web technologies. Although still a minority, the vendors using Semantic Web technology to supply tactical software solutions in these project areas would certainly expect to be measured against all the typical tactical metrics the industry has adopted.

In essence, when the buying organization is committed to information-centric operations and defines tactical success as measure of data flexibility, auditability, and reuse, the Semantic Web–based products will often be best-of-breed for those specific tactical needs. In particular cases, a vendor may specify which technologies are being used or choose to market the benefits the technology provides.

Oracle, IBM, and Software AG all leverage Semantic Web technologies in their SOA products, but you won't see them advertise the technology itself — only the features they provide.

So, contrary to popular belief, some Semantic Web technology can be very tactical in nature. And as is frequently observed, a little semantics goes a long way.

Viable partnering

Strong business relationships can trump other buying factors in most cases. The preference for sticking with a known vendor is a function of risk. If you've been successful with a partner previously,

> ✔ You inherently trust that vendor more.
>
> ✔ You view that vendor's suggestions as less risky than those of a new, unknown, vendor.

In most cases, going with the known quantity is just simple, smart decision-making. The Semantic Web can't explicitly bolster any particular partnership choices, nor can the technology itself help buyers overcome any personal doubts about a particular vendor's employees.

Consider this: Most large enterprise software vendors, and many small ones, have already begun to adopt Semantic Web technologies and embed them into their mainstream products. In fact, leading enterprise software vendors such as HP, IBM, Microsoft, Oracle, SAP, and SoftwareAG all currently provide applications and tools that support Semantic Web specifications.

Ask your partners about their plans to adopt Semantic Web standards for metadata and data. If your mainstream partners are unwilling or unable to articulate clear guidance about their roadmap for data and metadata management, there are many midsize vendors who would appreciate your time and can give you details about the future of Semantic Web technology for enterprise software.

Trusted relationships usually lead to good business decisions, but in the realm of technology and data management, your trusted advisors must be innovative as well as safe.

Seeing the technical superiority of the Semantic Web

Data is different than information. In the context of software, *information* is data that references or is referenced by a computational model. That information model is a necessary, logically consistent interface for accessing data. These information models are always accompanied by metadata about the model itself. The Semantic Web specifications (RDF, OWL, SPARQL, GRDDL, SAWSDL — refer to Chapter 1 for details) define consistent computational interfaces for enterprise software to declaratively interact with data.

Besides Semantic Web specifications, other computational metadata specifications for information models typically include

> ✔ Entity Relationship Model and DDL Scripting — all relational databases
>
> ✔ Meta Object Facility Models and Model Transformers — all UML compatible languages
>
> ✔ XML Infoset Model and Custom Program Implementations — all XML interchange

Databases, UML, and XML technologies constitute how the vast majority of enterprise software applications store and manage data today. But the Semantic Web presents a newer, more computationally powerful metadata specification that can be as reliable as a database, as portable as XML, and as powerful as native programming logic.

The Semantic Web specifications, in particular RDF and OWL, are the only technology specifications that were purpose-built for use as a metadata language, entirely dedicated to describing and linking data of all sorts at Web scale. More than 30 years ago, relational databases were conceived for the storage and consistently fast retrieval of data records. More than 15 years ago, UML was conceived as a unified approach for visually modeling structure software programs. Almost 10 years ago, XML was wrought from SGML as a way to give structure to documents and messages. Yet today, software developers routinely misuse XML, UML, and relational databases for purposes that they were not intended for.

Areas where RDBMS, UML, and XML technologies are misused, and where Semantic Web technologies excel, include specifications of

- Computationally sound business information models, such as technical data models that have a mathematical consistency that ensures consistent interpretation

- Linking and relationship (meta)data across physical data locations, like joining data and data models across system boundaries

- Dynamic structural logic and rules that are part of the data realm, such as the ability to influence interpretation directly from the data itself (not an application)

- A federation approach for geographically separate data records, like an agreed upon framework for distributing data using Web protocols

It isn't that RDBMS, UML, and XML technology can't be made to solve some of these technical challenges, but to do so, they must be contorted beyond what they are best at doing. Also, attempts to make them work have led to nonstandard, one-off, vendor-implemented, heuristics-based solutions that have absolutely zero portability and therefore no chance at solving enterprise-scale information problems. Semantic Web specifications are the only purpose-built solution for large-scale metadata intensive data problems in enterprise software.

Being purpose-built for change is a particularly striking difference between Semantic Web technology and conventional data languages. Conventional approaches rely on static data models and complex query logic, which cause a type of software development lifecycle that favors the up-front specification of system behavior. But software developers can rarely envision how a given system will be used in practice many years from the point that requirements were developed. In fact, application data will be always be used in unanticipated ways.

The Semantic Web specifications are different because they provide for continually changing data models, inferred classification of data and taxonomy, and all the richness and power of a declarative query language.

Key Semantic Web specifications were commissioned by U.S. and European government agencies in the early 2000s because their defense research scientists knew that RDBMS, UML, and XML technologies could not, by themselves, solve the information challenges of the next century. Even the standards bodies that control conventional data standards are selecting Semantic Web standards as a foundation for their own next-generation specifications. For instance,

- ✔ **Object Management Group,** which controls UML and CWM specifications, is adopting RDF and OWL as the centerpiece specification for its core Definitional Metamodels.

- ✔ The **International Standards Organization,** which controls various EDI and Metadata specifications, is adopting RDF and OWL within several ISO specification families.

- ✔ The **World Wide Web Consortium,** which controls XML and SOA specifications, is adopting RDF and OWL as extensions to existing XML and Web service specifications.

- ✔ **OASIS,** which controls many business domain-specific data specifications, is adopting RDF and OWL as a core feature in standards for Documents, Data Centers, Security, and Business Process Management.

But global conglomerates and federal agencies are not idly waiting for the enterprise software vendors and standards bodies to supply the Semantic Web on a silver platter. Specific situations are emerging from these end-user organizations that demonstrate both the necessity and power of the Semantic Web technical approach. Organizations are investing in this technology, in most cases, because there isn't a viable alternative that can address the size, scope, or complexity of their legacy data problems.

It should be plain to see that the Semantic Web specifications provide a superior technical capability for information-intensive enterprise software problems, which have a high degree of dependence on metadata for operational reliability, portability, and dynamic behavior.

Discovering the Semantic Web as a foundation for modern business

Hopefully at this point you understand the Semantic Web's superiority in the realm of metadata and data management, and you realize that it can be a safe, low-risk, and tactically oriented solution that's well supported by traditional partners. With that out of the way, I can turn to what you *really* want to know about: the business benefits of the technology.

Although the Semantic Web by itself cannot supply any magic revenue boost to the enterprise bottom line, it can provide a means to rationalize incredibly complex information ecosystems. Without Semantic Web technologies, businesses and federal agencies must use conventional RDBMS, UML, and XML technology combined with liberal amounts of expensive manpower, in order to rein in and achieve a modicum of clarity into their enterprise systems, information and data.

The Semantic Web can be tactically applied to many projects, as described in the "Tactical choice" section earlier in this chapter. The Semantic Web may also be strategically applied to the following business initiatives:

- ✔ Enterprise information management
- ✔ Enterprise governance and risk (including policy compliance)

The Semantic Web is itself an enabler. (Fortunately, it's a *positive* sort of enabler.) It enables systems to run more smoothly as a result of better metadata, enables less-expensive manual efforts to keep disparate information linked up, and provides much stronger capabilities for auditing, tracking, and defining actionable rules on top of shared enterprise data. The Semantic Web specifications are

- ✔ **Empower, directly and indirectly, new business capabilities** because they enable stronger and more consistent metadata linking, automatic inference for dynamic data structures, and a more declarative foundation model for shared business information
- ✔ **Throttle back IT expenditures** within medium and large businesses with reduced head-count requirements for the management of enterprise information assets, decrease the long-term costs of integration, and simplify decentralized data architectures
- ✔ **Transform the foundation of enterprise software** as all major software vendors adopt Semantic Web specifications within the context of their own mainstream tools

In short, the Semantic Web can help smash the silos of data that currently cost the enterprise time and money to make interoperable. Start training and planning for it. Talk to your vendors about it now.

Part II
Catch the Wave of Smart Data Today

The 5th Wave   By Rich Tennant

Tarzan - Lord of the Web

"...and then one day it hit Tarzan, Lord of Jungle – where future in that?"

In this part . . .

As it turns out, writing software is pretty hard. Data and software technology can be complex, and despite the best wishes of developers, there's only so much magic in those lines of code they write. This part of the book gives you a context for why the Semantic Web is technically different than the problematic types of data formats and metadata specifications that came before it.

Chapter 4

A Quick Semantic Web Primer

*T*his chapter provides a quick overview of the Semantic Web languages and specifications. You can scan it quickly in ten minutes for a summary of key features and examples of the RDF, RDFa, RSS, OWL, and FOAF specifications that you read about in Chapters 1 and 2. Or, if you prefer, you can take some more time with this chapter and really drill into the details.

In this chapter, I provide several simple examples of data formats and also some more complicated data examples that you can investigate to get started. You can type these examples into online code validators and see the results yourself, or you can simply download some developer software to start working with the examples immediately. Later, in Chapters 7 and 8, I supply a deep-dive, programmer-level explanation of RDF and OWL that goes beyond the basics presented here.

Getting Started with RDF Data

The Resource Description Framework (RDF) is the base language of the Semantic Web. It's a language used for describing data, metadata, and even other data languages. RDF uses a graph data format, in contrast to relational data formats (such as most databases) and hierarchical data formats (such as XML). Any data model or data language that uses RDF is a part of the Semantic Web.

The RDF graph is based on the idea that every data item should have a unique Web identifier, called a URI (Uniform Resource Identifier), and that every data item can be connected to every other item. A URI is different from a URL (Uniform Resource Locator) in that a URI may refer to either a

Web name or a location; a URL may refer only to actual Web locations. RDF makes URI relationships between data items the central attribute of the overall data model. Semantic Web programmers create data with URIs and link them together using relationships that are also named with URIs. In this way, an interconnected set of data may be distributed at global scale across the Internet.

Making a statement (Or two!)

In Listing 4-1, you see a basic RDF structure. Like anybody who is learning a new programming language, you may find it difficult to understand all the syntax at first, but don't be intimidated. After you get past some of the initial syntax questions, you'll see that RDF can be pretty easy.

Listing 4-1: A Simple RDF Graph

```
<?xml version="1.0"?>
<rdf:RDF
  xmlns:rdf="http://www.w3.org/1999/02/22-rdf-syntax-ns#"
  xmlns:dc="http://purl.org/dc/elements/1.1/">

  <rdf:Description rdf:about="http://me.jtpollock.us/">
  <dc:title>Jeff's Homepage!</dc:title>
  </rdf:Description>

  <rdf:Description rdf:about="http://me.jtpollock.us/">
    <dc:creator
     rdf:resource="http://me.jtpollock.us/foaf.rdf#me"/>
  </rdf:Description>

</rdf:RDF>
```

When you load the data structure in Listing 4-1 into any RDF-capable system, as described in Chapters 1 and 2, you get two new RDF data items. Each item is saying something about my relationship to a Web page. These RDF data items are usually called *triples,* or *statements.* (You can use the terms interchangeably.)

The first RDF statement is

```
<rdf:Description rdf:about="http://me.jtpollock.us/">
  <dc:title>Jeff's Homepage!</dc:title>
</rdf:Description>
```

It says that there is a Web page at the address http://me.jtpollock.us/, the title of which is "Jeff's Homepage!"

Chapter 4: A Quick Semantic Web Primer **71**

The second RDF statement is similar:

```
<rdf:Description rdf:about="http://me.jtpollock.us/">
  <dc:creator
   rdf:resource="http://me.jtpollock.us/foaf.rdf#me"/>
</rdf:Description>
```

This statement says that there is a Web page at `http://me.jtpollock.us/` whose creator is `http://me.jtpollock.us/foaf.rdf#me`. With RDF, every part of a statement may be a URI that points to another location. In this statement, the creator data simply points to another RDF resource that has a collection of data about me.

When taken together, these RDF triples provide two individual statements about the relationship between a particular Web page and some other data resources on the Web. The first triple simply names the page with a title, and the second triple identifies the creator by pointing to another set of data that describes me.

You can try validating this RDF yourself. Validating RDF is a lot like validating XML, HTML, or any other programming language: The validator simply checks to see whether there are any issues with your code. Navigate your Web browser to the W3C (World Wide Web Consortium) RDF validation service at `www.w3.org/RDF/Validator`. At this site, type in the code in Listing 4-1, choose the Triples and Graph setting from the Web page, and click the Parse RDF button. You should see results that look like Figure 4-1.

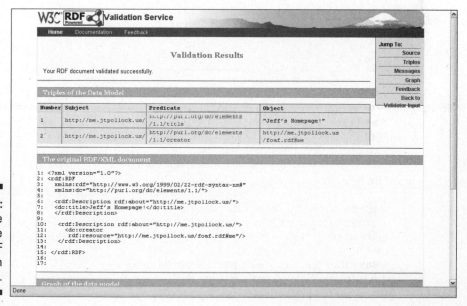

Figure 4-1:
An example from the W3C RDF Validation Service.

Figure 4-1 shows how the W3C Validation Service can take the example code you've copied, identify the two individual triples, and build a simple picture of how they're related in a graph.

Behold: A federated data graph

The simple set of two RDF triples in Listing 4-1 is actually a somewhat sophisticated data graph. The syntax of the RDF example uses several keywords to reference other parts of the example and also other parts of the Web. RDF statements that reference data vocabularies hosted in other parts of the Web are called *federated graphs*. Take, for example, the following statements:

```
xmlns:rdf="http://www.w3.org/1999/02/22-rdf-syntax-ns#"
xmlns:dc="http://purl.org/dc/elements/1.1/"
```

These two lines of code declare prefix variables that may be used elsewhere in the example. For instance, the xmlns prefix stands for *XML Namespace,* and you can use this keyword to create short-hand variables throughout your RDF documents. Throughout this chapter, I refer to it as simply a *namespace*.

In the example, you can see that the keyword prefix rdf is made equal to the URI http://www.w3.org/1999/02/22-rdf-syntax-ns#. The keyword dc is declared equal to the URI http://purl.org/dc/elements/1.1/.

With the RDF example shown in Listing 4-1, you can see tags that contain the two keyword prefixes dc and rdf. Whenever you see the shorthand prefix, you know that the computer will replace the shorthand with a fully qualified statement. For example, the tag <dc:creator> will be interpreted as <http://purl.org/dc/elements/1.1/creator>. This method is how you link data and data semantics across the Web.

The word creator means something to a human, but it doesn't mean anything to an XML parser. Typically, without the Semantic Web, a programmer would have to encode specific matching logic in a software program to interpret and react to the word creator when it appears in data. But in the Semantic Web, words can be defined as part of a vocabulary, providing context, definitions, and a model for interpreting the meaning of those words.

In the example, the word creator is defined to be a part of the XML Namespace http://purl.org/dc/elements/1.1/. This URI is a directory service that points to a vocabulary about publishing provided by the Dublin Core initiative. (The nearby sidebar, "Dublin Core initiative," gives you some insight into what Dublin Core is.)

Thus, the definition of the word creator is provided by the Dublin Core vocabulary, as you can see in Figure 4-2.

Persistent URLs (PURLs)

A Persistent Uniform Resource Locator (PURL) is a URL that defines an intermediate and more persistent Web location instead of the actual physical location of the resource being pointed to. Calling a PURL results in redirection (for example, via a 302 HTTP status code) to the current location of the final resource.

PURLs are an interim measure while Uniform Resource Names (URNs) are being adopted.

URL persistence problems are caused by the practical impossibility of every user having his or her own domain name, and the inconvenience and money involved in re-registering domain names, which results in WWW authors putting their documents in arbitrary locations of transient persistence.

Existing official PURLs (on Purl.org) will probably be mapped to a URN namespace at a later date.

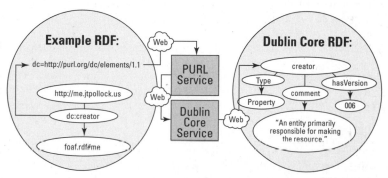

Figure 4-2: Logical view of how RDF models are federated across Web locations.

The definition of the word `creator` is much more than just the `description` or `comment` provided in the Dublin Core vocabulary. In Table 4-1, you can see that there is a specification that defines the vocabulary and usage of the `creator` term.

Table 4-1	Dublin Core: Creator
Term Name	*Definition*
Comment	An entity primarily responsible for making the resource.
Description	Examples of a creator include a person, an organization, or a service. Typically, the name of a Creator should be used to indicate the entity.
Full definition	`http://dublincore.org/documents/dcmi-terms/#elements-creator`

Dublin Core initiative

The Dublin Core metadata element set is a widely used standard to describe digital materials such as video, sound, image, text, and composite media like Web pages. The standard was defined by ISO in 2003 within ISO Standard 15836 and NISO Standard Z39.85-2007.

The semantics of Dublin Core is expressed in RDF and is maintained by an international, cross-disciplinary group of professionals from librarianship, computer science, text encoding, the museum community, and other related fields of scholarship and practice.

In fact, because the Dublin Core is considered to be one of the definitive sources of metadata terms, it serves as a canonical reference point for many other vocabularies. Saying that your software system understands Dublin Core metadata is like saying that you understand a particular dialect of English. The Dublin Core provides the set of words and terms that enables any software that shares this dialect to automatically interoperate.

In the example in Listing 4-1, I used a pointer to the Dublin Core term `creator`, which will allow anyone who understands that dialect to know what I mean when I say that something is the creator of something else.

The example includes some other pointers, too. The following are namespace pointers:

```
xmlns:rdf="http://www.w3.org/1999/02/22-rdf-syntax-ns#"
xmlns:dc=http://purl.org/dc/elements/1.1/
```

Here's an example of a RDF resource pointer:

```
rdf:resource="http://me.jtpollock.us/foaf.rdf#me"
```

The namespace pointer acts just like the previous Dublin Core example, by importing terms from external vocabularies. The `rdf:` shorthand prefix refers to the W3C specification for RDF syntax, which is used to define keywords like `Description` and `about`.

The RDF Resource pointer is interpreted by the RDF parser and may be navigated to find another RDF document that describes the creator (me). In this case, I have a Friend of a Friend (FOAF) vocabulary that defines who I am; it contains an RDF profile of who I know and what I've done. (For more on FOAF, see the section "Friend of a Friend [FOAF]," later in this chapter.) Therefore, the small example data graph I created is actually federated across several locations, as illustrated in Figure 4-3.

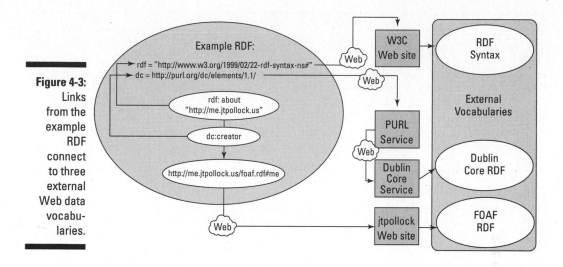

Figure 4-3:
Links
from the
example
RDF
connect
to three
external
Web data
vocabu-
laries.

In a nutshell, the power of the Semantic Web is that you can create new data models for yourself by reusing models that others have published. Additionally, the fundamental rules and syntax for how to define the data and link it are provided for by the W3C. The Semantic Web provides a blueprint for creating a large-scale, Web-based graph database. How cool is that?

Gleaning what the data model says

The first part of the model in Listing 4-1 defines the document type, syntax, and basic structure:

```
<?xml version="1.0"?>
<rdf:RDF  namespaces  />
```

These two lines are the self-describing aspect of the Semantic Web. Although RDF may be expressed in several different syntaxes, the examples in this chapter use the RDF/XML syntax that is officially part of the standard. That's what the first line — <?xml version="1.0"?> — tells you. The second line describes its own syntax as RDF <rdf:RDF . . . />.

The remaining RDF data exists between those tags:

```
<?xml version="1.0"?>
<rdf:RDF  namespaces  />

. . . RDF data

</rdf:RDF>
```

Recall how namespaces are declared in the RDF header:

```
<?xml version="1.0"?>
<rdf:RDF
   xmlns:rdf="http://www.w3.org/1999/02/22-rdf-syntax-ns#"
   xmlns:dc="http://purl.org/dc/elements/1.1/">

. . . RDF data

</rdf:RDF>
```

In the example, the remaining RDF data items are the RDF statements themselves:

```
<rdf:Description rdf:about="http://me.jtpollock.us/">
<dc:title>Jeff's Homepage!</dc:title>
</rdf:Description>

<rdf:Description rdf:about="http://me.jtpollock.us/">
   <dc:creator rdf:resource="http://me.jtpollock.us/
      foaf.rdf#me"/>
</rdf:Description>
```

In plain English, I've created a very small set of structured data that says the following two things:

- There is a Web page (`http://me.jtpollock.us/`) that has a title (where the term `title` is defined by `http://purl.org/dc/elements/1.1/title`) called "Jeff's Homepage!"

- There is a Web page (`http://me.jtpollock.us/`) that has a creator (where the term `creator` is defined by `http://purl.org/dc/elements/1.1/creator`) identified by the RDF Web resource `http://me.jtpollock.us/foaf.rdf#me`.

An astute reader would at this point ask how an RDF parser would know that one URI (`http://me.jtpollock.us/`) is a Web page while the other is referencing a person (`http://me.jtpollock.us/foaf.rdf#me`). The truth is that the RDF 1.0 specification does not address this ambiguity. In technical terms, both URIs are simply resources, and you know that they are related by a relationship called creator. Beyond that, there is room for interpretation. Work has begun in 2008 to revise the RDF specification and add a comprehensive notational system for resolving URI-naming issues (is the Web site the thing or is it about the thing?), so stay tuned for those new additions.

This chapter so far has provided a simple example of how you can declare, describe, and link graph data in RDF format. But you can create much more complex data vocabularies for specialized domains. In fact, RDF models describe numerous medical domain vocabularies that express hundreds of thousands of medical terms. People can use these vocabularies to increase the precision and reliability of data exchange in the insurance, life sciences, and clinical health care systems.

Keep in mind that this section is just a primer for understanding RDF concepts. I provide a closer look at all aspects of programming RDF in Chapter 7.

Exploring the Semantics of RDF

RDF is a data language intended to be used to express facts about data that can stand on their own (for example, statements or triples) using precise formal vocabularies. RDF was conceived from the start for access and use over the World Wide Web, and it's intended to provide a basic foundation for more advanced data languages with a similar purpose.

The exact meaning of an assertion in RDF in some broad sense may depend on many factors, including social conventions, comments in natural language, or links to other content-bearing documents. Most of this general meaning will be inaccessible to machine processing (automatic processing by software and computers). The exact semantics of RDF is restricted to a formal notion of data meaning. You can think of this formal definition of semantics as a common part of all other accounts of meaning that can be captured in mechanical (algorithmic) inference rules.

The formal base semantics of RDF is powerful enough to adequately capture data and data relationships of any other data language in a lossless graph format. For example, any relational database, UML model, or XML document can be fully expressed as RDF. But RDF's base semantics does not specify higher-order data concepts that would make these conversions simple or unambiguous in a standard way.

Because RDF is so powerful, yet so broad and unconstrained, many other data languages have been specified with RDF itself. Here you must keep in mind that the semantics of RDF can be used to specify the semantics of other data languages — which are in turn used to create software application models and complex data vocabularies.

Discovering Languages That Use RDF

Since 2004, RDF has served as a foundational data and metadata language for many other data languages and domain vocabularies. The following is a quick primer on some of the most important ones.

Really Simple Syndication (RSS)

Really Simple Syndication (RSS) allows Web users to view some of your site's content without actually having to visit your site directly. RSS provides a syndication infrastructure for content to be easily distributed and consumed. RSS is quite popular; in fact, the syndication Web site `www.syndic8.com` alone currently links to more than 500,000 RSS feeds worldwide.

Exactly what an RSS feed looks like depends on which version of RSS is being used. At the most basic level, a feed consists of a channel with its own elements (for example, title, description, URL, creation date, and so on) and a number of items each with their own attributes (for example, title, description, URL, and so on).

A picture of the basic RSS 1.0 structure is illustrated in Figure 4-4.

```
<?xml version="1.0"?>
<rdf:RDF
  xmlns:rdf="http://www.w3.org/1999/02/22-rdf-syntax-ns#"
  xmlns="http://purl.org/rss/1.0/"
  xmlns:dc="http://purl.org/dc/elements/1.1/">

    <channel rdf:about="...">
    .....
    </channel>

    <item rdf:about="...">
    .....
    </item>

    <item rdf:about="...">
    .....
    </item>

    <item rdf:about="...">
    .....
    </item>
```

Figure 4-4:
The basic
RSS
document
structure
showing
RDF types.

The information enclosed between the `<channel>` tags is used to describe the feed itself. The following code snippet illustrates a typical channel description:

```
<channel>
<title>CNN News | World | Top Stories</title>
<link>http://rss.cnn.com/rss/cnn_topstories.rss </link>
<description>CNN World Newsfeed</description>
</channel>
```

Each item in the RSS feed is described between `<item>` tags. At the most basic level, these include a title, links, and descriptions as illustrated in the following code:

```
<item>
<title>Semantic Web Conference Breaks Records</title>
<description>The fourth annual Semantic Technology
      conference in San Jose breaks all previous
      attendance records</description>
<link>
  http://www.prweb.com/releases/2008/05/prweb965744.htm
</link>
</item>
```

A complete snippet of RSS v1.0, shown in Listing 4-2, looks a lot like the first example of basic RDF from Listing 4-1.

Listing 4-2: An RSS Syntax Example

```
<?xml version="1.0"?>
<rdf:RDF
 xmlns:rdf="http://www.w3.org/1999/02/22-rdf-syntax-ns#"
 xmlns="http://purl.org/rss/1.0/"
 xmlns:dc="http://purl.org/dc/elements/1.1/">

  <channel rdf:about="http://example.com/news.rss">
    <title>Example Channel</title>
    <link>http://example.com/</link>
    <description>My example channel</description>

    <items>
      <rdf:Seq>
        <rdf:li resource="http://www.prweb.com/releases/
                        2008/05/ prweb965744.htm"/>
        <rdf:li resource="http://example.
          com/2008/05/22/"/>
      </rdf:Seq>
    </items>
  </channel>

    <item rdf:about="http://example.com/2002/09/01/">
<title>Semantic Web Conference Breaks Records</title>
<description>The fourth annual Semantic Technology
        conference in San Jose breaks all previous
        attendance records</description>
<link> http://www.prweb.com/releases/2008/05/
        prweb965744.htm</link>
    <dc:date>2008-05-22</dc:date>
  </item>
```

(continued)

Listing 4-2: *(continued)*

```
<item rdf:about="http://example.com/2002/09/02/">
    <title>News for May Twenty-second</title>
    <link>http://example.com/2008/05/22/</link>
    <dc:date>2008-05-22</dc:date>
</item>

</rdf:RDF>
```

RSS is a simple, but powerful, way of syndicating just about any kind of content you need to publish to a subscriber base.

Friend of a Friend (FOAF)

Friend of a Friend, or FOAF, is a machine-readable vocabulary for people to describe an online profile of themselves. You can use FOAF to describe yourself and link into social networks without the need for centralized databases or third-party services.

Computers use these FOAF profiles to navigate social networks and discover links between people and their interests. Each profile has a unique identifier (such as the person's e-mail addresses, a Yahoo! ID, or a URI of the person's homepage or blog), which is used when defining these relationships.

Tim Berners-Lee, the influential inventor of the Web, is highly supportive of FOAF as an on-ramp for creating the Semantic Web. He has been quoted as saying, "I express my network in a FOAF file, and that is a start of the revolution."

A simplified version of my FOAF profile looks like Listing 4-3.

Listing 4-3: Simplified FOAF Profile for Jeff Pollock

```
<rdf:RDF
  xmlns:rdf="http://www.w3.org/1999/02/22-rdf-syntax-ns#"
  xmlns:rdfs="http://www.w3.org/2000/01/rdf-schema#"
  xmlns:foaf="http://xmlns.com/foaf/0.1/">

<foaf:PersonalProfileDocument rdf:about="">
  <foaf:maker rdf:resource="#me"/>
  <foaf:primaryTopic rdf:resource="#me"/>
</foaf:PersonalProfileDocument>

<foaf:Person rdf:ID="me">
  <foaf:name>Jeff Pollock</foaf:name>
  <foaf:title>Mr</foaf:title>
  <foaf:givenname>Jeff</foaf:givenname>
  <foaf:family_name>Pollock</foaf:family_name>
  <foaf:mbox_sha1sum>
```

```
    1a444af3548b73c371f66ce79b32aebcd25acb9f
  </foaf:mbox_sha1sum>
  <foaf:homepage rdf:resource="http://me.jtpollock.us"/>
  <foaf:workplaceHomepage
    rdf:resource="http://www.oracle.com"/>
  <foaf:schoolHomepage rdf:resource="http://www.psu.edu"/>
  <foaf:knows
rdf:resource="http://www.w3.org/People/Berners-Lee/
        card#i"/>
  <foaf:knows
rdf:resource="http://www.w3.org/People/Connolly/#me"/>
</foaf:Person>

</rdf:RDF>
```

Just like the RSS example in the preceding section and my introductory example shown earlier in Listing 4-1, you should be able to see the following similarities of this RDF structure:

- The `xmlns` keywords contain the namespace definitions.

- Each keyword in the body of the RDF points to an `xmlns` for term definition.

- Each namespace contains a vocabulary of terms that can be reused across many different documents and databases.

RDF in Attributes (RDFa)

The Web contains an enormous number of pages that have been created and generated with HTML markup. These documents often contain a lot of structured data unavailable to most applications. Because HTML is not a structured data language and the Web is predominantly rendered in HTML, it's quite difficult to find or use any structured data on the Web.

Using RDF in Attributes (RDFa) is a way to encode data within HTML and XHTML Web pages — thereby enabling people and machines to supply structured data items directly embedded within Web pages.

The rendered, hypertext data of XHTML is reused by the RDFa markup so that publishers don't need to repeat significant data in the document content. The underlying representation of RDFa is RDF because it's flexible enough to let publishers build and evolve their own vocabularies while extending others with high degrees of data portability. RDFa structure is closely tied to the data itself so that rendered data can be copied and pasted along with its relevant structure.

RDFa is similar to microformats. Whereas microformats specify both a syntax for embedding structured data into HTML documents and a vocabulary of specific terms for each microformat, RDFa specifies only a syntax and relies on independent specification of terms (often called vocabularies or taxonomies) by others. Additionally, RDFa allows terms from independently developed vocabularies to be intermingled.

Listing 4-4 shows you a simple example of RDFa that consists of a basic HTML page with the addition of new xmlns namespaces and some new <span property> and <class property> tags.

Listing 4-4: A Simple RDFa Example

```
<?xml version="1.0" encoding="UTF-8"?>
<!DOCTYPE html PUBLIC "-//W3C//DTD XHTML+RDFa 1.0//EN"
      "http://www.w3.org/MarkUp/DTD/xhtml-rdfa-1.dtd">
<html xmlns:cal="http://www.w3.org/2002/12/cal/ical#"
      xmlns:contact="http://www.w3.org/2001/vcard
            -rdf/3.0#">
  <head>
    <title>Batla's Boisterous Blog</title>
  </head>
  <body>
...
  <p instanceof="cal:Vevent">
    I'll be hosting
    <span property="cal:summary">
      the big birthday party at the beach,
    </span>
    on
    <span property="cal:dtstart" content=
              "20080312T1600-0500">
      March 12th at 4pm.
    </span>
  </p>
...
  <p class="contactinfo" about="http://example.org/
            staff/jo">
    <span property="contact:fn">SA. Batla</span>.
    <span property="contact:title">Semantic Web
            Guru</span>
    at
    <a rel="contact:org" href="http://acme.org">
      Acme.org
    </a>.
```

```
    You can contact me
    <a rel="contact:email" href="mailto:batla@acme.org">
      via email
    </a>.
  </p>
...
    </body>
</html>
```

When these kinds of RDFa markings are embedded in Web pages, they can create structure where there previously wasn't any. Take for example the popular news Web site Digg.com, shown in Figure 4-5. It has embedded RDF tags to put structure in its content, thereby allowing external search engines to more intelligently mine its data.

After Web applications embed structured data within their pages, Web search engines can more intelligently mine those pages to find relevant search results. The Fuzzbot RDFa viewer, shown in Figure 4-5 loading the Digg.com triples, can display the embedded RDF triples from within any Web page.

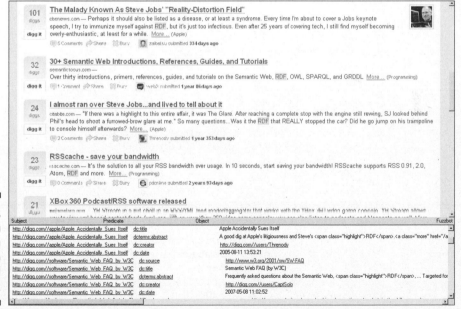

Figure 4-5. Digg.com shown in Fuzzbot with embedded RDF triples.

Yahoo! SearchMonkey is one example of a search engine adopting RDFa to simplify and improve its search results. Figure 4-6 shows what a more intelligent search result looks like on the Semantic Web.

Figure 4-6:
Yahoo!
Search
Monkey
search
results.

RDFa provides the on-ramp for regular Web pages to get onto the Semantic Web superhighway.

Web Ontology Language (OWL)

RDF provides a very simple model for graph data, but it does not specify complex semantics for relationships or advanced data models. Web Ontology Language (OWL; not to be confused with the Ordinary Wizarding Level tests from a certain boy-wizard series) is an extension of the RDF data model to supply a very rich set of semantics for building complex data models, vocabularies, and software logics. An instructional overview of OWL is provided in Chapter 8.

OWL supplies an object-oriented type of framework that links RDF triples to classes, associations, and other complex relationships. For example, OWL enables the kind of formal semantics to express in a data model a piece of logic like, *"A backpacker's destination is the intersection of all destinations that have budget accommodations and some type of sports or adventure activities."*

Unlike UML, relational databases, and XML, this type of powerful data semantic can be encoded directly in the data model. Later, when you query an OWL database that has that data model, you may simply use the query, *"find all backpacker destinations,"* and the database will know which records match your query based upon the logic defined in the data model — without ever having tagged the records as such!

Figure 4-7 shows an RDF graph using OWL semantics to express the following logic:

A backpacker's destination is the intersection of all destinations that have budget accommodations and some type of sports or adventure activities.

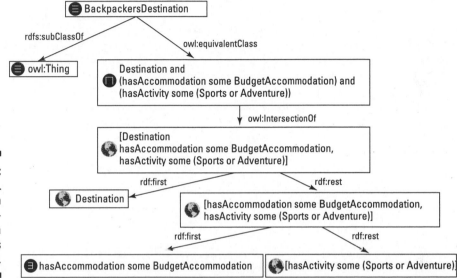

Figure 4-7:
An OWL
RDF graph
with pow-
erful data
model logics
included.

Because OWL is a more expressive language than other data languages, it can provide an umbrella modeling format for machines to understand how data is related. The RDF shown in the next example is in a simplified RDF format called Turtle:

```
:BackpackersDestination
  a       owl:Class ;

  rdfs:comment "A destination that provides budget
               accommodation and offers sport or
               adventure activities."^^xsd:string ;

  owl:equivalentClass
    [ a       owl:Class ;
      owl:intersectionOf
```

```
            (:Destination [ a owl:Restriction ;
         owl:onProperty :hasAccommodation ;
         owl:someValuesFrom :BudgetAccommodation]
      [ a       owl:Restriction ;
         owl:onProperty :hasActivity ;
         owl:someValuesFrom
           [ a       owl:Class ;
             owl:unionOf (:Sports :Adventure)]
      ])
    ] .
```

The standard `rdf:comment` keyword may look familiar from the earlier RDF examples in this chapter. But thereafter you see quite a few `owl:keywords` that aren't familiar. The OWL language provides many new extensions to RDF that enable robust data modeling; a few examples of those extensions are listed in Table 4-2.

Table 4-2	A Few Owl Extensions to RDF
OWL Relationships	**Examples**
SubClassOf	Author is a SubClassOf Person.
EquivalentClasses	Person is EquivalentClass to Homosapien.
DisjointClasses	Person is a DisjointClass from Canine.
SameIndividual	"President Bush" is SameIndividual "GW Bush".
OWL Class Constructors	**Examples**
ObjectUnionOf	Jeff is the union of Author and Employee.
ObjectIntersectionOf	Jeff is the intersection of Person and Male.

Many other extensions are available to OWL modelers; Chapter 8 provides a comprehensive explanation for each of them and a programming guide for getting started with the Web Ontology Language.

Other Semantic Web languages

Many other languages are being built upon RDF and OWL. Any new programming language or data language that uses RDF or OWL can be considered a Semantic Web language. Here are just a few of the most important ones:

- ✔ **SPARQL:** Simple Protocol and RDF Query Language (SPARQL) is the primary query language of the Semantic Web. It is like a more powerful SQL but for RDF graph data.

- ✔ **SWRL:** Semantic Web Rule Language (SWRL) bridges the gap to business rule and production rule systems that require more expressive logics than OWL permits because they would make OWL an inconsistent data language.

- ✔ **SAML:** Security Access Markup Language (SAML) uses RDF as a metadata feature for maintaining access profiles.

- ✔ **UML2 ODM:** The Ontology Definition Metamodel (ODM) is a standard within the Unified Modeling Language (UML) family that maintains an RDF and OWL profile for UML2.

- ✔ **SAWSDL:** Semantic Annotations for Web Service Description Language (SAWSDL) is designed to be embedded within WSDL 2.0 Web Service binding definitions as a way to encode powerful vocabularies directly within the Web Service API.

- ✔ **GRDDL:** Gleaning Resource Descriptions from Dialects of Language (GRDDL) is a W3C standard that defines a repeatable method for extracting RDF triples from HTML and XHTML document. GRDDL may be used, for example, to convert microformats into pure RDF.

- ✔ **ISO 15926, Part 7:** There are many industry-specific vocabularies that are adopting RDF and OWL. ISO 15926, Part 7 is one example focused on the exchange of data for different kinds of industrial plant operations — such as oil and gas drilling platforms.

Many other vocabularies are being built and used everyday throughout all industries. Governments in the United States and Europe are some of the most prolific adopters of Semantic Web technologies in all aspects of government. The life sciences and pharmaceutical industries have also been using RDF and OWL vocabularies for many years as a means to facilitate an easier exchange of business data.

A Little Semantics Goes a Long Way

One popular misconception among people who don't fully understand the Semantic Web is that all the data needs to be converted to RDF. But as you can see from this chapter, many Semantic Web languages are simply extensions of other languages to make a small portion of data accessible as RDF triples. No mass conversion is required. In fact, the Semantic Web works with regular non-semantic data precisely because a little semantics goes a long way.

Just a few well-placed RDF triples in a Web page, document, or database can make all the difference when somebody is searching for a particular thing. Unlike a search engine, the SPARQL queries on RDF graphs are deterministic (they don't rely on probabilities) and can inference (use logic and reasoning power) to create new data as they query. That means that you can be guaranteed to find the data you are looking for once it has been indexed by the RDF engine. It also means that the RDF engine can make better guesses at what you are looking for because it uses enriched vocabularies to cross-reference the results of your queries.

The idealistic vision of the Semantic Web may in fact be that giant global graph in the sky, but from where I stand today, there's much to be gained from a simpler view of the Semantic Web. The simple view is that RDF and OWL bring some very real and very fundamental new benefits to data and metadata languages. In any place where you may have considered using XML, UML, or relational formats for metadata, you should consider using RDF and OWL. Chances are, they would be a better solution.

Get started now using the Semantic Web and find projects where you can add a little bit of semantics — it will go a long way for you!

Chapter 5

Why the Semantic Web Is New Technology, Not Hype

*I*n mid-March 2008, a headline for a Times Online interview with Sir Tim Berners-Lee read, "Semantic Web could leave Google in the dust."

If proclamations like that don't quicken your pulse even a little, you might want to slowly set this book down and walk away. Unsurprisingly, both the business and technical crowds were all aflutter about this assertion, but for different reasons.

In the business community, analyst groups, and venture capital circles, the buzz is slowly building for the Semantic Web. Grand assertions about displacing Google may not be instantly believable, but they cause more than a few people to dig a little deeper. However, in the technical crowd, the Semantic Web geeks are busy trying to downplay the hyperbole. Every wise technologist knows that inflated expectations have buried more than a few good technologies over the years. As it turns out, even Tim Berners-Lee recanted the interview with Times Online and tried to squash any idea that he has it out for Google.

The Semantic Web is great — that's why this book exists — but it isn't a silver bullet for all your problems, and it probably isn't going to single-handedly displace any particular companies.

This chapter describes in some detail why the Semantic Web is different than other technologies and social movements like Web 2.0. The cautious reader must bear in mind that no technology is perfect, and the process of articulating why the Semantic Web is different requires pointing out some deficiencies of classical technologies. As such, many casual readers might dismiss the Semantic Web as "all hype." But the aim of this chapter is to carefully explain how the differences amount to very real, very tangible new ways of thinking about data.

Tracing the Roots of the Semantic Web

The Semantic Web is based on some genuinely different and powerful technology capabilities that haven't previously been widely deployed in software systems. It's a legitimately new set of specifications that may change quite a bit about how software is written.

Actually grounded in several old ideas from the artificial intelligence (AI) community dating as far back as the 1950s, the intellectual heritage of the Semantic Web can be traced back to some of the following roots:

- Graph systems, network databases, and semantic networks
- Frame languages and object-oriented systems
- Expert systems, description logic programs, and knowledge representation

Far from impractical, these central ideas from AI have been deliberately combined with Web architecture technologies like HTTP and the URI (Uniform Resource Identifier) to make AI more practical in today's Web-centric world.

Further, the Semantic Web architects carefully chose particular characteristics to ensure that the languages were a good fit for real-world demands. They specifically wanted to ensure that the core languages were deterministic like a database, more expressive than conventional modeling notations, and capable of being very fast.

The Semantic Web today consists of two core data languages (RDF and OWL) and a query language for accessing the data. Although there are many shared attributes with other technologies — including databases, integration platforms, and object-oriented programming languages — the Semantic Web remains distinct.

The Gartner Hype Cycle

As one of the premier business analyst firms in the software sector, Gartner's voice on technology trends carries far and is listened to intently. One of Gartner's established ways of defining the maturity of a new technology is to plot its progress on the Gartner Hype Cycle. This Hype Cycle is used to aid in Gartner's analysis of nearly every technology that it covers.

The key insight that Gartner shares with its Hype Cycle is that as technology is introduced, people often have very high expectations for it. These expectations result later in a type of blow-back effect of disappointment before the technology can ever reach any sort of stable and productive maturity.

If the Semantic Web were plotted on the so-called Gartner Hype Cycle in 2008, it would no doubt be rising toward the peak of inflated expectations. The Gartner Hype Cycle Figure shown here demonstrates how every new technology is subject to a kind of popularity ranking according to where it falls within this pattern of market adoption. Although the expectations may be too high today — for example, thinking that the Semantic Web will unseat Google as the king of search — you can rest assured that there are some very fundamental and very real benefits for the Semantic Web technologies.

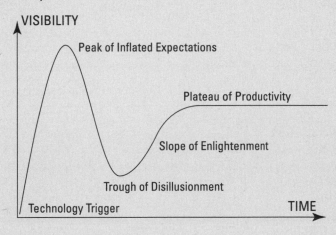

Realizing That the Internet Is Made Up of Pages, Not Data

The Internet, or the World Wide Web (WWW), is the basis for nearly every major software breakthrough since 1995. A simple idea really, the basis for the Internet's greatness lies in the notion that documents can be linked to one another. One simple standard, the URI (Uniform Resource Identifier), has since become the de facto way to link documents, pages, and just about anything else you can think of.

The Internet itself is made of documents, usually called Web pages. Sometimes these Web pages can be generated from databases or dynamically generated from XML, but when you see them via a Web browser, they're merely documents that contain links to other documents.

Advocates of the Semantic Web make this simple distinction: The Internet is a web of documents, and the Semantic Web is a web of data. Whereas a document might be a page with lots of text in it, the data itself isn't *structured* in a way that can be interpreted by a computer. Even though this paragraph can be understood by you, the human reader, it can't be interpreted by a computer because the words in this paragraph are not associated with any particular software syntax or structure.

On the other hand, structured data must follow some prescribed syntax and structure because it's used by software algorithms for data processing. Software algorithms must receive data in the structure and type that they expect; otherwise, an exception occurs.

Because the Internet is made up of pages of documents, it's really useful for people to browse. "Really useful" might be the understatement of the century; the Internet has revolutionized civilization itself. Many people take for granted that they can look anything up at any time. Whole nations, societies, and political revolutions are fueled by the access to information that the Internet brings people.

But information on the Internet is only for *people*. Alas, computers can't make sense of all those words on the Internet. If only everybody wrote things down exactly the same way every time. . . . Instead, there are different styles, colloquialisms, slang terms, and mistakes. As analog "machines" capable of high degrees of pattern recognition and an unparalleled aptitude for guessing, humans can usually make sense of what they find on the Web. Machines, on the other hand, cannot.

Take, for example, the way you search for information on the Internet. When you need to find general information via the Web, you usually start by using a search engine. Search engines aren't like the Dewey Decimal System in your local library, where you must know which categories of information to look within beforehand. Instead, you simply enter a few keywords in the search engine, and the search engine then matches them within a master index of pages that it has scanned. There is no intelligence in a search engine. Even in places where it seems as though the search engine has made a guess for you — such as Google's famous "Did you mean?" prompt at the top of its search results list — the search engine is still not truly intelligent. In all these cases, including the Google example, the search engine simply matches text in a list of words. Unlike with the Semantic Web, there is no complex logic or reasoning with the data: just simple keyword-matching algorithms.

If Semantic Web technologies were widely deployed, or if natural language processing systems were to create Semantic Web data from regular Web pages, the whole way you search on the Internet could change. Instead of looking for keywords, you might browse for ideas or data concepts; the search engines could help distinguish the meaning behind the words you typed in. Ultimately, you would get more results with greater levels of accuracy. Chapter 15 gives you examples of how Yahoo! and hakia are aiming to make these benefits a reality for you.

The true beauty and distinctiveness of the Semantic Web is that it's intentionally built on the same core principles and infrastructure as the regular Web. The distributed nature of the Web, achieved by using a decentralized network of servers, provides a global scale of data distribution and fault tolerance that is unmatched by any other technology that humans have created. The Uniform Resource Indicator (URI) and HTTP protocols ensure that servers all over the world are able to send requests for documents to any other place in the world. These Web pages and Web servers operate with metadata, tags, and markup in much that same way that the Semantic Web does. Just like the regular Web, the Semantic Web is another big evolution in the way people can find information from their computers.

Realizing That Web 2.0 Is for People and Semantic Web Is for Software

If you used the Internet in 2007 and have a pulse, you've heard about the Web 2.0 rage. Somewhere along the way, somebody noticed that the Internet could enable groups of people to collaborate in ways that they couldn't do without it. After a few Web sites that encouraged this group behavior were created, Web 2.0 was born.

Ever since group behavior became an important part of mainstream Web sites, companies have found numerous ways to exploit the behavior of Web surfers. Simple uses of Web 2.0 ideas include businesses like Amazon.com soliciting product rankings from consumers and offering shoppers hints of what others have bought. More overt notions of Web 2.0 include the many social networking Web sites that have tried to profit from the basic human need to connect with others. Facebook, MySpace, Friendster, Tribe, LinkedIn, Spoke, and countless others have looked to profit on connecting teens, communities, professionals, and just about any other type of demographic.

But the Web 2.0 phenomenon isn't based on any particular technological breakthrough beyond the Web itself. Sure, some new programming languages have surfaced — like Ajax, Flash, Ruby on Rails, JSON, and a more liberal use of XML — as shown in Figure 5-1, but these have been incremental improvements upon the existing Web platform and haven't fundamentally changed the fact that the Web is driven by documents and pages.

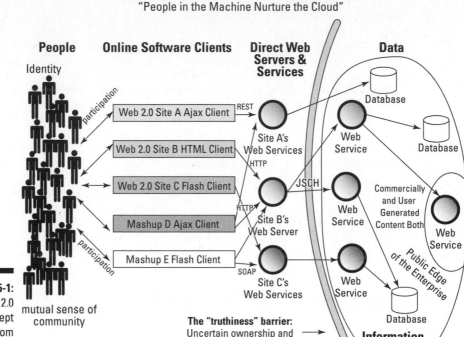

The Web 2.0 Architecture of Participation:
"People in the Machine Nurture the Cloud"

People · **Online Software Clients** · **Direct Web Servers & Services** · **Data**

Identity

Web 2.0 Site A Ajax Client
Web 2.0 Site B HTML Client
Web 2.0 Site C Flash Client
Mashup D Ajax Client
Mashup E Flash Client

Site A's Web Services
Site B's Web Server
Site C's Web Services

REST · HTTP · HTTP · SOAP · JSCH

Web Service
Web Service
Web Service
Web Service

Database
Database
Database

Commercially and User Generated Content Both

Public Edge of the Enterprise

Information "Cloud"

mutual sense of community

The "truthiness" barrier:
Uncertain ownership and data provenance past this point

Source: http://web2.wsj2.com

Figure 5-1:
Web 2.0 Concept from Hinchcliffe & Company.

The Web 2.0 phenomenon is more rightly described as a social and behavioral sea change. Instead of serving up static fixed content to Web surfers in the same way that television delivers static fixed content to TV watchers, the Web has become an interactive place for people to congregate and do things together — virtually. Web 2.0 is about the way people use Web 1.0, not about the Web itself. New ideas for harnessing the uncanny accuracy of crowd-sourcing opinions and predictions are driving a higher order of collective intelligence than anyone could have imagined a few short years ago. New ways to harness community tagging projects (where groups of people create hierarchies of tags) allow people to build *folksonomies,* which are vocabularies that evolve much like natural language evolves — in small pockets of communities. The term *mashup* is now a common part of the lingo, used to describe when people reuse other people's content in their own way.

A measured view of the Web 2.0 phenomenon is offered by Tim Berners-Lee, the true intellectual father of the Internet. In a podcast interview, Tim Berners-Lee described the term *Web 2.0* as a "piece of jargon," stating that "nobody really knows what it means." He went on to say, "If Web 2.0 for you is blogs and wikis, then that is people to people. But that was what the Web was supposed to be all along." Berners-Lee is clearly pointing out that this isn't a fundamental change in the technology infrastructure; it's just that people are evolving to use the full power of a medium that's already been there for several years.

I agree with Tim Berners-Lee's assessment. In fact, the Web 2.0 businesses that have matured in the past few years have exacerbated the fundamental limitations of the original document-based Web because they further proliferate data that cannot be easily reused. If you've ever belonged to more than one online social network, you know very well that you have to constantly re-type who you are, what you like, who your friends are, what your pet's name is, and so on. This repetitive re-typing reflects the plain truth that your data is owned by the network you join and each network you join is a silo unto itself. For all the noise about Web 2.0, it turns regular people — at least the ones with a lot of spare time — into data-entry robots who are typing and re-typing their personal information and favorites into every Web site that will have it.

In some cases, Web 2.0 sites are starting to use Web 3.0 (in other words, the Semantic Web) technologies. As Web 2.0 businesses start to utilize the power of metadata, they need more flexible ways to capture and define content on their own pages — they know that people want to reuse chunks of data, not just whole pages. Microformats, RDFa, and other tagging technologies are increasingly using Semantic Web technologies to achieve true portability and reuse. For more info, check out Chapter 4, where I introduce you to a few technologies that span Web 2.0 and the Semantic Web.

Databases Mean Business; So Does Semantic Web

The most recognized type of business software is the database. Businesses store their information, calculate their taxes, and manage their employees by using databases. The database is the perennial software used by businesses.

Databases come in all shapes and sizes. Relational databases, columnar databases, object databases, and graph databases are different ways to manage data records. The relational database is by far the most popular kind of database, but the other kinds are still very much part of the business landscape today.

Although the Semantic Web exists at *Web-scale* (meaning the data may be joined from any networked computer anywhere in the world), the detailed manipulation of the Semantic Web data still occurs inside a database platform. Whereas traditional databases require that their schemas (the way the data is organized) are defined before the data is loaded, the Semantic Web databases can have continually changing schemas at any time. Sometimes, the Semantic Web database is called a *knowledgebase* because (a) it's more logically expressive in what the schema can say about the data and (b) it can continuously evolve over time without major architectural impacts to the software.

But before I start to describe too much about the Semantic Web databases, take a look at the more conventional database platforms, as described in the following sections.

Relational databases

Compared to the Semantic Web knowledgebase, the relational database system is a less expressive but faster way to access structured data records. In a relational database, the structured data record, sometimes called a *tuple,* is arranged in tables. Tables were originally referred to as *relations* because the table itself is the relationship between the column names, which are sometimes called the object attributes.

Take for example a simple example table of Customers, shown in Figure 5-2. The table defines the fact that every record it contains is a type of Customer. Further, the table structure defines that every Customer must have a *primary key* (a unique identifier) and may have other *attributes* (descriptive fields) like FNAME, ADDR1, and so on. In this simple example, the definition of a Customer object is described by the table columns.

Figure 5-2:
A sample relational DB table with some data.

Customers				
SSN	FNAME	ADDR1	ADDR2	STATE
445542134	Jeff	123 Anystreet	NULL	CA
...	...	...	...	...

In more complex database schemas, collections of tables compose records. These collections are typically joined in one of two ways:

- ✔ **Directly in the data schema by using keys (primary, foreign, and synthetic keys are all kinds of unique identifiers):** These relations become part of the data model and are thus a dependable and consistent definition for the data.

- ✔ **Using Structured Query Language (SQL) statements to perform joins (such as UNION, INTERSECT, INNER, OUTER, and so on) on records at the time of retrieval:** These SQL-based data joins are obviously very useful for manipulating records and result sets, but they're impossible to reliably and consistently integrate into a separable information or data model.

The power of sets

When Ted Codd wrote his seminal paper on relational databases in 1970, there was little certainty that his ideas were valuable. Even his employer, IBM, dragged its feet in implementing his breakthrough concepts.

But the ideas about organizing data in sets, relationally in tables, solved a fundamental algorithmic challenge of the day — how to achieve computationally sound query results on large amounts of data. By restricting the data

model's semantics and eliminating an inherently slow hierarchical data structure (as was found in systems like IMS/DB), the relational data could be accessed with set operators such as UNION, MINUS, and INTERSECT.

Combined with efficient indexing strategies, there isn't a faster way to retrieve data from hard disks. Set-based relational systems are the pinnacle of fast structured data.

Key relationships in the relational model can be used in various patterns to create an efficient management scheme for collections of business objects within the database. Much like the various indexing techniques, the arrangement, constraints, degree of normalization, and overall shape of the data schema greatly impact the performance of a relational database.

Figure 5-3 shows how regular relational tables can each supply a key value for the SalesFact table. This logical construction allows for simpler analytic operations on complex combinations of loosely related data. This *star schema* approach is the most popular and widespread way of performing business intelligence queries because of its flexibility and performance in read-only type situations.

In contrast, the traditional OLTP database, with a second or third normal form relational data model (as defined by common relational data modeling practices), is the go-to standby for heavy transactional (write-intensive) use cases.

It should be easy to understand why the relational database is arguably the most successful and widespread software platform in the history of computers: It's fast, reliable, consistent, and flexible enough to be used for all different kinds of data-intensive use cases.

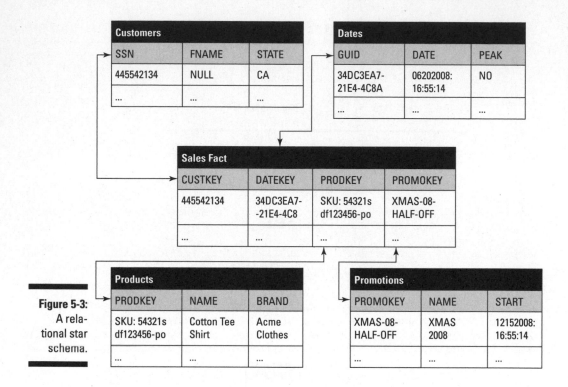

Figure 5-3:
A relational star schema.

But likewise, you should also be able to see why the relational database is being used for some use cases where it is not optimal. The need to optimize the shape of a relational schema differently for reads versus writes is a fundamental view into the reality of an essential fact about data management: When the extremes of performance and scalability are confronted, the relational database fails to be best at any particular use case. This view of the relational database as a generalist's tool is carefully considered in the provocative interview between two database pioneers, Margot Seltzer (inventor of Berkeley Database) and Michael Stonebraker (early pioneer of the relational database); the interview is called, quite aptly, "A Conversation with Michael Stonebraker and Margo Seltzer." (You can find the interview at `http://portal.acm.org/citation.cfm?id=1255430`.)

For more examples, here are some situations when relational databases aren't the best option:

✔ The best write performance can be achieved with an in-memory cache and not a separate disk-based database platform.

✔ The best read performance — reading data whose native structure is organized most like an index of tuples that is efficiently arranged on a hard drive — is achieved from a columnar-style database.

✔ The best storage structure for documents like XML and other messages is a hierarchical database structure.

✔ The best storage structure for frequently changing data, and data with very little formal structure at all, is a graph database.

The jury is still out on what technologies are best at any particular domain. The exciting thing about being a software engineer in this era is watching innovative ideas compete in the global market. With that in mind, in the following sections, I take a look at some new, and old, alternatives to relational databases.

Columnar databases

A relatively new entrant to the database segment is the column-oriented database, often referred to as a *columnar store,* or *c-store* for short, as shown in Figure 5-4. The key idea with a columnar database system is to optimize the database for very fast read operations. This extreme optimization for read access is achieved by physically arranging the data according to columns instead of rows.

Logical Data:

Customers				
SSN	FNAME	ADDR1	ADDR2	STATE
445542134	Jeff	123 Anystreet	NULL	CA
987656782	Samir	987 Main	NULL	RI
123432098	Sirus	12 Chestnut	Unit 2	NC

Row-oriented On Disk:

4455421234, Jeff, 123 Anystreet,, CA; 987656782, Samir, 987 Main,, RI;123432098, Sirius, 12 Chestnut, Unit 2, NC

Column-oriented On Disk:

4455421234, 123432098, 987656782 Jeff, Samir, Sirius; 123 Anystreet, 987 Main, 12 Chestnut; , , Unit 2; CA, RI,NC

Figure 5-4: Columnar databases arrange data by column, not by row.

In this approach, the physical layout of the data on disk, either within a file-based index or other binary format, is sequentially arranged so that all the similar column data is grouped nearby. The main idea is to prevent full table scans and eliminate the need for excessive indexing — both of which can become a major drag on performance when database sizes reach beyond a few hundred terabytes.

The columnar database approach can be applied to regular SQL and relational databases by providing a different records management system underneath the query interpreter and other planners. Likewise, the columnar approach can be applied to the indexing strategy of any search system to optimize for very fast regular expression text matching algorithms. In fact, the most successful columnar implementation is the Google BigTable system, which is how all your searches are answered so quickly.

In the final analysis, the columnar approach is a data optimization technique that can be applied equally to deterministic (with guaranteed accuracy) data management solutions like relational databases and inference engines or to non-deterministic (without computational guarantees that your queries are answered accurately) systems like search engine indices. In either case, the columnar system is a high-performance solution for reading data from very large data sets.

Hierarchical databases

Hierarchical databases actually predate the relational database. Before the advent of data modeling and the need for general-purpose data management, the central data management requirement was much more basic and centered around the need to save and inventory the bill of materials for large manufacturing and engineering businesses. The hierarchical data structure is perfect for this use.

The first databases were hierarchical. Because they simply took a transaction, or data record, and persisted it wholly as is, the default data orientation was very hierarchical or tree-like (another way of imaging how data relationships can branch out from a central trunk, like a tree), which is how any message is structured. Situations that call for very fast save operations and very fast lookups of data within a particular records structure still benefit from the hierarchical database engine. For these reasons, after more the 40 years in the marketplace, the IBM Information Management System Database (IMS-DB), a hierarchical database, is still being sold and implemented by businesses worldwide.

Figure 5-5 shows the tree-like nature of a hierarchical record and how the data values are arranged together as part of a single flat list. This structure can enable very optimized read-and-write use cases when the software needs to fetch and save records in their original fixed, hierarchical structure.

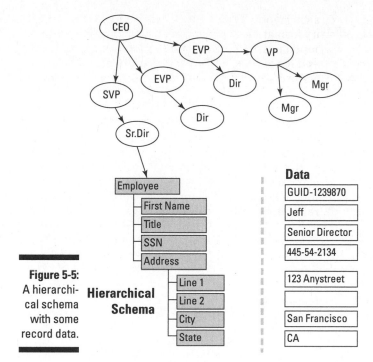

Figure 5-5:
A hierarchical schema with some record data.

Hierarchical Schema

Data

Another benefit that hierarchical databases provide is the ability to answer certain kinds of questions very quickly. For example, in a Human Resources system that contains lots of employees arranged organizationally and by hierarchy, hierarchical databases can provide quite simple and fast answers to queries like, "Find all employees in department XYZ." Similarly, for large engineering projects that contain many different assemblies and parts, a typical query might be, "Find all parts in this component."

When data records are arranged as they are in Figure 5-5, they can be searched very quickly to find all the parts of a whole. The most widely deployed type of hierarchical records store in the world is the commonly used LDAP (Lightweight Directory Access Protocol) security system.

The danger with hierarchical systems is that if the relationships get complex, or if records simply need to be joined together in a non-hierarchical way (for example, without using a parent and child type relation), the efficiency gains disappear, and the hierarchical system becomes a network or graph data model. A *network data model,* now more commonly called a *graph data model,* is usually hierarchical at its core, but it allows for more record-to-record relationships beyond the simple parent and child relation.

Graph databases

The graph database was one of the very first database types to emerge in the 1960s. Before the relational database gained dominance, there was quite a debate in the software field about whether hierarchical or graph database models were superior. Hierarchical systems were faster for some use cases, whereas graph data models were more natural modeling frameworks for many other use cases.

History has shown us that the relational database is the best general-purpose solution for data management, but just like the hierarchical database, the graph database has never really disappeared for specialty use cases. The Computer Associates Integrated Database Management System (CA-IDMS) is a mainframe system that still has a measurable foothold in certain industries. For geographical and spatial domains, the network data model continues to dominate — even the Oracle relational database includes a network data model feature for the spatial database option that's quite popular in the geo-spatial community.

Today, the primary data structure for the Semantic Web is graph-based. But instead of being localized to a particular database management system, the idea for the Semantic Web graph database is that it should exist at Web-scale. *Web-scale* means that the data may be joined from any networked computer anywhere in the world. This vision of a "database in the sky" has been espoused by a few prominent people, but the Semantic Web was actually *designed* that way.

The graph data structure itself is a type of semantic network. The semantic net is a classical artificial intelligence framework for working with directed graphs and was originally introduced to the computer sciences as a way to make human language interpretable by a processor. There are many types of directed graph operations, using different model theories and semantics. Until the arrival of the Semantic Web, there was no standard way to encode graph database records.

Object databases

Many considered object databases a failure in the past few years. The object database was originally conceived as an alternative to the relational database to become a more natural way of storing data for object-oriented software programs. The benefits were supposed to bring a simpler object mapping to storage and fast pointer-based object retrieval.

In practice, the object database is faster for some pre-planned data retrieval tasks where the data pointers can be optimized. However, due to the lack of a formal and mathematically sound data model (as exists with relational, hierarchical, and graph systems) and poor performance with ad hoc style queries that aren't planned for during system design, the object database marketplace to remain quite small in comparison to the relational market.

Further, the fact that many object databases are accessed via relational access points (like ODBC or JDBC) and many more are actually implemented using a relational database engine somewhat negates the originally desired benefits of an object-based system.

Software objects and the idea of object-orientation in general are old artificial intelligence concepts rooted in frame systems. A *frame system* is a type of software language that consists of frames and slots. A frame is simply a class, and a slot is an attribute. Thus, if you have a class called `Customer` and an attribute called `Address` (which may itself be a class), you have a frame system like the one shown in Figure 5-6.

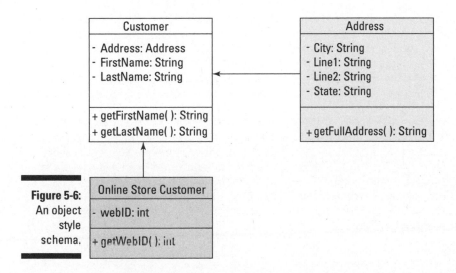

Figure 5-6:
An object style schema.

The object database is highly optimized for retrieval of data in this native frame style system. A software program may only have to instantiate an object with a trivial statement like this:

```
new OnlineStoreCustomer("445-54-2134")
```

The underlying object database fetches the appropriate attribute data as part of the complete record. The object style schema allows for data modeling characteristics like hierarchies and whole-part relationships. Object-orientation itself encourages data *inheritance* (one concept is a child of another) and *polymorphism* (a function could do one thing for one object, but another thing for a different object) for changing behavior and attribute constraints among different objects.

Unfortunately, there is no mathematical consistency across object-oriented languages, so it's not possible to create a general-purpose declarative data modeling framework. In simple terms, the classical object database is by definition a silo unique unto itself and not suitable for any large-scale information management problems.

What Semantic Web and databases have in common

After focusing so much on the differences between the major data management platforms and techniques, you must be wondering what these have in common with the Semantic Web. The Semantic Web specifications don't specify a particular technical implementation. In fact, Semantic Web solutions have been built upon every type of database platform described in the previous sections: relational, hierarchical, graph, and object.

Also, remember that the Semantic Web is itself a data and metadata specification for a *computationally sound, frame-based directed graph.* Or, to put it another way:

- ✔ The Semantic Web is based on formal mathematics *just like the relational database* — which means that any system that implements it can guarantee consistently reliable query answers that scale linearly with predictability.

- ✔ The Semantic Web is capable of native hierarchy definitions *just like a hierarchical database* — which means that tree-type data structures can be efficiently organized and retrieved.

- ✔ The Semantic Web is a semantic network *just like the network/graph database* — which means that it is exceptionally natural to model real-world data in the Semantic Web.

- ✔ The Semantic Web is a frame-based system *just like the object database* — which means that object-orientation can be preserved in the underlying data model.

The key Semantic Web specifications — RDF and OWL — were conscious efforts to combine the best attributes of the relational database (performance and consistency), the graph database (flexible, natural modeling easy to use with unstructured data), and the object database (powerful frame-based classification and logic-based relations).

Although the implementation of the Semantic Web database can be physically built upon any of the classical database engines, there are different tradeoffs to consider — I address those topics in Chapter 12.

Just like any database management system, a Semantic Web database would consist of a tuples-based data framework. (A tuple is just a fancy way of saying *data fact.*) And any Semantic Web–based system is capable of *set-based operations* (meaning the data can be organized and manipulated in sets rather than by one record at a time), although it's important to note that not every Semantic Web system is necessarily a set-based system. A well-implemented Semantic Web system should have many of the same characteristics as a conventional database, and yet it should also be capable of much more.

Grasping Why SOA/Integration Is for Messages, Not Data Structures

Ever since there have been computers in the world, there has been a demand for dedicated software integration technology. Integration platforms are responsible for assuring some level of consistency between two disparate software applications.

Integration technology itself comes in different styles, implemented with different patterns and for different purposes. Generally speaking, the biggest and most obvious difference between the Semantic Web and integration technologies is the focus on data movement. Whereas every type of integration technology depends on the specification of data movement over some protocol and with some guarantees about the delivery of that data, the Semantic Web is completely separate from how the movement of data occurs.

Some may say that because the Semantic Web is based on Web standards like the URI (Uniform Resource Identifier) it is inherently *federated,* or geographically distributed. That's true, but it doesn't answer for the obvious lack of a specification that arranges for the messaging, transport, or transformation of Semantic Web data.

Just as the integration platforms are not responsible for the data or metadata models, neither is the Semantic Web responsible for the mechanics of moving data across physical distance. But integration technology can be quite relevant to the same kinds of problems that the Semantic Web aims to solve in a business context. The historical ways of solving integration problems in business consist of the following approaches:

- ✔ Message-oriented middleware
- ✔ Enterprise application integration
- ✔ Service-oriented architecture
- ✔ Enterprise information integration
- ✔ Extract, transform, and load

Each of these technologies provides different tools that can be used independently, with each other, and with or without the use of Semantic Web technologies. More detail about the differences in these approaches follows.

Message-oriented middleware (MOM)

In the early 1990s, the message-oriented middleware (MOM) pattern arose as the predominant way to integrate applications via their APIs in a transactionally safe and flexible manner. MOMs are typically associated with the idea of a bus, whereby messages are published to several subscribers at once. Sometimes, this is called the *publish and subscribe* architecture.

Enterprise application integration (EAI)

The enterprise application integration (EAI) name is merely a super-set of the MOM functionality within a comprehensive integration product platform. As software vendors began to sell MOM-type products, they quickly realized that they required more functionality — like transformation engines, message management, error frameworks, and so on — so they bundled everything together for their largest customers and called it EAI.

Thus, EAI at its core is a message-oriented middleware system built around a publish and subscribe message bus.

Service-oriented architecture (SOA)

As the EAI products became more popular in the late 1990s, it became obvious that there was an interoperability problem among the different integration vendors — nobody's integration software worked with anybody else's!

The Web services scandal

I wrote an article for the Enterprise Application Integration Journal in 2002 titled, "Web Services Scandal." Somewhat tongue-in-cheek, the article pointed to some specific shortfalls of the then hyped-up service-oriented architecture (SOA) trends. Back then, Web services were supposed to solve all sorts of data-related problems.

From the dynamic assembly of services, the automatic orchestration of business processes, and the decoupling of service data bindings, the new Web service industry seemed to promise so much. But of course what sounds too good to be true usually is. In fact, SOA never really changed anything about directories, dynamic behavior, or data bindings. What a scandal!

The industry set about to solve this challenge with a new family of standards called *service-oriented architecture.* SOA is at its most basic level a standardization of the core message-oriented middleware architecture patterns that were almost 15 years old by the late 1990s. In most ways, the idea of SOA was really the software idea of EAI, but finally available with standardized formats.

Clearly, you can find some substantial positive differences in today's SOA compared with the original MOM systems. Here are a few:

- SOA focuses heavily on orchestrating long-lived processes.
- SOA implementations regularly use business rule engines.
- SOA is designed to work on Web protocols.

However, the shortfalls around dynamic discovery and loosely coupled data still remain. Finding services in large Web services frameworks is nearly impossible without a pre-ordained directory, and even with the popular rise of the XSD canonical data model (which is supposed to act as a common schema for messages), the bindings from application data formats to the wire-based XML are still extremely brittle and too easy to foul up when things start to change.

A balanced perspective recognizes the major steps forward in standardizing MOM-style integration frameworks while maintaining a clear head for how valuable that is in the big picture.

So despite falling short of some initial lofty promises, the service-oriented architecture movement has been a beneficial one, and those benefits will continue to be realized for years to come.

Enterprise information integration (EII)

Of the many kinds of integration technology, EII is the one most frequently confused with the Semantic Web. The term *enterprise information integration* was coined in the early 2000s and is distinguished by two central features:

- ✔ **The use of federated queries for data retrieval:** Unfortunately, EII has had trouble succeeding in the marketplace. Federated queries are typically such poor performers that the EII tool requires a substantial caching system to enable the EII platform to deliver data in a reasonable timeframe. This issue greatly diminishes the promises of realtime virtualized data access.

- ✔ **The use of a synthetic data model for viewing and accessing other disparate data models:** This second distinguishing feature has also proved troublesome. Various EII products have used synthetic data models of a classical nature. Typically, one or more of the following data model types have been used as the synthetic modeling language in the EII platform:

  - Relational data model
  - XML data model — XSD
  - Object data model — UML

  These are all perfectly acceptable synthetic modeling formats, of course, but each of them has well-known limitations that are common to their core modeling formats. In other words, the conventional EII synthetic models don't solve anything uniquely different about core data modeling and are therefore creating more silos unto themselves.

Each of the aforementioned issues is further compounded by a lack of any EII metadata standards, which means every vendor has implemented a solution in its own way — further isolating EII as a truly robust solution.

Extract, transform, load (ETL)

Extract, transform, load (ETL) is the granddaddy of enterprise-scale data integration. Highly optimized for large-sized data transfer and transformation, the typical ETL platform wastes no overhead on synthetic models and other inefficient data abstractions. Instead, the ETL platform is tuned for ultra-fast point-to-point data transformation that's all about getting data from Point A, Format A to Point B, Format B. Thus, the only meaningful semantics in an ETL platform is located in the highly optimized data transformation rules and the physical data models that are affected by them.

What Semantic Web has in common with other integration technologies

I started this section on integration technology by pointing out that the Semantic Web specifies data and metadata, whereas the integration platforms primarily focus on the mechanics of data movement. By now, you should appreciate the subtle but important differences between SOA, EII, and ETL. So it's fair to say that integration technology is apples to the Semantic Web oranges: They aren't in the same class of solution.

Yet there's more than a small bit of overlap. For instance, in a hypothetical utopia where every application publishes data in Semantic Web formats, there would be a drastically diminished need for integration software like SOA, EII, and ETL. Each application would instantly be able to share and consume business data without complex integration schemes.

Because the Semantic Web is a native part of the Web, all that data can be atomically delivered via HTTP. And because Semantic Web languages are much more expressive than relational, XML, or object style data models, the software applications themselves could achieve much more automated consumption of new data. Alas, we don't live in utopia, but the vision for our seamlessly interoperable applications of the future is at hand!

The integration platforms themselves have been tremendous letdowns. SOA delivers on only a fraction of its original promises: failing to fulfill the dynamic discovery and loosely coupled data promises. EII federated queries aren't fast enough, and the shared data models are too brittle for the kinds of dynamic mashups that developers really want to write. But this is another area where the Semantic Web standards can help!

A few ways that the Semantic Web can help with integration platforms, include

- ✓ Semantic Web–based inference engines are an ideal way to publish and find Web services — as network-based graphs.
- ✓ Semantic Web data models are an ideal way to abstract the data views within SOA and EII messaging systems.
- ✓ Semantic Web query standards are designed from scratch to accommodate federation at Web scale.

There isn't any silver bullet to making integration better, faster, and cheaper, but most of the work described in this section is already well underway. Later in this book, in Chapter 11, I go much deeper into the specific ways that Semantic Web will transform integration software of the future.

Realizing That XML Is for Documents, Not Data

When it was first introduced, many thought that XML would solve the data-integration ills of the world — many people are still under the impression that it will. But it won't.

First of all, XML and its schema language, XSD, are not true data models. They weren't intended to be. They're document models. The difference is in how strong the model semantics are required to be. One simple example is the nesting of tags. As shown in Figure 5-7, with XML you can declare that one tag is nested within the other. But what does that mean? Well, it can mean anything you want it to. It could mean parent-child, whole-part aggregate, whole-part composite, unidirectional association, bi-directional association, and so on. In its base definition, the nesting of a tag is simply an undefined relation. And because of those weak semantics, a particular XML Schema tag could mean just about anything.

```
<employee guid="1239870">
   <firstname>Jeff</firstname>
   <title>Senior Director</title>
   <ssn>445-54-2134</ssn>
   <address>
      <line1>123 Anystreet</line1>
      <line2></line2>
      <city>San Francisco</city>
      <state>CA</state>
   </address>
</employee>
```

Figure 5-7:
An XML
document
with some
data.

Those weakly defined structural semantics are precisely why XML became so popular — it's a document markup syntax and no more than that. If the standards bodies had tried to make it a data model, it never would have been adopted as widely as it has. The mistake people make is in thinking that it can be a data model or that it can be a general-purpose tagging and metadata framework for software applications.

In contrast, the Semantic Web languages are actual data models with very precise, mathematically grounded, model theoretic semantics. For example, I can define some arbitrary XML:

```
<employee> <firstname value="Jeff"/></employee>
```

This XML is syntactically sound, but no XML parser in the world can tell me that this means that there's a class of things called `Employee` and an instance of one called `Jeff`.

On the other hand, I can create an RDF triple:

```
<#employee><#firstName><#Jeff>.
```

As described in Chapter 4, any N3 RDF parser would understand the above syntax to mean that there is a class of data called `Employee` and that there is an instance of one `Employee` called `Jeff`. From there, I can add more employees, add more properties to an `Employee` class, and add more classes to assign people to.

Some people within the Semantic Web community actually feel that the association with XML is a burden. There was an early effort to build all the Semantic Web syntax in valid XML, but many find it much too verbose and complex. Thus, new RDF triples formats like N3 and Turtle have forgone XML as a syntax and instead advocate a much simpler triples format.

The nature of tagging is one area where the Semantic Web languages overlap with XML. When people think of tagging, they think of XML. Unlike XML, the Semantic Web languages can belong to a greater, more holistic data model, which is precisely why modern tagging languages are grounded in RDF. New tagging markup like microformats, RDFa, and GRDDL (Gleaning Resource Descriptions from Dialects of Languages) allow developers to encode RDF-based triples in their local syntax. By adopting a triples-compatible format, these modern tagging frameworks ensure a substantial degree of portability into the future.

Documents, not data models?

If you had a pulse and could program in the spring of 1998, you were probably excited about the arrival of XML. Java finally had something to do!

At that time, a lot of pundits speculated about the effect XML would have: It might change the way Java uses data, change object-oriented data markup, and maybe even cause the demise of the relational database. Not!

But as powerful as XML has proven to be — and indeed it's just about everywhere in almost all software — XML hasn't even come close to displacing the database. Fundamentally, XML is a document markup language, not a data modeling language.

Seeing Why Object Orientation Is a Heuristic

Object-oriented programming (OOP) is a software programming style that isn't grounded in an underlying mathematical model. Unlike the Semantic Web, which is grounded entirely on a complete mathematical model, the object-oriented heuristics offer an approach toward structuring software programs that is based upon rules of thumb and past experiences. Object-oriented heuristics cover both the structure of the data objects as well as their behavior.

There are various definitions of what makes something object-oriented, but no authoritative one. For the most part, people agree that the following are the definitive characteristics of object orientation:

- **Inheritance:** Parent to child relationships
- **Polymorphism:** Overloading and overriding class members
- **Encapsulation:** Hiding data behind operations

But there's a debate about these fundamental characteristics. Some people would add modularity as a fundamental characteristic of OOP, but others would rather eliminate the emphasis on inheritance. Still others decry the lack of formalisms for numerous constructs within object-oriented models.

Rather than dive in to the philosophical views about good object-orientation, the fact that there's a debate at all just goes to show the biggest weakness of OOP when it comes to data modeling — it's an informal heuristic with no basis in formal mathematics.

Unified Modeling Language (UML)

The Unified Modeling Language (UML), shown in Figure 5-8, began life as a simple visual notation for describing software programs. But nowadays some people consider it to be the pinnacle of software design and architecture.

But aside from all its inherent problems of largess, UML's main weakness is its lack of a formal mathematical theory. When it comes to modeling data, math is pretty darn important. Formal mathematical theory enables computer systems to make specific guarantees about the quality of their operations. For example, if I query a database, and there is a matching record in there, I am guaranteed that that record will be in my result set.

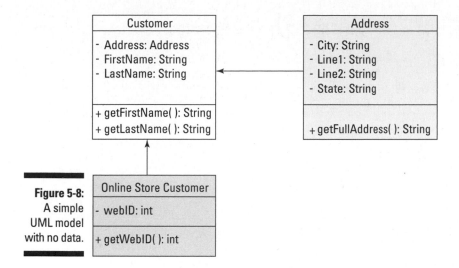

Figure 5-8:
A simple
UML model
with no data.

Because UML is a modeling heuristic — not a formalism — it means that there are no computational algorithms that can offer anybody a consistent and repeatable way to access data values written in a program that conforms only to UML. Sure, many algorithms can be modeled as UML, but just because I might model a relational database engine in UML doesn't mean that UML is as deterministic as the database engine!

Java

Like C++, SmallTalk, and Perl, Java is a programming language. Java is by far the most popular object-oriented language. Not all programming languages are object-oriented, but Java happens to be one that is. When any program, written in any programming language, is running, it executes in the computer's main memory. When it's executing in the main memory, many data objects are fully marshaled with various data attributes. But the way that these data attributes are connected, navigated, and operated on is a function of the software program itself.

Most programming languages operate with a fairly unconstrained, higher-order logic, which means that you can program pretty much anything you want so long as you use the programming languages syntax correctly.

Programming languages in and of themselves aren't suitable for encoding knowledge in software — precisely because they're too open. Too few constraints are imposed for how data may be related, constructed, and operated on algorithmically.

That's why people use programming languages to write data management software — the programming language itself (such as Java) is insufficient.

What the Semantic Web has in common with OOP

The Semantic Web specifications are built at the intersection of semantic nets and frame systems. And because object-oriented systems are also frame systems, the Semantic Web shares a few major attributes with OOP:

- ✔ The Semantic Web has classes as data concepts/categories.
- ✔ The Semantic Web has instances as actual data values.
- ✔ The Semantic Web supports inheritance among classes.
- ✔ The Semantic Web supports strongly typed data types.
- ✔ The Semantic Web supports whole-part relations.

But aside from these points, the Semantic Web is more rigorous and grounded in formalisms, using many of the mathematical foundations of semantic nets to further specify the types of relations that are allowable between classes and instances. Unlike UML, the Semantic Web assigns object and data relationships a first-class status in the data model.

The Semantic Web can't replace any programming language, nor is it intended to replace UML; however, it does provide a more common-sense way to model data than to rely on UML or depend solely on your programming language.

Seeing a New Beginning for Artificial Intelligence (AI)

Long in the doldrums, the AI winter has lasted decades. The *AI winter* is a phrase used by software industry insiders to describe the long periods when AI fell out of favor with mainstream software. Although many wish it weren't true, the Semantic Web is indeed built upon certain formalisms that emerged from the artificial intelligence community — but so are object-oriented systems, search engines, and relational databases. Nonetheless, it's still hip in some software circles to disavow any AI ancestry once a given technology becomes wildly popular.

Factually speaking, the roots of Semantic Web languages lie in both semantic nets (network data models) and in description logics (a type of frame logic that is a decidable subset of first-order logic). Both of these areas of AI fall within the category known as *knowledge representation*.

In the artificial intelligence community, the study of knowledge representation (KR) revolves around finding optimal ways to encode human knowledge in machine-understandable structures. This long-standing area of research has produced many different types of formalisms for encoding knowledge — several of which are the ancestors of the modern Semantic Web languages RDF and OWL.

Even the relational database structure is a type of knowledge representation — albeit a very restricted type.

Historically, the various techniques for representing knowledge in computer systems have been localized and built within silos that had few means to interact with data outside their own system. Prolog programs and large systems like Cyc have typically had to work with data that's held closely to their local format and semantics.

Following are the two biggest differences with the Semantic Web that haven't ever happened before in the span of computer science:

- ✔ The standardization of a formal model theory for data
- ✔ The intersection of an AI KR language with Web architecture

Taken together, the fact that there's a community standing behind the Semantic Web formalisms, and that it's built upon the Web architecture for boundary-less scale of distribution, this represents a breakthrough of substantial proportions beyond what AI has yet achieved.

Grasping How Semantic Web Is New and Different

If you're a software geek new to the Semantic Web and you aren't excited after reading this chapter, go back and read it again!

The Semantic Web is definitely at risk of being over-hyped, and you should keep in mind that it is no panacea. Further, many limitations currently exist, and many future developments have yet to occur.

In Table 5-1, I recap why this new technology is so different and cool.

Table 5-1	How the Semantic Web Is Different	
Conventional Technology	**Semantic Web Is Similar Because**	**Semantic Web Is Different Because**
Regular Internet	It's Web-based.	It's about data, not documents.
Web 2.0	It's Web-based.	It's about data, not documents.
	It's network-oriented.	It's machine-interpretable.
Relational database	It's declarative.	It's more expressive.
	It's deterministic.	It's Web-based.
	It's linear time.	
Columnar database	It's tuples-oriented.	It doesn't assert a physical strategy.
Hierarchical database	It can be very efficient for hierarchical data.	It's a graph.
		It's standards-based.
Graph database	It's a graph system.	It's Web-based.
		It uses frame logic.
SOA platforms	It can annotate legacy applications.	It isn't a messaging system or a software platform.
EII platforms	It can supply a neutral data view.	It isn't a software platform.
XML	It's a type of tagging.	It's a real data model.
		It's machine-interpretable.
Object-oriented/ UML	It's frame-based.	It's deterministic.
	It's model-driven.	It's declarative.
Java	It's a logic-based system.	It's declarative.
		It has formal data semantics.
Artificial Intelligence	It's an AI system! (It's a type of knowledge representation.)	It's a standard. (It uses the Web architecture.)

As a software geek who likes to think about the future, I can't imagine a long-term future where people still write Java programs that parse XML and read relational database data. Of course, those systems will still be around ten years from now, but as the predominant pattern for writing large software applications, I can't imagine it. Think about it: In 1996, XML didn't even exist. Java is less than 15 years old. Things can change fast in the software industry.

When we truly comprehend all the ways that Semantic Web specifications can improve upon and advance the way we professionals design and encode data, it's hard to imagine a future that doesn't have a Semantic Web at the very nucleus of just about every software system.

Chapter 6

The Problem with Metadata

Metadata is data about data. Now that I have that definition out of the way, what else is left to say? The unfortunate truth about that oft-quoted definition of metadata is that it's so vague that it's all but useless in practice.

When a software developer or architect talks about metadata, you have to be aware of the context. You see, the word *metadata* is so overloaded with different meanings that it can mean many different things. For example, the metadata in a word-processing document is different than the metadata in a document content repository, which is different than the metadata in the word processing software program, which in turn uses Web metadata for publishing the document format, and so on and so forth. You really have to pay attention to precisely what people mean when they use the word *metadata*. The real problem with metadata is that it should be a very serious and formal discipline for software development, yet it has become relegated to the trash bin of overused, meaningless catchphrases bandied about in an already jargon-filled industry.

Metadata is an important topic to understand because metadata is what the Semantic Web is really all about. Unlike the many kinds of conventional, informal, and undisciplined kinds of software metadata that I cover in this chapter, the Semantic Web was designed from the ground up to be about linking and references and model-driven.

In this chapter, I describe some of the most important metadata types and supply you with a framework for easily classifying metadata of all types. Then I describe a few of the ways that metadata is used in modern software systems. Finally, you find out how the Semantic Web can help unify metadata of all sorts and perhaps eventually fix the problem with metadata.

Grasping the Basics of Data and Information

Without data, there's simply noise. Noise is like the static on your AM radio when you're between radio stations; data is when you get the signal. Information is the meaning that you place on the data. As a human listener, you can hear the words of the radio station and interpret the audible information. Knowledge is the stimulus, or experience, of the information in action. (For instance, if you hear a recipe for hamburgers on the radio and then try to make that recipe, you're then knowledgeable about that recipe.) Wisdom is the understanding that comes from many experiences. (If you happen to be a decent cook, you might have the wisdom to alter the hamburger recipe to your taste.)

One way of describing how systems interact is "a continuum of knowledge." Popular among systems thinkers, philosophers, and information architects, the knowledge continuum is a way of understanding how people and systems move through a range of experiences at varying depths of cognition. Figure 6-1 is a popular view of the knowledge continuum, which shows how noise is a precursor to data, data is the basis for information, information leads to knowledge, and, with deep understanding, comes wisdom.

Figure 6-1:
Typical
knowledge
continuum.

Noise — Data — Information — Knowledge — Wisdom

meaning   stimulus   understanding

Metadata is simply a way to enrich data so that software systems can interact with information. Metadata about models, vocabularies, and even programming languages are simply ways to supply "data about data" so that an interpreter, processor, or algorithm knows what to do. There is no magic with metadata.

Even the most advanced types of metadata — take the Semantic Web metadata for example — are simply ways of enriching data and information so that it may preserve its meaning outside of its original context. This is why Semantic Web languages are part of a type of artificial intelligence (AI) called knowledge representation (KR). KR is one of the fundamental foundations of the entire AI discipline — the Semantic Web families of KR are just one type of modern KR format. (See Chapter 5 for more on KR.)

Semantic Web databases are typically called knowledgebases (KBs). KBs are different from RDBMs (Relational Database Management systems) in part because the KB allows much more expressive metadata that can be applied on the structure of data. Likewise, a KB allows more sophisticated algorithms to directly reason with inferences on the data structures. This kind of distinction between data, information, and knowledge may seem superficial to some or nothing but a semantic game for others, but for many, it's the mark of a fundamentally different and more powerful layer of metadata.

Devising a Framework for Classifying Metadata

Not all metadata is created equal. Nor is all metadata distinct. In fact, there are many typical patterns of how metadata can be used in practice. One framework for classifying metadata is to start with the data itself and become progressively more abstract. For example:

0. "300779834" is instance data.

1. "int ssn = 300779834;" is syntax.

2. "table PERSON; Primary Key = SSN" is structure.

3. "table ORDER; Foreign Key = PERSON.SSN" is a reference.

4. "object ORDERS from ANSI X12 EDI Order Series (855) Purchase Order Acknowledgment" is a domain reference.

The preceding examples are pseudo code, but regardless of whether I'm working with Java, C++, Relational Databases, XML messages, UML, RDF or OWL programs, the basic pattern of layered metadata is quite similar.

The following sections describe these different levels of data and metadata in more detail. Understanding these framework layers will help you recognize how Semantic Web formats and specifications can help in all areas of software development.

Level 0: Instance data and records

At the purest level, data exists without a data type and outside of a particular software programming language. For example, the facts and figures of your bank account balances are data that, regardless of the software used to process them, have an innate irreducible fact associated with its value. Likewise, string values like "Jeff Pollock" or "SA Batla" exist independently from whatever software context might be processing them at a given moment.

Level 1: Syntactic metadata

Syntax is the sugar with which programming languages are sweetened. Syntax makes it easy for humans to write programs because it abstracts the human programmer from the machine code that is eventually generated anyway. The way in which program variables and literals are defined is achieved with the syntax of a language. For document formats like XML and HTML, the syntax of angle brackets has achieved near synonymy with the term *tagging*. Syntax usually isn't the interesting part of a language, simply because most software programming and data languages are similar enough that learning new syntax is never too difficult.

Level 2: Structural metadata

Structural metadata is where things start to get interesting. Whereas the syntax of a language defines how to say things that the software compiler will understand, the structural metadata is a reflection of what can be said at all. For example, in XML and HTML you can use angle brackets to insert tags in a document, but XML documents may be associated with a schema (XSD) in order to enforce a prescribed structure of the document.

Every data or programming language that operates with a schema can be validated and checked for consistency against a governing model. Each programming or data language that has a governing model also has a measurable level of expressivity. The *expressivity* of a model defines how complex the structure that governs the data may be. For example, the structure of an XML Schema, an XSD, is itself defined by the XML Infoset specification, which is a relatively simple hierarchical definition of how tags may interrelate as part of a logical hierarchy. In contrast, database schemas usually comply with a common base relational model theory described mathematically in the 1970s and canonized within the ANSI SQL query standards.

When most tech-savvy people think of metadata, they're usually thinking of structural metadata. That old catchphrase, "data about data," is exactly what structural metadata is. Anyone who's been schooled in the basics of software programming understands the difference between an object and an instance.

Simplistically, the *objects* represent the structure, and the *instances* represent the data. For data models, the governing schemas can take four predominant forms:

- ✔ **Relational:** The data is organized in tables, like a spreadsheet.
- ✔ **XML:** The data is organized in hierarchies, like a tree's limbs.
- ✔ **Object:** The data is organized within a software program's main memory, in potentially any other type of format.
- ✔ **Graph:** The data is organized in a network where any item can link to another, like a spider's web fanning out and connecting to other webs.

The structure of data defines and limits the ways in which different software algorithms may navigate the structure and find what you or I may be looking for. For example, relational databases can be indexed very efficiently and therefore are very fast to query. On the other hand, graph databases — such as those used for the Semantic Web — can't be indexed as efficiently and take longer to answer queries. The structure of the data defines its use and limits for computing.

Level 3: Referent metadata

A *referent* is an object, action, state, relationship, or attribute that defines a relationship to anything real or imaginary. In the abstract sense, referent metadata may simply be the relationship between the string of characters on this page, "Jeff Pollock," and me, the human being typing on a keyboard. More practically speaking, reference metadata are the links between objects and instances. For example:

- ✔ The object/class of things called Purchase Orders contains a statement of items that have been procured; a Purchase Order definition may exist in a dictionary or as a part of a data model with other rules associated with it

- ✔ The instance/record of a particular Purchase Order would be a uniquely identifiable occurrence of a statement of items that have been procured by some particular entity.

Purchase Orders may be related to other objects or to other instances. For example, the Purchase Order object may contain one or more Line Item objects, or the instance of a particular Purchase Order may be related to others that have been created by the same customer.

In a model, the referent metadata is the set of allowable relationships that may exist between objects and instances. For example, here are some typical relationship types from UML (Unified Modeling Language), XML, and OWL (Web Ontology Language) models:

- Inheritance/superclass/subclass
- Aggregation
- Composition
- Hierarchy/taxonomy
- Unions
- Intersection
- Disjointedness
- Equivalence

Relationships may be statically declared after they're inside a model, or they may be objects themselves — instantiated for each new unique occurrence of a relation. For example, when I model domains in UML, there is exactly one kind of inheritance relationship. When I use an inheritance relationship once for modeling Purchase Orders as a type of Order, I use exactly the same inheritance relationship as I would in modeling Books.

In contrast, with Semantic Web languages like OWL and RDF, the references (properties) are first-class objects in the model that can be inherited and uniquely named just like any other object. This powerful feature of the Semantic Web data languages is one of the ways that it is different than every other popular data language.

Referent metadata may also include metadata that defines how objects and instances may be related across different schemas and domains. Typically in the form of point-to-point mappings — either declaratively in a map or programmatically in algorithms — this type of referent metadata may be materialized as ETL maps, XSLT maps, hand-coded transformation routines in any programming language, or automatically generated as part of some other tooling. In any case, this type of metadata defines the relationship among data items for the purpose of integrating data.

Level 4: Domain metadata

Domain metadata puts the structural and referent metadata in context. The Purchase Order object may mean something completely different in a SWIFT financial services domain model than it would in the NGOSS telecommunications standard models. It is domain metadata that's required for cross-system data exchange as a means to understand and relate foreign data into a local data model. Oftentimes, this domain metadata is understood only by the developer or data architect responsible for the data mapping. However, more and more modern systems link their local domain models to industry standards data models for easier portability and data exchange.

Logic and Rules in Your Metadata

Every metadata layer may be optimized with logic and rules. The syntax layers may define mathematical operators (+, −, /, and so on), conditional tests (>, >, =), and other inline techniques for manipulating data. Structural systems may incorporate rules and logic to help classify and organize objects and instances. Referent metadata may include techniques for constraining relationships in certain specific conditions. Domain metadata may include techniques for merging data while maintaining logical consistency. Rules and logic are a part of every data language.

The following section is a brief explanation of how rules are different than logic with a few simple examples in a data model context.

How rules differ from logics

Rules and logics are often discussed interchangeably, but they are quite different in practice for data models. *Logics* refer to the way the data model is constrained, whereas *rules* are typically actions that happen on the data once it is inside a procedural program. For example, data that violates the data model logics does not fit into the database or knowledgebase. In contrast, data that has rules applied to it may generate an action such as an event, or new data as an output. I cover more of these distinguishing factors in Chapter 9 when I describe Semantic Web business rule specifications.

Modeling constraints

Each software modeling language has certain, specific constraints that may be applied to the data and the data models. These constraints are part of the modeling metadata and typically have consequences that matter most at runtime. For example, if the constraints that have been modeled within UML, XML, or database models are violated during a software program's execution, typically some type of process exception will occur.

In a relational database, constraints may include

- ✔ Primary Keys
- ✔ Foreign Keys
- ✔ NOT NULL
- ✔ Various SQL Check Constraints
  - • Boolean
  - • Value Ranges, and so on

Unified Modeling Language (UML) constraints are typically captured in a language called Object Constraint Language (OCL). OCL enables UML modelers to describe constraints on classes, properties, attributes, and operations. The language uses very familiar operators (if, then, else, and, or, not, implies, and so on) that specify conditional expressions. The OCL itself is the foundation for several different model transformation languages that are used to transform MOF models within the OMG MDA specification. Unlike the database constraints, OCL isn't grounded in a formal mathematic model theory, so it behaves differently in different implementations.

 Constraints are an important part of metadata modeling because they enable a substantial level of richness and practicality to the data model — enabling software applications to focus on the business processing logic instead of always having to validate and re-validate data.

Discovering the Many Types of Metadata

Software applications, especially network-based applications, are some of the most complex man-made engineering accomplishments in the history of our species. Layers upon layers of logic and rules from billions of lines of code running on a silicon-based central processer work together to automate and simplify the business operations of Fortune 500 companies that generate more revenue than the gross domestic product (GDP) of most countries.

Without metadata, the whole framework for software development, deployment, and runtime execution would collapse. Metadata runs in every layer of that complex ecosystem from the central processor to the network transmission and protocol layers. Metadata is fundamental to every major aspect of software applications, software standards, network protocols, and database technology — there's so much to choose from!

The next several sections supply a more detailed example of conventional metadata formats used in different kinds of software architectures. In each section, I describe how metadata is normally used, and point out how it fits in the framework levels described at the beginning of this chapter.

Web metadata: HTML, XML, and Web services

Metadata on the Web is everywhere. The Web pages you browse are simply a veneer of pretty content assembled by a browser that understands metadata within the Web page. Tags, keywords, and special characters make up the basics of Web content encoded into pages.

The example in Figure 6-2 displays how a simple Web page like www.dummies. com is actually comprised of lots of metadata interspersed with a little bit of the content you see on the page displayed within the Web browser.

Any HTML or XML document for display uses metadata in this way. In fact, even the word processor I'm using to write this book uses XML encoding behind the scenes to define how my text and images should be displayed on a page.

Figure 6-2: A sample Web page with its source code visible.

Other Web content (such as Web services like those you may find from companies like eBay, Amazon.com, and Salesforce.com) also use metadata — but not for display. Web services metadata is used to define the APIs (application programming interfaces), bindings, and structure of messages and documents that are transmitted between different businesses. Web content of all sorts is built on top of metadata — without it, the World Wide Web would not exist!

Database metadata: OLTP, OLAP, and so on

Metadata inside business software applications is a necessity, but nowhere is this fact more true than inside databases. Databases are the most widely used software infrastructure in the world. Since the 1980s, businesses of all sorts have hosted mission-critical applications on relational databases.

Databases use a relational modeling approach that depends on the construction of schema, tables, and relationships between the tables called *keys*. Many more kinds of constraints and structural assignments can be made inside a database. The data integration tool from Oracle shown in Figure 6-3 makes some of these constraints, table column properties, and SQL-based mapping assignments visible. All of this is simply metadata to the database — the actual records, or data, are contained and viewed within the context of this descriptive metadata.

Other databases besides relational databases exist, but they all work in similar ways. Cube-style databases, called OLAP (online analytical processing), also depend on metadata for describing their dimensions, calculations, and other aggregation properties. Hierarchical databases and even newer graph databases built on top of Semantic Web languages all depend on system metadata and modeling metadata to make their records visible. Without metadata, the modern database would not exist.

Object-oriented language metadata: C# and Java

The way people model software programs depends on metadata. In fact, the very notion of modern programming is dependent upon structural and semantic metadata for modeling software.

Object-oriented programming uses common patterns for software development that include the use of inheritance, polymorphism, and encapsulation of data. The object-oriented programming languages all support these basic tenets of object design. The metadata notations shown in Figure 6-4 include the labels on the lines (relationships), the markers next to the text (visibility), and even the lines themselves (no arrows means a bidirectional, unqualified relationship), among others.

Languages like Java, C#, Smalltalk, and others all support the essential aspects of object design — the way they do so is to implement language features with metadata that allows developers to author their programs using object-oriented features. For example, take a look at some of the keywords used in this code sample:

```java
import java.util.*;

public class Backorder extends Order {
  public Date backDate;
  public Date estShipDate;
  //overrides the method from parent class
  public void checkForOutstandingOrders() {
    super.checkForOutstandingOrders ();
    System.out.format(super.orderNumber,this.estShipDate);
  }
}
```

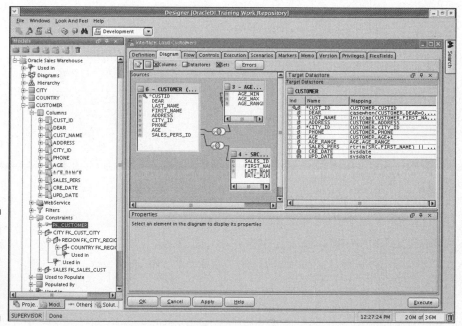

Figure 6-3: A sample application viewing database metadata.

The preceding Java example shows how you can implement simple inheritance in a software program by using the keyword `extends`. *Keywords* are used in code to tell the software compiler (or interpreter) how to link data that it is holding in main memory; they literally tell the computer how to build software programs. This type of keyword syntax is the type of metadata that makes simple fourth-generation programming possible. Without metadata, programmers might still be writing software applications directly in machine code.

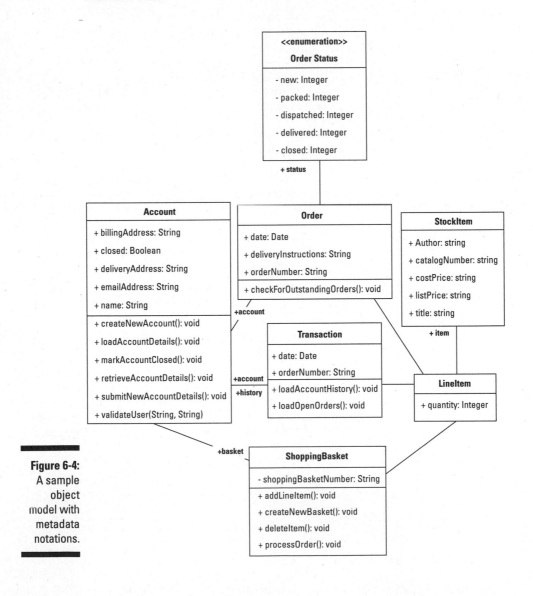

Figure 6-4:
A sample object model with metadata notations.

Programming framework metadata: IBM EMF, and Oracle ADF

Programming frameworks go beyond the basic language features to pre-implement additional features that developers can use to further simplify the construction of complex software applications.

Most of the major software providers have implemented their own frameworks, some of which are resold and some of which are freely accessible via open-source arrangements. IBM uses the Eclipse Model Framework (EMF), shown in Figure 6-5, which is the underlying programming model for any Eclipse-based project. Developers can use the EMF core (ECore) objects in their own applications to take advantage of prebuilt features that are available only to programs that use the ECore model.

Notice that the IBM EMF framework has an EClass object (in the center of the figure). If you were developing an EMF application, you might choose to inherit your Java object directly from the EClass object rather than have it be a plain-old Java object (POJO). When your objects were of type EClass, you could take advantage of all the features of EMF and enable the framework to handle the display and lifecycle of your business objects.

This ECore model is metadata at work because it defines a type of metamodel. When developers write an application that they build using IBM EMF, they must become deeply familiar with the characteristics and behavior of how the EMF works — this is called *model semantics.* By learning a framework and writing your own program in it, you've adopted the metadata and semantics of that framework.

The Oracle Application Development Framework (ADF) shown in Figure 6-6 is roughly analogous to the IBM EMF model, although Oracle's framework is more oriented around the Model-View-Controller (MVC) pattern than IBM's is. Like IBM, you as a developer may choose to implement your business objects as Oracle's ADF Entity Object rather than as a POJO. Along with other objects that you would inherit from, the Oracle framework would enable you to take advantage of many extra features that are not available in the base Java language itself.

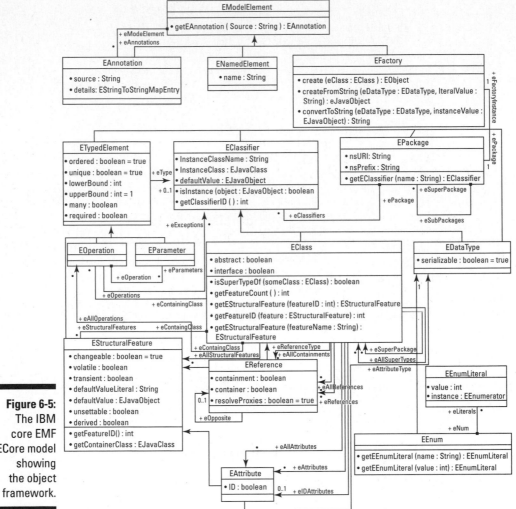

Figure 6-5:
The IBM core EMF ECore model showing the object framework.

Both the IBM and Oracle frameworks, and for that matter the Microsoft .NET framework, are extensions of a core programming language like Java and C#. The extensions are a program implementation itself, but the implementation depends on metadata and implied semantics about what the framework components mean and what they are supposed to do. Additionally, the EMF, ADF, and .NET frameworks all have some model-driven characteristics (where software behavior is declaratively driven from the model of the data, not just algorithms) and make extensive use of other declarative features such as business rules and late-bindings. Thus, these very popular frameworks, which the vast majority of business applications are written on, are themselves absolutely dependent on the metadata used to describe the framework.

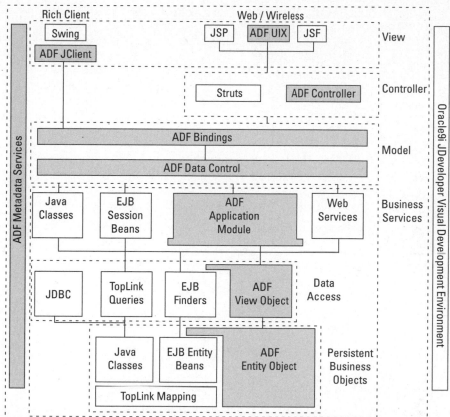

Figure 6-6:
The Oracle
ADF model
showing
the MVC
pattern.

Mainframe system metadata: Copybooks and JCL

When serious enterprise computing began in the late 1950s, COBOL was developed to fill specific demands that FORTRAN could not. Created by the Conference on Data Systems and Languages (CODASYL), COBOL was developed from the ground up as the language for enterprise business systems. COBOL's data types were limited to numbers and strings of text. This simplicity allowed for those data items to be grouped into arrays and records so that they could be tracked and organized better using metadata.

A COBOL program is structured much like a written essay, with four or five major sections that make up the finished program. COBOL program statements use a very English-like grammar, making it quite easy to learn — which is sometimes surprising for younger developers who often think of COBOL as an ancient and difficult software language.

The following example supplies a short fragment of COBOL, take note of the English-like syntax:

```
IDENTIFICATION DIVISION
PROGRAM-ID. SUM-OF-PRICES.
AUTHOR.
SOURCE.
ENVIRONMENT DIVISION.
INPUT-OUTPUT SECTION.
FILE-CONTROL.
  SELECT INP-DATA ASSIGN TO INPUT.
  SELECT RESULT-FILE ASSIGN TO OUTPUT.
DATA DIVISION.
FILE SECTION.
FD INP-DATA LABEL RECORD IS OMITTED.
01 ITEM-PRICE
  02 ITEM PICTURE X(30).
  02 PRICE PICTURE 9999V99.
  02 FILLER PICTURE X(44).
FD RESULT-FILE LABEL RECORD IS OMITTED.
01 RESULT-LINE PICTURE X(132).
WORKING-STORAGE SECTION.
77 TOT PICTURE 999999V99, VALUE 0, USAGE IS COMPUTATIONAL.
77 COUNT PCITURE 9999, VALUE 0, USAGE IS COMPUTATIONAL.
01 SUM-LINE.
  02 FILLER VALUE ' SUM ='PICTURE X(12).
  02 SUM-OUT PICTURE $$,$$$,$$9.99.
  02 FILLER VALUE ' NO. OF ITEMS ='PICTURE X(21).
  02 COUNT-OUT PICTURE ZZZ9.99.
01 ITEM-LINE.
  02 ITEM-OUT PICTURE X(30).
  02 PRICE-OUT PICTURE ZZZ9.99.
PROCEDURE DIVISION.
START.
  OPEN INPUT INP-DATA AND OUTPUT RESULT-FILE.
READ-DATA.
  READ INP-DATA AT END GO TO PRINT-LINE.
  ADD PRICE TO TOT.
  ADD 1 TO COUNT.
  MOVE PRICE TO PRICE-OUT.
  MOVE ITEM TO ITEM-OUT.
  WRITE RESULT-LINE FROM ITEM-LINE.
  GO TO READ-DATA.
PRINT-LINE.
  MOVE TOT TO SUM-OUT.
  MOVE COUNT TO COUNT-OUT.
  WRITE RESULT-LINE FROM SUM-LINE.
  CLOSE INP-DATA AND RESULT-FILE.
  STOP RUN.
```

COBOL programs typically consist of four divisions: identification, environment, data, and procedure. COBOL's environment division is a place for metadata that can help make programs easier to run on other systems because it forces the programmer to enumerate all the resources and facilities that the program requires. Traditional COBOL feature sets are primitive compared with modern computing languages.

Inside early COBOL systems, metadata is very basic: Only static data structures are supported, and numeric variables can only be binary or decimal. Support for range checking and output formatting, string manipulation support, and simple flow-control constructs are also provided for. Record structures and arrays are the primary means for organizing data, but no pointers or references are available. Although COBOL isn't considered to be a metadata-driven language in the modern sense, you can easily see that the structure, syntax, and format of even these very old programming languages contain quite a bit of implicit metadata and structure.

The term *JCL,* or Job Control Language, is used generally to refer to any scripting environment for mainframe systems. There are several varieties, but they are each pretty similar in function.

The following JCL example gives you an idea of the kind of syntax metadata used for these mainframe programs:

```
//TSOUSR123A JOB (12345),'JEFF POLLOCK',

// MSGCLASS=X,CLASS=A,NOTIFY=TSOUSR123
//* SAMPLE JOB
//STEP1 EXEC PGM=SAMPLE1
//STEPLIB DD DSN=TSOUSR123.LOAD,DISP=SHR
//INFILE DD DSN=TSOUSR123.DATA(MEMBER),DISP=SHR
//OUTFILE DD SYSOUT=*
//SYSOUT DD SYSOUT=*
```

In the preceding JCL sample, note some of the keywords like MSGCLASS, DSN, and DISP. Like all programming languages, the JCL scripts have a formal processing structure and semantics for allowable commands used in the mainframe environment to control operating system routines. Like COBOL, FORTRAN, and other legacy languages, JCL is *not* generally considered to be a metadata-driven programming language, but unlike any programming language, it's still entirely driven by a formal semantic and specification for its syntax and structure. As I further explore the wide range of metadata types and how they relate to the Semantic Web, I explain how even older legacy languages can be modeled and controlled from the Semantic Web framework.

Network and protocol metadata: TCP, 1P, HTTP, and FTP

Everybody who uses a computer nowadays uses it on a network. But networks are the most innocuous and forgotten about part of computing. In the surest sign of their absolute and total success, people just expect computing networks to work. But the few who write network firmware and build routers and switches know that it is anything but magic to get these complex systems to work.

One of the lowest levels of Internet communication protocols is TCP (Transmission Control Protocol). Along with IP (Internet Protocol) and HTTP (Hypertext Transfer Protocol), TCP forms the backbone of every Web link you've ever clicked.

TCP is a connection-oriented protocol whose transmission end points must establish a connection before transmission can begin. TCP protocol data units are called *segments*. Clients who send and receive TCP entities exchange data in the form of segments, shown in Figure 6-7, which consist of a fixed 20-byte header followed by a variable size data field.

16-bit source port number								16-bit destination port number	
32-bit sequence number									
32-bit acknowledgement number									
4-bit header	reserved	U R G	A C K	P S H	R S T	S Y N	F I N	16-bit window size	
16-bit TCP checksum								16-bit urgent pointer	
Options (if any)									
Data (if any)									

Figure 6-7: The structure of a TCP segment.

TCP is responsible for breaking down a stream of bytes into segments and reconnecting them at the other end. TCP retransmits any segments that are lost and also organizes the segments in the correct order. The segment structure is very tightly specified and includes information about the end points, ports, offset data, and security. User data, which might include the Web page data we browse for, is included after the end of the TCP segment header.

TCP doesn't work in isolation. The IP and HTTP protocols are layered above TCP to enable your Web browser to actually receive and render a Web page. For example, each time you click a link in your browser, it issues and transmits an HTTP GET command. The definition and behavior of the HTTP GET command are specified by the W3C standards for HTTP.

As you can see in the following standards snippet, the actual semantics of the GET commands may differ depending on the context of a given transmission. These kinds of semantics define behavior for most low-level protocols and are entirely driven by the syntax and structural metadata of the messages, and the network devices that route, switch, and deliver Web content.

```
8.3. GET

    The GET method means retrieve whatever information (in the form of an
    entity) is identified by the Request-URI. If the Request-URI refers
    to a data-producing process, it is the produced data which shall be
    returned as the entity in the response and not the source text of the
    process, unless that text happens to be the output of the process.

    The semantics of the GET method change to a "conditional GET" if the
    request message includes an If-Modified-Since, If-Unmodified-Since,
    If-Match, If-None-Match, or If-Range header field. A conditional GET
    method requests that the entity be transferred only under the
    circumstances described by the conditional header field(s). The
    conditional GET method is intended to reduce unnecessary network
    usage by allowing cached entities to be refreshed without requiring
    multiple requests or transferring data already held by the client.

    The semantics of the GET method change to a "partial GET" if the
    request message includes a Range header field. A partial GET
    requests that only part of the entity be transferred, as described in
    Section 6.4 of [Part5]. The partial GET method is intended to reduce
    unnecessary network usage by allowing partially retrieved entities.
```

OMG metadata: CWM/IMM, MOF, and MDA

The Object Management Group (OMG) is the international standards body that maintains many of the formal specifications for object-oriented and middleware software programming technologies.

MDA

One of the more popular, and controversial, standards efforts at the OMG is the Model-Driven Architecture (MDA). MDA represents an attempt by the OMG to provide a family of specifications, guidelines, and practices for separating the business and technical concerns in software programs. MDA is principally concerned with providing a platform-independent modeling framework that can allow software developers to work on the business problem in models while automatically generating the technical implementations.

MDA is itself more of a framework. Although the MDA specifies how to create a decoupled architecture for modeling, it leaves the actual language specifications to other implementation definitions. MDA, as shown in Figure 6-8, relies on the CWM (Common Warehouse Metamodel), MOF (Meta Object Facility), and UML (Unified Modeling Language) specifications for detail model guidelines. Likewise, MDA depends on regular programming languages like Java, .NET, and XML for the implementation profile of MDA compliance applications.

The core business model in the MDA architecture is the computation independent model (CIM) that shares many common characteristics of a Semantic Web ontology layer. The CIM is typically a model of the environment in which a system will operate and acts as a source of shared understanding and shared vocabulary for the given domain. The platform-independent model (PIM) represents a finer grained look at the application in question and describes the details of its operation — without specifying the technology in which it's implemented. Finally, the platform-specific model (PSM) specifies the details of a given technology or platform implementation of that PIM. Usually the PSM will reflect some technology design choice such as a J2EE or .NET platform decision.

MDA efforts in the OMG have focused on the difficult area of providing mappings between the various model specifications. Importantly, the mapping specifications between the PIM and PSM are crucial for the ultimate vision of the MDA to operate as promised. Mappings at this architecture layer provide developers the ability to generate functional code in multiple formats from common models — thus reducing the development time for new technology deployments.

As you can tell, the entire set of OMG, MDA, and related standards is entirely based on metadata! In fact, most of these standards are nothing but a set of agreed upon models and semantics, which must be used in a certain way to be within the standard. These are classic examples of structural, referent, and domain metadata.

CWM/MM

The Common Warehouse Metamodel (CWM) was created to facilitate the exchange of metadata among business intelligence systems and data warehouses. By virtue of its design, the implementation of the CWM relies on technology vendors to implement the CWM specifications inside their highly proprietary tools. Some vendors choose to adopt the CWM specifications as the core of their metadata repository, whereas others choose to offer import/export features to extract the metadata in the CWM specifications.

The CWM breaks down the classification of metadata into four main packages: Core, Behavioral, Relationships, and Instance, as shown in Figure 6-9.

The classes provided for in the Core package are the foundation upon which the rest of the CWM rests. In this Core model, you can see how the organization of core metadata concepts in the model is important to specialized communities that choose to implement with CWM and MOF ideals in mind.

One pragmatic result of the CWM standardization effort was to provide for an on-the-wire format for data warehouse metadata, which, when implemented by leading vendors, allows for the exchange of metadata in a common format. The design parameters for the CWM are consistent with other OMG efforts and other popular standards. CWM relies on the XMI model syntax to implement UML models and XML (using CWM XSDs) as the core exchange format for the metadata. Likewise, the CWM effort proposed the use of CORBA-like IDL (Interface Definition Language) interfaces for physical access to warehouse metadata in the CWM framework.

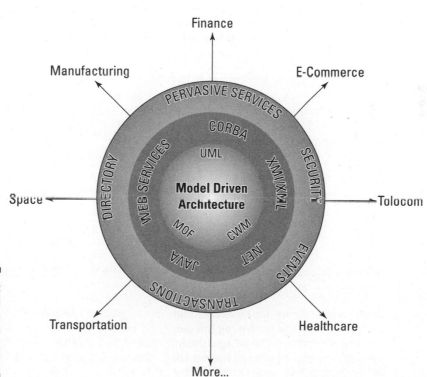

Figure 6-8: Graphical depiction of the MDA vision from OMG.

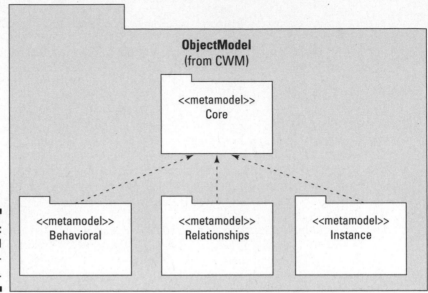

Figure 6-9:
The CWM
Core pack-
age model.

CWM was primarily intended to solve problems encountered by a fairly narrow range of applications — business intelligence and warehouse systems. Where CWM makes great strides is in the specification of models for metadata, and in the way it grounds them in a self-describing Meta Object Facility (MOF) to contain model-creep (when the model expands beyond its original purpose). MOF, depicted in Figure 6-10, is the overarching framework for UML, MDA, and CWM. These modeling advances are significantly beyond the scope of typical data warehouse and business intelligence applications.

One of the most important aspects of the CWM effort is that it provides a baseline understanding of how to approach the metadata specification problem. Whether a software architect is working with data warehouse issues, packages application issues, or information interoperability issues, the CWM can offer an approach for modeling and specifying the underlying business models and metadata infrastructure.

For example, the CWM scope also includes the definition of specialized types of metadata structures. OLAP (Online Analytic Processing) is a special kind of relational model that uses model dimensions as the central organizing feature of the model. OLAP models are extremely useful for analytic environments where pivoting the data is important. Typical software solutions for financial reporting, budgeting, forecasting, marketing, and general business reporting often use the OLAP model because it's faster and easier to work with than more traditional relational structures. CWM's standard definition of the OLAP model is as follows in Figure 6-11.

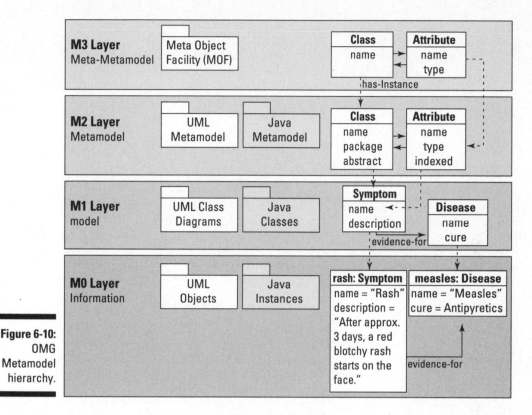

Figure 6-10:
OMG
Metamodel
hierarchy.

CWM efforts since 2005 have been focused on revamping the Common Warehouse Model. As successful as CWM has been, it hasn't served the original intent to create a high degree of interoperability between data warehouse and business intelligence vendor implementations. Nor has CWM been able to substantially contribute to the general purpose data interoperability challenge at the enterprise level. Therefore, newer efforts are underway to recast the CWM in an updated framework called the Information Management Model (IMM).

OMG's IMM initiative is an attempt to expand the relevance of the CWM metamodel into other information management domains. Particular focus from the OMG is being placed on making IMM suitable for XML-centric modeling, thereby providing an XML and data warehousing model profile inside the popular MOF/UML framework.

OMG Collaboration with W3C

One of the most unique things about the Object Management Group is that it sponsors more specifications work for metadata's own sake than any other international standards group. Both ISO (International Standards

Organization) and W3C (World Wide Web Consortium) have just as many standards that are metadata-centric, but only the OMG has really proactively taken the leadership role in saying that it views itself as the keeper of metadata-centric architecture specifications. Whether that's right or wrong, the OMG is certainly the principal driver of the model-driven development social meme.

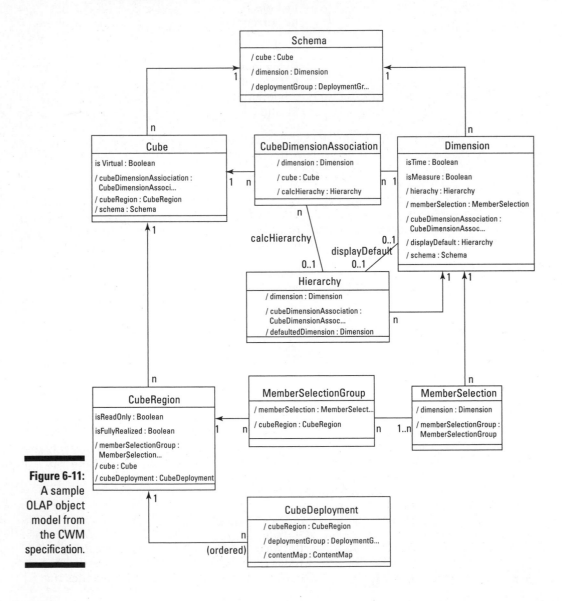

Figure 6-11:
A sample OLAP object model from the CWM specification.

A longtime criticism of the OMG metadata standards has been that they lack any sort of formal mathematical grounding. Unlike relational database theory (which is grounded in a formal algebra, the central feature of OMG's work), the MOF framework is simply a normative heuristic for defining metadata like classes, attributes, and relations. This foundational oversight means that in the OMG family of metadata specifications, there's no consistent way of performing *lossless model transformations* (where the original meaning of the model isn't lost) or guaranteeing correctness in the semantics of a metadata model.

To rectify this lack of an underlying mathematic formalism, the OMG maps its core metamodels to the W3C Semantic Web standards. For example, the OMG's Ontology Definition Metamodel (ODM) recommendation maps the MOF framework to the W3C RDF and OWL specifications, among others. The purpose of ODM is to supply a repeatable foundation for transforming MOF models and also to enable RDF and OWL to be modeled by the OMG visual notations such as UML.

This intersection of OMG and W3C work is one of the most promising areas for metadata standardization in the software industry. W3C brings strong foundations and a deep understanding for how Web infrastructure standards work in practices, and OMG brings focus to developer practices and a deep understanding for how layered business software applications are built.

You can't understand the problem and the potential of metadata without understanding just how much the OMG and W3C standards influence and impact every software application written anywhere in the world.

W3C metadata: Web infrastructure metadata

Throughout this chapter, I explain how various metadata formats affect every part of our computing environments. No standards body impacts all these software architectures more than the W3C. Responsible for ubiquitous metadata and infrastructure standards, the W3C's influence can be measured in societal terms and not just technical ones. Think of just how much the Web impacts elections, freedom of information, disaster awareness, and international aid programs.

Metadata, data, and protocol standards such as HTTP, HTML, XHTML, XML, SOAP, WSDL, and PNG define the ways in which people communicate over the Internet. Each of these standards is quite large, complex, and verbose. They contain a special syntax, a formal structure, and well-defined semantics that specify how interpreters should handle them in practice. All these features are provided for with metadata. Without the metadata defined for each of those standards, developers would be writing assembly code while trying to adhere to very precise instructions written in a standards document.

ISO metadata: 10303, 11179, Dublin Core, and others

The International Standards Organization (ISO) is a very active publisher of software specifications. In the software industry, they are more commonly known for their quality assurance standards (ISO 9000 compliancy), but ISO publishes standards for everything from paper sizes (A4), water-resistant watches, book numbering (ISBN), video standards (MPEG), and even the Portable Document Format (PDF).

ISO 10303, the STEP (Standard for the Exchange of Product Data) standard, is a vast framework for modeling and exchanging data about all sorts of things — anything that can be considered a product in any way. The STEP framework includes integrated resources that are made up of application modules and integrated constructs. STEP itself consists of many parts — application protocols, abstract test suites, and implementation modules.

STEP is intended to apply to the following domain areas: mechanical (2D drawings, 3D drawings, automotive, furniture, and so on); buildings; electrical (plants and so on); ships; technical data; fluid dynamics; and the list goes on. For example, the STEP formats would govern the structure of detailed data about automotive parts that is communicated between a supplier and a manufacturer.

More than 20 years of effort have been poured into the STEP family of standards. Vocabularies, metadata, and specialized modeling languages (such as EXPRESS) have been developed for nearly any kind of materials management problem domain. STEP contains metadata about data modeling, metadata about domain vocabulary, metadata about syntax, and structure of physical world items.

Recent STEP activities are moving toward more XML- and even Semantic Web–compliant notations. Support for RDF/OWL is already included in Part 3 of ISO 15926, which offers a Semantic Web compliant profile for ISO 10303 geometries. Likewise, the 15926 standard is defining an implementation method based on the Semantic Web architecture.

ISO 11179, the ISO standard for metadata registries, has attempted to define the standard for capturing business metadata in a metadata registry. The ISO 11179 specification is comprised of six parts:

- ✔ Part 1: Framework
- ✔ Part 2: Classification
- ✔ Part 3: Registry Metamodel and Basic Attributes
- ✔ Part 4: Formulation of Data Definitions
- ✔ Part 5: Naming and Identification Principles
- ✔ Part 6: Registration

Although ISO 11179 isn't considered a successful standard — very few organizations have ever made an attempt to become compliant — it's an important milestone in the area of metadata management because it was one of the first attempts to systematically decompose the problem and offer an industrial standard for the metadata repository itself.

Like many other metadata specifications that have followed, the ISO 11179 structure is an object-oriented type structure. The example in Figure 6-12 shows how a data element name is related to its object term and property term, thereby allowing for a systematic way of building and relating objects and properties.

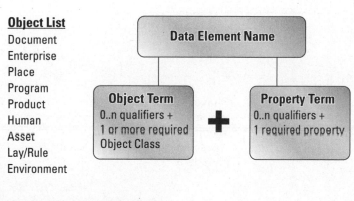

Figure 6-12:
Core ISO 11179 metadata framework data element construction.

Object List
Document
Enterprise
Place
Program
Product
Human
Asset
Lay/Rule
Environment

Data Element Name

Object Term
0..n qualifiers +
1 or more required
Object Class

+

Property Term
0..n qualifiers +
1 required property

Project List
Amount
Angle
Area
Code
Coordinate
Date
Dimension
Identifier
Mass
Name
Quantity
Rate
Temperature
Text
Time
Volume
Weight

Example Data Element Names
Document Abstract Text
Enterprise Name
Product Price Amount
Product Scheduled Delivery Date
Engineering Design Process Cost Amount

A much more successful ISO standard is ISO 15836, the Dublin Core Metadata Element Set. Created and maintained by a cross-disciplinary collection of librarians, computer scientists, and museum cataloging specialists, the Dublin Core consists of 15 metadata elements used for annotating items of any type. They are

Title	Format
Creator	Identifier
Subject	Source
Description	Language
Publisher	Relation
Contributor	Coverage
Date	Rights
Type	

Libraries and museums from around the world are using this set of metadata from the Dublin Core initiatives to encode information about their assets in a normative way that can be easily exchanged.

As I explain in Chapter 4, the Dublin Core technical encoding is expressed in RDF and can be used to annotate Web content. The following RDF snippet uses the Dublin Core metadata:

```
<?xml version="1.0"?>
<rdf:RDF
 xmlns:rdf="http://www.w3.org/1999/02/22-rdf-syntax-ns#"
 xmlns:dc="http://purl.org/dc/elements/1.1/">

<rdf:Description rdf:about="http://me.jtpollock.us/">
<dc:title>Jeff's Homepage!</dc:title>
</rdf:Description>

<rdf:Description rdf:about="http://me.jtpollock.us/">
  <dc:creator   rdf:resource="http://me.jtpollock.us/foaf.rdf#me"/>
</rdf:Description>

</rdf:RDF>
```

The second namespace definition `xmlns:dc` refers to the Dublin Core metadata models. Later in the snippet, I use the `dc:creator` identifier to denote that the Web page was created by a named resource. (In this case, it points to Jeff Pollock's FOAF description.)

The ISO standards are rich with data-centric models that define and describe vocabularies for all sorts of industries, metamodels about the encoding of data itself, programming languages, their syntax, and their structures. Just like we saw with W3C, OMG, and other technical metadata, lots of potential for overlap and redundant metadata definitions exist.

OASIS metadata: SAML, UDDI, and so on

No discussion of metadata standards would be complete without examining the work coming from the OASIS (Organization for the Advancement of Structured Information Standards). Originally conceived from within the SGML community, OASIS has matured into a strong international body for managing standards such as UDDI, SAML, UBL, XACML, and CAP. Oftentimes, as with ebXML and Open Doc standards, the OASIS community works closely with the ISO community in order to further validate a given standards framework.

Although OASIS is similar to W3C and OMG in many ways, the OASIS community tends to focus more on application standards and less on infrastructure and protocol standards. Whereas W3C is clearly a Web infrastructure body and OMG is a programming language body, the OASIS community focuses on areas such as word-processing document formats, application security, data center standards, and registry applications.

Application standards are very metadata-intensive. UDDI (Universal Description Discovery and Integration) is a registry application standard deployed along with most service-oriented architecture (SOA)–based infrastructure. The UDDI model consists of tNodes, which are essentially a taxonomy describing what services do, sort of like the Yellow Pages phone book categories. Likewise, the Security Access Markup Language (SAML) is a messaging and application specification for exchanging security details about policies. In Figure 6-13, you can see how the structure of a security assertion type is modeled as a set of XML attributes. These structural keywords — such as IssueInstant and saml:Conditions — have very precise semantics that are understood by the software interpreting SAML metadata from a SAML-compliant issuer.

Although the adoption of OASIS standards isn't as widespread as ISO, W3C, or OMG, many OASIS standards have existing or planned overlap with the Semantic Web family of standards. Likewise, OASIS standards such as UBL, UDDI, XACML, and SAML are frequently used in close deployment with W3C Web standards and OMG programming standards. As with all the other metadata types described in this chapter, the real problem with metadata is in the duplication and re-definition of basic principles of classification, relationships, and other metamodel features.

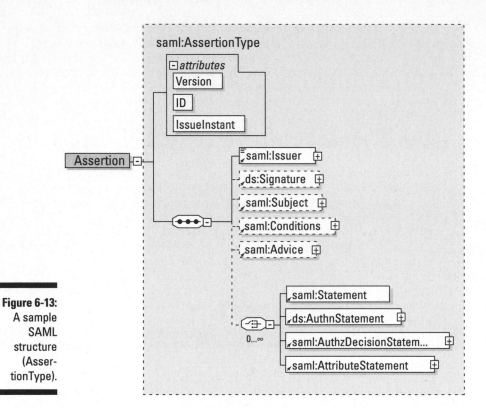

Industry vocabularies

The problem with metadata is that there is so much of it, yet so little reusability. Nowhere is this truer than in the industries where metadata is used to specify business vocabularies. All major marketplaces exchange data. Marketplaces such as automotive, aerospace, pharmaceuticals, defense, travel and tourism, consumer packaged goods, financial services, and insurance each specify their own unique data vocabularies for exchanging data among trading partners.

Example business vocabularies for a given domain may include hundreds of business entities, nouns, XML documents, UML diagrams, and other modeling and message metadata. Hundreds of domain-specific standards exist; some of the more popular ones include IATA (travel industry), NGOSS (telco), ACORD (insurance), HL7 (healthcare), and SWIFT (finance).

Business vocabularies may consist of several parts, multiple formats for consumption, and reams of documentation to explain how to use the standard. How many different technical standard formats do you imagine there are for the business entity called, "Address?" Too many, no doubt.

Business vocabularies are almost always developed in isolation, and those vocabularies that try to serve cross-purposes for several domains are often not considered useful. Universal Business Vocabulary (UBL) is one such vocabulary (in an XML format) maintained by OASIS; unfortunately, it is not widely adopted. ebXML (Electronic Business for XML) is another such cross-domain vocabulary that has not gained wide acceptance.

Far and away, the most successful business vocabularies are in the EDI (Electronic Data Interchange) data formats. With two major EDI formats (EDIFACT in Europe and X12 in the United States) the vast majority of business-to-business data interchange uses these formats. Trillions of dollars of banking transactions, retail orders, shipping/receiving transactions, and all sorts of other electronic processing happen in EDI data formats every day.

Business data vocabularies aren't an academic playground; they define how business gets done.

Semantics and Metadata

Semantics is truly a loaded word. Broadly, the semantics of data is just the definition of what that data means. But semantics in software is tied to all sorts of different code interpreters, compilers, database engines and other software algorithms. The semantics of Java is one thing, and the semantics of XML is another. Each data format or programming language has to be interpreted or compiled at some point — at that exact moment, the semantics of a given set of data or program instructions are perfectly clear, and if they aren't, the interpreter throws an exception.

The following sections give you an idea of the formal aspects of the Semantic Web's data and metadata formats. This should stand in stark contrast to the informal conventional metadata formats described earlier in this chapter.

Semantic Web model theory in a minute

Semantic Web is grounded in set theory. It is based in a model-theoretic viewpoint that says the behavior of data within sets should conform to a defined collection of theorems. The collection of theorems that a data language conforms to is called its model-theoretic semantics. Having a model-theoretic semantic context is important because it enables the software to make computational guarantees about finding the data you are querying for and allows the data container (a database or knowledgebase) to automate some of the hard work for us.

The Semantic Web has two data languages: RDF and OWL. Each language has its own model theory, and they aren't linked except for the fact that all OWL is also valid RDF.

Entailment, expressiveness, and closure

Semantic Web model theory differs from relational database model theory because it operates with an open-world assumption. In a database, if the data you're looking for doesn't exist inside a particular schema, the closed-world database assumes that data doesn't exist at all. With a Semantic Web knowledgebase, the knowledgebase knows the differences of answers that can be proven to be correct, those that can be proven to be incorrect, and those that are ambiguous. The Semantic Web open-world approach assumes that all answers are possible and then tries to find data that supports or refutes the query. More detail and examples about the open-world assumption are supplied in Chapter 8.

The expressivity of RDF and OWL are described in their model theory. Each language includes a domain, range, class extensions, and property extensions that define how the data model may be constructed and precisely how the model works in various mathematical proofs. RDF and RDFS languages specify several *lemmas* (like a logical proposition or mathematical theorem) used to prove the validity of a given model's interpretation, including the following examples:

- **Subgraph Lemma:** A graph entails all its subgraphs.

- **Instance Lemma:** A graph is entailed by all its instances.

- **Conjunction Lemma:** If entities are grounded, the vocabulary satisfies the entities if and only if it satisfies every RDF triple in all the entities.

- **Plain Subgraph Lemma:** If both of two entities are grounded, the first entity entails the second if and only if the second is a subgraph of the first.

- **Herbrand Lemma:** Any RDF graph has a satisfying interpretation.

- **Minimality Lemma:** If the vocabulary is a minimal satisfying interpretation of the entities, the vocabulary fails to satisfy every triple that has no instance in the set of entities.

- **Strong Herbrand Lemma:** Any RDF graph entities have a satisfying interpretation that does not satisfy any graph that is separable from those entities.

- **Merging Lemma:** The merge of a set of RDF is entailed by that same set and every member of that set.

- **Interpolation Lemma:** A set entails a graph if a subgraph of the set is an instance of the graph.

You can find the complete list of RDF model-theoretic semantics in the W3C RDF Semantics document, which is available at `www.w3.org/TR/rdf-mt/`.

OWL's model-theoretic context is quite a bit more complex to describe without a formal background in logic, but you should know that it's based upon a formal family of logics called description logics. This formal grounding captures and defines all the ways that the knowledgebase should respond to different kinds of data, models, and queries. For a complete look at the OWL semantics, check out the W3C document called Direct Model-Theoretic Semantics for OWL, which is available at `www.w3.org/TR/owl-semantics/direct.html`.

Decidability

One of OWL's most important characteristics is that even as an advanced knowledge representation language it remains decidable. *Decidability* is the ability for an algorithm to say for certain whether some bit of data belongs to a set. Relational databases are decidable — if you issue a SQL query to find all customers named "SMITH," you can be certain that the query has matched every record to your query. Many advanced knowledge systems introduce rich modeling constructs that have the unfortunate consequence of making those languages undecideable: This is sometimes generalized by saying that a language is *probabilistic*.

The challenge with using probabilistic data representations in practice is that you can't ever be 100-percent certain that your algorithms have found every match you need. For example, when you query using search algorithms such as Google, you see only a very small set of all possible matches to your queries — you may even see false matches as well. This probabilistic approach is fine, even desirable, for many human-involved search use cases, but it can't suffice for real-world software applications that need to have absolute certainty about the data they are working with (such as financial systems, healthcare record management, military launch control systems, and so on). That is why decidability matters and why OWL, because it has that feature, is quite a powerful data language.

Seeing the Semantic Web as a Superset for Metadata

The problem with metadata is truly that there is so much of it, yet so little of it actually works together. How can it be fixed? Yes, you guessed it: the Semantic Web!

There is no magic with the Semantic Web; after all, it's simply a data modeling specification. But for all the reasons you've read about so far — graph modeling with first-class relationship properties, open-world assumption, high expressivity, inference logic, and decidability characteristics — the Semantic Web data models are fully capable of becoming a superset language for most other metadata and modeling formats. Having a superset metadata language can go a long way toward fixing what is perhaps the most broken part of software development — metadata.

Having the Semantic Web function as an umbrella language for metadata, as depicted in Figure 6-14, isn't as far-fetched as it may initially seem. Efforts underway since the early 2000s have aimed at focused areas to map existing metadata structures into the Semantic Web's RDF and OWL formats. Numerous standards are migrating toward RDF and OWL support. There are tools and utilities to generate object-oriented metadata, even program code such as Java, from the Semantic Web's RDF and OWL formats. There are numerous utilities to generate RDF and OWL from relational databases, and vice versa. Semantic Web vocabularies are already commonplace in some industries such as life sciences, healthcare, and defense. So, while many people are still debating whether it's even possible, others are going out and doing it.

The Semantic Web as a superset metadata format for all data modeling may just be on the horizon for us all. If that vision becomes reality, it won't single-handedly rectify the metadata travesty — after all, the Semantic Web still isn't magic — but it will most certainly put us in a stronger position to get all that metadata working for us rather than against us!

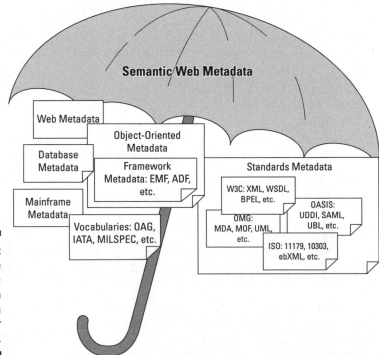

Figure 6-14:
The Semantic Web as an umbrella format for metadata.

Part III
Building the Semantic Web

"Would you like Web or non—Web?"

In this part . . .

On the Web, you can post documents about yourself, go shopping, and chat with your friends. But with the Semantic Web, you can create data about your interests, create a remix of data created by others, and link together unique ideas so that they're preserved for future generations of creative people.

In this part of the book, you find out how you can create your own corner of the Semantic Web, publish a profile about yourself, or just create a small ontology that describes your interests. Once you jump in, you'll see that it's not that hard.

Go ahead, admit it: This sounds like fun!

Chapter 7

Using the Resource Description Framework (RDF)

RDF is an acronym that stands for Resource Description Framework. There, that explains it, right? Well, perhaps not entirely . . . RDF is a standard data and modeling specification used to encode metadata and digital information. The Semantic Web vision revolves around and is predominantly based on the fundamental power of the RDF language. Currently, RDF is an approved recommendation for the Semantic Web at the World Wide Web Consortium (W3C).

In this chapter, I introduce you to the main elements of the Resource Description Framework. You discover how to build simple data graphs with RDF, the core structure of triples, the difference between resources and literals, how to use RDF Schema, and a few of the different encoding formats for RDF. Although you won't be an expert by the end of this chapter, you should be literate with the language and have a strong foundation for moving on to OWL in Chapter 8.

Breaking It Down to the R, to the D, to the F

Now that I have your head bobbing to RDF, I'm going to dive in a little further and break down an RDF statement. As I said, RDF stands for resource description framework. A *resource* in the RDF language can be anything you want it to be, as long as it can be uniquely identified by some kind of pointer, object reference, or even just a string literal value. *Descriptions* in RDF are encoded through the kinds of relationships assigned between sets of resources — these relationships take the form of a graph data model. Finally, the *framework* in RDF is a combination of the Web-based protocols (URI, HTTP, XML, and so on) that it's built upon and also the formal model theory (semantics) that defines the allowable relationships among data items in RDF.

Very simply stated, the concept behind RDF is that you can use it to describe a "thing" by making assertions about its properties. The "thing" is the resource you want to describe. Resources can be anything: books, people, places, customers, products, organizations, and so on. The set of properties that this particular "thing" has makes up the description of that resource — its attributes are its definition. Assertions that you make about attributes are axiomatic, you can treat those properties as facts about some "things." Thus, you describe resources in a standard framework, which gives us RDF.

Triplify me!

RDF has a model framework based on the idea of a triple. A complete RDF *triple,* or statement, must have the following three parts:

- ✔ The thing the statement describes
- ✔ The properties of the thing the statement describes
- ✔ The values of those properties the statement describes

Here's a look at a simple assertion you or I would write in plain English:

```
The Semantic Web For Dummies book is authored by Jeff
            Pollock.
```

Here's how you would identify the essential parts of that statement:

- ✔ The book `Semantic Web For Dummies` is the thing I'm describing.
- ✔ The book `Semantic Web For Dummies` has a property, `author`.
- ✔ The `author` property has a value, `Jeff Pollock`.

Additionally, I can derive other statements. Primarily,

- ✔ The thing being described is a `Book`.
- ✔ The `Book` has a property called title, with a value `Semantic Web For Dummies`.

To describe or define?

Often, the terms *describe* and *define* are used interchangeably. In fact, to most, the difference between describing something and defining something may seem minute, but in the area of data modeling, the two terms have very different implications. To a wordsmith, these differences may seem obvious, but I often hear the phrase "define a resource" when talking about the Semantic Web. Therefore, it's worth illustrating the distinction:

From *Webster's:*

✔ **Describe** means to give an account in words of something

✔ **Define** means to state the nature or meaning of something

When creating RDF statements about some data resource, you're simply giving an account of the characteristics or properties about it (typically through some observation or modeling activity).

You aren't necessarily defining everything that thing is. In fact, what I may want to call that thing or how I may want to understand its meaning is dependent on situational context.

Consider a common scenario on *Law and Order.* At the beginning of nearly every show, some sort of crime has been committed, and either the victim or a witness is asked the question, "Can you describe the assailant?" Notice that the questioned individual is not asked to define the perpetrator, but is simply asked to provide facts from his or her observation. In fact, often, the witness or victim tries to define the perpetrator anyway: "He was a loser, and a no-good punk," which of course is a definition based on that person's situation.

As opposed to the relatively messy real world, in the world of data modeling, you can choose your own frameworks and theoretical boundaries for defining situations, context, and semantics.

Does the structure of an RDF statement look familiar? It should. Take a moment to recall learning sentence structure in grammar school and apply what you learned to the sentence example. (For the purposes of this exercise, you're interested in the identification of the subjects, predicates, and objects of this sentence.)

What you might remember is the following:

✔ authored is the predicate.

✔ The book, Semantic Web For Dummies, is the subject.

✔ Jeff Pollock is the object. (The object helps to complete the predicate's meaning.)

The basic structure for sentences reacquaints us to the term *triple* as a grammar school concept. When formally speaking about the data specification, the term *triple* refers to the subject, predicate, and object (in that order) of an RDF statement. Because every RDF statement must have exactly these three items, it's also referred to as an *RDF triple* or just plain *triple*. Other terms sometimes used to describe the concept of a triple are *facts, assertions,* and of course *statements*.

RDF is a Web-based framework, and as such, it uses Universal Resource Identifiers (URI) as a mechanism for uniquely identifying the subject, predicate, and object of a statement. The subject, predicate, and object are each first-class citizens of the data model. As I discuss in previous chapters, these two unique features of RDF (Web-based and relations as first-class objects) are quite revolutionary for data languages.

If I rewrite the previously stated example as such:

Semantic Web For Dummies has an author, Jeff Pollock

I can now describe each part of the RDF triple completely with a URI:

- ✔ **Subject:** `http://www.dummies.com/books#Book-semanticweb_for_dummies`
- ✔ **Predicate:** `http://www.dummies.com/books#author`
- ✔ **Object:** `Jeff Pollock`

Note that my RDF subject is a resource, whereas my RDF object is a string literal named, `Jeff Pollock`.

Universal Resource Identifier (URI)

URIs are basically used to provide unique names in RDF. They look a lot like Universal Resource Locators (URLs), but have a different purpose. URLs are primarily locations (for example, Web pages) that you can address and go to on the Web. URIs *may* be but don't *have* to be addressable in this sense.

A URI's primary function is to provide a unique name. So, a URI could be `http://www.dummies.com` or `http://www.foo.com/ns/2008/v1` or anything that helps identify the domain context you are working in. A URI is also called a *namespace* when it is used as a qualifier for a specific set of names; however, not all URIs are namespaces. Because RDF is often used to describe federated data, the URIs are often addressable, but they don't have to be.

Here are examples of commonly used vocabulary namespaces in RDF:

- ✔ **RDF:** `http://www.w3.org/1999/02/22-rdf-syntax-ns#`
- ✔ **Dublin Core:** `http://purl.org/dc/elements/1.1/`
- ✔ **SKOS:** `http://www.w3.org/2004/02/skos/core#`
- ✔ **FOAF:** `http://xmlns.com/foaf/0.1/`

TECHNICAL STUFF

Resources versus literals

The key difference between resources and literals is that literal-valued predicates are constants, whereas resource descriptions may vary over time. You can't do much with literals programmatically, and they have no other attributes that describe them. Meaning is only discovered based on the observer's context. For example, the string pump could mean a water pump to some people, but to others, it could mean women's footwear.

In my example, the book *Semantic Web For Dummies* is authored by Jeff Pollock the resource, not Jeff Pollock the author. Because Jeff Pollock is a FOAF resource, you can now discover other wonderful things about me. Jeff Pollock, the resource, may also have facts that point to other resources, such as the company I work for.

Resource-valued predicates open the door to a world of rich and expansive data models.

Viewing RDF Data as a Graph

A collection of RDF triples is commonly referred to as a *RDF graph*. RDF graphs are mathematically grounded in formal set theory. Because a set can contain from zero to many things (according to set theory), even one RDF triple can be considered a graph, although quite a small one! A simple RDF graph based on our plain-English example looks like Figure 7-1.

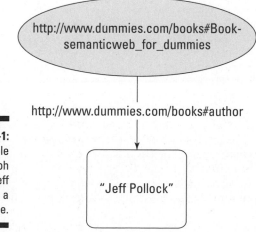

Figure 7-1:
A simple RDF graph with Jeff Pollock as a literal value.

In Figure 7-1, I have defined my name, `Jeff Pollock`, as a string literal value. But as it turns out, I happen to have a Friend of a Friend (FOAF) profile that describes me; this can be used instead of the literal value of my name. My FOAF profile contains all sorts of additional information about me, but my name is described there too. Figure 7-2 shows the small RDF graph pointing to my FOAF resource instead of a string value (the FOAF resource is identified by the namespace `http://xmlns.com/foaf/0.1/person#name`).

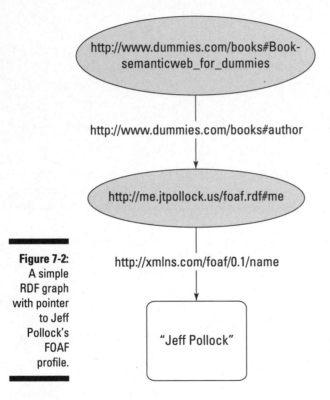

Figure 7-2:
A simple
RDF graph
with pointer
to Jeff
Pollock's
FOAF
profile.

There is a convention for reading RDF data graphs. RDF models show RDF triples as nodes (the ovals and rectangles) and arcs (the arrows). The subject and object are illustrated as nodes, and the predicates are illustrated as *directed arcs*. So, each RDF triple is represented as a node-arc-node linking pattern.

Now add the title of the book to the model, as shown in Figure 7-3. Use Dublin Core's "title" predicate in the example.

TIP

You may be asking yourself, "Why is one object a rectangle and the other object an oval?" Here's why: The author in this case is a resource. You can understand this fact by observing that the object is referring to an URI. The title of the book in this case is simply a string of characters, called a *literal*. We refer to these objects as resource-valued predicates and literal-valued predicates, respectively.

One of the main advantages of a graph data model when compared with hierarchical or relational data models is how flexible it is when working with rapidly changing data facts. In Figure 7-4, I can add an additional fact to the graph.

```
Jeff Pollock has a nickname "JTP"
```

You can probably see now how to go about creating RDF statements and how a statement may be related to one or more other statements. But, as easy as it might be for us humans to understand this RDF graph, it may not be so easy for a machine to understand it. The formal model theory behind RDF ensures that a model you develop in RDF is understandable to me when I compute it with my software. But how would you send your model to me? For software applications to understand RDF, we must have a portable format for exchanging it. The standard format designed for exchanging RDF is defined using XML.

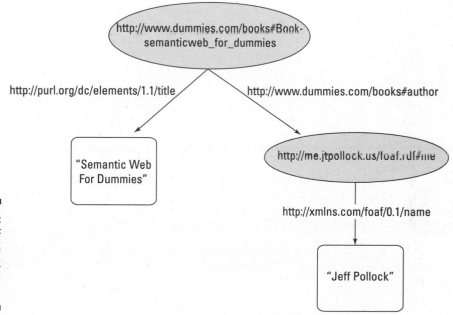

Figure 7-3:
An RDF graph with the book title as a string literal.

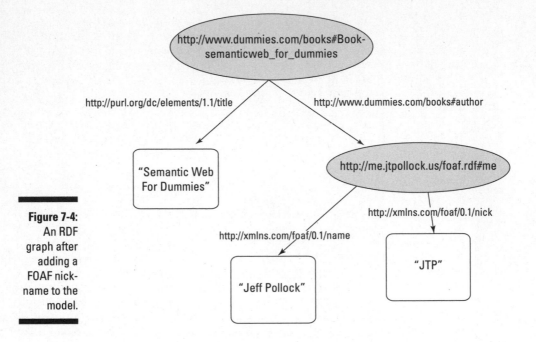

Figure 7-4:
An RDF
graph after
adding a
FOAF nick-
name to the
model.

Understanding That RDF Is XML

What do I mean when I say, "RDF is XML?" What I really mean is that RDF
provides an XML syntax for representing RDF graphs. Essentially, RDF is XML
(plus more). However, XML is not RDF.

Consider the plain-English example statement, `Semantic Web For
Dummies has an author Jeff Pollock`. The essential RDF for this state-
ment is

- **Subject:** `http://www.dummies.com/books#Book-semanticweb_
  for_dummies`
- **Predicate:** `http://www.dummies.com/books#author`
- **Object:** `http://me.jtpollock.us/foaf.rdf#me`

But what does the actual code look like for that RDF triple? Now, the moment
you have been waiting for! The XML syntax for this statement is expressed
here:

```
1. <?xml version="1.0"?>
2. <rdf:RDF
   xmlns:rdf="http://www.w3.org/1999/02/22-rdf-syntax-ns#"
3. xmlns:book="http://www.dummies.com/books#"
4. xmlns:foaf="http://xmlns.com/foaf/0.1/">
5.   <rdf:Description rdf:about=
      "http://www.dummies.com/books#Book-
      semanticweb_for_dummies">
6.    <book:author rdf:resource=
      "http://me.jtpollock.us/foaf.rdf#me"/>
7.   </rdf:Description>
8. </rdf:RDF>
```

As you can see, this looks a lot like valid XML syntax. It is. And because XML was designed for machines first, humans second, so was RDF. Not as pretty as a picture, but machines like it!

Line 1, "`<?xml version="1.0"?>`", is the XML declaration. It simply states that this file is an XML document that's using version 1.0 of XML.

Line 2 is the opening RDF tag. (The statement is closed on Line 8 with "`</rdf:RDF>`".) This tag indicates that all that follows is intended to conform with RDF syntax and semantics. Following this tag on the same line is an XML namespace declaration. Namespace declarations are almost like static variables in a programming logic. For example, the first declaration states that any tag starting with `rdf` is referring to this namespace: `www.w3.org/1999/02/22-rdf-syntax-ns#`. These syntax examples are the essence of the RDF vocabulary.

Likewise, Line 3 says that any tag beginning with `book` is referring to this namespace, `http://www.dummies.com/books#`. This namespace is referring to a vocabulary that's been established by the authors of this RDF model.

This at first appears to be quite a bit of overhead. Lines 1–3 are necessary housekeeping statements that let software programs know what to expect when they start to process the RDF. After you gain familiarity with common vocabularies and those in your own domain, creating these lines becomes second nature.

Moving on to Lines 5–7, this is where you get to the guts of it. These lines represent the RDF statements in Figure 7-2. Line 5 asserts that you're about to describe a resource with `<rdf:Description...` and that the unique identifier (the URI), `http://www.dummies.com/books#Book-semantic web_for_dummies`, is how you're going to refer to it. Quite literally, Line 5

states that the following assertion is a description and that it's describing (`rdf:about`) this URI. Line 6 makes the assertion that this resource has a property, `book:author`, with a value of `http://me.jtpollock.us/foaf.rdf#me`. Again, literally, it's saying that the resource's author is another resource (`rdf:resource`). Line 7 closes the description of this resource. For clarity, this example code excludes the portion of the graph that assigns the literal value "Jeff Pollock" as a `foaf:name` for `http://me.jtpollock.us/foaf.rdf#me`.

It is standard to save the file with the RDF/XML content with an `.rdf` or `.xml` extension. This method allows everyone to quickly identify the file's contents, and many tools natively understand how to process these file types.

Now add another property to the resource: the fact that the resource has a title. The following RDF represents the RDF graph in Figure 7-3:

```
1.  <?xml version="1.0"?>
2.  <rdf:RDF xmlns:rdf=
      "http://www.w3.org/1999/02/22-rdf-syntax-ns#"
3.    xmlns:book="http://www.dummies.com/books#"
4.    xmlns:dc="http://purl.org/dc/elements/1.1/"
5.    xmlns:foaf="http://xmlns.com/foaf/0.1/">
6.    <rdf:Description rdf:about=
        "http://www.dummies.com/books#Book-semanticweb_for_dummies">
7.      <book:author rdf:resource=
          "http://me.jtpollock.us/foaf.rdf#me"/>
8.      <dc:title>The Semantic Web For Dummies</dc:title>
9.    </rdf:Description>
10. </rdf:RDF>
```

Line 8 represents the fact that the resource now has a predicate called `dc:title`. This is a literal-valued predicate, and its syntax is different from the `book:author` predicate. In the case of literal-valued resources, the value is bookended by an open and end tag. It's noteworthy that the preceding RDF is actually an abbreviated version of the RDF graph in Figure 7-3. The logically equivalent but more verbose RDF for Figure 7-3 would look like the following (my remaining examples use the abbreviated style):

```
1.  <?xml version="1.0"?>
2.  <rdf:RDF xmlns:rdf=
      "http://www.w3.org/1999/02/22-rdf-syntax-ns#"
3.    xmlns:book="http://www.dummies.com/books#"
4.    xmlns:dc="http://purl.org/dc/elements/1.1/"
5.    xmlns:foaf="http://xmlns.com/foaf/0.1/">
6.    <rdf:Description rdf:about=
        "http://www.dummies.com/books#Book-semanticweb_for_dummies">
7.      <book:author rdf:resource=
          "http://me.jtpollock.us/foaf.rdf#me"/>
8.    </rdf:Description>
```

```
 9.
10.   <rdf:Description rdf:about=
       "http://www.dummies.com/books#Book-semanticweb_for_dummies">
11.       <dc:title>The Semantic Web For Dummies</dc:title>
12.   </rdf:Description>
13. </rdf:RDF>
```

Again, you'll note that for clarity I have excluded the portion of the graph that assigns the literal value "Jeff Pollock" as a `foaf:name` for `http://me.jtpollock.us/foaf.rdf#me`.

Using Typed Literals

Typed literals consist of a string and a datatype. To be perfectly clear, they aren't resources: They are indeed literal values. The datatype provides a space of eligible values. For instance, if I wanted to assert that the book `Semantic Web For Dummies` has 368 pages, I could do so by using the lexical form (the lexical form is simply a string of Unicode characters) of the literal, `368`, and a datatype known as an integer. In RDF/XML, there are a set of defined datatypes. The integer datatype declaration looks like this:

```
http://www.w3.org/2001/XMLSchema#int
```

There's nothing wrong with using literal values in your RDF statements. In some contexts, however, it may not be sufficient. Remember, as a human, you look at this value and realize it's an integer. You know it isn't a date, or a decimal value, and so on. You know this because you chose a great label, `pages`. But a program doesn't know what the label `pages` means, let alone what the string of characters following it means. You must provide some context if you intend to use the number in any way other than to just view it on a Web page. For instance, you might want to use the value to perform a summation, to compute an average or for performing equality or inequality operations. If you encountered a scenario where you had to find all *For Dummies* books that had fewer than 368 pages, you could do this quite easily, as long as the object was a typed literal. This task would be a lot more difficult to do if the object were just a string of characters with no context. The software would provide unpredictable results (or sometimes fail) because it wouldn't know what to do with the simple untyped lexical form of `368`.

Developers routinely build assumptions into the software that might make up for the absence of typed literals. For example, a developer could write code that would convert the value to an appropriate format for the operation. I suggest you can avoid these unchecked developer assumptions by simply using typed literals wherever possible. Using typed literals keeps your data models well constrained and easy to use.

Date is another common datatype. Software frequently tries to determine whether a given date is before or after some other date. If the software doesn't realize that `21 April 2008` is a date type (as opposed to some other literal), it might provide unpredictable results because the datatypes and conversion formats are not strictly adhered to.

The following snippet of RDF illustrates the use of typed literals in RDF/XML:

```
<rdf:Description rdf:about=
  "http://www.dummies.com/books#Book-semanticweb_for_dummies">
<book:pages rdf:datatype=
  "http://www.w3.org/2001/XMLSchema#int">368
</book:pages>
</rdf:Description>
```

You can see where I've used `http://www.w3.org/2001/XMLSchema#int` to denote that my page datatype is in fact a typed literal of type integer.

Identifying the Type of Resource

You may have noticed as you moved through the basic example (from the first part of the chapter) that I stopped referring to the resource `http://www.dummies.com/books#Book-semanticweb_for_dummies` as the book, `Semantic Web For Dummies`. This was not an oversight; it was intentional. Remember that earlier in this chapter, the plain-English statement says that the thing, labeled `Semantic Web For Dummies`, is a book.

```
The Semantic Web For Dummies book is authored by Jeff
                Pollock
```

You as a human can look at this statement and obviously see that the subject being described is a book. But you'd find it a bit harder to look at the RDF syntax in XML and come to the same conclusion.

Even if I had left out the word *book* from the plain-English statement, you could still come to a reasonable conclusion that the subject is some "reading material" (most generically), and with a little bit of context, you could reasonably conclude that it's a book. The context could vary, but if you're reading this book, the correct conclusion seems obvious. Throw in the predicate called `author`, and the case is even stronger.

You may be thinking, "Well, the resource's URI has the string 'book' in it, so therefore it must be a book!" Unfortunately (or fortunately), the URI could really be anything. The fact that you've seen something "meaningful" in the URI is a benefit to you as a human reader as you inspect the RDF, but a software program cannot and should not draw any computational conclusions based on strings of characters within the URI.

Reification

In RDF, *reification* allows the developer to make a statement about another statement. Reification can be a powerful way to use triples into multiple contexts, but it can also destroy the formal semantics of your model. Use reification with extreme caution!

Say that I want to alter the first plain-English statement from "Jeff Pollock is an author of the book *Semantic Web For Dummies*" to instead read that, "John Wiley & Sons says that Jeff Pollock is an author of the book *Semantic Web For Dummies*."

Using reification, I can simply qualify the first triple:

```
q:r1 subject book:sw_for_d ;
    predicate book:author ;
  object "Jeff Pollock" .
```

Then I can use that qualification in another assertion:

```
web:JW&Sons m:says q:r1 .
```

If I had only stated the assertion that Jeff Pollock is the author of *Semantic Web For Dummies* as part of my reification, that statement would only be provably true in the context of things that the John Wiley & Sons part of the model is asserting. It could still be true, but you don't know for sure except in John Wiley & Sons context.

As a general practice, I discourage the use of RDF reification as the semantics of reification in practice can be unclear and since reified statements are rather cumbersome to query with the SPARQL query language.

To solve this problem of classifying resources in a way that the software can understand, the RDF vocabulary has a predefined predicate called `type`. The predicate's semantics imply that the value of this predicate is a resource and represents a class of things. Furthermore, by assigning a "type" to the property, it implies that the subject of that property is also an instance of that class.

Adding this new information, that `Semantic Web For Dummies` is a type of book, to our RDF model, you now have the following:

```
1.  <?xml version="1.0"?>
2.  <rdf:RDF xmlns:rdf=
      "http://www.w3.org/1999/02/22-rdf-syntax-ns#"
3.      xmlns:book="http://www.dummies.com/books#"
4.      xmlns:dc="http://purl.org/dc/elements/1.1/"
5.      xmlns:foaf="http://xmlns.com/foaf/0.1/"  >

6.   <rdf:Description rdf:about=
      "http://www.dummies.com/books#Book-semanticweb_for_dummies">
7.      <rdf:type rdf:resource=http://www.dummies.com/books#Book/>
8.      <book:author rdf:resource=
          "http://me.jtpollock.us/foaf.rdf#me"/>
9.      <dc:title>The Semantic Web For Dummies</dc:title>
10.   </rdf:Description>

11. </rdf:RDF>
```

Now you know for sure that the subject (book:Book-semanticweb_for_ dummies) belongs to a class of things called Book because the rdf:type is http://www.dummies.com/books#Book.

Although it's unnecessary to describe the Book class, it's good practice for readability and reuse to describe the class with at least a label. (Remember, http://www.dummies.com/books#Book is just the URI.) Class structure and other properties are defined with RDF Schema, which I delve into in the next section.

Describing Stuff with RDF Schema

RDF classes are described with a separate modeling language called RDF Schema (RDFS). RDFS provides a vocabulary to describe resources, properties (predicates), classes, and subclasses. RDFS can be written in serialized XML just like regular RDF.

Add the Book class to the ongoing code sample:

```
1.  <?xml version="1.0"?>
2.  <rdf:RDF xmlns:rdf=
    "http://www.w3.org/1999/02/22-rdf-syntax-ns#"
3.     xmlns:book="http://www.dummies.com/books#"
4.     xmlns:dc="http://purl.org/dc/elements/1.1/"
5.     xmlns:rdfs="http://www.w3.org/2000/01/rdf-schema#"
6.     xmlns:foaf="http://xmlns.com/foaf/0.1/">

7.     <rdf:Description rdf:about=
       "http://www.dummies.com/books#Book-semanticweb_for_dummies">
8.       <rdf:type rdf:resource=http://www.dummies.com/books#Book/>
9.       <book:author rdf:resource=
         " http://me.jtpollock.us/foaf.rdf#me"/>
10.      <dc:title>The Semantic Web For Dummies</dc:title>
11.    </rdf:Description>
12.
13.    <rdfs:Class rdf:about="http://www.dummies.com/books#Book">
14.      <rdfs:label>Book</rdfs:label>
15.    </rdfs:Class>
```

In Line 5, I've added a new XML namespace declaration to include the RDFS vocabulary.

Lines 13–15 describe the Book class. You should notice that an RDFS class is also a resource, so this description looks similar to the resource I describe starting on Line 7, with a few differences:

✔ I use `rdf:Class` to state that what's being described is a RDFS Class.

✔ I give the URI: It should be the same as the URI used in Line 8.

If I were to end the resource there, with `</rdfs:Class>`, it would be sufficient, but it's good practice to give every resource some sort of label. I've done this in Line 14. (Line 10 serves this purpose for the first resource I described, but it uses the RDF vocabulary alone, not RDFS.)

Let me modify the example just slightly by changing the *type* of the original resource and adding a new class. I now assert that the original resource is now a `Dummies Series BookDummiesSeriesBook`, and that the `Dummies Series BookDummiesSeriesBook` class is in a class of things called Books. Because RDFS allows us to create subclass relationships, we can now say, "a Dummies Series Book is a subclass of Book."

The new model looks like this:

```
1.  <?xml version="1.0"?>
2.  <rdf:RDF xmlns:rdf=
    "http://www.w3.org/1999/02/22-rdf-syntax-ns#"
3.     xmlns:book="http://www.dummies.com/books#"
4.     xmlns:dc="http://purl.org/dc/elements/1.1/"
5.     xmlns:rdfs="http://www.w3.org/2000/01/rdf-schema#"
6.     xmlns:foaf="http://xmlns.com/foaf/0.1/">

7.  <rdf:Description rdf:about=
     "http://www.dummies.com/books#Book-semanticweb for dummies">
8.     <rdf:type rdf:resource=
         "http://www.dummies.com/books#DummiesSeriesBook"/>
9.     <book:author rdf:resource=
         "http://me.jtpollock.us/foaf.rdf#me"/>
10.    <dc:title>The Semantic Web For Dummies</dc:title>
11. </rdf:Description>
12.
13. <rdfs:Class rdf:about=
     "http://www.dummies.com/books#DummiesSeriesBook">
14.    <rdfs:label>Dummies Series Book</rdfs:label>
15.    <rdfs:subClassOf rdf:resource=
         "http://www.dummies.com/books#Book"/>
16. </rdfs:Class>
17.
18. <rdfs:Class rdf:about="http://www.dummies.com/books#Book">
19.    <rdfs:label>Book</rdfs:label>
20. </rdfs:Class>

21. </rdf:RDF>
```

By leveraging RDFS, we can now create a hierarchy of classes. Consider one possible Book hierarchy in Figure 7-5. Using subclass reasoning (also called *subsumption* reasoning), I can now infer that, `Semantic Web For Dummies` is a "John Wiley Book", even though I did not explicitly state that it is a John Wiley Book.

Because I asserted that it is in the `For Dummies` category and anything inside the `For Dummies` category is asserted to be a `John Wiley Book`, and a `John Wiley Book` is a "Book," you know for sure that `Semantic Web For Dummies` is a `Book`. This kind of inference yields an *economy of expression* when working with data.

For the most part, the terms *subclass* and *inheritance* may be used interchangeably. In fact, in everyday software development terms, there isn't much difference between the terms. Philosophically, there are some differences, but these can be quite esoteric and are not within the scope of this book. For RDF and OWL languages, a class B is a subclass of A if and only if all things in B are also in A. Stated another way, if all properties in B are also in A, B is a subclass of A.

In the example I discuss throughout this chapter, I assert that a `Dummies Series Book` implies a `John Wiley Book`. I've also said that any `John Wiley Book` is a `Book`. Therefore anything that's described as a type of `Dummies Series Book` is also a `Book`. The inverse is not the case however — something having been described as a `Book` doesn't imply that it's a `For Dummies Book`.

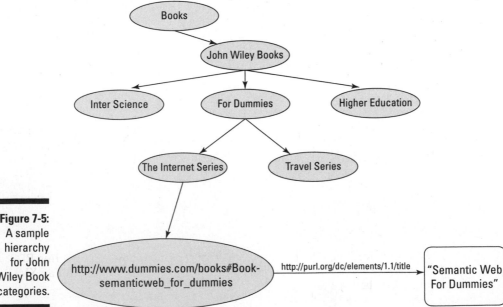

Figure 7-5:
A sample hierarchy for John Wiley Book categories.

The Venn diagram in Figure 7-6 illustrates this idea of subclass subsumption — the subsumed class receives the attributes of its parent.

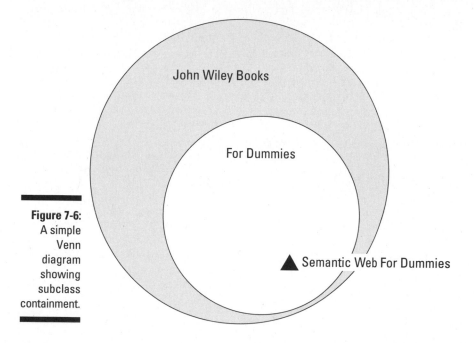

John Wiley Books

For Dummies

▲ Semantic Web For Dummies

Figure 7-6:
A simple
Venn
diagram
showing
subclass
containment.

Discovering Other Triple Formats: N3, Turtle, and N-Triples

Formats such as N3, Turtle, and N-Triples may also be used to encode RDF. In general, as long as you have the appropriate interpreters, it doesn't matter which of these formats you use. The knowledge is still in the triples logical format, and the physical syntax is really only syntactic sugar required by your particular model parser. (The term *sugar* refers to syntax that is added for cosmetic or usability reasons alone.) The following examples show serializations of the RDF graph in Figure 7-3 (shown earlier) in N3, Turtle, and N-Triples.

N3

N3 stands for Notation3 and is a shorthand notation for representing RDF graphs. N3 was designed to be easily read by humans, and it isn't an XML-compliant language.

```
1.  @prefix rdf: <http://www.w3.org/1999/02/22-rdf-syntax-ns#> .
2.  @prefix book: <http://www.dummies.com/books#> .
3.  @prefix dc: <http://purl.org/dc/elements/1.1/> .
4.  @prefix jtp: <http://me.jtpollock.us/me#> .
5.
6.  book:Book-semanticweb_for_dummies book:author jtp:name ;
7.    dc:title "The Semantic Web For Dummies" .
```

Lines 1–4 are general housekeeping items similar to the xml namespace declarations in RDF/XML. Line 6 is the start of the resource description: Notice the semicolon (;) at the end that indicates that the description of the resource is continued on the next line. The period (.) ends a line or description. N3 files typically have an .n3 extension.

Turtle

Turtle is a more verbose subset of N3 and an extension of N-Triples, which I discuss next. The previous N3 example is valid Turtle. Turtle stands for Terse RDF Triple Language. This particular serialization is popular among developers of the Semantic Web. Consequently, many tools are available to support this format. Turtle files typically have a .ttl extension.

N-Triples

The N-Triples is a plain and simple line-based format for expressing triples. Using the RDF graph in Figure 7-3 as an example, the N-Triples serialization looks like this:

```
1.  <http://www.dummies.com/books#Book-semanticweb_for_dummies>
    < http://www.dummies.com/books#author>
    < http://me.jtpollock.us/me#name> .
2.  <http://www.dummies.com/books#Book-semanticweb_for_dummies>
    <http://purl.org/dc/elements/1.1/title>
    "Semantic Web For Dummies" .
```

This format differs from the others in that there are no prefixes — the fully qualified URI is included in each statement. As with N3, the statements are closed by the period (.). Typically, files with N-Triples have the .nt extension.

The extensions typically used for these formats aren't necessarily a requirement. For the most part, there's no meaning in them from a machine's point of view (unless software has been developed that derives a particular meaning from those extensions). However, the extensions help us humans differentiate between formats. Therefore, these defaults are a common convention within the Semantic Web community.

Specializing in Microformats, RDFa, eRDF, and GRDDL

The largest opportunity, and challenge, for the Semantic Web is to encode existing data with Semantic Web–compliant markup. The following specialized languages are intended to fit within other more common data and document formats like XHTML and XML.

Microformats

The word *microformats* might suggest you need a magnifying glass to read material written in such a format. Well, the impact of microformats is not microscopic. Some people would say that microformats and RDF stand on opposite sides of the format spectrum: Microformats can be small and loose, whereas RDF is a little heavy and can be verbose. Although RDF itself is a framework, not just a format, many pundits can't resist comparing the two data languages.

Actually, either format is an appropriate and powerful way to encode more meaning into Web pages. Depending on what you want to accomplish, you may choose one or the other or both.

Microformats are a collection of formats (tags) for embedding document metadata within Web pages, XHTML, and HTML. Their ability to be embedded in HTML is seen by some as a major advantage over plain RDF. Later in this section, I show you how eRDF and RDFa allow you to achieve the same results. For now, I take a quick look at a few points regarding microformats to help differentiate between the two:

Microformats

- Were designed for humans first, machines second
- Solve a specific problem
- Reuse building blocks from widely adopted standards
- Are a way of thinking about data
- Are NOT a new language
- Are NOT infinitely extensible and open-ended
- Are NOT a panacea for all taxonomies and ontologies

RDF, on the other hand,

- Was designed for machines first, humans second
- Solves specific problems and also more general problems in representing metadata
- Reuses building blocks from widely adopted standards
- Is a way of thinking about data
- Is a new language
- Is infinitely extensible and open-ended
- Provides the foundation of OWL

Despite some of these substantial differences, both microformats and RDF are important contributors to the W3C's Semantic Web vision. The long-term value of microformats is a matter of debate in some circles. But both microformats and various flavors of RDF allow developers to encode metadata about the data into Web pages; and this is a good thing! Microformats happen to be a more rigid and brittle type of metadata, but for communities that have agreed on a vocabulary and syntax, they can be a quick and easy way to enrich Web pages.

RDFa

RDFa is a proposed set of extensions to XHTML. In case you're wondering, the *a* is for *attributes*. Its intent is to allow the inclusion of metadata in any XML document, but RDFa is primarily used in XHTML. RDFa allows machines to understand and leverage RDF semantics from within a Web page.

Many relevant objects can be found on a Web page such as media — videos, images, and audio — that has information about the creator, when it was created, length, and so on. If you've tried to buy something on the Web, you've seen tens or hundreds of pages of product information, describing things like the product's appearance, usage, price, and so on. Before RDFa, the information about such things was represented in XHTML elements: Only humans understood the semantics on those Web pages. With RDFa, there is now a standards-based approach to representing the Web page metadata just like you would with RDF.

Consider my working RDF sample resource, Jeffrey Pollock. I might create a simple Web page about myself that looks like Figure 7-7.

Figure 7-7:
A rendering of basic Web page containing semantic markup.

Information about Jeffrey Pollock

Mr. Pollock is an Executive business leader responsible for technology strategy, software product management, industry relations, and business development for enterprise software technology solutions.

© Semantic Web For Dummies

Using RDFa, the XHTML looks like this:

```
1.<!DOCTYPE html PUBLIC "-//W3C//DTD XHTML 1.0 Transitional//EN"
2.     "http://www.w3.org/TR/xhtml1/DTD/xhtml1-transitional.dtd">
3.<html xmlns="http://www.w3.org/1999/xhtml">
4.<head>
5.  <meta http-equiv="content-type"
          content="text/html; charset=iso-8859-1" />
6.  <title>Jeffrey Pollock </title>
7.</head>
8.<body>
9.
10.<div class="content"
        about="http://localhost/jeff_pollock.html"
        instanceof="foaf:person">
11.
12.  <h1>
13.    Information about
       <span property="book:foaf_firstName">Jeffrey</span>
       <span property="foaf:family_name">Pollock</span>
14.  </h1>
15.
16.  <img rel="foaf:depiction"
         class="flr"
         alt="Photo of Jeffrey Pollock"
         src="jeff_pollock.jpg"
         alt="Jeffrey Pollock" width="100" height="150"/>
17.
18.  <p>Mr. Pollock is an Executive business leader responsible for technology
          strategy, software product management, industry relations,
          and business development for enterprise software technology
          solutions.</p>
19.  <p>&copy; Semantic Web For Dummies</p>
20.</div>
21.
22.</body>
23.</html>
```

I assume that you have some working knowledge of HTML, so I focus only on the RDFa annotations — in this case, Lines 10, 13, and 16. Line 10 states this resource (the Web page) is an instance (about) a person. Line 13 states `Jeffrey` is the person's first name, and `Pollock` is the person's last name. Line 16 says the image is a depiction of the person represented on this Web page. Other information about different objects on the page may also be included.

As you can see, embedding RDF-based data can be an easy and straightforward task with RDFa.

eRDF

The very same Web page shown earlier in Figure 7-7 can be created using different encoding, eRDF. eRDF (Embeddable RDF) is similar to RDFa, and for the most part, they can be used interchangeably.

eRDF is a syntax for writing HTML in such a way that the information in the HTML document can be extracted (with an eRDF parser or an XML Stylesheet) into RDF. eRDF is not a W3C recommendation. Like RDFa, eRDF is embedded in XHTML documents. However, it differs from RDFa because eRDF is meant only for XTHML or HTML, whereas RDFa may be used in any XML-compliant document. Additionally, the RDFa markup in the XHTML must indicate the use of the RDFa profile.

Using the previous example, the eRDF version looks like this:

```
1.<head profile="http://purl.org/NET/erdf/profile">
2.</head>
3.<link rel="schema.foaf" href="http://xmlns.com/foaf/0.1/"/>
4.<div id="jp" class="-foaf-Person">
5.
6.
7.  <h1>
8.    Information about
      <span property="foaf-firstName">Jeffrey</span>
      <span property="foaf-family_name">Pollock</span>
9.  </h1>
10.
11.  <img src="jeff_pollock.jpg"
          class="foaf-depiction"
          alt="Photo of Jeffrey Pollock"/>
12.
13.  <p>Mr. Pollock is an Executive business leader responsible for technology
           strategy, software product management, industry relations,
           and business development for enterprise software technology
           solutions.</p>
14.  <p>&copy; Semantic Web For Dummies</p>
15.
16.</div>
```

GRDDL

GRDDL stands for Gleaning Resource Descriptions from Dialects of Languages. It's a W3C recommendation for extracting RDF out of XHTML documents using XSLT. Identifying an XHTML document (or any other XML document) as GRDDL-compatible is a simple case of adding a profile attribute in the head element and a link to a transformation script (typically XSLT).

Here's the previous RDFa example (with GRDDL annotations):

```
1.<!DOCTYPE html PUBLIC "-//W3C//DTD XHTML 1.0 Transitional//EN"
2.    "http://www.w3.org/TR/xhtml1/DTD/xhtml1-transitional.dtd">
3.<html xmlns="http://www.w3.org/1999/xhtml">
4.<head profile="http://www.w3.org/2003/g/data-view>
5.  <meta http-equiv="content-type"
         content="text/html; charset=iso-8859-1" />
6.  <title>Jeffrey Pollock </title>
7.</head>
8.<link rel="transformation" href="jeff_pollock.xslt" />
9.<body>
10.
11.<div class="content"
        about="http://localhost/jeff_pollock.html"
        instanceof="foaf:person">
12.
13.  <h1>
14.    Information about
        <span property="book:foaf_firstName">Jeffrey</span>
        <span property="foaf:family_name">Pollock</span>
15.  </h1>
16.
17.  <img rel="foaf:depiction"
         class="flr"
         alt="Photo of Jeffrey Pollock"
         src="jeff_pollock.jpg"
         alt="Jeffrey Pollock" width="100" height="150"/>
18.
19.  <p>Mr. Pollock is an Executive business leader responsible for technology
            strategy, software product management, industry relations,
            and business development for enterprise software technology
            solutions.</p>
```

Lines 4 and 8 are the modified lines. Line 4 indicates that there's at least one GRDDL transformation available. Line 8 identifies the transformation. Figure 7-7, shown earlier, still looks the same when described by this code!

Extracting the RDF

So, what's the point of all these standards and formats? First of all, they enable applications to find data where before they couldn't. Web pages have always been unstructured text in a document, but with microformats, RDFa, eRDF, and GRDDL, you can choose to turn each of your pages into small Web-based RDF databases.

As with most technology comparisons, there are distinct differences in what each of the technologies described enable you, the practitioner, to do. With any of the formats described here, the metadata may manifest itself as RDF in any syntax you choose. XSLT is a convenient, but at times limiting, mechanism to extract RDF from GRDDL documents. A variety of parsers available on the Web (as well as XSLT transformers) are great options for extracting RDF from RDFa and eRDF documents. In the end, you're looking for the RDF.

For the three examples previously given, the RDF looks like this (RDF house-keeping syntax has been excluded):

```
1.<rdf:Description
    rdf:about="http://me.jtpollock.us/foaf.rdf#me">
2.     <rdf:type rdf:resource="http://xmlns.com/foaf/0.1/Person">
3.     <foaf:firstName>Jeffrey</book:first_name>
4.     <foaf:family_name>Pollock</book:last_name>
5.</rdf:Description>
```

After the RDF data has been extracted from the Web page(s), I can easily load the RDF statements into an RDF database and start to perform some advanced query and analytic operations on them. The world has moved from the age of dumb Web pages assembled by servers to smart Web pages with atomic data items structured directly in the documents. Now is when data mashups really start to get interesting!

Getting to Know the Strengths of RDF

Many aspects of RDF should appeal to you. Technically speaking, XML as the transport for RDF is a tangible, nicely packaged, standard, serializable, and extremely portable format for data. These facts alone are reasons why many people choose RDF over a relational database format or a purely object-oriented approach — RDF is especially useful for transporting data while preserving the complex semantics of relationships.

Most of the earliest adopters of RDF are communities of practice that frequently need to exchange data, but cannot afford to strictly adhere to burdensome vocabulary standards. Industries such as biotechnology, pharmaceuticals, defense, and civilian environmental agencies have the need to exchange data whose formats are always changing and in flux. Therefore they need something more flexible than plain RDB or XML technologies.

If you look closely at RDF, and squint just a little, you can detect a hint of relational database type structure. In fact, both RDF and relational databases share some common underpinnings — both technologies use computationally sound mathematics as a foundation for their model theory. Set theory is the basis for both technologies, and, in fact, RDF data is frequently used to create database-driven applications.

I want to compare the structures of RDF and RDB technology more closely. Take a look at a snippet of my RDF example (to make it more interesting, I've added a FOAF resource for the Person Jeff Pollock):

```
1.<rdf:Description rdf:about=
   "http://www.dummies.com/books#Book-semanticweb_for_dummies">
2.   <rdf:type rdf:resource=http://www.dummies.com/books#Book/>
3.    <book:author rdf:resource=
       "http://me.jtpollock.us/foaf.rdf#me"/>
4.     <dc:title>The Semantic Web For Dummies</dc:title>
5.</rdf:Description>
6.
7.<rdf:Description rdf:about=
   "http://me.jtpollock.us/foaf.rdf#me">
8.   <rdf:type rdf:resource=http://xmlns.com/foaf/0.1/Person/>
9.   <foaf:firstName>Jeffrey</book:first_name>
10.  <foaf:family_name>Pollock</book:last_name>
11.</rdf:Description>
```

A simple database representing these resources might have two tables that look like Tables 7-1 and 7-2.

Table 7-1	Book	
GUID (Primary Key)	Title	Author (Foreign Key to Person GUID)
semanticweb_for_dummies	The Semantic Web For Dummies	jeff_pollock
other_books	...	...

Table 7-2	Person	
GUID (Primary Key)	first_name	last_name
jeff_pollock	Jeffrey	Pollock
other_persons	...	...

The similarities should be quite clear. Resources are analogous to table names, and predicates are analogous to columns. The primary key in the table is the resource URI (the subject), and the column values are the objects. It's a straightforward task to represent any relational database as RDF. This fact is true because RDF is a more semantically rich data modeling structure than RDB — it can fully contain the semantics of the basic RDB.

Although RDF doesn't look anything like object-oriented (OO) design, I can make an analogy between the two. (I'll spare you details of looking at Java or C# code.) A mapping of the terminology between OO and RDF, as shown in Table 7-3, should help you understand some of the similarities.

Table 7-3	OO to RDF Mapping	
RDF Terminology	*OO Terminology*	*Example*
Class Resource (a thing)	Class	`Book`, `Person`
Instance Resource (a particular thing)	An instantiation of a class	`semanticweb_for_dummies`, `jeff_pollock`
Predicate	Property	`title`, `first_name`, `last_name`

To be perfectly clear, I'm not suggesting that RDF and OO approaches are completely interchangeable. Each technology indeed has its own unique advantages or disadvantages, as I describe in Chapter 5. The requirements of the software system that you're creating should lead you down one particular path instead of another.

What's really going to drive your adoption of RDF — whether you're starting out fresh collecting new data or working with legacy data collected over years and years — is whether you want to decompose your data (knowledge) into smaller pieces of information (with meaning) and whether you want to express that knowledge in a decentralized way that is still consumable and open to anybody.

Simply put, if you need an easy way to assert data as very flexible statements, and if it must be structured so that a machine can easily read it, RDF — or a language derived from RDF — is probably a good solution for you.

Seeing Why RDF Is Only the Tip of the Iceberg

In this chapter, I present only a quick primer for RDF providing the essentials to get you started and feeling comfortable with reading the language — but it's only the tip of the iceberg for the Semantic Web. If you decide to really become an RDF developer, you need to spend some time on the W3C Web site (www.w3.org/2001/sw/) so that you understand most aspects of the RDF specification itself. The more time you spend with the various development tools for modeling RDF, the better you get.

RDF as a language is truly the foundation for the Semantic Web, but it is still only a small part of the total Semantic Web vision. Chapter 8 supplies the definitive primer for the Web Ontology Language, and Chapter 9 explains more details about several proposals still in process, including the use of business rules as a part of the Semantic Web.

Taken together, RDF, RDFa, GRDDL, OWL, business rules, and other coming features of the Semantic Web are an exciting evolution in the way people write software programs: Welcome to the 21st century!

Chapter 8

Speaking the Web Ontology Language

*O*WL stands for the Web Ontology Language. OWL builds on and extends RDF and RDFS by adding more vocabulary terms for describing sets of things called *classes,* facts about those classes, relationships between classes or instances, and characteristics of those relationships. OWL has quite a few additional model semantics compared to RDF — I discuss most of these later in this chapter. OWL 1.0 has been a W3C recommendation since 2004, and the OWL 1.1 specification is currently under development.

This chapter introduces you to the foundations of OWL including simple and complex classes, properties, individuals, assertions, and ontology development. You find out how to code simple OWL models and what pitfalls to avoid when developing a larger and more complex ontology.

Introducing OWL

As I briefly discuss in Chapter 3, the Web Ontology Language grew out of necessity from the late 1990s work in the U.S. Defense Department and European Defense community. Both research groups were looking for a data format that would be self-describing and dynamic so that intelligent agents might act autonomously on that data. After surveying various XML, object-oriented and database formats the Europeans and Americans simultaneously figured that new data languages would be required. The Europeans invented OIL (Ontology Inference Layer), and the Americans invented DAML (DARPA Agent Markup Language). Later, OIL and DAML were combined and eventually became the W3C specification that's now known as OWL.

Shouldn't it be WOL?

There's an endearing story about how the Web Ontology Language came to be known as OWL rather than WOL. Actually, OWL isn't a real acronym. The language specification started out as the Web Ontology Language with no special acronym. But after some time, the W3C Working Group disliked the acronym WOL and decided to call it OWL. The group became more comfortable with this decision when one of the members pointed out the following justification from the noted ontologist A.A. Milne who, in his book, *Winnie the Pooh,* stated of the wise character Owl, "He could spell his own name WOL, and he could spell Tuesday so that you knew it wasn't Wednesday, but his spelling goes all to pieces over delicate words like measles and buttered toast." I'm sure it didn't hurt the group's affirmation that Owl spoke with a Received Pronunciation (a uniquely prestigious and educated sounding British accent).

The syntax of OWL 1.0 is encoded as RDF/XML. OWL looks a lot like RDF/XML, but it has additional reserved words and special ways to format data. It's standard practice to save an OWL model in a file with an .owl extension. The following code listing gives you a look into a simple OWL model in its native syntax. To make it easier to follow along, I've added line numbers, which have no other significance:

```
1.<?xml version="1.0" encoding="UTF-8"?>
2.<rdf:RDF
3.xmlns:owl="http://www.w3.org/2002/07/owl#"
4.xmlns:rdfs="http://www.w3.org/2000/01/rdf-schema#"
5.xmlns:rdf="http://www.w3.org/1999/02/22-rdf-syntax-ns#"
6.xmlns:dc="http://purl.org/dc/elements/1.1/"
7.xmlns="http://www.dummies.com/owlexample#">
8.
9.    <owl:Class rdf:about="http://www.w3.org/2002/07/owl#Thing"/>
10.
11.
12.  <owl:Thing rdf:ID="semanticweb_for_dummies"/>
13.
14.</rdf:RDF>
```

As with the RDF models described in Chapter 7, Lines 1–7 are housekeeping items. Mainly, they specify the XML version and encoding, the beginning of the RDF, and namespaces in the model.

Line 9 exists in every OWL model. It says a concept called Thing exists that is the top-most class in any OWL hierarchy — it represents the superset of each and every "thing" in the model. Every other class is automatically a subclass of Thing, and every individual is a type of Thing.

Line 12 states there is an individual of type Thing with and ID `"semantic web_for_dummies"`. Notice that this resource has slightly different syntax than the resource example in Chapter 7. It's really just an alternative syntax. The previous example could also have been written like this:

```
<?xml version="1.0" encoding="UTF-8"?>
<rdf:RDF
xmlns:owl="http://www.w3.org/2002/07/owl#"
xmlns:rdfs="http://www.w3.org/2000/01/rdf-schema#"
xmlns:rdf="http://www.w3.org/1999/02/22-rdf-syntax-ns#"
xmlns:dc="http://purl.org/dc/elements/1.1/"
xmlns="http://www.dummies.com/owlexample#">

  <owl:Class rdf:about="http://www.w3.org/2002/07/owl#Thing"/>

  <rdf:Description rdf:about="http://www.dummies.com/owlexample#
          semanticweb_for_dummies">
     <rdf:type rdf:resource="http://www.w3.org/2002/07/owl#Thing"/>
  </rdf:Description>

</rdf:RDF>
```

Either of the two OWL models would be interpreted exactly the same by an OWL inference engine (referred to as a *reasoner*). The first example happens to be using native OWL XML syntax, whereas the latter example is using a more RDF-oriented syntax.

Old developer dogs learning new Semantic Web tricks

If you're a Semantic Web newbie and you're still interested in learning how to model and program in RDF and OWL, you're probably already a software developer. But when you create your own RDF and OWL models, you need to unlearn some of the tricks and practices that you've spent a lot of time immersing yourself in over the years.

For example, if you've come to the Semantic Web by way of an object-oriented programming background, you're probably pretty comfortable with the class model of OWL, but you have to unlearn the idea that classes are just a static datatype for objects at runtime and start to also think of classes as dynamic sets of instances that may change membership at anytime during runtime.

Database experts are more comfortable with the notion of OWL classes as sets, but they have to resist the temptation to normalize (as in second or third normal form) the data model using keys and instead focus on modeling accurate object hierarchies to represent the information model. Being a programmer before learning Semantic Web languages can give you a big head-start, but only if you're willing to unlearn some practices that you might take for granted.

Discovering the Various Species of OWL

The "species" of OWL, as I refer to them (the W3C calls them *sublanguages*), are specific versions of the OWL 1.0 language that are optimized for unique purposes and are distinguished by the language expressivity of the allowable axioms and constructors used in the OWL model. In OWL 1.0, there are three species to keep track of: OWL-Lite, OWL-DL, and OWL-Full. OWL-Lite uses only some of the expressivity available in OWL-DL. In OWL Lite, there are limitations on how a class can be asserted and the restrictions that can be placed on a class. OWL-DL allows full use of the core OWL language, but with some limitations on class restrictions. An OWL-Lite model is a valid OWL-DL model. OWL-Full is the most expressive of the three, allowing users to assert that classes can also be properties and instances.

In Chapter 9, I explain more about the recent extensions made with OWL 2.0, where new sub-species of the OWL language have been introduced so that vendors and implementers can easily distinguish what language properties they are adopting.

For this book, I explain and work primarily with OWL-DL, which is by far the most popular dialect of the many OWL species. Of the three, OWL-DL provides the ideal combination of language expressivity and performance — and therefore commercial viability. (In Chapter 12, I explain in more detail the impact of expressivity on large-scale Semantic Web applications.) The DL in OWL-DL stands for description logics — a family of knowledge representation languages that have historically been developed in the artificial intelligence community. (Chapter 16 busts the myth that the Semantic Web is just about description logics — it is indeed a key part of OWL, but the Semantic Web is about much more than just description logics.)

Here's a quick refresher on some basic terms:

- **Ontology:** An *ontology* is a formal representation of a set of concepts within a domain and the relationships between those concepts.

- **Individuals:** Describe a thing. Individuals may be members of one or more classes. Frequently in this book, I use the term *instances* to be interchangeable with *individuals*.

- **Properties:** Describe the relationships between individuals. A property in OWL and RDF is a first-class object in the model.

- **Classes:** Also known as sets. Members of classes share some properties or characteristics.

Because OWL classes are really just a description of a set of things, ontologies are often best visualized using Venn diagrams.

Figure 8-1 represents several assertions: 1) There is a class called Person; 2) Jeffrey Pollock is a Person; 3) S.A. Batla is a person; and 4) Jeffrey Pollock and S.A. Batla are related by the symmetrical relationship, hasFriend.

Figure 8-1:
Logical representation of two Person instances related by hasFriend property.

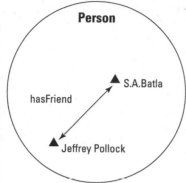

Exploring the Foundations of OWL

OWL's foundation rests on a family of knowledge representation languages called description logics (DL). DL allows you to describe concepts and logic-based semantics for a particular domain in a formal, well-structured way. DL is based on first-order predicate logic, which is a deductive reasoning system with foundations in mathematics. This means that, with OWL, you can express facts and rely on a proven query foundation based on mathematics to discover the implications of those facts. In a general sort of way, you can think of DL as a more powerful type of relational algebra that enables us to develop more powerful databases. That's why OWL databases are usually called *knowledgebases* — because they allow more expression and dynamism than regular databases.

Open-world assumption

The open-world assumption (OWA) is a monumental, cannot-be-exaggerated difference between Semantic Web data languages and regular relational databases. OWA is an assumption made in most formal logic systems that often confuses even the most seasoned ontologist. To explain the OWA, it helps to first explain its opposite — the closed-world assumption (CWA). The CWA is an assumption that states that any statement that is not known to be true is false. OWL, which is an OWA language, doesn't hold to this assumption. Instead, the OWA doesn't assume that an answer is false unless it can be absolutely proven that it is false — there are many questions that may have no provable answers at all.

Perhaps an example would help:

```
OWL Statement:
Jeff lives in San Francisco, California

Query/Question:
Does Jeff live Santa Fe, New Mexico?

Answer:
CWA: No
OWA: Maybe or unknown. (I could have residences in both
          places)
```

With an open-world assumption, the system is acknowledging that its knowledge of the world (or a particular domain) is incomplete. The failure to find a perfect answer doesn't imply the opposite must be the case. An OWA capable system such as the Semantic Web is sophisticated enough to acknowledge various shades of gray in the knowledgebase.

OWL is monotonic

Description logics are a monotonic logic and therefore so is OWL. A *monotonic* system based on deductive logic means that adding new statements (information) to our knowledgebase never falsifies a previous conclusion. If you later discover "Jeff lives in Santa Fe, New Mexico," this doesn't change any conclusion made from the previous statement. In some instances, the information might prove to be inconsistent, but from a reasoning perspective, previous conclusions, true or false, still hold. Modifying the example:

```
OWL Statement:
Jeff lives in San Francisco, California.

New OWL Statement:
Jeff lives in Santa Fe, New Mexico.

Query/Question:
Does Jeff live in San Francisco, CA?

Answer:
CWA: Yes.
OWA: Yes.

New Question:
Does Jeff live in Santa Fe, New Mexico?

New Answer:
CWA: Yes.
OWA: Yes.
```

Based on these simple assertions/statements, no OWL reasoner would complain about this apparent inconsistency because there are no known restrictions on how many places a person may live. How would the OWA answer the question if there was a restriction placed on "lives"? Such as "a person can only live in one place"? I address this inconsistency question later in the chapter, in the section titled "Inconsistency."

Understanding OWL Essentials

OWL provides a vocabulary for describing classes, facts about those classes, relationships between classes, and characteristics of those relationships. Some OWL axioms are somewhat esoteric, not very practical, and aren't covered in much detail in this book. I cover commonly used axioms in enough depth to understand their implications (and give you just enough information to make you dangerous with modeling basic OWL!).

The most intuitive way to get a mental picture of modeling with OWL is in terms of basic set theory: which things belong in different sets. I interchangeably refer to classes as *sets* and use Venn diagrams to visualize OWL assertions I cover in this chapter. This book isn't meant to be a primer on set theory, but where appropriate, I make basic references to explain some of the assertions and concepts in OWL.

As shown in my first example, an ontology can be very simple. At a minimum, all you need are some housekeeping items and the class Thing. But that's not very useful by itself. Now, I go a bit further by explaining how to assert classes, properties, and individuals.

Individuals (Also known as instances)

In Chapter 7, you discover how to create individuals. In our examples, the book, Semantic Web For Dummies and the author, Jeff Pollock, are individuals. I also introduce relationships between those individuals: I stated that Semantic Web For Dummies has an author, Jeff Pollock. In an ontology, these individuals and the relationship between them are known as the Assertional Box (Abox) or the data.

Individuals represent physical or virtual concepts the ontology is describing. At a minimum, individuals are members of the class Thing and don't necessarily need to be members of any other class. Individuals can belong to many different classes — multiple membership is fully allowable. Consider the individual in Figure 8-2: San Francisco International (SFO) Airport.

Abox and Tbox

In knowledge representation, the Assertional Box (Abox) is the assertional component, and the Terminological Box (Tbox) is the terminological component. The Abox holds the data facts associated with a Tbox, whereas the Tbox holds modeling knowledge such as descriptions of classes and properties. Assertions in the Abox are facts about instances that include relationships to literal values or to other individuals.

Some sample Abox statements:

```
Mary is a Student
Mary is 30
Mary knows Steve
```

Some sample Tbox statements:

```
All Students are Persons
There are two types of
    Persons: Students and
    Teachers
```

One easy metaphor is to think of the Tbox as a relational database schema and metadata fields. Think of the Abox as instance data or the records in the database.

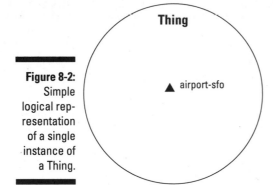

Figure 8-2:
Simple logical representation of a single instance of a Thing.

Now, the syntax in OWL/RDF:

```
<owl:Thing rdf:ID="airport-sfo"/>
```

This model doesn't represent anything too compelling, but it is indeed a complete OWL model. Nothing is implied in this model that wasn't already made explicit. Simply, there is an individual labeled "airport-sfo", and it is a Thing. Note, we humans are tempted to infer that "airport-sfo" is an

`Airport` (and that we are referring to San Francisco International). However, as it stands now, a machine doesn't have enough information to conclude this.

Properties: Datatype and object

There are two important types of properties in OWL: datatype properties and object properties. Datatype properties help describe individuals — they are not typically used to describe classes and are certainly not dependent on classes. The set of allowable values for datatype properties are typed literals. Typed literals are literal values (not abstract objects) with a specific datatype.

I'm going to assert a property in my model called `terminalCode`, which represents a code that refers to an airport terminal. Figure 8-3 below represents the assertion that `airport-sfo` has a `terminalCode`: SFO.

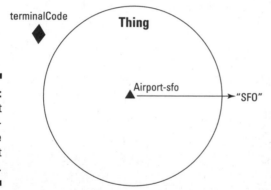

Figure 8-3:
Notice that SFO and ter-minalCode are not Things.

Now, the syntax in OWL/RDF:

```
<owl:DatatypeProperty rdf:ID="terminalCode"/>
<owl:Thing rdf:ID="airport-sfo">
<terminalCode rdf:datatype=
   "http://www.w3.org/2001/XMLSchema#string">SFO</
            terminalCode>
</owl:Thing>
```

As with our prior example, not much more is implied here than what has been asserted. In Listing 8-1, I introduce a class `Airport`, create another `Thing` called `airport-bos`, and make both individuals members of `Airport`.

Listing 8-1: An Airport OWL Example with Airport Class

```
<owl:DatatypeProperty rdf:ID="terminalCode"/>

<owl:Class rdf:ID="Airport">
 <rdfs:label>Airport</rdfs:label>
</owl:Class>

<Airport rdf:ID="airport-sfo">
  <rdfs:label>San Francisco International Airport</rdfs:label>
 <terminalCode rdf:datatype=
  "http://www.w3.org/2001/XMLSchema#string">SFO</terminalCode>
</Airport>

<Airport rdf:ID="airport-bos">
  <rdfs:label>Boston Logan International Airport</rdfs:label>
 <terminalCode rdf:datatype=
  "http://www.w3.org/2001/XMLSchema#string">BOS</terminalCode>
</Airport>
```

I've simply added a class called `Airport`, and asserted that `airport-sfo` is a member of `Airport`. I've also added another individual, `airport-bos`, with `terminalCode`, BOS. I now have two `Airport` types in this model, `airport-sfo` and `airport-bos`, with nice human-readable labels.

To make this ontology more interesting, in Listing 8-2, I now add a class called `Flight`. After all, what good are airports without flights?

Listing 8-2: An Airport OWL Example with Flights

```
<owl:DatatypeProperty rdf:ID="flightNumber"/>

<owl:Class rdf:ID="Flight">
 <rdfs:label>Flight</rdfs:label>
</owl:Class>

<Flight rdf:ID="flight-jb637">
  <rdfs:label>JetBlue 637</rdfs:label>
  <flightNumber>JB637</flightNumber>
</Flight>

<Flight rdf:ID="flight-jb638">
  <rdfs:label>JetBlue 638</rdfs:label>
  <flightNumber>JB637</flightNumber>
</Flight>
```

So what have I asserted? In this model, I have two classes, `Airport` and `Flight`. I've asserted two instances of airports, BOS and SFO, and I've asserted two instances of flights, JB637 and JB638. Obviously, I could provide a lot more information for each of the four instances, but this suffices for now. For legibility, the labels of each instance in Figure 8-4 have been left out of the diagram.

Quite a bit of description is missing from the instances, and information that links flights to airports is also missing. From the model itself, I don't know where these flights depart from or arrive. What I want to say about a particular flight is that it departs from one airport and arrives at another airport.

Object properties allow you to create associations or relationships between two individuals. That means the subject and the object the triple are both individuals. In this particular case, I want to create an association (a triple) that states a flight (the subject) departs from (the predicate) an airport (the object). Likewise, I also want to be able to say that a `Flight` arrives at a particular airport. In Listing 8-3, take a look at the complete OWL/RDF (without the housekeeping).

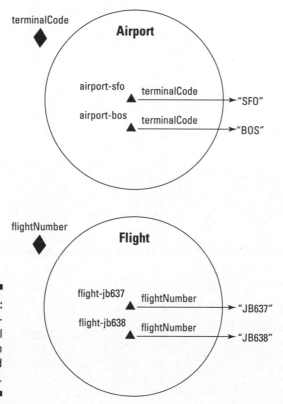

Figure 8-4: More complex logical model with Flights and Airports.

Listing 8-3:   The Complete OWL Airport Model

```
<!-- property assertions -->
<owl:DatatypeProperty rdf:ID="terminalCode"/>
<owl:DatatypeProperty rdf:ID="flightNumber"/>
<owl:ObjectProperty rdf:ID="departsFrom"/>
<owl:ObjectProperty rdf:ID="arrivesAt"/>
<!-- end property assertions -->

<!-- class assertions -->
<owl:Class rdf:ID="Airport">
  <rdfs:label>Airport</rdfs:label>
</owl:Class>

<owl:Class rdf:ID="Flight">
  <rdfs:label>Flight</rdfs:label>
</owl:Class>
<!-- end class assertions -->

<!-- individuals assertions -->
<Airport rdf:ID="airport-sfo">
  <rdfs:label>San Francisco International Airport</rdfs:label>
  <terminalCode rdf:datatype=
  "http://www.w3.org/2001/XMLSchema#string">SFO</terminalCode>
</Airport>

<Airport rdf:ID="airport-bos">
  <rdfs:label>Boston Logan International Airport</rdfs:label>
  <terminalCode rdf:datatype=
  "http://www.w3.org/2001/XMLSchema#string">BOS</terminalCode>
</Airport>

<Flight rdf:ID="flight-jb637">
  <rdfs:label>JetBlue 637</rdfs:label>
  <flightNumber>JB637</flightNumber>
  <departsFrom rdf:resource="#airport-bos"/>
  <arrivesAt rdf:resource="airport-sfo"/>
</Flight>

<Flight rdf:ID="flight-jb638">
  <rdfs:label>JetBlue 638</rdfs:label>
  <flightNumber>JB638</flightNumber>
  <departsFrom rdf:resource="#airport-sfo"/>
  <arrivesAt rdf:resource="airport-bos"/>
</Flight>
<!-- end individual assertions -->
```

The diagram in Figure 8-5 represents these same assertions within sets.

After studying the code sample above, you might be asking, "why not make *departsFrom* and *arrivesAt* datatype properties?" It's much more useful to have objects as resources, a topic that I cover in Chapter 7. As you read further into this chapter, I show you how some very interesting inferences can only be drawn when using object properties.

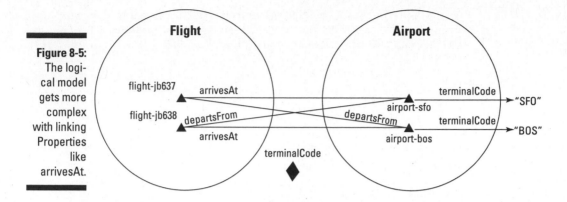

Figure 8-5:
The logical model gets more complex with linking Properties like arrivesAt.

If I were to only use the literal value approach, all an OWL reasoning system would really infer is that airports and flights have *departsFrom* and *arrivesAt* predicates whose objects are string literals — BOS or SFO. This is not any more useful than a regular database. However, when I use object properties, that same reasoning system infers that the flights depart from or land at airports and furthermore know which airports a particular flight departs from or lands (and other information about those airports). In the section "Complex Classes," later in this chapter, I dive deeper into determining Airport and Flight class membership.

Classes

I've demonstrated how classes are asserted in OWL:

```
<owl:Class rdf:ID="Airport"/>
```

This is the simplest class assertion. It's a good idea to provide a rdfs:label to all classes that give the class a text description. There may be other pieces of information to describe the class as well such as restrictions on membership in a class, which is something I get into later in this chapter.

Aside from this simple way of defining OWL classes, all you really need to understand about classes is the following:

✔ All classes in OWL are subclasses of owl:Thing;.

✔ Classes can share individuals. Individuals can be members of one (including Thing) or more classes.

✔ Membership in classes may be explicit or implicit. Up until now, I have shown you only the explicit variety.

Seems simple, huh? Not quite. It's time to revisit the open-world assumption and put it in the context of classes, properties, and individuals. Based on my existing OWL Airport Model shown earlier in Listing 8-3, the following statement is true:

```
A flight can be an airport, and vice versa.
```

Wait, please don't throw away this book — let me explain.

Using a simpler model to understand, consider three simple assertions in a higher education domain:

```
<owl:Class rdf:ID="Faculty"/>
<owl:Class rdf:ID="Staff"/>
<owl:Faculty rdf:ID="Jane"/>
```

So what does this model actually assert? The easiest way to understand the logic is to see the classes and the instances in a Venn diagram. Figure 8-6 shows what most developers might have thought I asserted; that Jane is a member of Faculty but not Staff. Figure 8-7 shows what I really said to the OWL reasoner; that Jane is a member of the Faculty and might also be a member of the Staff.

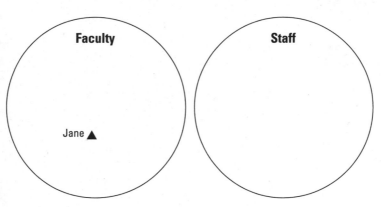

Figure 8-6:
What you may have thought I asserted. (Jane is Faculty, and Faculty are not Staff.)

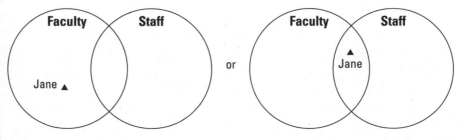

Figure 8-7:
What I really asserted. (Jane is Faculty and might also be Staff.)

Is this what I really meant? Maybe, or maybe not. There are two possible models in this little world as a result of those three simple assertions. Figure 8-7 shows the two possible interpretations of the world. This apparent ambiguity is what I get because of the open-world assumption. If I wanted to eliminate the possibility that Jane is Faculty AND Staff, I would need to assert one of the following:

- ✔ That a Faculty member could not be a Staff member (This concept is called disjointness, which I explain later in the chapter in the section "Disjointness.")
- ✔ That Jane is not a Staff member

Before you decide OWL isn't your cup of tea, you need to understand what you require from your knowledgebase. If you only want a system to report back to you exactly what has been asserted and no more (such as with a database), you don't need the features of OWL. You could certainly choose to use OWL for those cases, but it wouldn't be necessary and would probably be too much overhead. Relational database models do an excellent job of telling you what's been asserted (for example, the records in a database) and nothing more.

However, if you're looking for a system to draw inferences or to interpret the implications of your assertions (for example, to supply a dynamic view of your data), OWL is for you. Does that mean you have to assert that all classes in your data model are disjoint? Usually not. If you've determined that the questions you seek answers for require open-world reasoning (as opposed to the closed-world reasoning of relational database technology), it's unlikely you need to ensure that all classes in your model are mutually exclusive: Real life data eliminates possibilities naturally. If you do decide to make these assertions, you're manually closing the world of possibilities directly in the data model.

Now I want to ask my new Faculty ontology a couple of questions. First, you know there are two implications (or inferred models): We see them in Figure 8-7. One is the case where Jane is Faculty only, the other case shows that Jane is Faculty as well as Staff. There is no implication Jane is Staff only (because this possibility would be inconsistent with the assertion, Jane is a member of the Faculty class). Here's how I can confirm this:

```
Question:
Is Jane a Faculty member?

Answer:
OWA: Yes.
CWA: Yes.

Question:
Is Jane a member of the University Staff?
```

```
Answer:
OWA: Maybe.
CWA: No.

Question:
Is Jane a Flying Spaghetti Monster?

Answer:
OWA: Maybe.
CWA: No.
```

The following ontology is a great example of how the OWA can explode the world of possibilities with just a handful of assertions. Study the following OWL snippet.

```
<owl:Class rdf:ID="Staff"/>
<owl:Class rdf:ID="SocialCommunity"/>

<owl:Class rdf:ID="Faculty">
     <owl:disjointWith rdf:resource="#Staff"/>
</owl:Class>

<owl:Faculty rdf:ID="Jane"/>
<owl:Staff rdf:ID="Tom"/>
<owl:Community rdf:ID="Mary"/>
```

The new class assertion SocialCommunity says that membership in either the Faculty or Staff groups doesn't necessarily imply membership within the SocialCommunity. (At some universities in the United States, if you don't attend your school's sporting events, you aren't considered a true member of the university's social community!)

Our new disjoint assertion says that no Faculty can be Staff and no Staff can be Faculty. This fact is likely true in most real-world cases. In total, we have seven assertions (eight if you count the disjoint assertion as a symmetric relationship). Because of the open-world assumption, the SocialCommunity class intersects with Faculty and also with Staff. Figure 8-8 illustrates all the possibilities for how Jane, Tom, and Mary might fit.

(Admit it: You wanted to yell out, "Mickey Mouse!" when you saw Figure 8-8, didn't you?)

Because of the OWA, the model now has 12 possibilities. Notice I knew of only three facts regarding the individuals: their known memberships (computed by the ABox). But due to the OWA and my class assertions (inside the TBox), I now know that there are nine additional facts — inferred facts.

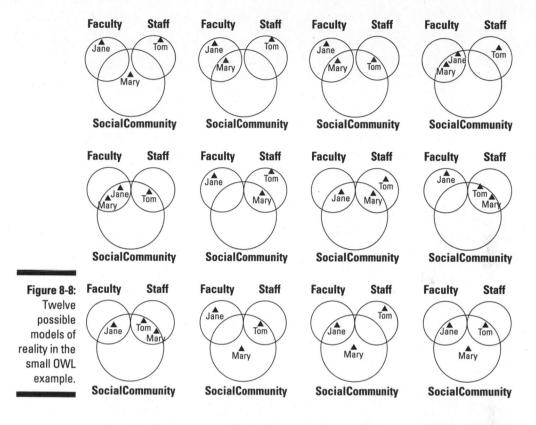

Figure 8-8:
Twelve possible models of reality in the small OWL example.

This example is trying to illustrate that it's *not* really a small world after all — not in OWL anyway. Think of the last time you said something seemingly simple and innocent that had numerous implications. Conveying the explosion of implications from facts you've stated in your data model is precisely OWL's main advantage. This feature makes your data models dynamic and multifaceted.

To understand Figure 8-8, start with the known facts (the classes), and then simply move the individuals (Jane, Tom, and Mary) around from class to class as long as you don't violate the simple assertions in the model. Do this until you've exhausted all possibilities.

Now I can ask the following questions:

```
Question:
Is Jane a member of the University Staff?

Answer:
OWA: No.
CWA: No.

Or put another way.
```

```
Question:
Is Jane not a member of the University Staff?

Answer:
OWA: Yes.
CWA: Yes.

Question:
Is Tom, without a doubt, a member of the University
          Community?

Answer:
OWA: No
CWA: No

Question:
Might Tom be a member of the University Community?

Answer:
OWA: Yes.
CWA: No.
```

The number of implications may increase or decrease depending on the assertions I make. For instance, take a moment and consider a model where all the classes are asserted as disjoint from one another. How would that impact the preceding model? And what would happen if new data arrives that violates my assertions? Say that new data arrives that states Jane is also Staff. I discuss this in the section titled "Inconsistency" a little later in the chapter.

Now I want to return to my earlier OWL example of airports and flights. Now you should fully understand why flights and airports can be the same thing unless I make those classes disjoint. Without explicitly stating Flight cannot be an Airport and an Airport cannot be a Flight, one view of my model really looks like the diagram in Figure 8-9.

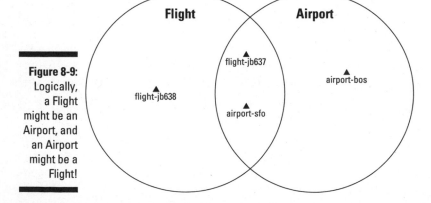

Figure 8-9:
Logically,
a Flight
might be an
Airport, and
an Airport
might be a
Flight!

Provable versus satisfiable

When querying an OWL reasoning system, there are mainly two types of questions another system or user will ask of it. One may ask whether something is provably the case or satisfiably (maybe) the case. A fact is provably true if, given what is currently known and considering all the possible cases, the fact is true in every case. A fact is satisfiably true if, given what is currently known and considering all the possible cases, the fact is true in at least one case.

Likewise, a fact is provably false, if given what is currently known and considering all the possibilities, the fact is false in every case. A fact is satisfiably false, if given what is currently known and considering all the possibilities, the fact is false in at least one case.

To further illustrate, consider the following statements:

✔ Anything that is provably true is also satisfiably true.

✔ Anything that is provably false is also satisfiably false.

✔ Anything that is NOT satisfiably false, must be provably true.

✔ Anything that is NOT satisfiably true, must be provably false.

✔ Nothing can be provably true AND provably false.

Thanks to the open-world assumption (OWA), the OWL reasoner must assume that any fact is potentially true unless it has been explicitly told otherwise. Anything unknown could be true or false, and a reasoner has to consider both possibilities. Therefore fact is provable if and only if it is true in every possible interpretation. It is satisfiable if it is true in *at least* one model. Solving these set theory problems are the two main uses of an OWL reasoner: to prove a statement or to discover if a statement is possible (satisfiable).

Applying open-world reasoning to my airports and flights model, if I were to submit the query, `Return a list of airports in the model.`, the OWA answer would be:

✔ `airport-sfo`
✔ `airport-bos`
✔ `flight-jb637`
✔ `flight-jb638`

But, if I query, `Return a list airports that we can prove are definitely airports.`, the OWA answer would be

✔ airport-sfo
✔ airport-bos

I can also ask other questions as well. Such as:

```
Question:
Which flights depart from Boston Logan International
          Airport?

Answer:
JetBlue 637

Question:
Which flights arrive at which airports?

Answer:
Boston Logan International Airport, JetBlue 638
San Francisco International Airport, JetBlue 637
```

The OWA allows one to ask questions about what may or may not be true and about what individuals may or may not be members of some class. When a software system needs to answer questions without all the information at hand, the open-world assumption can be a powerful reasoning tool.

Making Simple Assertions

Simple assertions of class, property, and individual, although critically important, don't have much implication beyond their explicit meaning. This section goes a little further into nuanced OWL assertions. I show you more about basic assertions that have broader implications that carry more potential impact. The simple assertions I show you here are the most useful and frequently used, but they aren't the complete set.

Equivalence

Equivalence assertions state that two things are the same. It's a simple notion, but it has powerful implications in OWL. You can assert equivalence for classes, properties, and individuals.

Class equivalence

Asserting that two classes are equivalent is a way of stating that every individual who is a member of one class is also a member of the equivalent class. This assertion is useful if you're resolving synonym issues across systems. Often in publishing, there is no distinction between author and creator. By asserting the Author class is equivalent to the Creator class, you are asserting that anyone who is an Author is also a Creator, and vice versa.

This is important because when you ask the question, `What are all known Authors in this system?`, the response includes both authors and creators in one query. The OWL/RDF looks like this:

```
<owl:Class rdf:ID="Creator"/>
<owl:Class rdf:ID="Author">
    <owl:equivalentClass rdf:resource="#Creator"/>
</owl:Class>
```

Property equivalence

By stating that two properties are equivalent, you're stating that the properties are interchangeable. Considering documents: Say you've asserted that the property has `Author`, which relates a `Document` to an `Author`. Elsewhere, if you find the property `hasCreator` has the same meaning as `hasAuthor`, you can use property equivalence to make them interchangeable.

Property equivalence allows you to query the system using either property. Say you know that `Jeff Pollock` is an author and you want to know what books he has written. If the model relates `Jeff Pollock` to one book with `hasAuthor`, and another book with `hasCreator`, asking the question `What books hasAuthor Jeff Pollock?` results in both books being returned. The OWL/RDF looks like this:

```
<owl:ObjectProperty rdf:ID="hasCreator"/>
<owl:ObjectProperty rdf:ID="hasAuthor">
    <owl:equivalentProperty rdf:resource="#hasCreator"/>
</owl:ObjectProperty>
```

Individual equivalence

Understanding individual equivalence is not as trivial as it is with classes or properties. Asserting two individuals are equivalent states that everything that is asserted about one is also true about the other. Regardless of their class membership, or properties they have, making two individuals equivalent is analogous to saying the two are one and the same thing.

Whenever you assert two things are the same, it's very important to think about the implications. This is especially true with individuals. Asserting equivalence should be done very carefully and is usually performed for resolving issues that come about from integrating different modeling contexts. In most practical situations, the description logics–based OWL reasoning system should be relied upon to determine whether individuals are equivalent.

```
<Person rdf:ID="person-135">
 <foaf:firstName>Jeff</foaf:firstName>
 <foaf:family_name>Pollock</foaf:family_name>
 <foaf:mbox>jtp@semanticwebfordummies.com</foaf:mbox>
</Person>
```

```
<Person rdf:ID="person-246">
<foaf:firstName>Jeffrey</foaf:firstName>
 <foaf:family_name>Pollock</foaf:family_name>
 <hasMiddleInitial>T</hasMiddleInitial>
 <owl:sameAs rdf:resource="#person-135"/>
</Person>
```

If both of these instances have the same referent, the author of this book, Jeff Pollock, you know that he has an e-mail address and a middle initial T and perhaps goes by either Jeff or Jeffrey — even though the facts themselves may be asserted on either individual.

Depending on your situational context, the accessibility of different data for the same person may be a positive or negative scenario for you. Either way, it is most likely significant. You may be resolving differences between systems and knowing that Jeff, the person, goes by either first name may be relevant to you. But, it may also suggest that your data is inconsistent. Being aware of these data inconsistencies is very likely important for your software application.

Disjointness

Disjointness assertions explicitly state that two things are different. One common mistake is to think that disjointness means "opposite." It doesn't — it means only that two things are not the same. Disjointness can be asserted between classes or individuals.

Class disjointness

Recall that individuals can be members of more than one class. In fact, they can be members of *any* class unless they are provably otherwise. (Remember the many possible worlds in Figure 8-8.) So, asserting that two classes are disjoint states that any member of one class cannot be a member of the disjoint class. This means that disjoint classes can have no common members. If I assert that Flight is disjoint from Airport, my absurd statement earlier, "A flight can be an airport, and vice versa," can no longer be true. In the Venn diagram in Figure 8-10, you now see what you might have thought that I originally asserted in the OWL Airport Model.

In OWL, the assertion that makes Flight disjoint from Airport looks like this:

```
<owl:Class rdf:ID="Airport">
 <rdfs:label>Airport</rdfs:label>
</owl:Class>

<owl:Class rdf:ID="Flight">
 <rdfs:label>Flight</rdfs:label>
 <owl:disjointWith rdf:resource="#Airport"/>
</owl:Class>
```

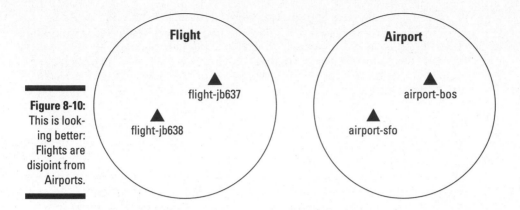

Figure 8-10:
This is look-
ing better:
Flights are
disjoint from
Airports.

Individual disjointness

Disjoint individuals means something quite different than disjoint classes. This assertion actually instructs an OWL reasoning engine to remove the idea that the two individuals are equivalent from the set of possibilities. In other words, if two individuals are asserted to be disjoint, the OWL reasoner will always conclude that those instances are provably not equivalent.

Consider for the moment that I have a "notable names" ontology and there are two references to Jerry Lewis. One of these individuals refers to the Comedian/Actor, and the other refers to the Congressman/Politician. Asserting that the two Jerry Lewis instances are disjoint means that an OWL reasoning engine never considers the possibility that they are the same.

Does this mean that you have to assert individual disjointness on every binary relationship in our ontology? Thankfully, you don't. In reality, almost all individuals in an ontology are disjoint. Remember, for two individuals to be equivalent, what is true about one individual is also true of the other. This is rarely the case in real-life data. Even if there were such cases, most prac- titioners would rather know that an OWL system found two instances to be equivalent — it could mean there's a problem with the data arriving from one or more data sources.

Here's an example of asserting two individuals as disjoint in OWL:

```
<Person rdf:ID="person-123">
 <foaf:firstName>Jerry</foaf:firstName>
 <foaf:family_name>Lewis</foaf:family_name>
</Person>

<Person rdf:ID="person-456">
 <foaf:firstName>Jerry</foaf:firstName>
 <foaf:family_name>Lewis</foaf:family_name>
 <owl:differentFrom rdf:resource="#person-123"/>
</Person>
```

In the previous example, if there is no disjoint assertion on `"person-456"`, an OWL reasoner takes into consideration that the two individuals could be equivalent, and in fact concludes that they are satisfiably equivalent. As with the equivalent individual assertion example, this is an important conclusion. It may be a strong indicator that there are inconsistencies in your data that may need resolving.

Subsumption

Subsumption is one of the most basic principles in set theory (and therefore OWL). If you think of OWL classes as sets of things, subsumption expresses a *subset of* relationships. Subsumption can be asserted on classes and properties, not individuals. Because subsumption exists in OWL, so does the concept of *supersumption* — taking a group of existing classes and making them subsets of a new class. But whether you need subsumption or supersumption, in OWL, the syntax is expressed using the `subClassOf` keyword.

Subsumption logic states that if an individual is a member of a class, it is provably a member of its superclass or superclasses. There is no restriction as to the number of sub or superclasses a class may have. To illustrate subsumption, take a look at Figure 8-11 — a Venn diagram of the book hierarchy depicted in Figure 7-5 in Chapter 7:

Unique Name Assumption

The Unique Name Assumption (UNA) is a concept that assumes individuals with different names always refer to different entities. OWL doesn't make this assumption. It isn't assumed that because two individuals have different names that they must be different. However, OWL does provide a vocabulary for making two individuals equivalent or distinct.

Human thinkers typically follow the UNA — especially when it comes to solving riddles. Here's a riddle that provides a clear metaphor.

Two sons and two fathers went to a pizza restaurant. They ordered three pizzas. When they came out, everyone had a whole pizza. How can that be?

Most people would assume that there were four people who entered the pizza restaurant, "two sons and two fathers," and focus on the word *whole* as some attempt to trick them. But in fact, there were three people: a grandfather, a father, and a son.

Remember the absence of the Unique Name Assumption when you're using OWL.

You can see that the individual, `Semantic Web For Dummies`, is a member of the class, `The Internet Series`, which is a subclass of `For Dummies`, which is a subclass of `John Wiley Book`, which is a subclass of things called Book. Therefore it is provably true, that the thing, `Semantic Web For Dummies`, is a `Book`. You also know that the individual labeled, `Introduction To Modern Set Theory`, is a member of `John Wiley Book` (and therefore provably a `Book`), but you can't prove that it is a `Higher Education` book or `Inter Science` book or `For Dummies` book. The OWL/RDF looks like Listing 8-4.

Listing 8-4: A John Wiley Book Ontology

```
<owl:Class rdf:ID="Book"/>

<owl:Class rdf:ID="JohnWileyBook">
 <rdfs:subClassOf rdf:resource="Book"/>
</owl:Class>

<owl:Class rdf:ID="ForDummies">
 <rdfs:subClassOf rdf:resource="JohnWileyBook"/>
</owl:Class>

<owl:Class rdf:ID="HigherEducation">
 <rdfs:subClassOf rdf:resource="JohnWileyBook"/>
</owl:Class>

<owl:Class rdf:ID="InterScience">
 <rdfs:subClassOf rdf:resource="JohnWileyBook"/>
</owl:Class>

<owl:Class rdf:ID="TheInternetSeries">
 <rdfs:subClassOf rdf:resource="ForDummies"/>
</owl:Class>

<owl:Class rdf:ID="TravelSeries">
 <rdfs:subClassOf rdf:resource="ForDummies"/>
</owl:Class>

<ForDummies rdf:ID="SemanticWebForDummies"/>

<JohnWileyBooks rdf:ID="IntroductionToModernSetTheory"/>
```

All `For Dummies` books have the string `"Dummies"` in the title and therefore, as a human, you could conclude that the book, `Introduction to Modern Set Theory`, is provably not a `Dummies` book. But unless I make the assertion that `All Dummies series books have the word Dummies in the title`, you cannot interpret that fact provably.

There can be no disjointness between sets that have a subset relationship. If an individual is a member of a set, and therefore provably the set's superset, the two sets cannot be disjoint.

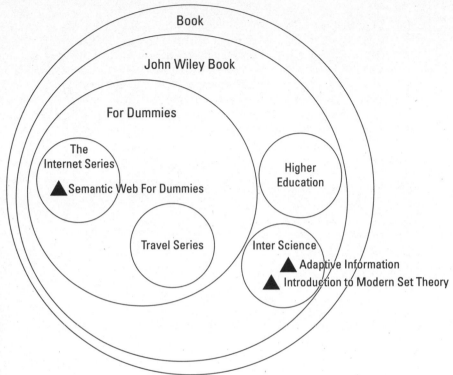

Figure 8-11:
Semantic
Web For
Dummies
is a type of
John Wiley
Book.

In practice, *sibling sets* (sets who share the same parent/superset) are typically disjoint. Therefore, asserting that they are disjoint in OWL is common practice. If, upon investigation, you can't determine the sibling sets should be disjoint, the sets in question may be better suited to having a subset relationship.

Subsumption in properties is used when using one property implies the use of another. A very common example used to illustrate this is `hasParent` and `hasAncestor`. It's important to note that this isn't property equivalence — these properties are not interchangeable. One implies the other. In this case, `hasParent` implies `hasAncestor`. The OWL/RDF is

```
<owl:ObjectProperty rdf:ID="hasAncestor"/>

<owl:ObjectProperty rdf:ID="hasParent">
 <rdfs:subPropertyOf rdf:resource="#hasAncestor"/>
</owl:ObjectProperty>
```

Inconsistency

Remember that OWL is monotonic: Adding new statements (information) to a world knowledge base never falsifies a previous conclusion. This behavior opens the door for modelers to make inconsistent assertions. An OWL reasoner doesn't complain about inconsistency. In fact, you can still ask questions of an inconsistent ontology and get sensible conclusions, but sometimes the results may not make sense. When this happens, asking the OWL reasoner to tell you whether a model is consistent is a good idea. All good OWL reasoners have this capability.

What makes an ontology inconsistent? A number of different scenarios can, and I can't cover them all here. One thing is for sure, however: An ontology without individuals will never be inconsistent, even though it may contain contradicting assertions. Consider the following ontology:

```
<owl:Class rdf:ID="A"/>

<owl:Class rdf:ID="B">
 <owl:disjointWith rdf:resource="#A"/>
</owl:Class>

<owl:Class rdf:ID="C">
 <rdfs:subClassOf rdf:resource="A"/>
 <rdfs:subClassOf rdf:resource="B"/>
</owl:Class>
```

Remember, OWL is based on set theory. So, if the ontology contains no individuals, an OWL reasoner knows that every set (A, B, and C in this case) is *empty* — including the set `Thing` — meaning that there are no members in any set and, therefore, no conclusion can be drawn that the assertions are contradictory. However, if you introduce an individual into the ontology (regardless of its *asserted* membership):

```
<C rdf:ID="someIndividual"/>
```

The reasoner now has enough information to tell the user whether the ontology is consistent. In this case, it is not. The OWL reasoner approximates this kind of logic-checking process: If the individual is a member of A, it is not necessarily a member of C and is provably not a member of B; therefore, it is okay. The same logic applies if the individual is a member of B.

But in our case, the individual is a member of C, and is therefore provably a member of A and B (by subsumption), but A and B cannot have common members (because of the disjointness assertion). Therefore, the entire model is inconsistent.

Consistency can be checked in an ontology. Checking whether future assertions contradict a previous assertion is a powerful tool for quality assurance. If an ontology becomes inconsistent, there may also be issues with the quality of data arriving from your data sources. An often-used test is to query your ontology for "empty" classes or unclassified individuals. Either situation may be an indicator that the model needs to be reconsidered in light of the actual system data. In fact, in the biomedical research industry, new protein combinations have been discovered exactly this way by researchers using OWL reasoning systems with real drug discovery data.

Examining Property Characteristics

Throughout this chapter, I review the implications of OWL's simpler assertions. In this section, I dive into assertions that have deeper and more complex impacts on the data model.

First, I examine property characteristics. The best way to understand the simple assertion of a property is in terms of datatype sets. Consider the following OWL:

```
<owl:DatatypeProperty rdf:ID="productClass"/>
```

With this simple assertion, I've created a new class (unnamed for now) that contains all things with the property `productClass`. Introducing a property in an ontology is equivalent to asserting an anonymous class of all things that have that property assignment. If I assert the following:

```
<Product rdf:ID="product-123">
  <productClass>Electronics</productClass>
</Product>
```

I've created an anonymous set of things that have a property called `productClass` with a value `Electronics` whose member is `product-123` (and perhaps other members). Figure 8-12 shows the anonymous class.

Anonymous classes may be created from `ObjectProperty` assertions as well. For instance, if `product-123` has a property called `assembledFrom` with a target `product-456`, another anonymous set of things is created that are all those things that are assembled from `product-456`.

Be sure to understand that properties are features of an individual that either include or exclude the individual from a class or category. Characteristics of a property refine that inclusion or exclusion.

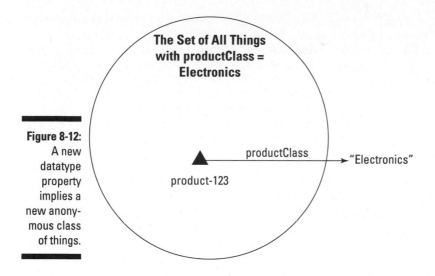

Figure 8-12:
A new
datatype
property
implies a
new anony-
mous class
of things.

Functional

Functional properties allow me to assert that a `Person` can have only one biological mother. For instance,

```
<owl:ObjectProperty rdf:ID="biologicalMother">
<rdf:type rdf:resource=
 "http://www.w3.org/2002/07/owl#FunctionalProperty"/>
</owl:ObjectProperty>
```

This characteristic has some very interesting implications. The preceding assertion states that for any given subject engaged in a `biologicalMother` relationship, it can have only one object. But this is not a constraint in traditional terms. Remember, OWL being monotonic, I can assert later that a particular individual has yet another biological mother. For instance,

```
<foaf:Person rdf:ID="person-123">
 <biologicalMother rdf:resource="#person-123456"/>
</foaf:Person>
later...
<foaf:Person rdf:ID="person-123">
 <biologicalMother rdf:resource="#person-123456789"/>
</foaf:Person>
```

Using the OWA, an OWL reasoner doesn't complain about that second assertion. In fact, if you ask the reasoner to check on consistency, it reports back as consistent. What the heck is happening here? The reasoner correctly concludes that `person-123456` and `person-123456789` are equivalent! Because `biologicalMother` is a functional property, the reasoner concludes that the objects of both assertions must be the same individual and therefore equivalent.

Functional properties are a very important property characteristic to understand. In general, assertions in OWL are used to force an OWL reasoner to eliminate from consideration certain possibilities. Its function is not to decide which assertions appear contradictory or nonsensical and throw them out of consideration.

A healthy debate exists about the use of functional properties when applying OWL in real life (whether or not to use Functional Properties to eliminate possibilities in the model), and both points of view have good arguments. One simple thing to keep in mind is that you want to build your ontology as close as possible to the real world, but you also need to understand how it may be used by the software applications that need it. For example, it might be a widely accepted fact that a person has only one biological mother, and therefore you might argue *for* this assertion in an OWL ontology about clinical healthcare. But if data later comes along that suggests there are two individuals who qualify to be a biological mother of a person (as with transplanted eggs), I would want the reasoner to tell me about that too. If somebody makes a new assertion for two birthmothers, perhaps my data might be corrupt or indeed the two (OWL) individuals have the same referent, but just different URIs. Either way, this is important knowledge for my system.

Inverse

In the stated terms of the triple, inverse properties suggest the same relationship, but with the subject and object reversed. This means that a declared relationship in one direction implies the inverse relationship in the other direction.

Every object property has an implied inverse. For example, `partOf` is a natural choice for the inverse of `assembledFrom`. But it is implied or unnamed. In other words, the subjects of `partOf` are the set of all objects of `assembledFrom`. A Venn diagram in Figure 8-13 illustrates this point.

In the figure, `product-123` is engaged in the `assembledFrom` property, and its object is `product-456`. In the inverse scenario, the subject and object are flipped in the `partOf` property relationship. By labeling the inverse property of `assembledFrom` with `partOf`, we can refer to it in the ontology and therefore use it for querying. The assertion looks like this:

```
<owl:ObjectProperty rdf:ID="assembledFrom"/>

<owl:ObjectProperty rdf:ID="partOf">
  <owl:inverseOf rdf:resource="#assembledFrom"/>
</owl:ObjectProperty>
```

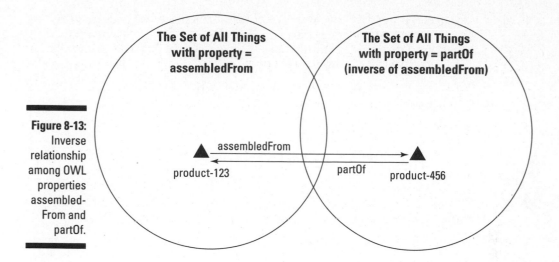

Figure 8-13: Inverse relationship among OWL properties assembled-From and partOf.

It is important to note here that because string literals are not allowed to be the subject of a property relationship in OWL, there are no implied inverses of datatype properties. In other words, it cannot be asserted that the literal `Electronics` is the `productClassOf` of `product-123` (from Figure 8-12).

Symmetric

Asserting that a property is symmetric allows the modeler to state that given a property relationship between a subject and object, the property relationship in the other direction is also given. A perfect usage of this characteristic is the *sibling* relationship:

```
<owl:ObjectProperty rdf:ID="sibling">
 <rdf:type rdf:resource=
   "http://www.w3.org/2002/07/owl#SymmetricProperty"/>
</owl:ObjectProperty>
```

The symmetry of the relationship means that it can hold going in both directions. I am the sibling of my brother, and my brother is also the sibling of me.

Transitive

A good way to understand the OWL transitive property is to remember back to your primary school education. "If A equals B and B equals C, then A equals C" is how you probably learned about transitivity. In this example, the *equals* operator is transitive (and also symmetric).

Located In is another great example of a transitive property. For example, if the Golden Gate bridge is located in San Francisco, and San Francisco is located in California, the Golden Gate bridge must be located in California. Here's the transitive property assertion in OWL:

```
<owl:ObjectProperty rdf:ID="locatedIn">
  <rdf:type rdf:resource=
     "http://www.w3.org/2002/07/owl#TransitiveProperty"/>
</owl:ObjectProperty>
```

Property characteristics such as inverse, symmetric, and transitive allow you to ask an OWL reasoner if an instance of data provably or satisfiably participates in a relationship (as well as the object of that relationship). In other words, you can ask pretty interesting questions about the data in a knowledgebase because our object relationships are very expressive.

Complex Classes

Because OWL ontologies are based on Set Theory, I can use complex class assertions to define how sets are related to other sets. Just as I can perform regular Boolean operations on sets, I can do the same thing with OWL classes. In the following sections, I describe three of the most important class combinations: intersection, union, and complement.

Complex classes allow for dynamic categorization based on class membership criteria. Rather than asserting class membership explicitly, the idea is to specify the criteria for inclusion and then allow the OWL reasoner to determine membership by considering an individual's unique characteristics.

Intersection (And)

A class described by the intersection of two or more classes includes exactly all the individuals that are common to all the classes listed in the intersection. For example, say that you're a compliance officer for your organization and you want to describe someone who has a Purchase Order Creator role *and* a Purchase Order Approver role as a potential compliance violation. Here's how you would describe such a class:

```
<owl:Class rdf:ID="POCreator"/>
<owl:Class rdf:ID="POApprover"/>

<owl:Class rdf:ID="IllegalRole"/>
 <owl:intersectionOf rdf:parseType="Collection">
  <owl:Class rdf:about="#POCreator"/>
  <owl:Class rdf:about="#POApprover"/>
 </owl:intersectionOf>
</owl:Class>
```

With the OWL in Figure 8-14, I've created a new set called `IllegalRole` whose members are those individuals that are in both `POCreator` and `POApprover` sets.

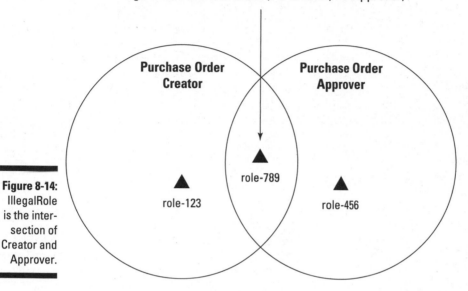

Illegal Role = intersectionOf (PO Creator; PO Approver)

Figure 8-14: IllegalRole is the intersection of Creator and Approver.

Union (Or)

A class described by the union of two or more classes includes all the members specified in the union. Say that you're a travel agent in New England and you want to describe a class called `WinterGetaway` that includes Florida, Aruba, and Bermuda getaway packages that you offer. Here's how you would describe such a class (see Figure 8-15):

```
<owl:Class rdf:ID="FloridaGetaway"/>
<owl:Class rdf:ID="ArubaGetaway"/>
<owl:Class rdf:ID="BermudaGetaway"/>

<owl:Class rdf:ID="WinterGetaway"/>
 <owl:unionOf rdf:parseType="Collection">
  <owl:Class rdf:about="#FloridaGetaway"/>
  <owl:Class rdf:about="#ArubaGetaway"/>
  <owl:Class rdf:about="#BermudaGetaway"/>
 </owl:unionOf>
</owl:Class>
```

In a real situation, I might model the getaways as subclasses of a class called `Getaway`, and also make each getaway subclass disjoint from its siblings.

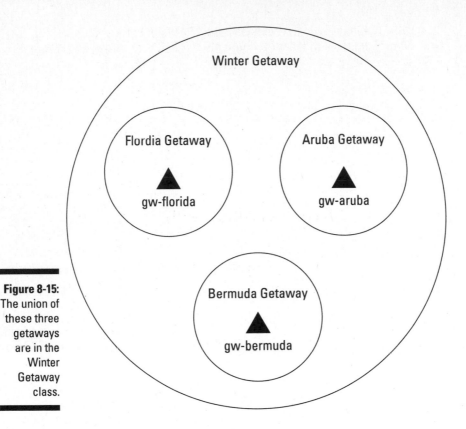

Figure 8-15:
The union of
these three
getaways
are in the
Winter
Getaway
class.

In this case, every individual in any of the three classes is a member of the `WinterGetaway` class.

Complement (Not)

A complement describes a class that includes all the members that provably do not belong to a specified class. Asserting an individual is provably not a member of class A implies that it is satisfiably a member of all the other classes that are provably not equivalent to class A. By itself, complement isn't very useful, but combined with intersection, it can be quite helpful. With an intersection, you give that individual more meaning. Here's what the OWL looks like:

```
<owl:Class rdf:ID="NotAReplacementPart">
 <owl:complementOf>
  <owl:Class rdf:about="#ReplacementPart"/>
 </owl:complementOf>
</owl:Class>
```

Without an intersection with a class called `Part`, members of `NotAReplacementPart` may include *anything* (a member of any class that is not equivalent to `ReplacementPart` of course).

Restriction classes

Restriction classes are very powerful classes packed with reasoning implications. *Restriction classes* have property restrictions placed on them. These restrictions dictate which individuals get included in or excluded from the class. This is often the preferred approach to determining class membership — to specify class membership criteria and let the reasoner decide if an individual is a member as opposed to explicitly asserting the fact.

For example, in my OWL `Airport` and `Flight` ontology, I could set the criteria for being an `Airport` instead of explicitly asserting `airport-sfo` and `airport-bos` to be members of the `Airport` class. Here's one simple way to define the main characteristic of an airport:

```
An Airport is anything that a Flight departs from.
```

In OWL, it looks like this:

```
<owl:Class rdf:ID="Airport">
 <owl:equivalentClass>
  <owl:Restriction>
    <owl:onProperty rdf:resource="#hasDeparting"/>
    <owl:someValuesFrom rdf:resource="#Flight"/>
  <owl:Restriction>
 </owl:equivalentClass>
</owl:Class>
```

The `owl:Restriction` is the criteria I'm setting on the class `Airport`. It's stating that to be an `Airport`, an individual must have the property `has-Departing`, and the object of that property relationship must be a `Flight`. Furthermore, with `owl:someValuesFrom`, I state that only one such triple needs to exist to satisfy the criteria. This statement implies that if there are other property relationships, that the individual is involved with that those are irrelevant.

Study the following change to our `Airport` class and `Airport` individuals, shown in Listing 8-5.

Listing 8-5:   An Updated OWL Airports Ontology

```
<owl:Class rdf:ID="Airport">
  <rdfs:label>Airport</rdfs:label>
  <owl:equivalentClass>
    <owl:Restriction>
      <owl:onProperty rdf:resource="#hasDeparting"/>
      <owl:someValuesFrom rdf:resource="#Flight"/>
    </:w
owl:Restriction>
  </owl:equivalentClass>
</owl:Class>

<Thing rdf:ID="airport-sfo">
  <rdfs:label>San Francisco International Airport</rdfs:label>
  <terminalCode rdf:datatype=
"http://www.w3.org/2001/XMLSchema#string">SFO</terminalCode>
  <hasDeparting rdf:resource="#flight-jb638"/>
</Thing>

<Thing rdf:ID="airport-bos">
  <rdfs:label>Boston Logan International Airport</rdfs:label>
  <terminalCode rdf:datatype=
  "http://www.w3.org/2001/XMLSchema#string">BOS</terminalCode>
</Thing>
```

This is much different from my earlier example of Airports and Flights in Listing 8-3. This time, I've made `Airport` a restriction class, and I've changed the individuals, `airport-sfo` and `airport-bos`, to be in the `Thing` class — I want the reasoner to determine their membership in the `Airport` class.

Note that `airport-sfo` has at least one property relationship with `hasDeparting`, and the object of that relationship is known to be a `Flight`. The reasoner in this case concludes that `airport-sfo` is provably an `Airport`. But what about `airport-bos`? There is no such data for `airport-bos`. In this case, the reasoner concludes that `airport-bos` may be an `Airport`, but can't prove it. In fact, it may even be a `Flight` (but it can't be both because of the disjoint assertion).

This a very critical point to understand. If you ask an OWL reasoner for all things *proven* to be members of the `Airport` class, you get `airport-sfo`. If you ask for all things that *might* be in the `Airport` class, you get `airport-sfo` and `airport-bos`. The reasoner doesn't return the members of the `Flight` class because their membership is explicit and flights cannot be airports.

Can you apply similar membership criteria to a `Flight`? You can. Consider this statement:

```
A Flight arrives at an Airport.
```

You can model this in OWL:

```
<owl:Class rdf:ID="Flight">
 <owl:equivalentClass>
  <owl:Restriction>
    <owl:onProperty rdf:resource="#arrivesAt"/>
    <owl:allValuesFrom rdf:resource="#Airport"/>
  <owl:Restriction>
 </owl:equivalentClass>
</owl:Class>
```

The restriction placed on the `Flight` class is similar to the one put on `Airport`. In this case, the property relationship is `arrivesAt` with the object being an `Airport`. There is one minor syntactical but major semantic difference — `owl:allValuesFrom` means that *all* the objects of `arrivesAt` property relationships must also be members of the `Airport` class. Listing 8-6 illustrates the change in the example.

Listing 8-6:   An Updated OWL Airports Ontology with Flights as Restrictions

```
<owl:Class rdf:ID="Flight">
 <rdfs:label>Flight</rdfs:label>
 <owl:disjointWith rdf:resource="#Airport"/>
  <owl:equivalentClass>
    <owl:Restriction>
     <owl:onProperty rdf:resource="#arrivesAt"/>
     <owl:allValuesFrom rdf:resource="#Airport"/>
    </owl:Restriction>
  </owl:equivalentClass>
</owl:Class>


<Thing rdf:ID="flight-jb637">
   <rdfs:label>JetBlue 637</rdfs:label>
 <departsFrom rdf:resource="#airport-bos"/>
<arrivesAt rdf:resource="airport-sfo"/>
</Thing>

<Thing rdf:ID="flight-jb638">
<rdfs:label>JetBlue 638</rdfs:label>
<departsFrom rdf:resource="#airport-sfo"/>
<arrivesAt rdf:resource="airport-bos"/>
</Thing>
<!-- end individual assertions -->
```

Note that both `flight-jb637` and `flight-jb638` have at least one `arrivesAt` property relationship, but only `flight-637`'s participation is with a known `Airport`, airport-sfo. I know `flight-jb638` arrives somewhere, but I don't know where for sure. Because I can't prove airport-bos is an `Airport`, I can't prove `flight-jb638` arrives at an `Airport` and therefore can't conclude that it is provably a `Flight`. But, there is another implication here: The reasoner can't conclude that `flight-jb637` is provably a `Flight` either! It may be, but the reasoner can't prove it. Remember, *all* `arrivesAt` properties must have `Airport` as the object. Even though the one assertion I see satisfies this restriction, the next new assertion that gets added to the model (where the object participating within the `arrivesAt` relationship with `flight-jb637` is disjoint from `Airport`) may or may not satisfy this restriction (due to the open-world assumption).

Asserting restrictions like `owl:allValuesFrom` are based on value of the object (in this case, `Airport`), whereas `owl:someValuesFrom` is based on number of relationships (at least one). In practice, `owl:someValuesFrom` is most commonly used. You can see where the implications from `owl:allValuesFrom` may cause a lot of sleepless nights.

Domain and range

Domain and range restrictions are global restrictions on properties (as opposed to local property restrictions like functional, transitive, and so on). They apply to every instance of the property in an ontology. The most important thing to understand about domain and range is that they are not used as constraints (as in mathematics). They're used to infer an individual's membership in a class or classes, which is why I describe them in the "Complex Classes" section of this chapter.

In mathematics, the *domain* of a function is the set of all values that can be inputs, and the *range* is the set of values that can be outputs. You can use domain and range in this case to test if a value is allowed as an input or output. This is not the case in OWL. Here are some examples:

```
<owl:ObjectProperty rdf:ID="capitalOf">
 <rdfs:domain rdf:resource="#City"/>
 <rdfs:range rdf:resource="#AdministeredRegion"/>
</owl:ObjectProperty>
```

With the preceding OWL, I asserted that the subject of the `capitalOf` property must be a `City` and the object must be an `AdministeredRegion` (a region with an administrative seat). To illustrate the implication of domain and range in OWL, I'll assert something absurd: The Atlantic Ocean is the capital of Spain.

```
<Thing rdf:ID="AtlanticOcean">
  <capitalOf rdf:resource="#Spain"/>
</Thing>
```

This doesn't make sense to a human, but an OWL reasoner doesn't complain and in fact makes perfect sense out of these facts. Domain is used to infer subject membership in a class; range is used to infer object membership. Given this, the OWL reasoner concludes that `Spain` must be an `AdministeredRegion` (which sounds reasonable), but it also concludes that the `AtlanticOcean` must be a `City`. This last conclusion sounds unreasonable. This example highlights the potential power of domain and range reasoning such as being able to conclude membership in a class without all of the information available. But it also exposes a misconception.

The way to really think about domain and range in OWL is to ask yourself what types of things *are* the subject and object of a property, rather than what types of things *can* be. If you find yourself asking the latter, avoiding domain and range restrictions is wise. In most cases, using restriction classes would be a better way to go. The distinction between things that *are* or *can be* are subtle, but consider this for our example. Cities *can be* capitals of administered regions, but *are* they necessarily? No. Perhaps a subclass of `City`, called `Capital` (or `CapitalCity`) would be better suited as the domain of `capitalOf` because they *are* capitals of administered regions.

Consider how the open-world assumption applies to these two property restrictions. Remember, the absence of an explicit property relationship between two individuals does not imply that one does not exist. Also, remember that you can't assert that a property doesn't exist between two individuals.

Going back to the `Airport` and `Flight` ontology: I haven't set domain and range restrictions on `arrivesAt` and, due to the OWA, the reasoner thinks it is possible that an `Airport` can arrive at a `Flight`. This doesn't make sense. To keep the reasoner from drawing this conclusion, I simply state that `arrivesAt` has a domain of `Flight`. This eliminates the possibility that an airport can be in the domain of `arrivesAt` and therefore makes that property relationship no longer satisfiable.

Domain and range are powerful but often misunderstood in the context of OWL. As shown in these examples, they may help remove some nonsensical possibilities but may also introduce them as well. In some cases, as in the first example, using restriction classes is the better option.

Distinguishing Necessary from Necessary and Sufficient

One of the greatest powers of representing knowledge in OWL is the ability for you and me as modelers to choose between subsumption (subclass relationships) and equivalence class assertions.

Subclass relationships provide *necessary* conditions for class membership, but this is only a partial definition. For instance, examine the Figure 8-16 (a slight modification of Figure 8-14). For an individual to be an `IllegalRole` in this model, by definition of the `IllegalRole` class, the individual must be a `POApprover` and a `POCreator`. But the fact that the role is both a `POApprover` and `POCreator` is not sufficient by itself. You can't prove that if an individual meets these two criteria alone that it is provably an `IllegalRole`.

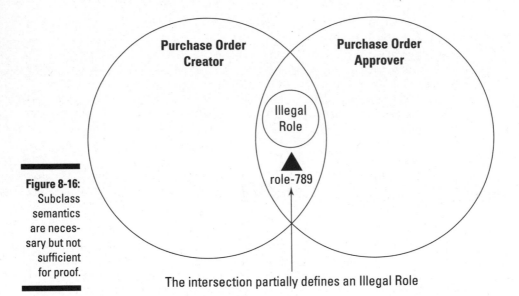

Figure 8-16:
Subclass
semantics
are neces-
sary but not
sufficient
for proof.

The intersection partially defines an Illegal Role

However, when you use the `intresectionOf` constructor, you're using equivalence semantics by default. Equivalence relationships provide necessary and sufficient semantics — a complete definition. For example, Figure 8-17 shows an OWL intersection that `An IllegalRole is a POCreator AND a POApprover`. I'm using equivalent class semantics. `IllegalRoles` are *exactly* those individuals that have both a `POCreator` and `POApprover` roles. There's no other definition of an IllegalRole. If an individual does not have both roles, the individual is provably not an `IllegalRole`.

This distinction between simple subclass reasoning and more advanced complex class reasoning is one of the powers of OWL — you can specify a rich set of relationships, rules, and constraints directly onto your data, and you can reclassify that same data on-demand.

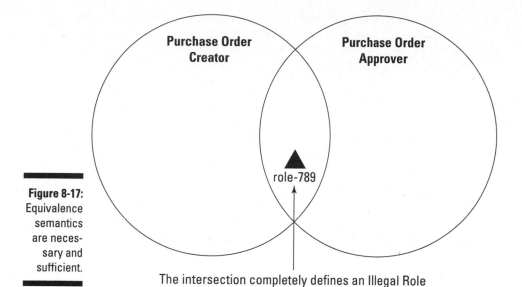

Figure 8-17: Equivalence semantics are necessary and sufficient.

The intersection completely defines an Illegal Role

Understanding Why OWL Is Different

Throughout this chapter, I make comparisons between OWL and other forms of knowledge representation — such as relational databases and object-oriented systems. Generally speaking, good code written by smart people can certainly give the illusion that some type of reasoning is happening, but only OWL supplies a standard semantic that can be reliably and repeatedly applied to data in different locations.

In this book, I describe many benefits to using OWL (and reasoning engines that consume OWL) that data practitioners can take advantage of. The following three benefits are the key reasons why OWL matters to data architects and data modelers.

Precision

Declaring a data assertion to be true (or false) without having all the evidence leaves open the possibility that your facts may be incorrect. In my University OWL example, if I were to assert `Jane` is a `Faculty` member at a `University`, but the properties for `Jane` do not support this assertion, then I would have an inconsistency in my data. However, if I describe what a `Faculty` member *is* (requiring an employee ID, a status, or some combination of criteria), a reasoner always draws the correct conclusion for every person in the knowledgebase (or it would at least tell you that it doesn't have enough information to answer with certainty — if you ask it). There may be other class memberships you want to discover as well; for instance, based on years of service and other criteria, a `Faculty` member may be a `TenuredFaculty` member, and so on.

In contrast, one must write complex queries in a database, or complex logic in an object-oriented program to determine class membership for a particular instance of data. With databases, the important semantics are in the query itself, not in the database model. Simply put, with a database, the fact that a record exists means that the record belongs to the set of things in that table, nothing more.

Dynamism

Dynamic categorization is the action a reasoner takes every time new knowledge enters the system. As new data comes into the system, the reasoner is asked to re-categorize all the individuals (based on the knowledge you've given it — the TBox and ABox), and it infers class membership for all individuals. If new information about `Jane` the `Faculty` member comes into the system that meets the criteria of the `TenuredFaculty` class, she becomes a member of that class.

Dynamic categorization is very important in time-sensitive applications where records or documents change "state" frequently. Notions of stale data, safe-harbor documents, day/week/month old documents, classified data, and so on are based on metadata about a document or data, and that metadata may change frequently. Modeling different data states or document states is very easy with OWL, as you can see in this chapter's examples. Instead of tagging everything explicitly, you let the OWL reasoning engine draw the logical conclusions for you.

There's no such thing as dynamic categorization in relational database or in object-oriented design. Database queries and code contain the real semantics — and they typically represent very specific and narrow contexts for truth.

Expressiveness

In OWL, you can create a simple model that represents knowledge that looks just like a relational model. On the other side of the spectrum, one can create a model that is very open and has numerous implications (and a lot of them are of no use to us). Somewhere in between is where your model will fit. Which side it favors depends on various factors: your domain and how explicit you need to be or how vague you can afford to be; whether you choose to use object properties rather than datatype properties; whether you use subclass semantics or equivalence semantics; whether you use domain and range; whether you eliminate possibilities with disjoint axioms; and so on. Oh, and there's that thing about satisfying your system requirements and use cases.

This flexibility in knowledge representation is unseen in database and object-oriented technologies. A combination of primary key/foreign key relationships and triggers in relational databases simulate "reasoning" (as well as writing code), but again, they're tied to very specific and narrow contexts.

Developing OWL Ontologies

After you decide that you want to develop OWL ontologies for a project, you will want to develop your real-world data models without having to hand-code OWL or gaze at Venn diagrams. When developing an OWL-based system, you constantly need to keep a clear distinction between the instances (ABox) and the models (TBox). Because OWL allows you to change the models on-the-fly, this distinction is somewhat trickier to bear in mind because both the data and the models may change at any time due to application behavior.

For the moment, I'm going to set aside the details about how to work with OWL individuals (ABox) during development; in any case, that discussion is essentially a discussion about RDF triples. How to go about creating RDF resources for your data is covered in Chapter 7 — there are numerous methods.

But how should you model the (TBox) class and property assertions? As with RDF/S, there are many tools on the market. For ontology modeling, tools that have a graphical user interface, are scalable, and have a lightweight reasoning engine to reason about and allow querying are the most practical tools.

Chapter 9 gives you more details about these OWL modeling tools and describes other essential extensions of the Semantic Web that can make your applications even more powerful.

Chapter 9

Exploring Semantic Web Enablers

*I*f you've read the first eight chapters of this book, you probably understand by now that the Semantic Web is a multifaceted and dynamic topic that spans technical and social domains. In this book, I try to supply you with the breadth of understanding and the context to apply Semantic Web languages in your own projects. In particular, I focus this introduction to the Semantic Web predominantly on the RDF and OWL languages. For technical purists, RDF and OWL are the heart and soul of the Semantic Web. However, several other "neighboring" technologies may not be considered as core to the Semantic Web, but are no doubt essential to its success. Natural Language Processing (NLP) technology, business rule languages, and various data vocabularies built with RDF/OWL may all be instrumental to the long-term success of the Semantic Web despite the fact that many people do not consider them a central feature of the core technologies. These various Semantic Web enablers are the topic of this chapter.

Revisiting the Semantic Web Stack

The defining picture of the Semantic Web is sometimes called the "layer cake." The logical architecture diagram in Figure 9-1 is the visual depiction of how the core technologies of the Semantic Web should fit together.

In practice, the technology represented by each of these individual architecture layers is in a different state of maturity. Figure 9-2 shows which technologies are highly mature, mostly mature, and still immature. Taken as a whole, RDF and OWL are clearly the cornerstones of the Semantic Web and, since their standards recommendations in 2004, have been proven to be quite stable even in their early revisions.

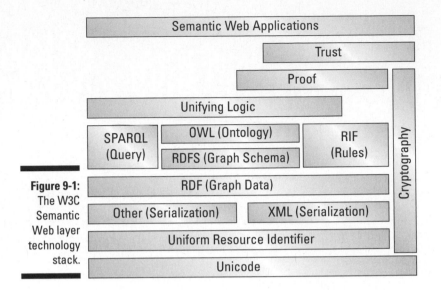

Figure 9-1:
The W3C
Semantic
Web layer
technology
stack.

One point that may not be obvious to a casual observer is that the technologies described in Figures 9-1 and 9-2 are not nearly enough to write an entire software application. In fact, to put it into context, the entire family of Semantic Web languages is only capable of replacing some of the data definition aspects of conventional object-oriented programming languages and relational databases. To put it bluntly, there is no such thing as a "pure" Semantic Web application: There will always be some sort of procedural application code required to surface the Semantic Web data into regular software applications.

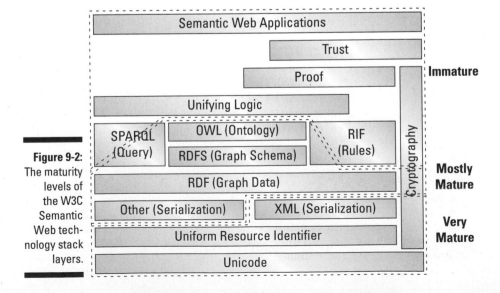

Figure 9-2:
The maturity
levels of
the W3C
Semantic
Web tech-
nology stack
layers.

So what does the Semantic Web really give us? In the next few sections, I recap Unicode, XML, RDF, OWL, and SPARQL, as well as other Semantic Web languages that are defined in more detail in Chapter 6.

Unicode and URI

As the standards-bearer for the Semantic Web, the World Wide Web Consortium (W3C) has been committed to the Unicode text standard as its foundation. Unicode is actually an ISO standard (as published in ISBN 0-321-48091-0) that provides a common representation and technical encoding for text in any language. This is important because as data travels between regions of the world, different kinds of alphabets and other characters that people use to communicate all need to be represented. The Unicode standard is the baseline text standard that ensures that computer text is compatible with all types of software. The most common Unicode formats are UTF-8 (multi-byte) and UTF-16.

The Uniform Resource Identifier (URI) is the foundation of the World Wide Web and essentially provides the address for how to find any kind of Web resource. A URI may consist of a name and/or a locator. URIs are the basis for finding Web pages inside browsers and linking RDF data objects across the vast expanse of the Internet.

XML

The eXtensible Markup Language (XML) is a language for marking documents and messages with tags that can make it simpler for machines to parse data from files. The XML standard supplies a grammar and syntax for tagging (the famous angle brackets <tag>) and also a behavioral standard for parsing those tags.

XML is a hotly debated topic in the Semantic Web community because the first versions of the RDF and OWL specifications were encoded exclusively in XML, but the inelegance of XML for encoding has prompted a movement to enable Semantic Web languages encoding in other formats. A few of those alternative formats, like N3, Turtle, and N-Triples, are described in Chapter 7.

RDF and RDFS

The Resource Description Framework (RDF) and RDF Schema (RDFS) are truly the backbone of the Semantic Web. As you can see from Figure 9-2 (shown earlier), the RDF and RDFS formats are mature data formats that truly serve as the central defining feature of the Semantic Web. RDF provides the core model semantics for an open and extensible graph data model of interconnected data items linked by URIs. The RDF schema provides the core model semantics for describing simple class taxonomies (concepts) that group the RDF data into more complex sets that can be organized and queried via different query languages. Chapter 7 provides some hands-on exercises to get to know RDF.

OWL

If RDF and RDFS are the foundation of the Semantic Web, OWL is the load-bearing support system for the Semantic Web. OWL brings an advanced, computationally stable way of defining highly complex and interdependent data models in the Semantic Web. OWL adds data modeling semantics that are more powerful than conventional databases, but maintains their essential reliability and correctness guarantees that make them so valuable for software applications. OWL is what gives the Semantic Web an element of grounding and stability for defining the meaning of data in an unambiguous yet powerful data model that rests upon a strong mathematical foundation. Chapter 8 is a fuller explanation of logical modeling with OWL.

SPARQL

The Simple Protocol and RDF Query Language (SPARQL) standard is a query language for RDF. Developments are under way to make sure that the SPARQL standard can work with OWL. Like SQL and XQuery, the SPARQL language provides a declarative interface for interacting with an RDF database. Critics of the SPARQL standard believe that instead of inventing a new grammar for SPARQL, the W3C should have leveraged the work already put into XQuery or SQL. As ANSI SQL helped popularize the relational database, many supporters hope that the SPARQL standard will help encourage adoption of the Semantic Web technologies.

RIF and SWRL

The Rule Interchange Format (RIF) is a Working Group (an approved action committee) within the W3C. Its charter originally set out to define a standard format for the exchange of business rules between various kinds of software engines. The RIF Working Group has since decided to develop a family of languages aimed at solving specific kinds of problems because the complexity of defining a single technical language for all types of business rules became undesirable. By far, the most widely deployed focus area for business rules are *production rule systems*. Production rule systems are the backbone of fraud detection systems, anti-money-laundering applications, and most computer security programs installed inside any major business. As it relates specifically to the Semantic Web, the business rule topic is mainly about interoperability so that OWL and RDF data models can be further extended and constrained with complex business rule definitions.

Unifying Logic layer

The Unifying Logic layer of the W3C technology stack is still only vaguely defined. One interpretation on the intent of this layer is to describe a formal mathematical logic that reconciles all the different model semantics of the parts (RDF, RDFS, OWL, SPARQL, and RIF) into a consistent and holistic model theory. The central tenet of this proposed layer would be to provide a single logical interface to the Semantic Web of data and rules so that software applications could be more easily written to this single facade rather than to the individual parts. However, the technical implementation or details about this unifying logic are undefined and nonexistent in the practical sense.

Software frameworks (open source, or from commercial vendors) that supply all the component parts of a Semantic Web framework in a single collection exist, and they've each implemented their own unifying logic to make everything work together, but each of those software frameworks do the unification in a different way. Thus, although the RDF and OWL remain standard and portable, the implementation of the application does not.

Proof, trust, and cryptography

The various security frameworks defined for the Semantic Web are still deep areas of research. Because the Semantic Web depends on unprecedented levels of intelligence at the data layer, the software needs to be capable of explaining what kinds of intelligence have been automated. For example, if a future Semantic Web software application is constantly monitoring sensor data about the health of a person, or even the health of our national borders, it could recommend drastic actions if certain conditions have been met.

The "proof" element of the Semantic Web technology stack is intended to supply a mathematically correct way of explaining which inferences and which business rules have led to a particular conclusion or recommendation. It's a way for humans to validate what the software machine has inferred. The "trust" element of the Semantic Web supplies a means to rate data in terms of trustworthiness so that we can distinguish data that is likely to be good from data that is more likely to be bad. Finally, the cryptography work in the Semantic Web is building upon the encryption techniques defined for lower layers of the stack like Unicode and XML.

GRDDL, SAWSDL, RDFa, and SKOS

Although some programming languages are specifically built with the RDF and OWL formats, or are developed explicitly to provide interoperability with the Semantic Web languages, they typically aren't included in the W3C architecture stack depicted in Figure 9-1. In some ways, this is a shame, because the W3C itself has sponsored new standards that are key enablers for the Semantic Web vision. Here are some of those other key standards enabling the Semantic Web vision:

- ✔ **Gleaning Resource Descriptions from Dialects of Languages (GRDDL)** is a W3C standard for encoding XML and XHTML with extra metadata that can be parsed by XSLT and converted to RDF.

- ✔ **Semantic Annotation for Web Service Description Language (SAWSDL)** is a W3C standard for annotating service-oriented architecture Web services with RDF or OWL (or any other ontology) metadata to aid in the simpler discovery of services.

- ✔ **Resource Description Framework in Attributes (RDFa)** is a W3C standard that can be used to define new attributes in XHTML that can be parsed automatically and structured as first-class RDF objects. RDFa is commonly used by developers to add machine readable data directly within their Web pages.

- ✔ **Simple Knowledge Organization System (SKOS)** is a W3C standard that is built upon RDF and used to provide a starting point for developers looking to create their own vocabularies. As it turns out, many classification schemes and data models follow similar principles, and RDF by itself doesn't provide enough of a framework to prevent duplicative work by developers in different communities. Thus, SKOS is an optional RDF language that modelers can choose to inherit from as a way to jump-start their own modeling and ensure some degree of conformance with best-practices.

Each enabling language (GRDDL, SAWSDL, RDFa, and SKOS) helps to bring the Semantic Web to a wider developer audience and supply a higher level of automatic interoperability among different Semantic Web implementations.

Digging a Bit Deeper into SPARQL

In Chapters 7 and 8, I give you a view of what it looks like to work with RDF and OWL, but when you decide to jump in and start coding your own application, you also need to know how to query those RDF and OWL models. Realistically, many RDF databases do not yet implement a standard query language, but when they do, it will most certainly be the Simple Protocol and RDF Query Language (SPARQL) — a W3C standard that defines a standard query language for RDF.

SPARQL is both a standard query language and data access protocol, which means that you can query not only RDF graphs, but also other data sources that can be mapped to RDF. Since January 2008, SPARQL has been an official W3C recommendation.

SPARQL allows the user to write queries that consist of triple patterns, *conjunctions* (logical "and"), and *disjunctions* (logical "or"s). In SPARQL, as with most declarative query languages, the query is actually specifying a pattern in the data that should be matched in a result set. Given a particular triple pattern in a query, a SPARQL processor considers sets of triples in the target RDF model that match the pattern. Here's an example:

```
PREFIX rdf:<http://www.w3.org/1999/02/22-rdf-syntax-ns#>
PREFIX owl:<http://www.w3.org/2002/07/owl#>
PREFIX books:<http://www.dummies.com/books#>

SELECT   ?book
WHERE {
        ?book rdf:type books:Books .
        ?book books:author
            http://me.jtpollock.us/foaf.rdf#me .
       }
ORDER BY ?book
```

Simply stated, this query is looks for books authored by Jeff Pollock and orders the resulting list. Notice that in the WHERE clause, I'm specifying triple patterns. The first pattern matches on all RDF instances that are of rdf:type Book. The second pattern matches all those RDF instances that have a book:author relationship to Jeff Pollock. The fact that these two patterns are inside the braces in the WHERE clause implies a conjunction. The ? in front of the word book, indicates a variable — the thing you are looking for. To round off the syntax, the "." signifies the end of a triple pattern in the WHERE clause.

This code returns the list of URIs of all the resources that match these patterns. In the case where we had a fully populated RDF model in structure I used in Chapter 7 and 8, I should get two books in the result:

```
http://www.dummies.com/books#Book-semanticweb_for_dummies
http://www.wiley.com/books#Book-adaptive_information
```

This fully qualified result set doesn't look very nice for a human reader, but you can leverage the dc:title predicate from Dublin Core and print out a nicer result:

```
PREFIX rdf:<http://www.w3.org/1999/02/22-rdf-syntax-ns#>
PREFIX owl:<http://www.w3.org/2002/07/owl#>
PREFIX books:<http://www.dummies.com/books#>
```

```
SELECT ?title
WHERE {
        ?book rdf:type books:Books .
        ?book books:author
           http://me.jtpollock.us/foaf.rdf#me .
        ?book dc:title ?title .
    }
ORDER BY ?title
```

This query gives a nicer-looking result:

```
Adaptive Information: Improving Business Through Semantic
   Interoperability, Grid Computing, and Enterprise
   Integration
Semantic Web for Dummies
```

SPARQL queries can be very easy to write for RDF data. For experienced developers, they are very similar to SQL queries for relational databases and can be used in much the same way. Future work on the SPARQL standard will include more advanced keyword support to do pattern matching with OWL inference engines. This capability will give developers a standardized way to harness the full power of Semantic Web data languages.

Developing Easy RDF Models

Say that you understand RDF, OWL, and SPARQL, and you think this stuff is the best thing since you learned how to upload photos on Facebook. But if you've honestly and truly been following along with the technical examples, you probably realize that you would never want to put up with the hassle of creating RDF, OWL, or SPARQL by hand-coding it into your favorite text editor while having to cut and paste from a spreadsheet containing your business data in another window. So how can you *easily* create RDF?

You can create RDF data and OWL ontology models many different ways. Tools to create Semantic Web models (whether from scratch or from importing data from another format) are abundant. Graphical tools allow the user to draw diagrams similar to the graphs earlier in the chapter. Connect those drawings to a relational database, and then with one click, you get RDF/XML. A variety of tools are available to harvest the RDF out of GRDDL, eRDF, and RDFa as well. Then there is the tried-and-true custom code route as well. Consider RSS and Atom feeds, for example: You could write a simple program in Java that parses these standard formats and produces plain RDF. This would be a programmatic, bottoms-up way of creating Semantic Web data.

In the next few sections, I detail some popular graphical tools to help you start modeling your Semantic Web masterpiece from the top-down, model-driven perspective:

Protégé

Protégé is one of the oldest and most widely deployed ontology modeling tools. It was originally conceived as a frame-based modeling tool for rich ontologies in accordance with the Open Knowledge Base Connectivity protocol. Later iterations of Protégé have expanded to include a plug-in that is now widely used for OWL and RDF modeling. Figure 9-3 shows a sample OWL model inside the Protégé tool.

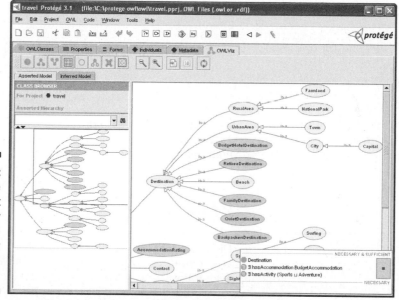

Figure 9-3: Protégé is the first widely deployed ontology modeling tool.

Although Protégé is most widely used in the academic community, its fully featured support for OWL and RDF is garnering it a wider following in commercial enterprises as well. Because it's free, Protégé may well continue to be a leading ontology editor. The source code is also freely available under the open-source Mozilla Public License (MPL).

XML Spy SemanticWorks

XML Spy from Altova (see Figure 9-4) is one of the most popular and acclaimed XML editors in the software industry. Altova decided to stick close to its roots and offer editing tools for other kinds of XML-based models too — including the Semantic Web. The SemanticWorks product line from Altova gives developers a friendly way of building ontologies that is familiar to any XML developer. The tool itself can work with multiple encodings of RDF to produce RDF/XML and also N-Triples.

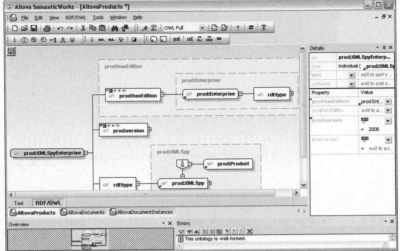

Figure 9-4:
XML Spy
Semantic
Works
brings
Semantic
Web
markup
to XML
developers.

The Altova product is particularly important because it breaks down barriers between the XML development community and the Semantic Web development community. This tool from Altova provides complete support for RDF and OWL with syntax, format, and semantic validation on the models.

TopBraid Composer

TopQuadrant is a long-time pioneer in the Semantic Web field. Traditionally focused on consulting engagements, the company's shift toward software products started with the very successful TopBraid Composer, shown in Figure 9-5. The Composer tool comes in multiple editions and is more than just a modeling tool: It's like a toolbox for developing complete Semantic Web applications. Beyond the class modeling, data modeling, SPARQL queries, and source code editing, the Composer tool also enables data source mappings, geography mapping, form generation, scripting, and various conversion utilities for XML and e-mail messages.

TopQuadrant is also expanding TopBraid to go beyond the development tooling areas and push forward into more mainstream enterprise software areas like business intelligence and data integration. The Composer product is a good start for TopQuadrant as it moves toward these mainstream markets.

Regardless of which modeling toolkit you choose to use, these products can be excellent ways to jump-start your programming efforts and enable you to rapidly develop your own Semantic Web applications.

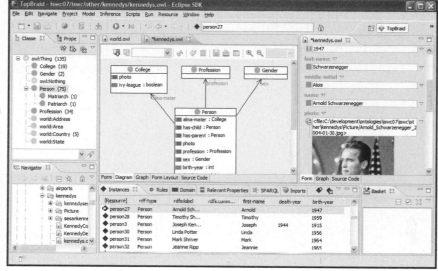

Figure 9-5:
TopBraid
Composer
sets the
standard for
graphical
Semantic
Web
modeling.

Finding Out Why Business Rules Are a Good Thing

The Semantic Web is a powerful set of technologies, but it's still incomplete. Both RDF and OWL work within a constrained set of logical expressiveness. In contrast, business rule systems, non-monotonic reasoning, and fuzzy logic can greatly extend the core power of the Semantic Web.

The Semantic Web of today is for defining data and metadata — it doesn't define any languages that give you actions (not withstanding SPARQL for querying). To really build functional software, a developer needs the power of events and actions to work with. These are foundational tools for doing the following things inside your code:

- ✔ **Looping:** In other words, "if something is true, then do some action."

- ✔ **Working with case statements:** For example, "in the case where something matches a condition, then do the next thing and move on."

- ✔ **Using mathematical operators:** Say, "if x is greater than y, then do something."

Details about different programming languages like Java, C#, or Perl are outside the scope of this book, but most languages provide a very high level of capability for writing logic and rules inside that programming framework. Although this approach to writing business rules is powerful, it places the content of the rules and the execution of the rules in a highly technical domain that only very specialized developers can work with. In contrast, a business rule engine attempts to remove the specification and execution of certain rules and logics from the domain of programmers and into a place where business users can control them.

This decoupling of the business rule from the programming framework is what enables higher levels of reuse, portability, and greater dynamism of software behavior. Mainstream business rule engines are the main enablers for some of the most important financial and national security software currently in production worldwide.

Business rules are largely an arbitrary and proprietary endeavor. Different software vendors use different mathematics and heuristics to implement their business rule systems, making it impossible to accurately classify, extract, or pinpoint the types of rules you've encoded inside their software. This tactical problem for business rule vendors provides key motivation for the W3C Rule Interchange Format Working Group.

RIF: A family of dialects

The Rule Interchange Format (RIF) Working Group at the W3C originally started with the charter to specify an exchange format for business rules so that they can be used across diverse systems as a common language into which established and new rule languages can be mapped, allowing rules written for one application to be published, shared, and reused in other applications and other rule engines. As the RIF has evolved, it has become clear that a single language for business rules cannot solve the enormous scope and complexity of the many vendor implementations and theoretical use cases that must be considered. Therefore, the RIF group has defined a family of different dialects that will be specified (see Figure 9-6), including

- **Framework for Logic Dialects (FLD):** This specification is the overarching formalism used for specifying the other dialects of rule languages supported by the RIF group. This logic defines both the syntax and semantics that are commonly used for various logic languages. The design of FLD is intended to be broad enough to encompass the semantics of future logic dialects and specific enough to require deep technical justification when newer logics can't map directly to FLD.

- **Basic Logic Dialect (BLD):** This specification is a core part of the FLD specification and contains the syntax, semantics, and XML serialization format for the interchange of basic business rules. From a logic theory standpoint, this specification corresponds to the language of definite Horn rules with equality and standard first-order logic (FOL) semantics. In layman's terms, it's a pretty powerful rule language even though it's called "basic!"

- ✔ **Datatypes and Built-ins (DTB):** This part of the RIF specification specifies the list of primitive datatypes along with built-in functions and predicates. Input from the XML Schema datatypes and XPath-Functions are the starting point for this RIF foundation library.

- ✔ **Production Rules Dialect (PLD):** This is a key specification that will enable production rule systems (behavior, action-oriented rule systems) to exchange rules in the proper semantics while using a common syntax. Unlike logic rules, the production rule usually contains a THEN statement that describes an action that may add, delete, or modify a knowledge base.

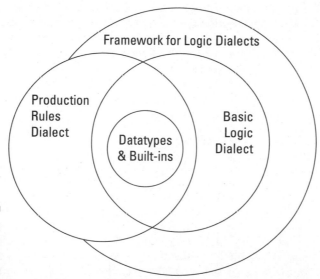

Figure 9-6:
RIF families
of dialects.

As it turns out, having a family of dialects for business rules is very important to prevent side effects when exchanging logic and production rules. Side effects need to be scrupulously avoided because even the smallest error in interpreting a rule could have disastrous effects (wrong answers to highly sensitive questions) in the software application that it is executing within. Because business rules are so important to the business and developer communities, development of the RIF portion of Semantic Web is moving a very deliberate pace intended to ensure that no mistakes are made along the way.

Non-monotonic reasoning

The many foundation math theories that comprise the Semantic Web are much too complex to cover here since I want to engage a wide range of readers, but one very important theoretical concept that you should remember is the distinction between monotonic and non-monotonic logic.

Put simply, *non-monotonic* reasoning is the ability of the reasoner to accept new facts that might contradict previously held beliefs. In contrast, when a *monotonic* reasoning system learns new facts, it cannot reduce the set of facts that were already known, and the system must remain consistent (no contradictions).

Business rules can be either monotonic or non-monotonic. But in the Semantic Web defined by OWL and RDF, only monotonic logics are allowable. This difference in logical foundations is one of the central mathematical differences between pure Semantic Web data languages and other knowledge representation techniques such as business rules.

Consider a simple OWL data model that defines the class `Birds`. Because your data model is about flying things, you have another class called `ThingsThatFly` from which you inherit your `Birds` class. You want your OWL data model to automatically classify any new `Birds` you add as `ThingsThatFly`. This works great while you are adding `Eagles`, `Sparrows`, and `Robins`, but then you add `Penguins` and `Emus` and realize that your system won't work out. So, knowing a bit about OWL, your natural reaction is to add a *disjoint* relationship (disjoint asks the reasoner to exclude instances from belonging to the disjoint classes) between your flightless birds and the class called `ThingsThatFly`. Whoops!

Because OWL is a monotonic logic, you get inconsistency warnings when you try to load this data model. Because you have a data record (`Penguin`) that is inherited from the class `Bird`, which is inherited from the class `ThingsThatFly`, you cannot then say that something of type `Bird` is incapable of flying (by assigning disjoint between `Penguin` and `ThingsThatFly`). That creates a problem for answering queries like, "return a list of all things that can fly." The query engine would find an inconsistency because, on one hand, all kinds of `Birds` can fly, but these specific animals are defined as being different from anything that can fly. Which is it?

A non-monotonic logic system wouldn't care. Instead, it might give you results for `Penguins` in both sets of "things that fly" and "things that don't fly," or it might choose to let the disjoint statement override the generalization at the `Birds` class level — but you might not know which case the engine has selected. Non-monotonic logic systems are by far the most widely used logic in logic systems in software and are at the very core of most kinds of statistical analysis like data mining, fuzzy logic, Natural Language Processing (NLP) Web-based search engine algorithms, and business rule systems.

The use of monotonic logic systems for the Semantic Web is a deliberate choice to offer explicit, consistent, and strict data modeling logic for ontologies used at Web scale. This has the advantage of creating a more relational database–like guarantee for correctness of query results (without the weakening or statistical thinning used by most non-monotonic reasoners).

Fuzzy logics, statistical mining, and how they relate to the Semantic Web

Fuzzy logics, statistical data mining, and many other types of advanced logic programming are close cousins to the Semantic Web, but remain distinctly different. For example, fuzzy logics supply *approximate reasoning,* whereas the Semantic Web description logics provide *exact reasoning.* Thus, the statistical approach to data analysis depends on a willingness to accept approximate query results instead of guaranteed query results. A greatly simplified example of this is the difference between searching for a query on Google versus searching for a query in your company's financial database. The Google results are fast and usually pretty accurate, but they're only an approximation of your real search. (When you submit a query, the Google technology doesn't search the whole Web or the entire cache of data; instead, the results are primed in advance and sorted by keywords.) Conversely, the query you send to your financial database is guaranteed mathematically to find any matching data according to the precise semantics of the query you sent it. This guarantee is crucial for business systems that depend on repeatable and correct results.

It's possible to apply fuzzy logic and statistical mining to structured database data or unstructured text data. These fuzzy algorithms perform cluster analysis according to rules that a given algorithm defines. Depending on the complexity of the algorithms, these fuzzy logics can

- ✔ **Correlate words in massive amounts of text using distance algorithms and frequency.** Words that are frequently located close to one another are more likely to signify related concepts.

- ✔ **Find patterns in scientific data.** Cluster analysis of average surface temperatures over time shows areas on our planet that are warming faster than others.

- ✔ **Spot fraudulent activities in banking software.** Hackers are known to use specific kinds of multi-step attacks and can sometimes be stopped after the algorithms spot a likely break-in before it is finished.

Semantic Web and fuzzy logics (statistical reasoning) are like apples and oranges — they're both part of the same family of techniques for working with data, but they are distinctly different varieties to consider. Although business rules and fuzzy logics are not yet formally considered as part of the core Semantic Web family, they are already a necessary ingredient for most implementations and will always be considered for use alongside RDF and OWL datasets in Semantic Web applications.

Grappling with Natural Language Processing (NLP)

One place where the statistical (fuzzy) analysis techniques are particularly important is for use with Natural Language Processing (NLP) engines. An NLP engine is capable of applying algorithms to completely unstructured text in order to produce structured data or a data model. A typical approach is to encode grammar rules or clustering rules into algorithms that then create a cumulative score for how data and concepts are extracted from raw text.

The value of the NLP domain in general is to bring some semblance of order to chaos. It's true that humanity is creating more new information this decade than in all of recorded human history. Most of this new data is in the form of unstructured text and binary media such as photos and videos. NLP engines are one of the only viable technologies that can automate the extraction of valuable structured data from all this new unstructured noise.

NLP engines are used in fraud detection, anti-terrorism software, mortgage financing software, anti-money-laundering systems, network security software, publishing software, business intelligence reporting, and many other software applications that need to work with huge volumes of unstructured text. The more common NLP systems and frameworks are

- **General Architecture for Text Engineering (GATE)** is an open-source framework for applying text mining and NLP programs to raw text. The GATE technology is a framework because it allows developers to create new NLP components that can be plugged in to the existing architecture and used with pre-existing NLP algorithms. This flexibility is important because real-world problems typically require a series of NLP algorithms applied serially to achieve a high accuracy rate. Commercial users of GATE include Glaxo Smith Kline, AT&T, Thomson Reuters, and Garlik. (See Chapter 15 for more information about Garlik.)

- **Unstructured Information Management Architecture (UIMA)** is an architecture framework for NLP that was developed by IBM and is commercialized in its OmniFind product. A version of UMIA has been moved into the open-source domain as an Apache project.

- **Inxight** is a long-time leader in the commercial text-extraction area, the Inxight products were acquired by Business Objects, which was subsequently acquired by SAP.

- **Thomson Reuters Calais** is a new entry into the NLP sector, the Calais product was created from the ground-up to be Semantic Web–ready. It's the only product or framework to plug in directly to the Linked Data initiative started by Tim Berners-Lee. (For more on Calais, see Chapter 15.)

NLP: A necessary evil

For most practitioners of information management, the NLP engine is considered a necessary evil. It's necessary because there is so much unstructured data in the world that human beings cannot possibly organize it all. On the other hand, NLP is evil because after 30 years of research and development, there still isn't a reliable NLP engine that works well for all types of data.

In very specific domains (like healthcare, law, or security), practical NLP implementations achieve a reasonably high degree of accuracy (where high accuracy is measured by how successful the algorithm is at classifying a document or producing a new data model from raw text). But for most general purpose applications, the quality of NLP engines is dismal — usually achieving only a 60–70 percent accuracy level. Further, the typical NLP engine isn't very good at defining what a given document is about. For example, a given document might have dozens of references to `Cars` but actually be about `Environment Protection`.

Even in cases where the accuracy level for NLP is low, many businesses still find it worthwhile for uses where they don't care about *false negatives* (situations where the NLP engine classifies some data or documents incorrectly). In these situations, the usefulness of the *positive matches* outweighs the *false negatives*.

The good news about NLP and the Semantic Web is that they're highly complementary technologies. A good NLP engine can produce RDF, which in turn can be networked and linked to rich OWL data models. Thus, unstructured text can be brought into the Semantic Web and made part of this giant database in the sky.

However, the hype has greatly exceeded reality. In fact, the steep hype curve of expectations for NLP had been considered a significant handicap for decades preceding the Semantic Web. So although the whole of the Semantic Web plus NLP exceeds the sum of their parts, they also bring along baggage from long over-inflated expectations.

A crucial step for Semantic Web pioneers is to build compelling applications with RDF, OWL, and the enabling technologies such as business rules and NLP without getting burned by past failures attributed to these technologies. Only through the rise of successful and compelling applications (see Chapter 15) will the sullied reputations of NLP and business rules cease to diminish the new thinking behind the Semantic Web data formats.

Enabling New Operational Models

Semantic Web software applications should be useful and supply meaningful new capabilities in order to bear the inherent risks of using them. The relative immaturity of the tools and technologies creates far too many risks to haphazardly try Semantic Web applications. In this section about enabling new kinds of operational models, I identify a few key capabilities that the Semantic Web can bring to your business applications that use it.

Handling uncertainty

Typical business applications leverage relational databases and XML data processing techniques. But relational databases and XML depend on pre-defined data definitions (schema) that are difficult to change after they've been implemented. Likewise, those relational and XML formats operate on the basis of a *closed-world assumption,* which means that they assume that the data they contain is the only data relevant to a given application. On the other hand, the Semantic Web formats operate on an open-world assumption, which I describe in some detail in Chapter 8. The *open-world assumption* empowers a Semantic Web knowledgebase to distinguish between data facts that are provable and those that are satisfiable. A satisfiable query result can be useful to an application because it tells the application that there's some uncertainty in the answer.

One extreme, but illustrative, example of this open-world characteristic is to consider a software application that helps doctors with the decision about whether to operate on a patient. With a Semantic Web application, you can ask the knowledgebase whether there is data to support the decision to oper-ate, and the knowledgebase might answer in one of four ways: provably yes, provably no, satisfiably yes, or satisfiably not. The two satisfiable answers are interesting because they indicate that some of the data indicates a yes or no answer, but that there are not enough facts for the system to answer with complete certainty. This ability to handle uncertainty is useful for a large number of business applications and, rather than depending on procedural code to deduce that uncertainty, the knowledgebase can supply those results directly.

Dynamic classification

Dynamic classification is the ability to say whether a particular data item belongs to a class of things without having to directly tag all the data. For example, a Semantic Web knowledgebase can answer a query to find all pos-sible evacuation facilities without having to require developers to predefine each and every facility. A single OWL model can define the properties of a suitable evacuation facility by defining a specific elevation above sea level, a certain size in square feet, and the availability of specific facilities like water, restrooms, and beds. From there, a Semantic Web query can evaluate data from all sorts of different sources about facilities like churches, schools, hotels, stadiums, or shopping malls and match the facilities that meet the model definition of an evacuation facility. One of the principal benefits is that these data items can be matched according to a model, and they don't have to be hard-wired into one or more queries that depend on the local syntax of a given data source. Several examples of this type of dynamic classification are given in the Enterprise use cases described in Chapter 11.

Ad hoc modeling and browsing

Ontologies are a conceptual model of a domain that may or may not map to physical data sources. Because these conceptual models can exist completely outside of the physical systems, they can be independently manipulated, altered, and evolved over time. Although there are other ways to achieve this logical abstraction, the Semantic Web provides a standards-based approach that's more portable and much less ambiguous than other techniques. The principal benefits for using ontology this way are that business analysts and other information workers can change the models on-demand and browse the data that matches their conceptual models without having to learn all the details about the underlying physical sources and physical data models.

Unstructured data pipeline

A significant emerging challenge for any large business is how to rationalize content within documents with data within databases and XML. Whereas database and XML data are inherently structured, the contents within documents do not typically have much structure that can be leveraged for useful queries and joining with structured data. The Semantic Web formats like OWL and RDF supply an ideal format for joining unstructured and structured data because they are a graph structure rather than more rigid tabular and tree-like data structures.

Some organizations such as governments and the financial services industry have substantial amounts of content that needs to be understood alongside database data, and they are using a combination of Semantic Web technologies and Natural Language Processing (NLP) techniques to perform those analytics. In their fully realized form, the NLP processes can operate as a pipeline to inject and refine unstructured content into more structured formats like RDF/OWL. After it is structured, that content may be analyzed alongside or with structured content for many different kinds of business purposes. For example, the business intelligence examples provided in Chapter 11 explain how that works.

Open-source data

Unstructured data pipelines enable a new class of analytic applications that may use freely available data from the Web in powerful analytic engines that previously worked only on structured data. Freely available data is sometimes referred to as *open-source data* because it is open for anybody to find.

The open-source data trend is one of the most exciting and promising movements in the intelligence community because the explosion of new content on the Internet means that data is sometimes available that can help identify and prevent malicious attacks on our community interests. Semantic Web formats can help with the challenges of knowing what data can be trusted and how to find data without knowing what to ask for. By converting data to RDF/OWL, more efficient machine automation can be applied to that open-source data to rate its trustworthiness and automatically classify millions of documents according to NLP and inference rules. Without a doubt, there are many unsolved challenges in the open-source data movement, but the Semantic Web has opened new frontiers and offered new solutions to age-old problems that simple search engines like Google can't solve.

Setting the Truthiness Dial

By combining reasoning techniques from different Semantic Web languages and business rule systems, a software vendor could choose to give developers the ability to change entailment levels. *Entailment levels* define what rules the query engine follows when answering queries. For example, if your data model shows that a `Web Shopper` is a type of `Customer`, and you submit a query asking for all `Customers`, that query may include people who are directly classified as `Customers` and/or those who are classified as `Web Shoppers`.

For the purposes of a Semantic Web application, the entailment level of the query defines the truth of the data. As the entailment levels change in a reasoner, so does the logic of the data and therefore the truth of it. So, if you have a reasoner that can change entailment levels, you are thereby changing the facts and concepts that are considered when the system answers a question. Thus, although the reasoner can't answer from its gut (since it doesn't have one), you can still think of this as a *truthiness* dial!

Because OWL ontologies are quite advanced in terms of what can be expressed, and because there are many kinds of logics that may or may not be considered while answering a query (including monotonic or non-monotonic logics), a particular knowledgebase must conform to one or more expressiveness levels during a particular query.

Have you ever seen one of those art posters that are composed of many different colors and look like nonsense when viewed with the naked eye, but when you wear special tinted glasses, the pictures materialize and make sense? The *expressiveness* of querying a knowledgebase is a little like that. Using one level of expressiveness, the knowledgebase might deliver one set of results, but using another expressiveness level, the knowledge base might deliver an altogether different set of data.

The newer OWL 1.1 specification has begun to define fragments of OWL logics that can be safely used as self-contained entailment levels, with well-defined consequences for moving from one level to the next. The following list describes a few of the more commonplace entailment levels that are commonly used today:

- **RDFS:** This formal specification includes basic RDF graph navigation semantics plus the simple RDF schema class inheritance semantics.

- **OWL Prime:** This informal specification implemented in the Oracle database supports the most widely used semantics for practical applications (as viewed by Oracle). Support is included for the following axioms:

    - rdfs:domain
    - rdfs:range
    - rdfs:subClassOf
    - rdfs:subPropertyOf
    - owl:equivalentClass
    - owl:equivalentProperty
    - owl:sameAs
    - owl:inverseOf
    - owl:TransitiveProperty
    - owl:SymmetricProperty
    - owl:FunctionalProperty
    - owl:InverseFunctionalProperty

- **OWL 2 DL:** This is considered a major dialect of the OWL 2 specification. It's a syntactically restricted version of OWL Full. OWL DL restrictions produce a language that's fully deterministic and much more practical for vendors to implementation solutions for.

- **OWL 2 Full:** This is a major dialect of the OWL 2 specification and is generally considered to be a more straightforward extension of RDFS, but it introduces the possibility of some non-deterministic and resource-intensive query results.

✔ **OWL 2 EL++:** This is a profile of OWL 2 that's defined to provide highly optimized behavior for large and complex ontologies that depend on complex class definitions. Example domains that should consider OWL 2 EL++ include life sciences, manufacturing, retail, scientific, and other domains that may require complex conceptual models.

✔ **OWL 2 QL:** This profile of OWL 2 was formulated specifically as a way to capture the model semantics of databases and UML (Unified Modeling Language) and is intended to aid in the use of OWL as a data integration language.

✔ **OWL 2 RL:** This profile of OWL 2 was built for optimizing the intersection of rule programs with description logics. It's intended to provide a profile for implementing reasoning systems on top of existing rule engines or other hybrid-based approaches for using increased expressive power.

Future Semantic Web knowledgebases and platforms may eventually include seamless ways to change expressiveness on-the-fly using a user-controlled dial for changing levels, but these capabilities are still in their infancy today. Once in place, this kind of hypothetical truthiness dial will enable applications and information workers to apply entailment levels as a kind of filter to analyze the same data from different perspectives, different performance characteristics, and different answers to the same questions.

Part IV

Putting the Semantic Web to Work

In this part . . .

Alas, the Semantic Web can be pure fun only for hobbyists and academics. For the rest of us schmucks, we have to worry about putting it to work. Thankfully the Semantic Web can offer a lot to the average big business by laying the groundwork for a stable and flexible information management infrastructure.

Far from being another IT fad, the Semantic Web offers some unique alternatives to the same-old tired data architectures. This part of the book explains how you can make it work for you!

Chapter 10

The Rise of the Information Worker

*I*f you've already decided to read a book about the Semantic Web, you probably intuitively understand that the world of work is changing. Regardless of your role in a white-collar, blue-collar, or even green-collar industry, you're probably using computers and electronic information in ways that would have been unimaginable just a few years ago. The pace of change is speeding up, and workers all across the globe are being asked to become smarter, faster, and more productive — in other words, they're being asked to become information workers.

Information workers, in the broadest sense, are people with everyday jobs who must learn to be more productive by using technology to aid in the automation of their routines. Even the largely manual blue-collar jobs of today are using more automation in the form of robotics, navigation systems, and other technology-driven machinery to push the envelope of productivity in their industries. Desk jobs especially are using software to increase productivity and automation. ERP (Enterprise Resource Planning) systems, social networking for businesses, workplace collaboration suites, and desktop automation systems all push forward what's possible with technology. Pretty much any job can have elements of IT injected into its core to turn workers into information workers.

In a more narrow sense, information workers are also emerging as a specialty workforce that's in charge of the data assets of big businesses. Increasingly, and smartly, big companies are starting to treat their corporate data as what it is — a business asset. *Capital assets* are material assets like trucks, buildings, and machinery that contribute to a business's value. Human capital consists of the minds and output of the people employed by business. *Data assets* are the digital information that fuel business software. Forecasts, budgets, inventory, logistics, and any critical data about a business's health are types of corporate data assets. The people who know how to take care of these data assets in very detailed ways are the new class of emerging specialty information workers.

In this chapter, I explain in detail the new types of specialty information worker jobs, the businesses that most heavily depend on them, and how the Semantic Web will influence the evolution of these jobs.

Taking a Look at the Global 2000

The pace of change in business since the mid-1990s is breathtaking. The ubiquity of the Internet and the aggressive adoption by businesses of Enterprise Resource Planning (ERP) software systems in just ten short years have forever altered our notions of big business.

Whereas businesses used to close the books on their finances once per quarter, many of the largest companies now close their books nightly. Large manufacturing and retail businesses used to take it on faith that their logistics shipments and product movements were on time, but today they use Global Positioning Systems (GPS) and Radio Frequency Identifiers (RFIDs) to track where their merchandise is. Yesterday's businesses used to operate in virtually unregulated territory, leaving it to the pressures of the marketplace to enforce fairness. Today's businesses, though, face the most highly regulated global environments ever as Sarbanes-Oxley, BASEL 2, and other financial regulations are forcing companies to play fair, report about their money consistently, and prove to governments that they're following the rules.

A *Global 2000* business is one of the top 2000 businesses in the world by measure of its gross revenues. These are the most important businesses in the world, whose success drives the vast majority of the global economy and the U.S. economy, and provides the economic stability for small businesses to thrive. These Global 2000 businesses are pushing the envelope of information management — using information as a way expand their lead on the competition and to proactively change the rules of their industries.

Since the role of information in Global 2000 companies is now seen as an instrument of competition, the Semantic Web is primed to transform how businesses compete on an international stage. The Semantic Web's core innovation is that it brings the rigor of science and logic to the management of data, models, and business rules. In times past, it was possible for database administrators and software architects to locate all the data; large-scale data processing was only possible with people in the process to help out.

Global 2000 businesses have now gone beyond the time when major business decisions were entirely driven by the gut instinct of a few powerful people; today, the entire infrastructure of the business is built to supply good information about the business facts so that decision makers make their calls without just guessing. Global 2000 businesses now regularly use scenario modeling and financial planning software to assist their understanding of the future and influence their decisions today. Now more than ever, the systematic and near-scientific institutionalization of innovation is the driving force that separates the global leaders from the has-beens.

The information supply that drives innovation and separates the leaders doesn't magically appear for some and not for others. This information supply can't be bought off the shelf and installed to make any business a Global 2000 company. Rather, a deep commitment by some companies to invest in the development of new competencies — information worker competencies — separates the winners from the rest. These information worker competencies are not ethereal ideas about people looking at information all day and thinking deep thoughts. Instead, these competencies enable businesses to execute more efficiently because they put in place more streamlined processes and repeatable ways to make smarter, better informed decisions.

Understanding the Tactical Role of Information in Business Economics

The Semantic Web has tremendous potential to change the everyday job of the typical information worker throughout the world. The skills and competencies of these information workers impact a business's bottom line in big ways. The everyday operations of a Global 2000 business, quarterly reporting, and even customer satisfaction can depend on how reliable the businesses information is. After all, people build the reports, put data in the enterprise software, and link together customer data from different systems. Information influences the most tactical of business operations.

Take, for example, the act of balancing the ledger. Just like you balance your checkbook, every business has to balance its general ledger and report to the government what its balances are. These ledger statements impact everything from a company's tax burden to its stock market valuation. The process of balancing big business ledgers used to require armies of accountants working with paper, pencils, and calculators. But with the widespread deployment of ERP systems, that process has become easier.

The ERP system is like a big, advanced calculator, but just as with the calculator, you still have to get the data into the ERP system. And this data gap, from the sources of the ledger transactions to their entry into the ERP system, can still be error-prone and cause substantial impacts to the bottom line or even shareholder stock valuation problems. Working on ledger data may seem like a geeky technical problem, but it has a critical impact on the actual and perceived health of the business.

Like ledger data, the data about a business's products is crucial to the operations of those businesses. Major retailers and packaged goods manufacturers (like Wal-Mart, the Gap, Proctor & Gamble, and so on) depend on product data as the lifeblood of their business. The data about their raw materials, their manufacturing processes, logistics, and supply chain information and inventory levels can't be too accurate or too current. These are software systems that enable those companies to operate efficiently, and it is information workers who enable those software systems to function correctly.

The process of taking orders and fulfilling them is also an information-intensive process. Businesses that streamline the order-to-cash processes eliminate costly manual steps in order-taking, debiting payments, updating inventories, and scheduling logistics. These lifecycle processes may also include the steps to issue quotations, accept bids, and initiate the bookings. Each step in these complex, global, and multisystem interactions require good quality information and efficient software systems. Once again, the modern information worker acts as the caretaker for these critical business systems that are the lifeblood of well-run companies.

Accurate data and information aren't luxuries for modern competitive businesses: They're a tactical necessity. No longer can a company expect to thrive without paying attention to its data as an asset, instead of treating it as an afterthought. As more Global 2000 businesses leverage Semantic Web data in their own enterprise software systems, they gradually shift the attention of information technology (IT) away from the technology and back to the information. Part and parcel of this shift in attention is how the role of the specialist information worker changes to become the key enabler for these newer, more streamlined software systems.

Getting to Know the Types of Information Workers

Specialist information workers are not technical software developers who write code. They are not simply database administrators who take business requirements and make databases, nor are they regular business employees who have business line responsibilities for a profit center. The specialist information worker is a catalyst for bridging the gap between businesspeople and information technology (IT) specialists. They usually think in terms of the business but act on IT assets that are consumed by software systems. A few of the key information worker roles are

- ✔ Business analysts
- ✔ Corporate librarians
- ✔ Information architects
- ✔ Taxonomists
- ✔ Ontologists
- ✔ Data stewards
- ✔ Database architects

Many of these roles have emerged just in the past three to five years, as the necessity of their functions gained importance in the new economies of Global 2000 businesses. As these roles continue to evolve, they will be using the Semantic Web in their everyday jobs. Whether by using tools that generate RDF or by designing ontologies directly, these information workers are also becoming Semantic Web developers.

The following sections provide explanations of these roles and have been validated by numerous interviews with people who hold these titles. Try searching for these jobs yourself on your favorite job board!

Business analysts

A *business analyst* is the most widespread information worker and is also the closest to the main business operations. Typically, the business analyst doesn't have a particular horizontal skill set that effectively maps between industries. More often, the business analyst has some kind of business degree and is an expert in a particular industry or domain and has skills that are transferrable among companies in that domain. For example, a business analyst in the insurance industry may be expected to have strong working knowledge of catastrophic modeling and underwriting, whereas a business analyst in the financial services field may be expected to have expertise in the areas of order management and billing.

Information worker skills for the business analyst include

- ✔ Is comfortable being a catalyst between businesspeople and IT people
- ✔ Has a detailed understanding of the business processes that are unique to a given industry

✔ Has a detailed understanding of the data contained within the IT systems that enable various business processes

✔ Can translate the business requirements into actionable IT objectives that can be successfully implemented by technologists

✔ Has expertise using the following kinds of software tools: desktop productivity tools such as Word and Excel, and ERP applications

✔ May be able to use various database management systems and Master Data Management (MDM) applications

The business analyst advises the IT team on behalf of the business and sets objectives for the management and dissemination of high-quality and reliable business information.

In a word, the business analyst plays the role of a *catalyst*.

Corporate librarians

A *corporate librarian* is an information worker who specializes in the organization of complex information. Often, the corporate librarian's job requires a Library Sciences degree, and by their nature, corporate librarians are not necessarily specialists in a particular industry or marketplace. (Some fields, such as law, do prefer corporate librarians trained specifically in their discipline.) Since the rise of the Internet, modern librarians are expected to understand how to produce search strategies that can be applied to various search engines and other online catalogs.

Information worker skills for the corporate librarian include

✔ Is comfortable working with large volumes of complex content

✔ Can produce detailed classification rules for content that is unique to a given industry

✔ Has a detailed understanding of the data contained within multiple cannons of information used to enable various business processes

✔ Can translate the business requirements into actionable searches that can be repeated and automated by businesspeople

✔ Has expertise using the following kinds of knowledge management tools: Autonomy; Enterprise Content Systems (SharePoint, Stellent, Documentum, FileNet); Portal software; and online resources such as Docline, PubMed, and Lexis/Nexis

✔ May be a power user of various internal and external content management systems and Master Data Management (MDM) applications

The corporate librarian's core duties are to locate, enrich, organize, and disseminate corporate data. Although corporate librarians help locate information, research, enrich found information, and organize information to a taxonomy, they may or may not actually create the taxonomies, repair bad data, or set requirements for application-specific data formats. Corporate librarians should be experts in locating, organizing, and disseminating business information. They work with predefined tags/taxonomies to manually classify information and further enrich it for distribution.

In a word, the corporate librarian plays the role of the *cataloger*.

Taxonomists

Often confused with the corporate librarian role, the *taxonomist* typically has a much more technical background. For example, whereas the corporate librarian may read, organize, and classify documents, the taxonomist is the person responsible for defining the category system and tags. This is a more technical role because the category systems and tagging systems are usually part of a bigger systems picture where taxonomies are consumed by automated software programs and may be maintained in technical formats like XML documents and indexed master files. A taxonomist may be required to specify and maintain complex taxonomies with IT dependencies that require a deeper technical understanding of code syntax and programming skills in order to produce technically valid IT inputs.

Information worker skills for the taxonomist include

- Is comfortable working with complex technical data formats and data models

- Can produce detailed hierarchies, create taxonomy standards, and define the taxonomy strategies unique to a given set of IT systems and technologies

- Has a detailed understanding of the systems and system architectures that consume taxonomy and drive various business processes

- Can translate the business lists, codes, and hierarchies into organized information models that can be inserted into specific IT systems

- Has expertise using the following kinds of tools: Autonomy, Synaptica, Omnifind, XML Spy; also, can work with the raw formats of Java, Cobol, C++, and other programming languages that consume ordered taxonomy data from master files or properties files

- Is a potential power user of an ontology modeling toolkit

A taxonomist must work closely with the business analyst to understand the business requirements and translate them into IT requirements for the many uses of that corporate information and reference data. Taxonomists work with model hierarchies, ontologies, tag sets, file lists, master files, property files, and some relational data models or indices. They create and maintain the classification systems (manual and automated) used to organize structured, semi-structured, and unstructured content. These classifications may be applied to Master Data Management systems or exported for use in other information management systems, such as content management systems. Taxonomists respond to business user, librarian, and steward requirements by improving the findability of corporate data that is organized by structured lists.

In a word, the taxonomist is the *definer* of terms, categories, and master files.

Ontologists

Ontology experts can be thought of as senior taxonomists, or as senior information architects — the evolution of either role will lead to expertise in the ontology field. Whereas a regular taxonomist may start with expertise in the structure and organization of category trees, such as being skilled in defining the broader and narrower definitions of terms in a thesaurus, the *ontologist* is skilled in a definitional logic that is much more expressive than thesaurus-style lists. Similarly, the information architect (see the next section) may be skilled in producing models in the UML (Unified Modeling Language) or ERD (Entity Relationship Diagram) formats, whereas the ontologist supplies a higher-level of modeling experience using formats like OWL, KIF (Knowledge Interchange Format), or SCL (Simple Common Logic).

Information worker skills for the ontologist include

- ✔ Is comfortable working with specialized technical data formats and data models

- ✔ Can produce detailed modeling standards and define the rules for consistency that are unique to a given set of ontology assets

- ✔ Has a detailed technical and linguistic understanding of the vocabularies, terms, and concepts that drive various business processes

- ✔ Can translate taxonomies, data models, and system architectures into organized ontologies that can be reliably reasoned with inside conventional expert systems

- ✔ Has expertise using the following kinds of tools: Protégé, TopBraid, Oracle Spatial, OpenCyc, NLP engines; also capable of working with the raw formats of OWL, RDF, SPARQL and other programming languages that enable ontology-driven applications

- ✔ May need to be a power user of an ontology modeling toolkit

As you see in Figure 10-1 (which shows a recent job listing), ontologists are an emerging breed of specialists that are working at the pinnacle of their disciplines, capable of the hard-core logic and mathematics for writing the most complex software systems. They choose to focus on the discipline of information modeling, structured data definitions, and description logics.

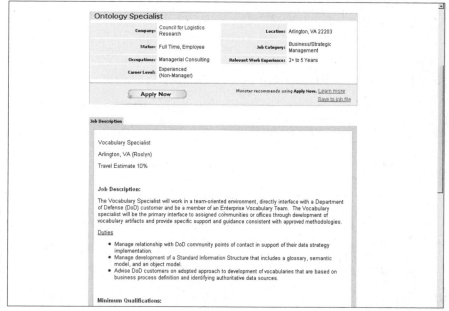

Figure 10-1:
A recent job posting for an ontology specialist.

Information architects

The *information architect* position is an often overloaded one. In some communities, the information architect role is attributed to jobs that focus entirely on making large Web sites easier to navigate. However, I'm referring to an information worker role that specializes in the informational aspects of software architecture. The job of the information architect is truly a cross-disciplinary specialty that may often be detached from any particular industry that the information architect works in. Instead, information architects are experts on the underlying software technologies and systems that supply the lifeblood of data throughout a large business.

Information worker skills for the information architect include

- ✔ Is comfortable working with complex IT systems and data models
- ✔ Can produce detailed information standards and strategies unique to a given set of IT systems and technologies

- ✔ Has a detailed understanding of the design patterns and reference architectures of IT systems used to enable various business processes

- ✔ Can translate the business requirements into information models that can be implemented within specific IT systems

- ✔ Has expertise using the following kinds of tools: Enterprise Architecture Modeling tools (XML, UML, OWL, RDF, ERD), Business Intelligence platforms, Master Data Management (MDM), Information Lifecycle Management (ILM), and DBMS and Data Warehouses

- ✔ Is a potential power user of an ontology modeling toolkit

The information architect understands the business requirements well enough to build models from them, and he or she works within IT objectives to create new data formats while staying within design limitations of various technologies selected by IT. The information architecture role may also be known as software architect, database architect, or systems architect.

Information architects are experts in the IT systems that feed and are fed by the information management applications; they make decisions about latency requirements of data, scheduling of system updates, and ensure end-to-end dependability of enterprise data and system resources. Additionally, the information architect responds to requirements set by analysts and stewards for new systems participating in the data ecosystem, and sets requirements and objectives for developers and DBAs working on implementation design and construction.

In a word, the information architect fulfills the *blueprint* role in the data-driven organization.

Data stewards

The *data steward* ensures that business data conforms to the corporate models and ontologies and improves the quality and eliminates redundancy in the data itself. Whereas most of the information workers described earlier in the chapter (taxonomists, architects, librarians, and so on) are principally concerned with the models, categories, and organization of the data, the data steward looks after the data itself. The power and influence of the data steward should not be minimized by the use of the relatively passive word *steward;* perhaps the term *data governor* is a more benefitting job title, but that term isn't commonplace in the industry. However you say it, the data steward's responsibilities are both broad and deep.

Information worker skills for the data steward include

- ✔ Is comfortable working with complex technical data formats and data models

- ✔ Can define, plan, and supervise the establishment of data governance rules for the use and management of corporate data assets

- ✔ Can produce detailed standards and define the strategies for the management of master data and *golden records* (trusted, clean, guaranteed data)

- ✔ Has a detailed understanding of the data cleansing and parsing operations that ensure high-quality data drives important business processes

- ✔ Can translate the technical requirements into a metadata management strategy that can be inserted into specific IT systems and business applications

- ✔ Has expertise using the following kinds of tools: master data management applications, data quality systems, and metadata management systems; also, can working with the raw formats of XML, ERD, DBMS, and other modeling languages that drive application data, metadata, and business rules

- ✔ Is a potential power user of an a metadata management toolkit

Data stewards are experts in finding and navigating the data within the MDM applications; they know what data can be changed, by whom, and how to do it. They interact with human workflow systems, as a team of stewards, to respond to tasks that have been set by SMEs and business analysts. The data steward is principally responsible for ensuring good data.

In a word, the data steward *governs* corporate data for its full lifecycle from cradle to grave.

Database architects (DBAs)

The term DBA has always been somewhat ambiguous; it could mean database administrator or database architect (DBA). In these classical definitions, the administrator is usually a more junior version of the architect. For my purposes, I'm referring to the *database architect (DBA)* as a specialty information worker. In practice, the DBA's skills strongly overlap the information architect skills defined previously, but with less focus on non-database models and more focus on performance optimizations for relational databases.

Good DBAs are capable of working directly with the business analysts and taxonomists to understand the system requirement. They then must be able to produce a database data model that can match those business needs with the IT requirements for scalability, performance, and tolerance. Many DBAs end up with specialty roles unique to a database engine like Oracle, DB2, or Teradata; they may also develop specialties in areas of data warehousing, transactional databases, or OLAP cubes. However, for DBAs to be truly successful, they must be able to see the big picture from a business perspective and understand the database technology is merely an enabler.

Understanding the Needs of the Information-Centric Company

Information workers are especially important for businesses that are dependent upon information for their competitiveness. Although many of these information-intensive businesses are in the Global 2000, many small businesses are transitioning from manual processes to more efficient levels of automation. This continual drive toward efficiency and automation is precisely the reason that the Semantic Web will be critical for tomorrow's information-centric company. But in the future, *every* company, large or small, will be information-centric.

For example, I worked with a small dry-cleaning business operating from the Midwestern United States. This business had 18 locations in three states and could certainly operate as a profitable company without high levels of automation. However, the company wanted to grow and automate the process of balancing its books, so it looked to a software-based solution for synchronizing its cash receipts every night. In this particular case, a relatively simple database-replication process was installed, enabling the business owner to track progress and balance budgets continuously.

You don't have to be a multibillion-dollar company to be information-driven.

One way to appreciate the importance of information workers is to see how entire industries are changing the way data is used to drive business operations.

Automotive manufacturing

Margins are tight in the automotive sector. Unlike 30 years ago, there is very little room for error in the process of manufacturing vehicles. Labor costs have been steadily rising, downward pressures on pricing have accelerated due to more competition from automakers in emerging markets, and materials costs haven't diminished. So where do carmakers innovate?

Although labor automation through the use of robotics has garnered the most attention from the industry, successful car makers like Toyota, Mercedes, and Audi have also been innovating in other areas. Increasing the reliability of vehicles through simulation, understanding market conditions through scenario planning, and optimizing supply-chain operations for materials management are all ways that information-driven jobs are helping some automotive manufacturers get an edge.

I've worked with ontologists and data stewards from major automotive manufacturers who are building next-generation systems to streamline the car-making process. From concept to dealer lots, the manufacturers can control their products and get feedback from buyers through the smart use of software systems. Building data models, managing master data, and maintaining corporate taxonomies are new ways to streamline and improve older manufacturing information systems.

Consumer packaged goods

Information management has always been a key element of the consumer packaged goods (CPG) industry — but no one ever called it that. The secrecy of Coke's recipe for the world's favorite cola has gained almost mythological status. But Coke's secret recipe is just one small example of how CPU closely manages information. Proctor & Gamble (P&G) is one of the largest CPG companies in the world, and it has some of the most sophisticated, and secretive recipe-management systems in the world. Some of the P&G products are legendary for the amount of research and development that went into producing a consumer hit — Pringles potato chips, for example — and P&G rightly wants to protect and preserve the information about what did and did not work to make those products.

Research and development plays a hugely important role for CPG companies as they try to create the next hit products. But the manufacturing and marketing aspects of CPG are also crucial to their success. CPG companies that understand the buying patterns, shopping patterns, and tastes of their customers have a clear edge in that cutthroat business. The information about their consumers and retailers is used to create real-time business intelligence for CPG executives to make decisions about huge investments in new products. Information workers enable every aspect of those information flows — from recipe management and supply-chain data, to customer relationship management. Data architects and corporate librarians are the workers who keep the successful CPG companies producing at high efficiency.

Publishing

By definition, the publishing industry is information-driven, but you might be surprised to discover that the major publishers have only recently begun to truly automate their business operations electronic software systems. Business operations for a publishing company are the processes by which they manage the lifecycle of content. Content, for the publisher, is the raw material that is assembled, packaged, and sold for huge profits.

Major publishers like Thomson Reuters, McGraw-Hill, and Reed Elsevier control a healthy percentage of the world's content. Everything from magazines, journals, electronic libraries, business information, and book contents is owned and copyrighted by a publisher. Even the content of this book in your hands is copyrighted by John Wiley & Sons. Some of the publishers, like Thomson Reuters and Reed Elsevier, license their content libraries to businesses all over the world.

Accessing these publishing systems can be easy, but finding what you want can be difficult. Therefore these publishers employ armies of corporate librarians, taxonomists, librarians, ontologists, and data stewards to make sure that their content is easy to find, high quality, and secure. Perhaps more than any other industry, the publishing industry intuitively understands why the emerging class of specialty information workers and the Semantic Web as a whole are keys to its future.

Financial services

The historic innovators of the information-driven economy have always been the financial institutions, by necessity. Long gone are the days where banks and trading houses dealt with any material assets: Everything from bank transfers to mortgage payments and stock trades is electronic these days. Every financial transaction has a data model associated with it. The last time you used an ATM to withdraw cash, you sent an electronic transaction through a central software system designed by information workers many years ago.

Today, every large bank or investment company has hundreds of different IT systems responsible for keeping billions of dollars accurately accounted for. The people who manage these software systems, keep them running, and help them evolve are information workers.

Business analysts, database architects, and taxonomists keep the records straight. They ensure that the general ledger codes are accurate. They maintain multiple lists of legal entity codes that map to their business operations in different parts of the world. They maintain the auditing requirements for how they must show which debits and credits were applied as part of closing their books. They organize the many versions of their data models that are constantly evolving in response to changing market conditions. Without the information workers, modern banks could not operate with any efficiency, nor could they comply with government regulations that ensure fair reporting of their activities.

Energy/oil and gas

Long-time stalwarts of business-scenario planning, oil companies practically invented the discipline. Used as a way to aid the decision-making processes of the energy companies, the scenario planning models typically looked at how the global energy markets would respond to real and hypothetical political changes among nations. More than just a group of smart people imagining situations, the scenario planning of the energy companies is a science unto itself. It's information-driven, almost to a fault.

But the scenario models of energy companies aren't the only ways information workers contribute. The more mundane everyday business operations of multinational companies require hyper-flexible software systems that can react to constantly changing conditions. Knowledge-based systems for connecting people, overseeing seismic and drilling projects, and maintaining billions of dollars in oil rig and refinery operations are dependent on experienced knowledge workers who create and maintain the data models, geography taxonomies, and accounting codes that fuel their business operations.

In the past few years, I've worked with data architects and data stewards at major oil companies who are working with data-intensive software systems that are a decade old. I've also worked with ontologists and taxonomists at those same oil companies who are working to build the next generation of knowledge systems — many of which will be based on Semantic Web technologies.

Aiding Information Workers with the Semantic Web

Information workers and information-driven companies have existed without and are not dependent upon the availability of Semantic Web technologies. However, each of the information worker roles and information-driven industries previously described are already benefiting greatly from emerging technologies of the Semantic Web.

Search optimization

One of the most important core business functions in the publishing industry is to assist customers in finding the right information at the right time. Unlike a search performed via a search engine like Google, the publishing industry depends on very rich and sophisticated taxonomies to guide its customers to the right content. Whereas the typical search engine employs sophisticated algorithms to find search terms and frequency, publishers categorize their content according to term lists, keywords, and data models. Historically, organizing and tagging content have largely been manual tasks. Partially automated techniques depend on software to categorize this content according to nested taxonomies of words, similar to a traditional thesaurus.

Newer technologies coming from the Semantic Web field are aiding these processes in several ways:

- The process of automating the classification of documents is now being driven by much more powerful Natural Language Processing (NLP) algorithms. Although NLP itself predates the Semantic Web, newer NLP approaches use Semantic Web–based ontologies as a way to seed their data models with more dynamic and powerful taxonomies.

- The output of NLP systems in the publishing industry has traditionally been fed into standard relational data models, but newer approaches populate RDF databases with graph data that's far more flexible and more easily navigable.

- The old way of specifying master files was usually done with relatively flat word lists, generally as text documents. Newer master file structures are actually encoded as proper ontologies with all the additional richness and power of a complete business logic for linking word descriptions.

The business benefits of the Semantic Web technology for search optimization are not revolutionary per se, but the incremental benefits do impact the bottom line. Customers of the publishing companies that use Semantic Web technologies — such as Thomson Reuters, Dow Jones, Elsevier, and Time Inc., to name a few — experience faster and simpler navigation of paid content and are generally more satisfied with the services that they already subscribe to. In some cases, publishers are able to offer more customization, more features, and higher value service levels. The net effect, of course, is more revenue.

Business intelligence

Business intelligence solutions are broadly part of the $10-billion decision-support market category. These systems are built and employed to aid decision-makers with scenario planning, forecasting, visibility into operational systems, analysis of market conditions, and various kinds of reporting. The business intelligence and decision support systems can service and support all types of organizations, including commercial businesses as well as governmental agencies. For decades, these decision support systems have depended on the relational database as their central data management software. In fact, decision support is one of the main reasons why the relational database was invented. The structure of data in those relational business intelligence systems has historically taken one of two forms: the normalized model or the multidimensional star model. Multidimensional models make up the vast majority of those data models today.

Semantic Web systems are improving upon the business intelligence category in both incremental and revolutionary ways. For many of the classical business intelligence systems, the investment in the multidimensional data model approach is too entrenched to change quickly: Systems have been optimized for that data structure for nearly 20 years. But incremental improvements have been embraced where graph data — like RDF and OWL — can aid in the uptake of unstructured documents into the classical business intelligence systems. Using the Semantic Web in this way is an incremental but important way to improve business intelligence systems.

On a more revolutionary front, some newer decision support systems are being built entirely around the Semantic Web data structures. The advantages of Semantic Web data structures are particularly valuable in industries that face exceptionally dynamic data that needs to be assembled in new ways without the overhead of rigid multidimensional data models. Life sciences, defense, and disaster preparedness are all areas where newer business intelligence systems are rapidly moving toward a Semantic Web–based approach.

The benefits of the Semantic Web for business intelligence are many-fold, but the dominant factors tend to prevail when the industry or market has special data needs. For example, in the life sciences industry, researchers from all sorts of different companies and universities are constantly generating new research data. Sometimes this research data is proprietary and secret, but increasingly there's a wealth of public data becoming freely available in the public domain. The challenge for researchers is to be able to consume this free data and rapidly make effective use of it. Semantic Web formats like RDF and OWL are ideal because they can be used as a place to easily put data coming in very diverse formats and structures. Once the data is in the Semantic Web format, new links and analysis can be performed on that diverse data without a lot of overhead caused by rigid multidimensional data models. This method produces better research analysis faster, which can be the difference between finding a patent on a new drug or being a has-been.

Similarly, the defense industries from most of the large nations use Semantic Web data as a place to consume and analyze open-source intelligence gleaned from public sources. Disaster preparedness systems built by government agencies and university systems use Semantic Web business intelligence systems to deliver more flexible analysis because, in times of crisis, it can be very important to consume unexpected data very quickly without having to rebuild data models and recompile software applications. These benefits of adaptability, agility, extensibility, and flexibility may matter more for some than for others, but for those who place a premium on those attributes in business intelligence, the Semantic Web technologies are very attractive.

Metadata management

The challenges of metadata management are known to only a few but are felt by many. Typically accounted for in the $5-billion software integration market, the metadata management problem surfaces whenever two or more software systems are linked together. At a very basic level, the issue has to do with the problem of relating the structure of one set of information with the structure of another set of information. This problem is a required part of integrating software systems, and integrating software systems is now a required part of doing business in any large company.

Today, most integration technologies have some level of metadata management. A few even separate the discipline into its function. For example, several commercially available and popular systems employ a metadata management repository that acts as a central storehouse of all metadata used in an integration platform. The features of the metadata repository might include the import and export of various formats and sophisticated version management of all kinds of metadata, including data definitions, file formats, software programming interfaces, business processes, and so on. Existing popular metadata repositories have been built using relational database technology, which has yielded some successes and many limitations.

The main underlying limitation with using relational subsystems is that the more flexible you try to make them, the less you can leverage the inherent power of the data models. To put it another way, a very powerful metadata system has to have a level of modeling flexibility that isn't inherently available in the relational database.

Some newer metadata management systems that use the power of the Semantic Web are beginning to emerge. The benefits that these systems yield come from the ability to enable extremely rich modeling while maintaining a built-in dependence graph that can be used to find how all the millions of metadata items are related to one another. When based on the Semantic Web, this dependency model is in a standard and portable format with well-known algorithms for finding and navigating the dependencies. Although some companies have been able to force similar capabilities into older technology, the Semantic Web approach holds much promise for raising the bar substantially for what you can expect from flexible, extensible, and traceable metadata repositories.

Data accuracy and quality

The bane of any business executive is inaccurate data. It seems that there's a regular outpouring of retracted financial statements, investor reports, and sometimes bad earnings announcements that impact the valuation of many public companies. More often, the public doesn't hear about the cases where bad customer data or bad product data cost a company millions.

Existing traditional approaches to fixing data quality are generally provided for with rule-based systems that trap bad data and then supply a fixed version of it. Other modern approaches use a statistical technique that looks for clusters of data and then reports to you the statistical outliers, which are usually good indicators of bad data. A semantics-based approach uses a different technique: first attempting to organize data according to the concepts that the data appears to belong to, and then normalizing that same data based on consistency rules that can be inferred from other related data.

No particular approach to data quality cleansing appears to be entirely dominant. Each technique excels in its own problem domain, but the Semantic Web concept-based approach has been proven to provide better data quality and cleansing operations in very complex data domains such as product and business data, where the conceptual alignment of terms may be the best way to find like items in a sea of noise.

Enterprise content visibility

Second only to the problem of having data that you think is correct but isn't is the problem of not being able to get the data that you know is there somewhere. For content management, the management of documents, there are two important markets to watch: enterprise content management (ECM) and information lifecycle management (ILM). The ECM and ILM markets combined are worth close to $3 billion. ECM is focused on the management of content for Web site pages and corporate business documents. The ILM market also covers that type of content but focuses on the deep storage part of the problem, essentially dealing with the archival problem. Most medium-to-large-size businesses have one or more ECM solution (Microsoft essentially gives one away called SharePoint), and most large businesses will have some type of ILM strategy. The biggest and most complex content visibility issues come from companies or government agencies that have several of each kind of system.

Technically speaking, a single ECM or ILM system may contain several terabytes of data (the entire print collection of the U.S. Library of Congress would consume about 10 terabytes of space), and most large companies have several ECM systems and several ILM systems comprising the content equivalent of many petabytes (several hundred U.S. Libraries of Congress) — that's a lot of data. That much data is difficult to search, organize, and find things in. Making matters worse is that each software system that holds a fragment of the big picture would typically have its own taxonomy, term list, search algorithms, and underlying software engine.

Semantic Web technologies can be used as a kind of enterprise ontology to unify the taxonomies of different content systems and provide a single data model to retrieve content through. I've personally been a part of several projects where OWL and RDF have supplied a common ontology to bridge ECM systems from Microsoft, IBM, and Oracle, as well as some home-grown proprietary ECM systems from a major aerospace company. This kind of shared visibility and unified view is very difficult — if not impossible — to achieve without a rich, flexible ontology language.

Forecasting the Information Worker of Tomorrow

In some ways, information workers of tomorrow will look a lot like the information workers of today. However, there will be an increased level of appreciation and specialization of the information worker roles as more business executives become aware of their importance. Most of the jobs that I describe in this chapter have only come into being since the late 1990s, and I'm among the first to point out that this collection of jobs is really a new category of worker — not quite traditional IT people and not quite traditional businesspeople. More and more businesses will start to become more effective at defining these roles, recruiting for them, and incentivizing their best people to take those extremely important information worker jobs.

Tomorrow's information workers will still be working with data models, taxonomies, master files, master data, and data quality tools, but those formats and tools will continue to evolve. In the future, there will be many more formats using RDF and OWL. Generations beyond may be using new business rule standards and formats that haven't yet been invented. One thing that's for certain is that things must change. There is simply too much new information being generated every year to keep using the current generation of information formats successfully — new innovation and more powerful formats are necessities, not wishes.

The good news for information workers is that instead of manual scripting and 1980s-era data formats, the Semantic Web brings a new generation of formats and tools that can make them more productive, more connected, and more innovative. In light of the many generations of information workers to come, we're still at the earliest and most rudimentary beginnings today. The Semantic Web is not the destination: It's merely the next step.

Chapter 11

Discovering the Enterprise Semantic Web

*Y*ou're surrounded by them every day, but most people have no idea just how dependent they are on enterprise software systems that big businesses run. Swipe your credit card at Starbucks for a coffee, and millions of electrons fire up inside software from IBM and Oracle. Ride a bus in most major cities and your movements are being followed through a satellite and software from IBM, Oracle, or Microsoft. Buy some milk at your local supermarket and the inventory software automatically calls for a bit more milk replenishment on the next shipment. Even when you're watching television at home, your channel selections are copied into large data warehouses in Florida to report on how many people are watching. Yes, enterprise software isn't just somebody else's problem: Everyone is influenced by it.

But enterprise software is complicated and challenging. Professionals labor their entire careers on projects to build it, billion-dollar companies rise and fall selling it, and implementing it results in far more failures than successes. Enterprise software is as complicated and important as anything that humanity has created. Our biggest achievements — space travel, particle accelerators, humanitarian aid programs, and so on — wouldn't operate without it.

The Semantic Web is already being inserted into the biggest and most complicated enterprise software programs in the world. This chapter explains a little bit about how those enterprise systems work and why they need more of the Semantic Web.

Discovering the Roles within the Software Industry

The software industry is a big, dynamic, and borderless space, but people still try to draw boundaries around the different kinds of software as a way to segment the industry. For example, most observers make a distinction between business applications and software infrastructure. A *business application* is software that's predominantly used by a nontechnical business person as part of an everyday job. These business applications might include the cash registers at your favorite retailer or restaurant, the payroll systems at a big company, or the software that helps buyers manage the inventory for stores like the Gap, Macy's, and Wal-Mart. These applications usually have a specific function and businesspeople to interact with them throughout the duties of their jobs.

In contrast, *software infrastructures* rarely have businesspeople using them directly. Instead, the infrastructure is built and maintained by technical specialists who work for the same companies as the businesspeople, but who focus entirely technical specialties. Infrastructure software may include the database management systems that store the application data, the middleware systems that operate like the plumbing in your house by connecting appliances running in different rooms, and security systems that centrally track and authorize businesspeople using all different kinds of applications.

The purpose of a business application is to provide a business function — like making payroll, distributing healthcare benefits, or tracking a package. The purpose of infrastructure software is to provide a technical function — like storing data on a hard drive or sending a message from one datacenter to another. The Semantic Web does not supply any unique business function: It's inherently about providing new and more efficient technical functions.

In Chapter 10, I describe in some detail the role of information workers in Global 2000 businesses, but infrastructure developers are not part of the definition I provided. Infrastructure developers are hard-core technology experts: They may have a specialty or be a generalist, but they're predominantly concerned with the technology itself. Usually, the infrastructure developer isn't expected or needed in the business discussions. As you know, infrastructure developer is very different from the information worker (business analyst, taxonomist, corporate librarian, ontologist, and information architect) who absolutely must deeply understand the processes and models of the business.

Infrastructure developers are a lot like surgical specialists — they're not usually concerned with why a system exists or any measures of its overall health. They're the deepest experts in a particular field and a particular set of tools. In practice, infrastructure software specialists tend to orient around platforms (databases, middleware, security); or languages (Java, .NET, Ruby); or vendors (Oracle, IBM, SAP, Microsoft). Improving the productivity and practices of these specialists is the focus of Semantic Web in enterprise infrastructure systems.

Creating Semantics for Enterprise Systems

Nobody but academics enjoy the Semantic Web for its own sake. The Semantic Web has to bring some value to people's jobs or lives for it to matter at all. Enterprise infrastructure software is already a maturing area with known challenges and solutions. To the extent that Semantic Web is important, it should provide some unique value to things that people are already doing, or even eliminate the need for things that people spend time on. This section describes some existing areas of software infrastructure work that the Semantic Web can dramatically transform and improve.

Semantics for data integration

Ever since the world's second computer was built, there has been the need for data integration. What is today a $3-billion software market only scratches the surface of the data integration problem — far more data integration projects are still taken care of the way they always were: with brute-force custom-coded solutions that employ armies of skilled labor.

Data integration challenges come in many shapes and sizes. The basic requirement for data integration is to enable the data of one system to work effectively inside a completely different system. As I describe in Chapter 6, this seemingly innocuous requirement is beset by plenty of landmines in the syntax, structure, and semantics of the data. Data integration software is built to handle all of these complexities and is therefore quite complex. The Semantic Web can help, but not in all areas.

Because the business applications that companies wish to integrate come in so many shapes, sizes, and architectures, many different styles of data integration are used in the real world. As seen in Figure 11-1, business applications may sometimes be integrated at the database tier, the logic tier, or sometimes even the interface tier (not shown). Applications may sometimes need to have nearly instantaneous integration, and sometimes it may be more appropriate to integrate on daily or weekly cycles. Sometimes data integration occurs from many systems into a single large system, and sometimes data integration needs to replicate data equally among many different systems.

Being complex, the data integration marketplace has several different kinds of specialty areas, including

- **Extract, transform, load (ETL):** Technology for making massive amounts of updates from one system to another as fast as possible.

- **Enterprise information integration (EII):** Technology for merging and reading data from many sources at once.

✔ **Data replication:** Technology for keeping databases in perfect synchronization at all times at any given moment.

✔ **Data services:** Technology for creating components inside a service-oriented architecture (SOA) that expose composite data components as Web services.

✔ **Object-relational mapping (ORM) toolkits:** Technology for developers to build their own data objects inside custom applications.

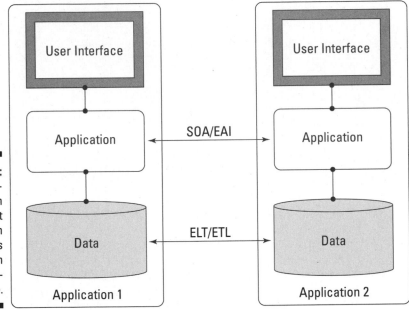

Figure 11-1:
Data integration from different places in the business application architecture.

Semantic Web technologies may have a role to play in each of these data integration market areas, but it's unlikely that the Semantic Web will have a transformative effect in these existing market categories. Because most of the established data integration marketplace is strongly driven by performance-optimized solutions, the Semantic Web technology set is at an inherent disadvantage because it always requires additional processing overhead.

For example, ETL technologies are predominantly judged on the raw performance of moving and transforming massive amounts of data, and they have been optimized to eliminate unnecessary overhead in their processes. The Semantic Web offers nothing in terms of performance gains to ETL; in fact, it's just the opposite — Semantic Web is such a new technology that it isn't at all strongly optimized in relative terms. But all is not lost for the Semantic Web: Large gains can still be made in the data integration space using Semantic Web technologies. Table 11-1 shows how.

Table 11-1	Semantic Web for Data Integration
Existing Data Integration Challenge	**Semantic Web Opportunity**
ETL and replication solutions are typically part of a larger solution that may include business intelligence, analytic applications, or other data integration solutions — but incompatible system metadata results in lost productivity and unplanned system outages.	Leverage OWL/RDF as a common metadata framework for enterprise infrastructure (because it's so powerful and expressive) and derive substantial new benefits from higher reuse, better developer productivity, and end-to-end impact analysis features that prevent unforeseen technical outages.
EII, Data Services, and ORM solutions typically offer developers a way to create a new data model that maps to many underlying sources, but these new data models either (a) are standard formats with weak expressiveness, or (b) have powerful flexibility but no portability outside a specific vendor toolkit.	Leverage OWL/RDF as a data model view layer so that developers can build their unifying views in a format that is both highly expressive (powerful) and exceptionally portable (reusable).

The most practical path forward for businesses to receive benefits from the Semantic Web in data integration use cases is for technology vendors like IBM, Oracle, and Microsoft to begin using the technology within their already popular data integration solutions. However, that process will only begin to accelerate when the customers of those solutions demand the productivity, openness, and flexibility benefits that the Semantic Web will yield.

 Finally, it must be noted that the long-term promise of the Semantic Web for data integration is actually to displace existing tools, not to make them better. The central challenge with any of the existing mainstream data integration tools is in the physical integration of differing data syntaxes, data structures, and data semantics. The central benefit of the Semantic Web data languages is that, after data is in those formats, they largely eliminate the difficult and complex brute-force design work required to make different data work together. If you haven't already, check out Chapters 9 and 10, where I discuss how RDF and OWL data can be easily recombined in new ways.

The most optimistic Semantic Web advocates see a future where most business software applications make their data available in Semantic Web formats. After this utopian ideal materializes, the need for traditional data integration tools will begin to fade away. In this vision, the RDF/OWL data would be directly accessible from the business applications and that data could be easily linked, joined, and reused without having to rely entirely on infrastructure developers to manually connect the data together in advance.

Although this optimistic vision is absolutely possible, it remains improbable for the foreseeable future. The reality of business applications is that they're infrequently upgraded after they're installed, and the application vendors rarely add features for purely altruistic reasons. For those reasons, it will probably be decades before Semantic Web technology will even begin to displace the need for even some of the more conventional data integration solutions that are around today.

Semantics for service-oriented architectures

One of the hottest markets in enterprise infrastructure is the service-oriented architecture (SOA) market. Since 2001, the SOA market has been building and building based on the promises of lower-cost and more flexible integration. Unlike the data integration technologies, the SOA technologies are built primarily to integrate business applications at their logic layers using messages and transactions. Historically, these kinds of integrations have been fulfilled by technologies called enterprise application integration (EAI) platforms, but SOA raises the bar on features and offers a more standardized way to ensure long-term flexibility.

As a technology, a typical SOA is actually made up of several subsystems that comprise the whole solution. Just as with the data integration marketplace, the Semantic Web is not a replacement or panacea technology for SOA. Instead, the Semantic Web benefits may be selectively applied to certain SOA components for incremental benefits.

Any enterprise SOA has an enormously complex collection of metadata that's required to make the solution work. Inside these SOA platforms there's always some type of metadata repository to govern the lifecycle of these assets. The Semantic Web can't replace this SOA repository, but it can provide substantial new capabilities to improve how these subsystems work. Today, large SOA providers such as IBM and Oracle are using RDF and OWL to augment the functionality of their SOA metadata management subsystems. These uses for Semantic Web technology can be as simple as proving a better way to annotate existing SOA metadata, or as comprehensive as using the RDF/OWL as the primary metadata model for expressing the relationships among SOA assets. Large vendors and smaller niche vendors will no doubt be offering more Semantic Web capabilities inside SOA repositories in the years to come.

A related but distinct area within SOA is the registry. Like the repository, the SOA registry is comprised of mainly metadata, but unlike the repository, the registry's purpose is to enable the runtime and design-time discovery of active services that are available for use. Whereas the SOA repository is like a file cabinet for placing items, the SOA registry is like the Yellow Pages directory that you use to locate services. If you need to brush up on your SOA fundamentals, you can find out all you need to know about from the recently updated 2nd edition of *Service Oriented Architecture For Dummies* (Wiley).

Because the Semantic Web is an excellent way to create powerful taxonomies and data models, as you discover in Chapter 10, you can guess that these RDF/OWL formats can also be a powerful way to store the structure of SOA Web services and publish them for consumption. Instead of depending entirely on the limitations of XML Schema, or the limited power of UDDI's (Universal Description, Discovery, and Integration) TNode approach, the OWL/RDF semantics can empower SOA developers to write more dynamic programs that can locate and leverage Web services more independently and with higher accuracy.

Some vendors are also exploring ways to use Semantic Web technology to generate business processes at runtime. Instead of the way the BPEL (Business Process Execution Language) standard works today — where the developer must define the process in advance — it's possible to construct business processes on-the-fly by using inference engines to make the data-level bindings more automatic. Although these highly dynamic use cases aren't for every business, some companies that depend on close operations with partners can use this Semantic Web extension to BPEL as a way to be more flexible and dynamic.

Again, the Semantic Web does not displace the need for SOA: It merely offers a better alternative to basic XML as a metadata layer when the situation calls for it.

SOA is a quickly growing market that is already worth billions, but critics are quick to point out that SOA hasn't fundamentally made working with data any easier. Using SOA is akin to pressing harder on the gas pedal when you're driving down a dark road without your headlights on: You need lights, not more speed! The Semantic Web is one way to shine more light on the data-level issues inside SOA. The aforementioned uses for Semantic Web in the SOA registry, SOA repository, and SOA process engines are all ripe for semantics.

Likewise, the data integration use cases like data services can inject semantics into SOA as a kind of canonical data model for XML messages. Unlike the limited power of XML, the RDF and OWL models can supply a genuine data framework for viewing and retrieving data inside a SOA architecture. Someday, the SOA may even be the preferred place to access data — bypassing the database and SQL for a more middle-tier, silo-less approach for data. Nonetheless, that kind of major shift in technology is still far away.

Semantics for business intelligence and data warehousing

Despite guidance from database vendors, few businesses store all their data in a global single database. Mergers and acquisitions, upgrades, legacy systems that are essential and can't be phased out, internal politics, and simple common sense ensure that multiple and heterogeneous databases will continue to exist for the foreseeable future. Much of the useful information in many organizations is contained in the spreadsheets and single-user databases on users' desktops, and this reality is also unlikely to change.

Yet, organizations recognize that the quality of their information is a key competitive factor. Streamlined internal information flows and high-quality reporting are considered essential to a modern business — but the required information is fragmented, held in several online transaction processing (OLTP) databases and dozens or hundreds of small, hand-crafted reporting systems, all of which have different definitions of terms as well as different scopes, user interfaces, and goals.

A data warehouse aims to crystallize all of this different information into a single, central system, with real-time querying of data properties based on frequently updated operational data. These online analytical processing (OLAP) systems may store many terabytes of data and support queries from thousands of users. A data mart is a smaller version of a warehouse, with its structure optimized for a particular department or business function; these may still run to tens or hundreds of gigabytes.

A typical data warehouse or data mart contains three components:

- A relational database optimized for queries
- One or more multidimensional aggregations stored in some custom data structure, typically a hypercube
- A way of transforming data from multiple OLTP schemata into a single schema for the warehouse

The optimized relational database typically uses a star or snowflake schema. A star contains a single, large table of facts, and several dimension tables that map identifiers to values. There may be several separate stars in one warehouse. A four-dimension example for a retailer is shown in Figure 11-2.

The fact table holds identifiers for the various dimensions and numeric values. Rows contain the finest level of detail available through the warehouse. Each dimension has one associated dimension table that holds all its data. In this example, there are four dimensions: product, location, time, and payment method. This dimensional modeling approach allows a user to move between levels efficiently and to drill down to more detailed information. Sometimes a dimension table is complex enough to be split into its own star. This split produces a snowflake schema, as shown in Figure 11-3.

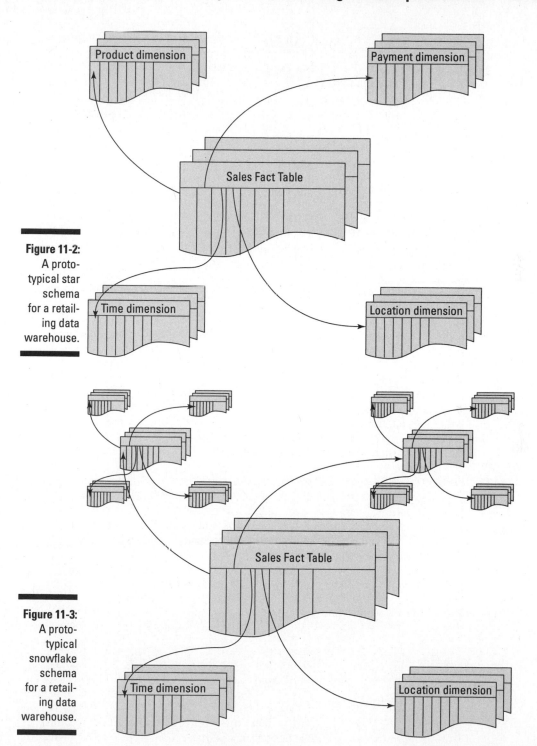

Figure 11-2:
A proto-
typical star
schema
for a retail-
ing data
warehouse.

Figure 11-3:
A proto-
typical
snowflake
schema
for a retail-
ing data
warehouse.

Both the star-schema approach and the more complex snowflake approach are built with relational databases. As I describe in Chapter 5, relational databases are good at storing large volumes of similar data and retrieving small parts of that data. They're less successful at calculating summaries, such as totals, over large parts of that data. As a result, other types of technology have been created for storing and aggregating those summaries. Multidimensional OLAP cubes allow summary data to be queried more quickly and efficiently than any other technique.

A typical cube has three dimensions — for example, time, location, and payment method. If it's divided up on all three dimensions into many tiny cells, it can store combinations of three OLAP dimensions in those cells. Each cell corresponds to one possible combination of values. A multidimensional cube is simply a cube with more than three dimensions. It's more difficult to visualize, but simply allows the same cell construction with more complex fact tables.

Business intelligence, reporting, and analytic applications use cubes and the underlying OLAP database as alternative ways of retrieving information. Top-level summary information is usually obtained from the cube; as a user drills down to smaller amounts of data, queries are run against the underlying relational database.

When typical business intelligence (BI) and analytic systems work with star-schema, snowflakes, and OLAP cubes, they typically have to work directly against the physical structures of that data. These physical tables, as you can well imagine, may be very complicated to navigate and understand. Very few businesspeople or information workers are productive when working against the raw physical sources of data warehouses.

Newer, more advanced BI solutions offer some layers of indirection; some vendors even call these indirection models a "semantic layer." But what these BI solutions are really doing is allowing the BI developers to create more business-friendly logical dimensions and fact tables on top of the physical fact tables and dimensions. Although this is incrementally useful, it doesn't change the reality that fact tables and dimensions are an extremely unnatural way of looking at business data. Therefore, the BI and analytics industry as a whole continues to face much criticism about the specialty developers that have to be continually on-call for the businesspeople in order make truly useful BI dashboards and reports. This manual and labor-intensive solution is quite expensive for big companies.

Another challenge for these star-schema and cube-based analytic and data warehouse systems is their ability to work with semi-structured and unstructured data. Although these BI platforms have all generally evolved to work pretty well with relationally structured data, they haven't really applied any innovative methods to leverage unstructured and semi-structured data inside BI. These unstructured data requirements are becoming more important each year that the Internet becomes more pervasive and the more that large companies look to organize and use the enormous amount of documents that exist in parallel but disconnected systems. Thus, there are two important opportunities for the Semantic Web technology based to incrementally improve and expand upon BI and data warehouse systems, as shown in Table 11-2.

Table 11-2	Semantic Web for BI and Data Warehousing
Existing BI and Warehouse Challenges	*Semantic Web Opportunity*
BI and data warehouse tools usually require users to work on the physical data tables directly or sometimes through a dimensional logical layer. Both of these kinds of data models are extremely non-intuitive for business users to set up, query, and maintain, thereby causing enormously expensive and inefficient BI solution footprints.	Leverage OWL/RDF as a data model view layer so that businesspeople can build their enterprise data views in a more natural graph data format that is highly expressive (powerful), exceptionally portable (reusable), and strongly deterministic (important for formulating DBMS queries).
Businesses are placing a rising importance on their document-base content and making it part of the overall BI imperative. Unstructured and semi-structured content should be capable of being analyzed alongside normal data warehouse data in order to provide a more complete and accurate picture of the business-to-business leadership.	Leverage OWL/RDF as an intermediary format for parsing unstructured data into a more highly structured format. Because OWL and RDF are graph formats, the text parsers have an easier time extracting data into them, and the resulting data can be more easily combed for useful analytics alongside traditional warehouse systems.

Few, if any, vendors are pursuing this complementary vision of the Semantic Web augmenting the data warehouse and business intelligence platforms — at least not publicly. As you can see by the conceptual idea captured in Figure 11-4, the idea is really a loose coupling between the BI system, the data warehouse, and the Semantic Web technologies. The benefits are a simplified user interface for the businesspeople as well as an improvement in the BI system's ability to cope with documents and unstructured data.

Perhaps more interestingly, more efforts are being placed into newer business intelligence and analytic applications that rely entirely on the Semantic Web for infrastructure. As I point out in Chapter 10, these newer systems are being constructed because certain industries place a premium on adaptiveness, agility, and flexibility. For those who prize those attributes over raw speed and raw scale, it's possible to construct a purpose-build BI system to aid in decision support directly on top of Semantic Web repositories and data formats.

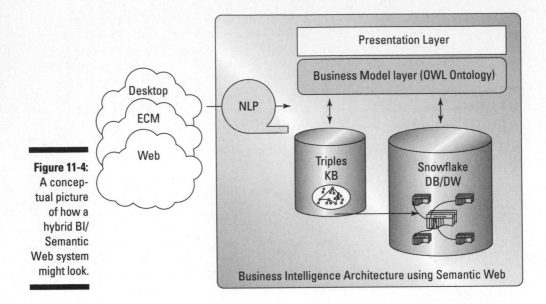

Semantics for enterprise governance

Governance is one of the most catchy, overused, and ill-defined buzz words in enterprise software. Depending on who you talk to, it could mean something as trivial as making sure you have a strong password, or something as all-encompassing as surviving a Sarbanes-Oxley audit by the government. Governance is big business today, but mostly for the professional services organizations that supply auditors and technical staff to help shore-up and stabilize the enterprise computing environment. In fact, governance is a broad collection of management, security, and audit processes that span many different kinds of IT systems.

For the purposes of this discussion, I refer to the following broad categories of IT governance:

✔ **Data governance:** The process of managing the complete lifecycle of data models, data records, data hierarchies, and data rules. Typically, this area is fulfilled by the master data management and metadata management marketplace.

✔ **SOA governance:** The process of managing the complete lifecycle of SOA metadata for design-time and runtime XML metadata. Typically, this area is fulfilled directly by the SOA platform provider, but specialty solutions such as Oracle Enterprise Repository and Software AG CentraSite also provide standalone solutions.

- ✔ **Security governance:** The process of enabling single sign-on infrastructure and a common identity framework across business systems. Typically, this area is fulfilled by the identity management software sector.

- ✔ **Application governance:** The process of managing the risk and compliance factors for how people can use or abuse application-level functions inside business software of any type. Typically, this problem area is addressed by the governance, risk, and compliance (GRC) marketplace.

- ✔ **Network governance:** The process of managing the hardware devices, their configurations, and their connections inside a large company. Typically, this problem is solved by systems management and configuration management databases like HP OpenView, Tivoli, and Oracle Enterprise Manager.

Each of these broad categories is treated somewhat independently from the others in the marketplace and, although some overlap does occur among them, they tend to solve different enough problems to describe how the Semantic Web can help in each area.

Each of the infrastructure governance categories I've defined have unique properties and work on substantially unique kinds of data. But they also share much in common. The fundamental questions that users of each of these systems want to know are

- ✔ Can I see an end-to-end picture of how things are logically connected?

- ✔ Can I generate a report to show me if something will break when I make changes?

- ✔ What happens if a newer version of this data becomes available?

- ✔ Are my systems ready to pass an audit?

In the case of SOA governance, those questions might apply to changing WSDL (Web Service Description Language) interfaces or BPEL processes. The data governance questions may apply to changing database schemas or accounting codes. Security governance staff may ask those questions about users, roles, and permissions, whereas my application governance personnel might be wondering about new functionality in the billing system and whether certain application users can now approve invoices.

Today, these solutions are partially addressed by dedicated systems, but I cannot use a SOA governance platform to watch my data models or a data governance platform to watch my segregated application function points. The opportunity for the Semantic Web is both within and across these existing governance solutions, as shown in Table 11-3.

Table 11-3	Semantic Web for Enterprise Governance
Existing Governance Challenges	*Semantic Web Opportunity*
With each existing governance category (Data, SOA, Security, Application, and Network), there's a common need for being able to identify technical and business concepts that can be easily connected and navigated. However, creating data graphs with XML or relational formats is complicated and non-deterministic, making it impossible to build a solution that can gracefully change over time.	Leverage OWL/RDF as the conceptual model for things (SOA artifacts, data model entities, devices, application functions, people, and roles, and so on) and then rely on the power of the inference engine to do dependency analysis and ensure that business rules are consistently and deterministically applied to the data about the environments being governed.
Governance as a market is still in its early days, as evidenced by the five unique areas mentioned in this section. Over time, the opportunity will be to link together governance practices from each of these areas into a common framework for governing data assets, SOA assets, security assets, application usage, and network assets from a unified place, but today's fragmented systems cannot offer that ability because of incompatible and inflexible software systems built without using Semantic Web metadata.	Existing governance platforms could be abstracted into a single OWL ontology of assets, people, and policies and connected via a middleware for governance. Or alternatively, specialty governance solutions could employ OWL models from the beginning and continuously evolve into new areas by expanding the ontology and application functionality.

It's a near-certainty that the enterprise governance markets will continue to grow, thrive, and become even more important as regulatory pressures worsen. The opportunity for existing governance solutions to leverage the Semantic Web, even on a tactical basis, is quite strong. A few companies are already heading in that technical direction. But a larger challenge is looming on the horizon: the challenge of integrating the governance platforms. This may be a kind of long-tail problem that doesn't materialize for a decade or more, but some forward-thinking businesses are already investigating what it will take to align data governance with SOA governance with application governance, and so on.

Enterprise metadata on steroids

Data integration, SOA integration, and enterprise governance all depend on metadata. The common opportunity for Semantic Web technologies to assist those software markets swirls around the general metadata problem space. As I describe in Chapter 6, metadata can come in all shapes, sizes, flavors, and uses, and it comes with its own set of technical strengths and weaknesses. Until the Semantic Web, there really wasn't a viable candidate for making metadata interoperable in a one-size-fits all kind of manner. The universal promise for Semantic Web technologies in the enterprise computing sector is to leverage a powerful, deterministic, and flexible standard for defining system metadata — that's the common thread running throughout each of these enterprise Semantic Web use cases.

Discovering a Single Source of Truth for the Enterprise

For many years, enterprise IT departments have sought the ability to present a single view of truth about business operations to the business community. This single view of the truth would tie together disparate business applications into a rational and complete view of data about key business assets such as customers, products, supply chain operations, human resources, orders, and general ledger statements. This objective has spawned and fueled the significant IT spending patterns for many years. The client-server boom of the early 1990s, the ERP boom of the mid-1990s, and the business intelligence boom of the early 2000s have all, to a substantial degree, been an attempt to create a single global source of truth for businesspeople to understand their operations.

Unfortunately for businesspeople and IT staff alike, these attempts have yielded only incremental gains and in most cases have only worsened their problems. ERP systems for human resource planning, financial accounting, and customer relationship management have multiplied instead of consolidating. Business intelligence systems and data warehouses have been capable of solving only narrow business problems in specific domains, and innumerable one-off attempts to leverage enterprise information models have been too complex and were resounding failures. These effects haven't just been felt by businesses. State and federal governments have tried for the same goals and also had to abort their efforts.

This description of failure in meeting the larger goal of an enterprise source of truth is not to imply that ERP and BI systems have been failures; to the contrary, they've been quite successful in achieving more narrowly defined goals. The main enemy of a single source of truth has always been change. During the many months of any IT project, businesses change many times over. Changing market conditions drive business decisions like mergers, acquisitions, new products, new promotions, new accounting practices, new sales territories, and so on. ERP systems and BI systems can keep pace with that change in only very narrow circumstances, under just the right conditions, and with no small amount of effort to keep pace.

Every ERP or BI system is a terribly complex collection of software. Layers of business objects, business rules, data models, and application interfaces manipulate data along predefined execution paths. These predefined execution paths prevent easy changes. How can a system designed over the course of many years respond to a business's 180-degree turn on a moment's notice? It can't.

When ERP and BI systems depend on underlying relational models or hardwired business entities and contrived flex data elements, they cannot change midstream. To many people, the kind of desired flexibility required for generating and maintaining a single source of truth is an impossibility. Some have compared the single source of truth idea to the idea of trying to change a jet airliner's engines while it is flying: a nice idea, but a fantasy nonetheless.

Ontologies and the Semantic Web do not magically solve this decades-old problem, but they do offer an intriguing path forward to try yet again what some have deemed impossible. Semantic Web ontologies provide some new, unique capabilities that haven't been available previously: new capabilities that directly address some of the short-comings of previous attempts at a single source of truth. First, OWL/RDF ontologies provide a superset of data model expressiveness, which means they are technically capable of capturing the semantics of existing IT systems with lossless accuracy. Second, OWL/RDF ontologies are computationally consistent, which means that there is grounded unambiguous level of truth when interpreting them. Third, OWL/RDF ontologies can change in real time, which means that consistency can be maintained while changing or asserting new facts into the global data model.

The Semantic Web is not itself the Holy Grail for an enterprise source of truth, but it does offer compelling clues to what the next stages of that journey might look like. So far, there have been several early tries at using Semantic Web languages for these purposes, and some early patterns are emerging. In the following sections, I look at these early patterns and give you some pros and cons to consider about their usefulness.

OWL knowledgebase

An OWL knowledgebase can describe data/records, schema, and business rule–type metadata within a single repository that can be always kept consistent. In this approach, the data models contain taxonomic/schema concepts connected to OWL-based records that are essentially RDF triples. After the data is accessible via OWL and in the RDF format, more powerful and expressive connections can be made on the records themselves to link them together, define datatype properties, and perform algorithmic inference operations on the data directly.

The defining characteristics of this approach are

✔ **OWL as the model representation:** The business models are syntactically and semantically held within an OWL framework.

✔ **Taxonomic and associative data linking:** The OWL is leveraged via a TBox and an ABox, which means that records must be converted and stored into the OWL/RDF formats. See Chapter 8 for more information on TBox and ABox components.

✔ **Mappings connect records to RDF triples:** A mapping directs extraction engines to convert business application data into RDF triples.

✔ **Data retrieval by the OWL knowledgebase:** The physical retrieval of data must now occur directly from the OWL knowledgebase.

✔ **Advanced inference may occur on data:** The OWL knowledgebase can classify and assert new facts (axioms) onto the data according to how the OWL taxonomic models have been defined.

The main substantial limitation to this approach is that the OWL knowledgebase does not and cannot ever scale to the levels of a relational database. Both in terms of query speed and in amount of data, the OWL knowledgebase is always behind a comparable relational database. (The facts behind this tradeoff are explained further in Chapter 12.) Secondarily, because the data itself is now part of an OWL knowledgebase, there will always need to be background processes that copy data from the point of origin into the knowledgebase. In other words, the data in this approach is always a copy (as shown in Figure 11-5) and not the actual data that is active in the business application.

Figure 11-5:
The OWL knowledgebase approach for a single source of truth.

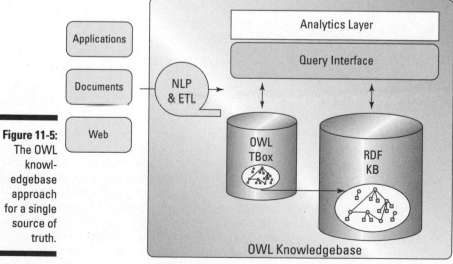

The benefits of this approach to business are in the analytic power of the OWL knowledgebase. If the business is willing to sacrifice scale and speed, the graph format of the data allows for much more powerful algorithms to manipulate the data inside the OWL knowledgebase. The most important new capabilities are the ability to continually evolve the data model, how the data is organized, and how the data is connected to other data — essentially overcoming the barriers to changing data models directly in the knowledgebase itself. These capabilities are reasons why some industries like life sciences, defense, and financial services are looking to OWL knowledgebases for use as decision support systems.

RDFS view layer

The RDFS view layer is technically similar to the OWL view layer, but with limited model expressiveness. In this case, the models are limited to the RDFS level semantics, as defined in Chapter 7. Instead of using OWL ontologies for defining the business view, the information workers use simpler taxonomies and business models that don't exceed RDF Schema's semantic capabilities. This method yields a simpler architecture for viewing a single source of enterprise truth, but it greatly limits how powerful the business models can be.

The defining characteristics of this approach are

- **RDF Schema as the model representation:** The business models are syntactically and semantically held within an RDF Schema framework.

- **Mappings connect concepts to records:** A mapping of RDF concepts links the model to underlying data schema such as relational models or XML Schema (RDF Façade, as shown in Figure 11-6).

- **Data retrieval by regular systems:** The physical retrieval of data still occurs in the legacy data tier using SQL, XQuery, or other commonplace data recovery techniques — although the upstream software clients may issue an RDF query such as SPARQL.

Limitations to this approach include a lack of modeling power and inability to manipulate data directly at the record level. Because the RDF Schema is acting only as a view, the physical records of business applications remain in their relational or XML formats. This would yield a good way to link different IT system data models, but the records themselves would not be any more unified than before. RDF Schema offers some advantages over relational modeling because it's a graph format that allows for class inheritance and a more intuitive way of structuring data hierarchies — which are commonplace in business systems — but its degree of power in defining complex concept associations is far less than OWL and only somewhat comparable to even UML.

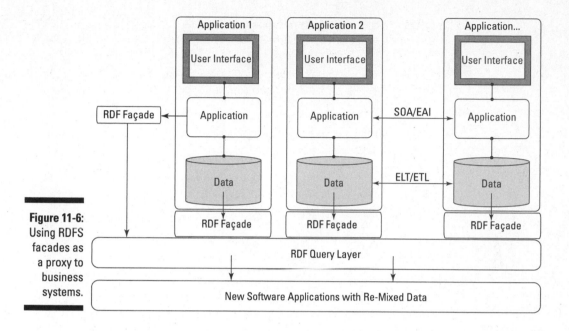

Figure 11-6:
Using RDFS
facades as
a proxy to
business
systems.

The benefits of this kind of approach can be useful as an alternative to some more commonplace data integration techniques, namely EII and data services, but the overhead and relative immaturity of the approach may make the benefits insufficient to justify the risks.

OWL view layer

One promising approach is to extend the RDF Schema layer in order to leverage OWL ontologies as a common logical modeling layer on top of existing enterprise business applications. Because OWL is technically capable of accurately expressing data models of any type, business models can be generated by information workers and mapped through layers onto existing IT systems. After it's in place, the OWL model becomes the consistent view through which enterprise data is used by client software that requires a unified single source of truth.

The defining characteristics of this approach are

- ✓ **OWL as the model representation:** The business models are syntactically and semantically held within an OWL framework.

- ✓ **Taxonomic models only:** The OWL is leveraged via a TBox only, which means that the data records are not converted and stored into the OWL format. See Chapter 8 for more on TBox.

✔ **Mappings connect concepts to records:** A mapping of OWL concepts links the ontology to underlying data schema such as relational models or XML Schema.

✔ **Data retrieval by regular systems:** The physical retrieval of data still occurs in the legacy data tier using SQL, XQuery, or other commonplace data-recovery techniques.

One limitation of this approach is that it leverages only the taxonomic power of the OWL ontologies. This limitation means that it would not enable deeper connections and linking to occur between the physical records. For example, I could create an ontology that says that two different relational database columns, CUST and ISV_PART, are both conceptually a corporate customer, but it would not enable me to say that two data records, ACME and ACME Consulting, are the same. Thus, I get the incremental benefits of conceptually linking many different kinds of schemas, but I can't directly link the physical records in the view itself.

Businesses can benefit from this approach most when they need to work directly with the data models as the dominant source of truth. Certain kinds of problems lend themselves to using the data model as a way of defining allowable relationships, views, and business rules, and OWL is a likely format for enabling that. Secondly, sometimes the business's main challenge is linking together many different applications from the schema level in order to know where data is and how to get at it; answering questions about what data you have and where it resides is sometimes the biggest part of a business's problem. Finally, giving information workers an exceptionally powerful, flexible, and dynamic way of building enterprise business domain models can move them beyond the limitations of other formats like relational databases, XML Schema, and UML (Unified Modeling Language), which aren't as expressive and far more brittle and inflexible than OWL.

RDF knowledgebase

Just like the OWL knowledgebase approach, the RDF knowledge base supplies a landing spot for data copied from other places. But instead of viewing that data via a powerful and expressive ontology, the RDF knowledgebase by itself only allows for RDF Schema–level models to be applied to the physical data.

The defining characteristics of this approach are

✔ **RDF Schema as the model representation:** The business models are syntactically and semantically held within the RDFS scope.

✔ **Data record–level linking:** The RDF triples are leveraged via the RDF repository directly, which means that records must be converted and stored into the RDF format. See Chapter 7 for more information on the concept of a triples store.

- ✔ **Mappings connect records to RDF triples:** A mapping directs extraction engines to convert business application data into RDF triples.

- ✔ **Data retrieval by the RDF knowledgebase:** The physical retrieval of data must now occur directly from the RDF knowledgebase via a query language such as SPARQL.

- ✔ **Some RDFS-level inference may occur on data:** The RDF knowledgebase can classify and assert new facts (axioms) onto the data according to how the RDF Schema models have been defined: for example, to build new classification schemes based on subsumption-level inference (see Chapter 7).

The benefits and limitations to this approach roughly mirror those of the OWL knowledgebase. Instead of working with a more powerful ontology language like OWL, the modeling formats are limited to the power of the RDF Schema model semantics. Although many people would prefer the more advanced ontology formats, others make the point that RDF by itself is less constricting and easier to work with. Essentially, RDF gives users a blank canvas with their data, and they're free to manipulate and recombine it without having to comply with possibly limiting data models. Whereas some information workers want the control to enforce consistency on the data through the ontology, others prefer the flexibility to add and retract facts in the knowledge base with fewer constraints. In those cases, particularly where there's a lot of previously unknown data that must be consumed, an RDF knowledgebase approach would be more desirable than an OWL knowledgebase.

Hybrid implementations

As the Semantic Web approaches evolve, knowledgebases will likely spawn hybrid capabilities that enable business to mix up these different styles (see Figure 11-7). There are valid business reasons why one source of truth may require powerful and consistent data models expressed in OWL, whereas other business drivers may require the flexibility to consume new RDF triples without constraining them to a particular business model. Likewise, the need to balance operational requirements might direct one solution down the path of viewing data in the place where it's used, whereas other requirements might necessitate copying data into a knowledgebase for more advanced analytics. The benefits of a Semantic Web–based approach is that these differing needs could be accommodated in a single platform, while still enabling the cross-pollination of data into different data views.

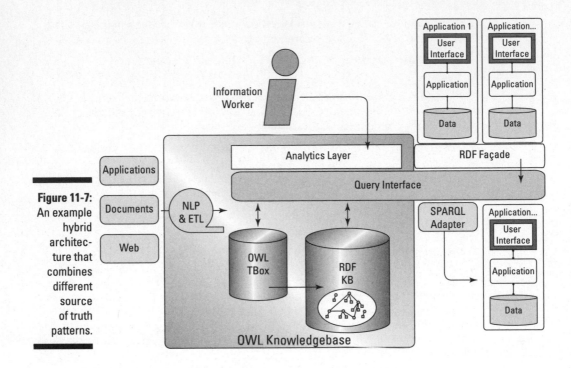

Figure 11-7:
An example
hybrid
architec-
ture that
combines
different
source
of truth
patterns.

Exploring Some Enterprise Semantic Web Use Cases

All the ideas presented in this chapter would be theoretical and mostly useless if there weren't real examples of the technology in action. Unfortunately
for researchers, many of the most interesting examples of the Semantic Web
are unpublished classified projects considered too strategic and too important to promote widely. Fortunately, a few companies are willing to share
their successes with the industry and have made all or part of their Semantic
Web projects public in one form or another. Many of the use cases presented
here were drawn from the growing collection of examples hosted by the W3C
Semantic Web Education and Outreach initiative.

NASA: Expert locator service

Like many large organizations, the U.S. National Aeronautics and Space
Administration (NASA) can sometimes have trouble locating the right people
for a particular job. Working together with Michael Grove from Clark &
Parsia, NASA has developed a Semantic Web application called POPS (People,
Organizations, Projects, and Skills) that aims to make it easier to find the
right people when you need them.

According to the use cases published on the W3C Web site and many public blogs, POPS application development started in the 2006/2007 timeframe and finally went live in the early part of 2008. At the time of launch, it used RDF data generated from internal NASA LDAP (Lightweight Directory Access Protocol) directories and other data sources to enable the correlation of people, their skills, NASA projects, and the organizations that fund those projects. The POPS application itself contains RDF data about 70,000 to 80,000 NASA employees and third-party contractors.

Instead of trying to change NASA's culture, the POPS application team worked hard to incorporate ways to augment typical business practices like calling co-workers for references. The POPS application works much like a social network, showing details about how the staffing manager is connected to the potential candidate. Even if they don't know each other, the staffing manager can call people she knows for references. Other benefits from using the Semantic Web include an easy-to-use and consistent data architecture (RDF) and the rapid integration of new source information (by converting to RDF and merging).

Eli Lilly: Targeted drug assessment

In the pharmaceutical industry, researchers are the main drivers of innovation and profits. Their work to find new drugs and chemical compounds are the first steps in a long process of producing medicines that help people stay healthier and live longer. But making new medications is a long and costly process. Often a drug that seems promising at an early stage may not produce the expected results later in the development cycle. Likewise, the costs for finding new compounds early in the stages of drug development are soaring to billions of dollars.

Data integration is a key part of the drug discovery process. Because the data about targets and drug compounds is analyzed at early stages to eliminate or select candidate drugs, the better the data is, the better the company's chances of making good decisions, saving money, and finding the right drug compounds early.

At Eli Lilly, the Semantic Web is used to extend the capabilities of the Target Assessment Tool (TAT). Scientists and researchers use TAT to evaluate candidate drugs in light of scientific and business requirements. Industry terminologies are stored and manipulated as RDF and OWL models. Other kinds of data models were not as efficient and flexible when working with the diverse data sources that TAT requires. Because RDF and OWL is a graph language, researchers can navigate through the relationships more naturally without having to use artificial keys and indices. The Semantic Web provides a more powerful way for the pharmaceutical researchers to work on data directly, discover information as they navigate the set of knowledge, and view all data that's related to the entities of interest.

Renault: Intelligent automobile diagnostics

The production of the technical documentation that's used daily in automotive repair shops for diagnostics and repair is an intricate process. It requires precise modeling of the workings of vehicles and the aggregation of data from many sources. These processes are further challenged by the growing complexity of cars, which is a consequence of their many electronic components.

Improving this process, as well as allowing new uses of the knowledge that gets produced, requires the availability of an increasing part of this information as machine-understandable data.

Implementing the linked data principles inherent to the Semantic Web is a first and very significant step. For example, data entities that are part of the field gain unambiguous identification — an obvious prerequisite for data integration — and existing data repositories get turned into simple services. These simple services can be achieved through unobtrusive methods with respect to the legacy systems involved (for example, the conversion of XML as RDF, RDF facades in front of SQL databases, and mapping between equivalent terms used in different systems).

After they're unambiguously defined, the terms of the published vocabularies can be safely used as metadata to describe the documentation, which can therefore be queried with SPARQL. On these easy-to-use services, you can implement the application that mechanics use to access the information they need for a given repair.

You then can build on OWL's greater expressivity to model more precisely the concepts of the field. For instance, defining with OWL the relations between car components, part failures, symptoms, diagnostic tests and failure rates, Renault has built a prototype diagnostic engine. Reusing a probabilistic induction tool developed in-house for other purposes, it computes on the fly procedures that minimize the total cost of diagnostics. This is clearly an example of the innovative applications that linked enterprise data and sharable Semantic Web–type modeling can make easier to develop.

Pfizer: A drug compound knowledgebase

Multinational pharmaceuticals like Pfizer fund hundreds of concurrent projects to develop new chemical compounds in the hopes of discovering some useful ones that can be used for new drugs. These companies spread risk by supporting projects at all different phases of the development lifecycle: Some compounds are very early in development, whereas others are quite mature with well-known attributes and behaviors. Most compounds developed don't reach the market in an approved drug or medication by a long shot, but that doesn't necessarily mean that they aren't useful in some situations.

Because these pharmaceutical companies end up with massive databases of drug compound information, most of which aren't being fully utilized, it raises the question of whether that existing research and knowledge can be mined for new uses or combined in new ways. Pfizer is trying a new Semantic Web approach to aggregate and mine its corporate knowledge of these drug compounds (some of which may be many years old or residing in different IT systems) in an effort to help scientists collaborate and reuse the knowledge gleaned from previous investigations.

Pfizer's approach is to keep the primary compound data records in their original source formats, but to export the key attributes as RDF. This is a kind of RDF view–layer approach as described earlier in this chapter. The benefits that Pfizer is happy about include a balance between the ease of maintenance and ease of use of the data. A version of the MIT SIMILE technology was leveraged to combine different RDF result sets and help the researchers make better decisions and find compounds that may have been cancelled for one project, but could still be useful in another. Without the Semantic Web technologies, it would be much more difficult for researchers to work effectively with such a huge body of information while remaining efficient and productive.

Finding more enterprise Semantic Web use cases

For more information about the use cases described in this chapter, and for additional information about more enterprise Semantic Web use cases like those in the following list, point your Web browser to the W3C Semantic Web Education and Outreach Web site at www.w3.org/2001/sw/sweo/public/UseCases. This site includes a large number of case studies, including those from the following companies and organizations:

- ✔ **Vodaphone:** Mobile content search and discovery
- ✔ **British Telecom:** OSS systems integration
- ✔ **Audi:** Manufacturing parts assembly
- ✔ **Chevron:** Oil and gas research knowledgebase
- ✔ **Cleveland Clinic:** Clinical research knowledgebase
- ✔ **UK Ordnance Survey:** Geographic referencing framework
- ✔ **AGFA Healthcare:** Radiological orders validation
- ✔ **Oracle:** Technology network search engine

Chapter 12

Scalable Architectures

• •

• •

Sometimes technical people take a little while to internalize the systemic advantages of the Semantic Web data formats: Simply put, it takes awhile to "get it." Newer ideas like making data available with Web identifiers combined with older ideas from artificial intelligence–like graph data networks and inference algorithms make for some unusual reactions to learning more about the Semantic Web. But eventually, as the power of this approach sinks in, folks naturally start to think about how to put it to work.

But then the reality of the Semantic Web sinks in — its Achilles heel and main weakness has always been *scalability*. Scalability means different things to different people, but for the purposes of discussing Semantic Web architectures, scalability questions are typically about the following:

✔ How much data the system can take

✔ How expressive the reasoning on the data can be

✔ How fast the system can calculate the newly inferred data

Since 2004, a wealth of new startups in the enterprise and consumer software sectors have looked to solve old problems in new ways using the Semantic Web. Entrepreneurs are increasingly looking at the Semantic Web as a technology that can give them an edge against more well-established businesses. But as soon as the technology is aimed at mainstream software problems and applications, they get a nasty wake-up call about the relative maturity of Semantic Web architectures. All that new data processing power of the Semantic Web comes at a price, and that's a price that most technologists haven't had to consider: data scalability.

This chapter builds on the topics covered in Chapter 11 and introduces you to the most important technical and scalability considerations you should think about when putting together your own plans for a Semantic Web application. I discuss the tradeoffs of using *inferencing* (calculating the newly inferred data and reasoning with it), and I cover the various ways you can reliably expose Semantic Web data to consuming applications. Finally, I conclude with a "buyer beware" message to urge you stay pragmatic when adopting Semantic Web technology — inflated expectations are the greatest cause of failure among most Semantic Web projects.

Recognizing That This Is Not Your Father's Database

As cool as the Semantic Web is, it doesn't change the fundamentals of software. Software requires programs for processing, places to store data, and user interfaces to work with it. Nothing fundamental has changed. But the infrastructure that people use to process and store Semantic Web data requires different tools than what long-time professionals are used to. In particular, working with RDF and OWL demands a different kind of database that has never been widely used before.

Mainstream relational databases have been around in roughly their same form since the early 1990s. The relational database core patterns were defined nearly a decade before that. Any software professional who has implemented commercial, scalable software must have used the relational database for the vast majority of his or her projects.

Relational databases have features that people simply expect to be there, but that aren't there yet for most OWL/RDF databases. Some of these expected features include

- Scalable query listeners
- Backup and fail-over utilities
- Bulk loading programs
- Multilevel security controls
- Flexible view management
- Embedded procedural programs and functions
- Powerful partitioning utilities
- Query planning and indexing wizard

The list could go on. It's not that the makers of OWL/RDF repositories are inferior, but most of the robust utilities and features of a relational database need to be rethought in terms of a new and different data structure. Security on a graph is different than security on matrixed data. Query processing and planning are different when inference is involved. The notion of what a view is and how to manage it changes when OWL ontologies enter the picture. Partitioning and indexing depend on how the data is written to disk, and optimizing disk writes for RDF data is different than the same features for relational data.

Of course, none of these concerns are stopping developers from prototyping. Heck, you don't even need an RDF database to prototype a Semantic Web application! One popular prototyping framework, Hewlett Packard's Jena toolkit, doesn't even require a database to work. But planning how an application can be successfully transitioned from one or two users to thousands of concurrent users takes a high level of engineering foresight, planning, and tooling. Simple logic dictates that Semantic Web database features will always be behind the curve when relational databases are the benchmark.

Noting Semantic Web Tool Patterns

Fortunately, not every Semantic Web application requires the maximum level of functionality offered by Semantic Web languages. Sometimes a specific part of a larger application can benefit from Semantic Web languages. Sometimes a large application requires a pervasive but relatively efficient part of the Semantic Web. And in those cases where a large application requires a substantial number of Semantic Web features, you can employ certain strategies to overcome some of the barriers to scalability. The following sections describe a few known and repeatable patterns for using Semantic Web alongside more traditional software systems.

Ontology as static metadata

An ontology in the OWL format can be used in many different ways. In Chapter 8, I describe how OWL can be used to model a domain and how the inference capabilities of OWL are used with that model to empower active data models. But OWL can also be used in a more static way.

OWL is itself a data model. Without using any inference features whatsoever, OWL is still a data model. You can build an OWL model and deploy it as an XML document without having to use any query or inference capabilities

at all. When used in this way, it is similar to how many software projects use
XML Schema or the Unified Modeling Language (UML) — as a conceptual
model for understanding a larger data set. Figure 12-1 shows a simplified
view of how you can use ontology management tools (like those described
in Chapter 9) to manage static OWL files, or OWL models in a DBMS, and the
links among them.

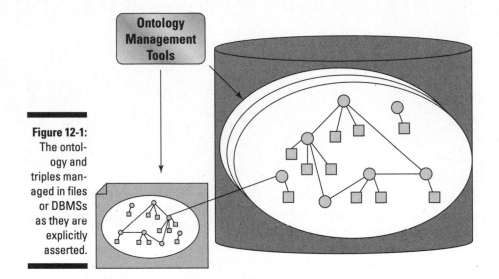

Figure 12-1:
The ontol-
ogy and
triples man-
aged in files
or DBMSs
as they are
explicitly
asserted.

Usually an application that requires a separate conceptual model has a
requirement to work with domain concepts, terms, entities, and data vocabularies independently from the physical data records. Healthcare applications,
financial systems, and decision support systems of all types often have these
kinds of requirements. OWL can be a very useful alternative to XML Schema
and UML because it has a more expressive structure (the standard for defining classes and relationships) than either of those formats.

Even though this general pattern for using OWL might not fully leverage
all the strengths of logic and inference that OWL can provide (which are
described in Chapter 8 and again later this chapter in the section "Scaling
Semantic Web Tools"), it's still sufficient to supply a robust and more standardized way of building model-driven applications. Importantly, it also
starts to enable high-level Semantic Web capabilities without the overhead
and costs associated with the scalability problem that a fully featured OWL
subsystem entails.

The U.S. Air Force Space Wing project

The U.S. Air Force Research Laboratory has developed DEEP (Decision Explanation Engine Platform) in support of the U.S. Air Force's 45th Space Wing Knowledge Management Initiative. Launch operations staff at the 45th Space Wing are required to make mission-critical decisions about whether to launch a vehicle into space based on large amounts of distributed, fragmented information. DEEP first worked to solve the biggest issue facing launch operations by using OWL ontologies to unify fragmented and disparate data. The solution addressed the most pressing fragmentation issues first without any advanced inference, and only later added capabilities for decision reasoning: how to focus the ontology (or model) and reasoner on the subset of facts and relationships necessary to answer the decision-maker's question.

The tooling for this solution was the Modus Operandi Wave semantic data services platform, which applies an OWL semantic model to federated data that can enable a flexible and powerful search and query capability over real-time events for launch decision support. Modus Operandi President and CEO Peter Dyson emphasizes that, "Ensuring America's preeminence in space launch involves high tempo operations that rely on timely, trusted information. The 45th Space Wing is underway with an initiative to increase the level of integration of its disparate data sources. We are targeting this important and exciting challenge on the DEEP project in support of launch operations. The resulting new technology speeds the cycle time for making informed decisions."

Ontology as active metadata

Sometimes the system demand is for a much more powerful set of capabilities that include advanced reasoning algorithms for changing metadata structures on-the-fly. These kinds of systems are typically very dependent on having accurate up-to-date information on system events that could vary widely or change suddenly, with profound and complex implications to the behavior of the software application.

Some of the software applications described in Chapter 11 are good examples of active metadata systems. The Audi maintenance application uses business rules and ontology models to assess a vast array of potential problems, and the state of the software applications changes with each new data point added to the knowledgebase. Likewise, the targeted assessment models used by the pharmaceutical companies profiled in Chapter 11 rely heavily on the inferred combinations of proteins and drug compounds to inform scientists about the results that can be expected from new data as it becomes available. Of course, many of these active metadata problems can be solved with conventional software applications, but they would require developers to understand and code for all the possible combinations of data in advance — which is impractical for most complex systems and impossible for some.

A typical approach for solving these sorts of problems would be to leverage an OWL ontology reasoner to build an associative model for the ontology and build the inferred data from the data that has been asserted by the system. You can see in Figure 12-2 how the OWL model may contain explicit data (in black) and inferred data (using dashed lines) that is generated by inference engines. This level of sophistication and inference complexity leads directly to massive scalability limitations in large systems.

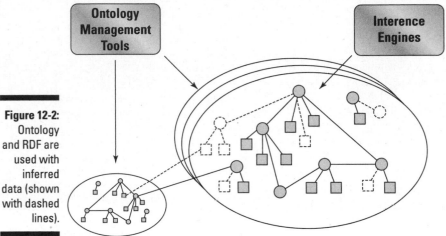

Figure 12-2: Ontology and RDF are used with inferred data (shown with dashed lines).

An active metadata approach that uses an OWL reasoning platform depends heavily on powerful, computationally intensive algorithms to compute inferences on data. Because these features are more intensive than simpler storage and query algorithms, they always require more overhead for processing. In some systems, the computations are calculated during the time that a query is asked, but for other systems, the calculations occur in the background. The advantage of applying inferences at the time of query is that you always get accurate inferred data, but the downside is that your query could take many minutes or even hours to answer. Active metadata systems that apply background calculations always have faster query responses, but the answers to your queries might contain information that is no longer accurate because the system might still be calculating the inferences in the background.

Most newer OWL systems can employ the background classification approach. Applications tend to have a stronger demand for fast query responses and can sacrifice accuracy in the short term. This approach also allows for the OWL-based systems to scale to reasonably large levels up to 10 billion RDF triples. Depending on the number of relationships and overhead in the model, that could be as many as a 50 billion database records.

For some applications, a billion records might be a lot, but for perspective, such a database could not even hold the names of all the citizens in China, never mind any additional attributes about them or relationships among them. This relatively low ceiling is just the nature of where scalability limits exist at this point in time.

Issues and concerns about how much data an RDF/OWL database can contain or query are only one dimension to consider. Equally important are the various kinds of operations you can perform on that data. For example, the algorithms used to infer the implications of deleting data are much more complex than those required for inserting new data. Likewise, updating existing records is computationally more difficult than inserting data. Sometimes the processes for retracting and updating are handled separately and in parallel to other database operations, and may necessarily take more time.

These performance considerations and further distinctions between the kinds of OWL/RDF database implementations are explained in more detail as part of the assessment strategies offered in Chapter 13.

Triples databases

Commercial databases that support RDF/OWL are still maturing and in a relatively early stage. The state of the market today is characterized by different technical approaches to working with vast amounts of RDF, and there haven't been any clear winning technologies defined as of yet.

RDF to relational mapping approach

One of the most conventional and mainstream approaches to working with RDF data is to leverage a typical relational database and simply structure it in a three-column table (for the RDF subject, predicate, and object parts of the triple) and then use SQL (structured query language) to retrieve the data. Technology frameworks consisting of pre-built Java classes for working with relational databases are commonplace as a way to enable this pattern. The Sesame project and Hewlett Packard's Jena software are popular frameworks that employ this approach. Likewise, many other projects have created their own implementations using a relational database and proprietary extensions for working with RDF.

Oracle hybrid approach

One of the software industry's most popular databases is the Oracle database. Primarily a relational system at its core, the Oracle system also offers an interesting hybrid implementation of an RDF/OWL database as part of its Enterprise Edition Spatial features. Oracle's Spatial subsystem is highly optimized for working with graph data due to the long-time demands from the geography and mapping industries. Because that system is already optimized for graph operations, it's a natural extension to include RDF/OWL support. Today, Oracle's implementation is in its third generation and arguably offers some of the most robust and feature-rich RDF/OWL capabilities because of its association with the exceptionally feature-rich core database platform.

Native RDF and columnar approaches

Other, more native RDF databases also exist. The Franz Technologies AllegroGraph database is a Java and Lisp-based platform that works natively with RDF triples on disk. Because of that company's long-time investment in native object-oriented databases, Franz implements a number of useful features for flexibly working with object-type systems inside the product. Likewise, the Franz team has some of the most advanced technology for working with Lisp, so companies and research teams using that programming environment naturally find a lot of synergy with that approach. Franz invests heavily in its core database but also builds semantic applications and APIs for enabling companies to make rapid progress on their projects.

An interesting development happening since 2006 has been that data warehouse appliance vendors are also starting to consider how they can optimize for RDF-driven analytic data warehouses. As described in Chapter 5, the data warehouse appliance usually employs a shared-nothing backend architecture (where hardware nodes, especially disk drives, are not shared with a single master process), which is particularly good for handing read-optimized queries on very large datasets. Vertica is one data warehouse appliance vendor that has demonstrated a columnar database (see Chapter 5) that works with RDF. One of the most popular warehouse appliances is the Netezza system: It also leverages a shared-nothing backend architecture and the company has also considered how it can optimize for RDF/OWL applications.

Another recent development has been the experimentation with distributed B+tree systems like Google BigTable, Yahoo! Hadoop, and specialty Semantic Web implementations like the open-source projects called BigData and Mulgara.

Whereas data warehouse appliances use grid software to manage dozens or even hundreds of compute nodes (each node with its own CPU, hard drive, and random access memory [RAM]), the biggest of all data grids are used to answer Web-based search queries. Both Google and Yahoo! have built massive data centers with thousands of interconnected servers that help answer the billions of questions that people send to them every day. Grounded in a popular algorithm called MapReduce, Google's BigTable and Yahoo!'s Hadoop both achieve incredible levels of scalability and reliability.

These columnar-style approaches are extremely promising because they are leveraging open frameworks like MapReduce for data scalability and federation. In contrast to many of the more proprietary approaches used by data warehouse vendors, there is more worldwide activity being applied to these open alternatives that could realistically produce the next big breakthrough in massively scalable Semantic Web computing.

In-memory approach

Another trend in triples databases has been to develop *in-memory systems,* which operate in random access memory (RAM) to avoid the extra overhead of disk-based input and output. These systems build the entire graph of RDF/ OWL inside the main memory of a software application and use that for the basis of answering queries. Because the main memory for most hardware platforms is limited to roughly 3GB and even more advanced systems only offer up to 16GB, another layer of data federation has to be used. Data grid technologies from Oracle Coherence and Gigaspaces can be used to link together main memory from several machines to achieve a virtual main memory footprint that exceeds the terabyte level. RDF/OWL databases that use this approach can support billions of triple in main memory, thereby achieving performance advantages over disk-based systems. One implementation of this approach is by Siderean Software, which uses RDF/OWL to build a graph of knowledge about content to aid more advanced searches.

Understanding the tradeoffs

Each of the approaches described in the preceding sections comes with tradeoffs:

- ✔ **The conventional RDF approach** with relational systems can be built with free software, but it's limited in size, scale, and flexibility.

- ✔ **The Oracle hybrid approach** offers the best overall robustness and features for commercial users, but it doesn't include some of the advanced capabilities offered by shared-nothing and main memory approaches.

- ✔ **The native RDF, columnar, and in-memory** approaches have compelling scalability attributes, but they typically require much more setup time and programming to be efficient in the context of an actual Semantic Web application.

Reasoners, inference engines, and rule systems

As I describe in Chapter 9, business rule engines are a natural part of the Semantic Web ecosystem. *Inference engines* are a special kind of rule engine that work on more narrowly defined logics and standardized formats. Implementations for inference engines can be wide and varied. The tuning and optimization for dedicated standalone inference engines (versus inference and rule platforms that ship within more mature products) can sometimes be a bit of a black art, but thankfully most of the RDF triples databases described in the previous section offer some built-in inference engines that scale with more predictable characteristics.

The following list describes the most common types of inference engine implementations:

- ✔ **Chain-based rule engine:** The most popular type of inference engine for OWL is built using forward or backwards chaining production rules. A production rule system that uses rule chains applies rules to data in a hierarchy, moving up and/or down the hierarchy to test the data and create new data when a rule pattern is triggered. Chain-based rule engines tend to operate very efficiently on smaller data sets and can be quite fast (sub-second) when there aren't many rules to apply. As data sets grow to become quite large, or the rule system gets quite complex, the rule chain approach can bog down easily and become the main bottleneck for applying inferences. Another limitation of rule-chaining approaches is more theoretical; they cannot guarantee the computational correctness of their aggregate inferences because one rule chain is not directly aware of another rule chain working on the same data. This correctness guarantee is important in only a few critical kinds of applications.

- ✔ **Tableau reasoning system:** Another common OWL reasoning technology is based on the tableau system. A *tableau reasoning system* applies inferences within datasets that are kept consistent as part of its core operations. Thus the tableau reasoning system can guarantee computational correctness, but it trades efficiency, especially on smaller datasets.

- ✔ **FOPC-based approach:** Some Semantic Web systems are based on artificial intelligence (AI) technologies that leverage a first-order predicate calculus (FOPC) for managing the units of data. One powerful advantage is that these FOPC-based approaches can seamlessly move between expressivity levels up to OWL and beyond, but there isn't a standard accepted way of defining the allowable expressivity levels beyond OWL. The Simple Common Logic (SCL) standard and Prolog programming language are based on this FOPC approach. FOPC-based applications typically place a strong emphasis on the reasoning capabilities of their systems and less importance on how consistent they are with any standards. Historically, all kinds of AI expert systems have used this approach for building really smart systems.

Finally, there are many different kinds of theorem provers, mostly in the university context, that specialize in different logic subsets. These theorem provers can be used to directly enable Semantic Web applications or similarly advanced AI systems that require very agile and adaptive data structures.

Scaling Semantic Web Tools

Although comparing different technology approaches to the Semantic Web can be a little like comparing apples to oranges, I can still compare the functional output of different technologies to assess both fitness and performance. For example, regardless of the particular technology at hand, normal scalability metrics like throughput, failover, response time, and so on all apply equally to any technology. These scale and performance dimensions are particularly important when sizing Semantic Web applications.

The following sections give you some ideas for functional performance comparisons between Semantic Web technologies, which should help you make the best decision for your project.

Query entailment and distribution

Regardless of which kind of Semantic Web infrastructure you consider, you should be thinking about some of the following questions:

- How complex might the models be?
- Which OWL axioms and class constructors can be used?
- May the system selectively close the world, or is open-world assumption (OWA) always intact? (OWA is described in Chapter 9.)
- How complex can your queries be? Full SPARQL, or with custom functions?
- Does your application data need to be in one physical location or may it be federated?
- If your data can be federated, how is the data partitioning handled?

Rulebase speed and scale

A *rulebase* can be a database, a business rule engine, or an inference engine/reasoned. Any rulebase you select will have finite limits. You should be thinking about what your application requirements are and how the technology choices will fit:

- How many rules can you put in the rulebase?
- Are answers computed with rule chains or some other approach?
- Can you tune the engine to demand provable execution of full chains or partial execution for speed?
- Can you change your rule entailment by model? By instance? Dynamically at runtime?
- Does the rulebase offer the ability to prove why some inferences were made? In what formats?
- Can rules be asserted on-the-fly, or is recompilation in the background required? At what cost?

Memory-resident knowledgebase

Main memory approaches can be very fast when high-performance is the number-one requirement, but the infrastructure demands and knowledge-base attributes are quite unconventional. Here are some of the factors you should take into consideration when you're examining the use of a main-memory approach for your application:

- ✔ What is the maximum number of hardware nodes allowable for a memory cluster?
- ✔ Does each machine offer a single main memory blackboard or several?
- ✔ How is query partitioning handled? With a firmware hash? Is it index-driven?
- ✔ What grid technology is used underneath the knowledgebase? Oracle Coherence? Gigaspaces? Open Source JGroups?
- ✔ What hardware platforms can be in the cluster?
- ✔ Is the access pattern via a query listener, or via APIs?

Relational knowledgebase

By far the most popular infrastructure for Semantic Web applications, the relational database offers a number of advantages and also some unique areas of concern for scalability. Here are the critical questions to answer when you're selecting a triples database:

- ✔ How many triples can be stored?
- ✔ How many triples can be efficiently queried at a given query entailment?
- ✔ Are the triples written directly to core relational database tables or to an intermediary data model?
- ✔ Which built-in database features can and cannot be used with the RDF subsystem? Security controls? Bulk loading utilities? Partitioning? Query plan optimizations?
- ✔ Do you query the system with SQL, SPARQL, or something else?
- ✔ Can the system make inferences on OWL models?
- ✔ How is the OWL graph persisted and computed?

Change management and security

Any triples system should provide features that allow you to work with changing data that is befitting of the power of RDF and OWL. Likewise, because RDF and OWL are relatively immature with respect to enterprise systems, you should be asking plenty of questions that help you determine the appropriate security controls on the data that you require:

- ✔ Does the RDF query language support inserts, deletes, and updates?
- ✔ Does the system allow model versioning or data snapshot capabilities?
- ✔ How are views computed, and how many views can be layered on the same triples?
- ✔ Do deletes cascade to inferences, or are orphaned triples allowed?
- ✔ Does the system compute updates or translate updates to inserts?
- ✔ Is security at the model level? The triple level? Computed for inferences?
- ✔ Are triples stored as quads or quints, or do they require an external security model?
- ✔ Is security role-based? User-level? Can security levels be inferred?

Getting a clear picture on the scalability and functional attributes of your triples database can be the difference between your project's success and failure. Because of the wide differences in platforms on the market today, my general advice is to develop your Semantic Web application requirements in parallel with your technology selection process. By exploring the limits of the available technologies, you'll find yourself more accurately understanding how your system architecture will look and be more likely to get the best match first. In a nutshell, don't assume that your previous experiences with building applications necessarily apply in the world of Semantic Web: Do your due diligence on the data layer fresh, with open eyes, and in consideration of how unique RDF/OWL can be.

Understanding Patterns of Architectural Usage

It's a plain fact that the Semantic Web isn't ready for all types of enterprise needs; therefore, the judicious application of semantics for specific use cases should dictate a realistic scalability architecture. Specific functional use cases are driven by the application requirements, and the degree to which the Semantic Web infrastructure should scale is a reflection of those requirements. A few different patterns of scaling and deploying Semantic Web infrastructure are becoming more widespread today, and I look at them in the next few sections.

Three-tier application approach

In the case where a large number of triples must service an application, or a set of applications, a centralized knowledgebase can be utilized. Of the triples repository types described earlier in this chapter, the most common fit for this use would be the conventional relational database as an RDF knowledgebase or the data warehouse appliance. Figure 12-3 shows a conventional three-tier application approach being sourced from a common, shared data repository.

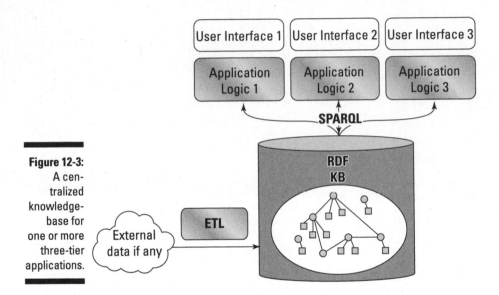

Figure 12-3:
A cen-
tralized
knowledge-
base for
one or more
three-tier
applications.

This pattern would typically involve a knowledgebase that is self-contained and operating within a fairly narrow domain. Because the knowledgebase is working, for the most part, with local data, it is considered to be the source of truth for the data it contains. Data input and output are predominantly via the applications directly, or through tightly controlled back-end processes like ETL (extract, transform and load) services.

For scalability planning, this approach is like any three-tier architecture: The consideration of load from the application queries is a central concern. The knowledgebase must be capable of handling the level of concurrency and result set load from the applications. Your application requirements for static or active metadata also place a ceiling for what the scalability of the knowledgebase can accommodate in terms of the amount of data. *Latency* (the processing time between software steps) is a topic that is one-part traditional (network and system latency) and one-part unique to the Semantic Web (classification latency). For system planning, your architecture should consider how frequently new facts will be asserted to the knowledgebase, what level of inference you plan to support, and what the acceptable amount of time is from the point new data is added to the point your applications must have access to that data and its inferred implications.

Data classification as a service

Using a knowledgebase as a service on a service-oriented architecture (SOA) can be a powerful way to augment an integration architecture with some additional smarts. The central scalability limits of the knowledgebase are not that different than in any other situation, but the typical use cases would be. For example, with a Web service front-end, the knowledgebase may have a more fixed interaction pattern (repeating query patterns) that can be heavily optimized by the developer. This is because the Web service itself may publish an API of allowable bindings that is limited to a set of specific features.

Many of the companies using this approach are using the Web service as a kind of vocabulary server. Figure 12-4 shows an RDB knowledgebase exposed via SPARQL end-points in a Web service cloud. In industries that have very complex localized terminologies (such as healthcare and defense), the service may be published to allow end-users to look up terms and term relationships. The terms themselves would of course be maintained and managed in an RDF/OWL format. Cancer researchers worldwide use a vocabulary system like this from Stanford called the National Cancer Institute (NCI) ontology: This ontology is used as a way to streamline communications and ensure consistent use of medical terms.

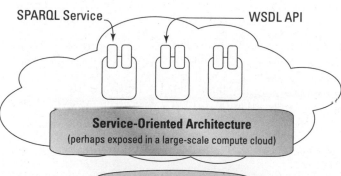

SPARQL Service — WSDL API

Service-Oriented Architecture
(perhaps exposed in a large-scale compute cloud)

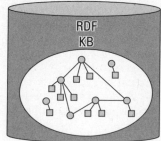

RDF KB

Figure 12-4:
A shared classification service driven from a shared RDF knowledgebase.

Other data classification or vocabulary services may leverage an ad hoc interface so that upstream clients can issue dynamically formatted queries that are not tightly controlled by the Web service, but these systems can yield highly unpredictable performance stresses and should be handled with caution. Because the RDF/OWL knowledgebases are inherently lower performing than conventional databases, they are much more susceptible to malformed queries and bad records that cause prolonged classification processing. Web service front-ends can certainly be set up to restrict problematic functions, but that kind of preventive ability requires a lot of preplanning and implementation time to enhance the robustness of the Web service.

The data classification service may also be used within a SOA for internal metadata services, but the software architecture for that setup might be vastly different than how an end-user would deploy a knowledgebase in a SOA. Vendors like IBM, Oracle, and Microsoft are already using RDF inside their SOA products, but each vendor takes a different technical approach to wiring the knowledgebase to the SOA components.

Composite data graph

A popular vision for the Semantic Web is to leverage it as a unified data integration layer for disparate enterprise data sets. Unfortunately for the pundits, using Semantic Web data formats in this way is not inherently any easier than other more conventional techniques — it can actually be much harder. Certain tools can enable this sort of vision more easily than building it from scratch. For example, Oracle Data Service Integrator, formerly the BEA Data Service Platform, can be paired with Modus Operandi Wave's OWL ontology layer to supply a unified data model across data services, which are in turn mapped to one or more enterprise data sources.

The main benefit of this federation approach is to provide a consistent, model-driven view of enterprise data — the OWL ontology provides that view — and then be capable of issuing queries to that view without detailed knowledge of how those queries are fulfilled (as shown in Figure 12-5). In order for this composite approach to work, the following architecture patterns must be applied:

1. The knowledgebase must expose the OWL concepts for query.

2. The OWL concepts must be mapped to physical data services provided by an enterprise information integration (EII) platform.

3. The EII platform must be mapped to the actual physical application sources that maintain the data.

The resulting architecture pattern requires a lot of query re-writes and result set filtering at runtime — which can be a substantial performance drag — but many use cases tolerate the relatively poor query performance for the benefit of having a rationalized model-driven view of their data assets.

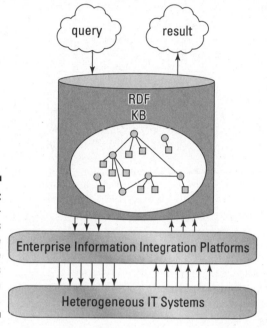

Figure 12-5:
A knowl-
edgebase is
a composite
of multiple
domains
and system
data.

Because this approach is predominantly about the scalability of the queries at runtime, the primary place to look for optimizations is in the runtime components. Tuning the mappings from ontology to data service, and from data service to source, can yield substantially better results than simply rely-ing on the infrastructure to build the best SQL queries or XQueries. In this approach, there is not a substantial amount of data localized in the RDF/OWL structure. Most data caching occurs inside the EII platform itself, and you refer to that architecture for tuning hints.

One last important aspect to consider when using this pattern is the require-ment for the OWL platform to easily supply mixed views and secure access — be sure to fully define your required view management needs and your secu-rity requirements up-front and match those to the OWL platform that is acting as the view layer.

Intelligence at the edge

The promise of the Semantic Web for applications has much to do with its ability to access and work with data transparently from its physical location and original purpose. Achieving this goal requires pushing intelligence to the edges of a large-scale network of systems working together and enabling applications to use other application data directly, without a dedicated integration layer. As described in Chapter 11, if all business applications were to use RDF data starting tomorrow, the need for data integration software would drop precipitously. Each RDF-enabled application could work with local or remote data graphs via the URI naming infrastructure and without much overhead dedicated to transforming data into and out of different structures and syntaxes.

In this forward-looking view, each application may have a local RDF knowledgebase (as a database, but also likely as an in-memory system) and the ability to join together other RDF resources using Web protocols. So, if you build an RDF application and expose your data on the Web, I can build my RDF application and use your data without much integration effort at all. As shown in Figure 12-6, this kind of low-level data interoperability could dramatically reshape the way software applications work together over the Web.

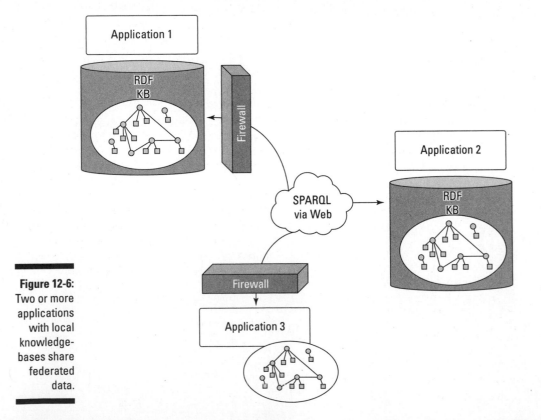

Figure 12-6:
Two or more applications with local knowledgebases share federated data.

In large systems, these different RDF applications could act individually or as a collective. Early adopters of this approach are military intelligence agencies that have the need to distribute complex application behavior to remote places, ensure that those applications have a high level of resilience to network outages, and still be able to leverage constantly changing remote data whenever it happens to be available. Imagine a battlefield situation where a single application running on a laptop in a tent needs to be capable of running effectively with no network access, yet automatically connect to and use data from other nearby command centers (tanks, planes, boats) as well as data coming all the way from Washington, D.C., via a Global Information Grid (GIG). RDF/OWL applications offer an extreme level of resilience and flexibility around constantly changing data sets and structures, making it an ideal format for those high-demand use cases.

Buyer Beware!

The fancier your proposed Semantic Web application sounds, the less likely it will scale. The laws of physics can't be broken. Ultimately, the Semantic Web is still about moving bits and bytes through software algorithms that execute inside silicon. The algorithms that power the inference-ready Semantic Web are substantially more intensive than what you're probably familiar with for databases.

In the not-too-distant future, Semantic Web formats may be able to be quickly and easily deployed for any application, but that time is not yet here. As I describe in Chapter 3, there are many good, rational, and low-risk ways to begin experimenting with the Semantic Web. Your reasons for exploring that direction can be an effective way of hedging against the certainty that today's mainstream technologies are hitting their upper limits of flexibility. But the key to success is to proceed with extreme caution into new areas. Many products and services sound good on paper but turn into snake oil once you invest your capital.

 If you're a buyer of Semantic Web technologies, you should ask your selected vendors to provide support for extended presales proof-of-concept projects. If you're a designer or an architect, prepare for an unusually long period of time spent assessing how the Semantic Web technology impacts your ideal architecture — and be prepared to change course when you find out what the practical limits of the technologies really are.

Chapter 13

Assessment Strategies

● ●

In This Chapter

▶ Determining whether your project is ready for semantics

▶ Framing a business problem as a Semantic Web opportunity

▶ Being aware of technical implications

▶ Assessing your application's fitness for Semantic Web

● ●

*L*ike the old saying goes, "When the only tool you have is a hammer, every problem looks like a nail." The Semantic Web is an exciting new collection of technologies and a new way of thinking about data, but it shouldn't be used for every type of software problem. Say that you've read the chapters in this book that describe the tremendous social impact that semantics is already having on the Web, and you've learned enough of RDF and OWL to want to go try them, but you're still not sure whether the Semantic Web makes sense for your project. The assessment strategies in this chapter tell you the right questions to ask and give you the techniques for identifying a good opportunity to try the Semantic Web yourself.

Understanding the Business Problem

A new software project always begins with a defined business problem that you want to solve using software. With the Semantic Web, the core part of this process is just like any other software project: You have to supply the cost-benefit analysis that says your project is worth the amount of time, effort, and money that it would take to complete it. There isn't anything inherently different about making this business assessment when the Semantic Web is in the picture. However, the technical implications of using the Semantic Web should change the cost structure of your analysis, and perhaps it could even change the benefit side of your equation.

First, you should understand how to map the technical power of the Semantic Web back to your business problems. The business problem should be one that the core technical strengths of the Semantic Web can help solve. If mapping the technical strengths to the desired business outcomes doesn't drive new value in your project, you have some serious thinking to do about the cost side of your equation.

The following sections identify a few key ways you can map the Semantic Web value to a business problem.

The problem requires handling of unpredictable data

Applications written with Semantic Web data provide a dynamic and flexible way of handling data and relationships in formats that could not be predicted at the time the software application was first written. As described in Chapter 8, the Semantic Web operates with an open-world assumption (OWA). Compared with traditional data structures, the Semantic Web data can enable your application to automatically make the distinction between data that is provably true versus satisfiably true.

A Semantic Web database can answer some queries with records that might possibly match, or it can separately tell you which records are absolutely a match (see Chapter 11 for some practical examples). Many business use cases can benefit from seeing uncertain data, and Semantic Web technology gives those businesses a more comprehensive set of tools to work with.

The problem requires dynamic classification of data

The Semantic Web technology can use inference engines to enable property-driven classification of data instead of more labor-intensive and error-prone manual tagging. An inference engine follows the rules of an ontology to classify data, as described more fully in Chapter 8.

For example, if you had a software application that was responsible for listing emergency evacuation centers, you could manually review data about buildings and locations to tag the buildings that are potential evacuation centers, or you could ask an inference engine to find possible matches based on rules in the ontology. These property-driven rules could contain criteria such as "elevation must be greater than 50ft above sea level, facilities must have more than three restrooms, building must be greater than 10,000 square feet of open space" and so on. Then your application could ask a simple question like, "Which buildings are potential evacuation centers?", and the Semantic Web database would know how to infer which structures were a good match.

The exceptionally valuable point about this technique is that you could easily redefine the rules in the ontology, and the inference engine reacts in real time to give you new matching data. No recompilation of software or dropping and rebuilding of data models are required!

The problem requires ad hoc modeling and data browsing

The Semantic Web supplies a conceptual model that is also computationally sound and an international standard. No other technology shares those attributes. Conceptual modeling and data layering can provide easier ad hoc navigation of data because you don't have to understand the physical layers of how data is represented. There are many other technical means to achieve a conceptual data layering architecture, but none like the Semantic Web that can provide an open and portable window into the core data structures, conceptual models, and data relationships. For business problems that need the conceptual modeling and would benefit from high levels of openness, the Semantic Web is a clear choice to make.

The problem requires understanding unstructured data

The Semantic Web is an ideal semi-structured format for describing data within a multi-step process flow that converts text into more structured data formats. Natural Language Processing (NLP) approaches (described in Chapter 9) that can take completely unformatted text in any language and give it some basic structure are algorithmic miracles. These NLP engines can ideally store the output of their conversions into RDF triples and be chained together serially or run in parallel to improve the ability to find structure in chaos.

Many kinds of business problems can benefit from taking e-mails, documents, text, Web sites, and other unstructured content and converting them into structured data that can be merged and reused with other database sources. The Semantic Web languages are not a requirement in this process, but they can substantially augment the NLP algorithms by giving them ontologies for classifying data and inference engines for generating new facts where the data supports it. However, if your application's core functionality is dependent on these NLP engines, approach the Semantic Web cautiously and deliberately because these technologies inject additional technical risks of failure into your project.

The problem requires open-source data

Many modern software applications make heavy use of public data from the Internet: This is what I call *open-source data*. Information and content that resides on Web pages is extremely useful for a range of software applications. Customer service applications that need to provide tips and hints for how to solve problems and even national security applications looking for information about people can be greatly enhanced by open-source data that's free on the Web for anybody to browse and reuse. The Semantic Web is an ideal format for merging that open-source, unstructured data with more structured business information. Really an extension of the need to support the understanding of unstructured data, the open-source domain is a particular niche where the Semantic Web has a major role to play.

Avoiding Common Traps in Planning Your Semantic Web Application

It's easy to get excited about the Semantic Web, but it's difficult to find a software problem that's uniquely suited to it. You should be wary of some common folk wisdom when you're thinking of areas where you can leverage the Semantic Web successfully:

✓ **Build another data integration solution.** Many Semantic Web pundits think that the problem area of data integration is the Holy Grail of business use cases for the Semantic Web technologies, but it isn't. Data integration is a multibillion-dollar marketplace that depends on mission-critical, high-performance software that is strongly optimized for data warehouses and business intelligence systems — none of which currently leverage the Semantic Web. At some point in the future, the Semantic Web may become more prevalent in the enterprise software ecosystem, but until then, the conventional data integration technologies already solve major parts of the real problems faced by IT professionals. Don't be fooled into thinking that the Semantic Web circa 2009 can solve problems that regular data integration tools can't!

✓ **Become the next Google star.** It's a popular pastime for many to dream about becoming the next Google, a company that starts with just a few people in a dorm room and morphs into a hundred-billion-dollar juggernaut. Some folks think that the Semantic Web will change the game for search engines and that the next breakthrough will be a semantic search company. But in 2008 Microsoft snapped up Powerset (a semantic search company), and Yahoo! deployed SearchMonkey (a semantic application of search results), so it should be obvious that the Semantic

Web is more of an additive technology rather than a fundamental power-shift. Google and others are keeping a close eye on the Semantic Web evolution and won't be blindsided by a new startup that ruins their business. If you're looking for the next software juggernaut, don't look in the search industry!

✔ **Tackle Web-scale problems.** Because the Semantic Web is inherently a Web technology and is sometimes billed as "functional at Web scale," early adopters often try to solve problems using huge amounts of Web data (search engines, blog engines, semantic Wikipedia, and so on). But a realistic assessment of your first project with the Semantic Web should start much smaller. Why confront the many limitations of scale (see Chapter 12) if you don't have to? Start small, act fast, and build a system that can grow with you over time!

Identifying Semantic Web Opportunities

Even though everything you see may eventually start to look like a Semantic Web opportunity — trust me, I've been there — it pays to work hard to understand whether you're looking at solving a fundamentally different problem than has been solved before, or solving an existing problem in a new way.

Blue Ocean Strategies

A *Blue Ocean Strategy* is defined in the book of the same name written by Chan and Mauborgne. Essentially, this is the idea that, in a particular market, you're either competing in a crowded marketplace where products become commodities and growth is increasingly difficult over time, or you're competing in new industries that are largely untainted by competition. The Blue Ocean is where demand is created and the rules of the marketplace have not yet been defined. The Red Ocean is where competition is cutthroat and the waters are bloodied. Many purveyors of the Semantic Web core technology foundations have essentially viewed themselves as Blue Ocean innovators, producing software that is fundamentally a new way of doing things that dramatically disrupts the old ways.

However, this can be a risky foundation to rest on because often the business model is unproven and there few other competitors in that area that can justify your own existence by validating a strong source of revenues. Your project may seek to exploit Blue Ocean forces by differentiating in major and fundamental ways, but in the early part of your Semantic Web explorations, I strongly recommend that your project be dedicated to solving a known and recognized problem.

Operational efficiency strategies

At the other extreme of Semantic Web solution areas is the project that seeks to solve an existing long-time problem by producing a more efficient solution than the other guys. These are projects that already have solutions, or may even have many competing solutions, but a new project using the Semantic Web is seen as attractive because it offers an incrementally better way to achieve some results.

This is a very risky strategy because an incremental improvement may not justify other risks that inherently surround the new Semantic Web technology. Rarely do you find a known problem area, with many existing software solutions, that can be completely and fully solved by software based in the Semantic Web. The simple fact is that the Semantic Web is merely a foundation, but a conventional, more mature software application would have evolved over many years to provide specialized and highly robust application layers (beyond just a foundation) for control on a given problem set.

If you plan to use the Semantic Web on a very mature problem area when there are already many other alternatives, you should proceed cautiously and seriously investigate whether the Semantic Web gives you enough benefits to justify other shortcomings that are likely to exist due to the immaturity of your foundational data choices.

Social and political implications

Many people feel that the Semantic Web is inherently good because it's more open than other technologies. Of course, leveraging the Semantic Web provides some inherent openness to any solution, but the value of that openness may lead different people to different opinions. Openness isn't always viewed as an absolute positive benefit. Sometimes openness of the data just doesn't matter, or worse, sometimes a software application may purposefully seek to encapsulate the data away from any direct manipulation. These encapsulation principles have been a defining aspect of object-oriented programming for almost 20 years. In the modern Web culture, openness is generally seen as a virtue, but don't assume that all software architects agree with that value judgment.

Using the Semantic Web automatically attaches a stigma to your application. Because this is a new technology, some of your stakeholders may automatically view it as cutting edge, but others may see it as doomed for failure. Don't underestimate the backlash or blowback that builds up with any new technology paradigm. For every person who is excited about the new breakthrough, probably two more are overtly skeptical of the promised features, and five more are just downright indifferent. Selecting the Semantic Web as a technical foundation for your project subjects your choices to the judgments of others, and their preconceived notions may or may not match your own!

Technical implications

Using the Semantic Web is just like using any other software foundation, except harder. The designer and architects of Semantic Web–based solutions must pay special attention to the weak areas of the Semantic Web (see Chapters 12 and 14) to counter-balance the relative immaturity of the solutions in the domain. Using the Semantic Web absolutely introduces some front-loaded technical risk to your projects, but if you get it right, and use the Semantic Web judiciously, the payoffs could be huge.

Reviewing Your Assessment Checklist

This section provides you with a series of scorecards to help you think about whether your project is a good fit for the Semantic Web. I offer a way for you to score each section and a range of total scores to assess if your project is a Strong Fit, a Possible Fit, or a Weak Fit for leveraging the Semantic Web.

To start this assessment, you should have a specific software project in mind and have thought about the business problem you want to solve with that software. For the purposes of this checklist, I assume that the hypothetical Semantic Web–based application is leveraging an OWL+RDF data layer to enable these advanced semantic capabilities.

To use the assessment, check the box of each answer that applies to your project. At the end of the assessment, you will be asked to add up the scores for each item that you have checked. Then you can see how good a fit your project is by comparing your score to the grading scales provided at the end of this assessment.

Application behavior requirements

First, assess your project from a behavioral standpoint.

Open world or closed world

Does the application directly benefit from being able to distinguish between absolute and possible answers to database queries? A closed-world relational database has absolute unambiguous query results. An open-world RDF/OWL database may provide both absolute and possible result sets. Review Chapter 8 for a refresher on these topics.

- ❏ A closed-world normal database would be fine. (+1)
- ❏ Perhaps some open-world behavior would be useful. (+2)
- ❏ My application definitely needs open-world behavior. (+3)

Correctness levels

For the data that your application is using, does it absolutely need to be guaranteed as correct and repeatable? For example, a search engine result set is very useful but not guaranteed or fully repeatable. A relational database is fully correct and fully repeatable. Sometimes an application may need some data as statistical (not guaranteed) and correct (guaranteed). Review Chapter 5 for a refresher on these topics.

❑ My application should primarily use a statistical method of data retrieval like a search engine. (+1)

❑ I need some statistical behavior and also guaranteed queries. (+2)

❑ I need 100-percent correctness guarantees in the data used by the application — for searches and elsewhere. (+3)

Amount of structured data

If you need to store and query RDF/OWL data efficiently, pay attention to how low the ceiling is. Especially if inference and data classification is required, ensure that the repository and query platforms you select are scalable to your maximum peak levels. Review Chapter 12 for a refresher on these topics.

❑ I need more than 1 terabyte. (+1)

❑ I need between 100 gigabytes and 1 terabyte. (+2)

❑ I need less than 100 gigabytes. (+3)

Unstructured data

Requiring Natural Language Processing (NLP) technology outside the scope of the Semantic Web can create double the risks of immature and bleeding edge technology. For mainstream systems, be positive that the business solution you actually need is provided by the NLP systems feeding your Semantic Web repository or application. Review Chapter 9 for a refresher on these topics.

❑ The application depends on automatic linguistic parsing. (+1)

❑ The application needs to parse some data linguistically. (+2)

❑ The application doesn't need any unstructured data. (+3)

Entailment levels

If you find yourself needing an unrestricted level power for rules and logic in your data language, or if you only need SQL/RDBMS levels of power, consider alternative languages besides RDF and OWL for your data. Within the scope of RDFS or OWL data semantics, your application can take on a lot more expressive power while retaining openness and portability. Review Chapter 8 for a refresher on these topics.

❏ I need an unrestricted level of logic. (+1)

❏ I need SQL/RDBMS-type queries only. (+2)

❏ I need RDF/S or OWL Prime expressiveness. (+3)

❏ I need OWL OWL DL, EL++, QL, or RL expressiveness. (+4)

Application security

Systems with a need for exceptionally robust and flexible levels of data security shouldn't be considering RDF/OWL-based systems. As of 2009, there are very few widely deployed RDF/OWL platforms that can compare with built-in data level security features of most relational databases. Of course, if the benefits of RDF/OWL justify the expense, a robust multilevel security system can be implemented within the ontology and graph data models themselves. Research efforts into trust and proof security problems using inference have already broken ground on these topics. Review Chapter 11 for a refresher on these topics.

❏ The entire system is a high-security system. (+1)

❏ A trust system is required (open-source data). (+2)

❏ Security must remain correct with inferred nodes. (+3)

❏ Role/user-based data filtering is required. (+4)

Data integration

The infrastructure requirements for data integration almost always involve systems with data that isn't in RDF/OWL formats. If your project involves using a lot of existing data in your Semantic Web application, be prepared for the costs and timelines necessary to convert the physical and logical data into your application. A Semantic Web application doesn't automatically help with any practical aspect of data integration. Review Chapter 11 for a refresher on these topics.

❏ I need to import hundreds of millions of existing records. (+1)

❏ I have some data imports, but they aren't excessive. (+2)

❏ My data is mostly self-contained to the proposed solution. (+3)

Application interface requirements

Next, examine your proposed project from a software interface standpoint.

Human interface

Using ontology for the items on graphical user interface (GUI) can make a user experience more dynamic, but the most important part of human experience is how quickly the system responds to new data. A fast system is required for trading applications and call centers, but applications like reporting systems and back-office business software can usually wait for data several minutes at a time. Because it can sometimes take a while to infer new data on the Semantic Web, which is really what the Semantic Web is all about, you can sometimes expect your application to need precious time (or more hardware) to work with lots of new data coming from its users. Review Chapter 12 for a refresher on these topics.

❏ The interface must be highly dynamic and extremely responsive in real time to new data. (+1)

❏ The interface must be dynamic, but is largely driven by pre-existing data. (+2)

❏ The interface is fairly static, and new data may take several minutes to assess correctly. (+3)

Machine interface

Some software systems are built for handling massive numbers of small transactions, the debits and credits of a trading center for example. Other systems are built for handling huge sets of data all at once, a business data warehouse for example. Depending on your Semantic Web application's needs, you may have to watch for use cases that depend on extreme transaction speed — these won't necessarily be the best fit for process-intensive Semantic Web data. Review Chapter 11 for a refresher on these topics.

❏ The system has a high degree of transactional input and output. (+1)

❏ The system has a high degree of transactional input, but not output. (+2)

❏ The system has bulk inputs for large amounts of data. (+3)

❏ The system is self-contained, with very little input or output of any kind. (+4)

Application development requirements

Finally, in this section, assess your development requirements.

Team size

How large does your development organization need to scale to?

❑ Large team (greater than 30) (+1)

❑ Medium team (10–30) (+2)

❑ Small team (less than 10) (+3)

Visualization during development

How important is visualizing your data architecture or analyzing your data during development?

❑ Visual modeling and analysis of data are essential requirements for developers. (+1)

❑ Visual modeling and analysis are nice-to-have features for developers. (+2)

❑ Visual analysis and modeling of the application data aren't really required during development. (+3)

Skills planning for staffing

What kind of skills do you have access to today? Review Chapter 10 for a refresher on these topics.

❑ Semantic Web skills are definitely required, but nobody on existing staff has used them before. (+1)

❑ Semantic Web skills might be required, and a few developers have learned the basics. (+2)

❑ Semantic Web skills might be required, and I already have architects and developers who know them well. (+3)

Skills planning for management

How much experience does your management have with Semantic Web applications? Review Chapter 10 for a refresher on these topics.

❑ No management experience with Semantic Web projects (+1)

❑ Some management experience with Semantic Web projects (+2)

❑ Good management experience with Semantic Web projects (+3)

Skills planning for scalability

More than many other aspects of your proposed Semantic Web project, you should be ready to confront the scalability and performance limitations that are inherence in the Semantic Web technology base. Skilled scalability architects from any discipline will rapidly add value to your project. Don't worry too much about direct Semantic Web background; find the scalability experts and train them into the Semantic Web. Review Chapter 12 for a refresher on these topics.

❑ No scalability architect is on staff. (+1)

❑ Some senior developers or existing architects know some things about scalability in software. (+2)

❑ I can get a scalability architect on loan from another group. (+3)

❑ I am directly ready to staff a dedicated scalability architect to the project. (+4)

Scoring the Checklist and Understanding Benefits

Now, add up your scores from each check box that you marked in the previous sections. Depending on how high your score is, your project might be a strong fit for Semantic Web technology. A possible fit means that you should dig a little deeper and perhaps explore some Semantic Web technology to see if it would work. A weak fit means that it is unlikely that your project would work well with Semantic Web technologies.

For Application Behavior, your results map to these recommendations:

✔ **A score of 18–higher** means that the Semantic Web is probably a Strong Fit for your project. The answers you gave indicated that the Semantic Web is likely a low-risk and high-value proposition for your proposed project's application behavior.

✔ **A score of 13–17** means that it's a Possible Fit. You should probably investigate the Semantic Web a bit more thoroughly for your project. Take time to review the answers you gave that were scored as a 1 or 2 and read the appropriate chapter that discusses that topic more thoroughly.

✔ **A score of 7–12** means that the Semantic Web is probably a Weak Fit for your project. There are too many areas where the technology doesn't match your requirements or the importance of certain behavior is too risky for depending on the Semantic Web.

For Application Interfaces, your results map to these recommendations:

✔ **A score of 6–higher** means that the Semantic Web is probably a Strong Fit for your project. The answers you gave indicated that the Semantic Web would not significantly jeopardize your software application interface requirements.

✔ **A score of 4–5** means that the Semantic Web is a Possible Fit. You should investigate the Semantic Web a bit more for your project. Take time to review the answers you gave that were scored as a 1 or 2 and read the appropriate chapter that discusses that topic more thoroughly.

✔ **A score of 2–3** means that the Semantic Web is probably a Weak Fit for your project. There are too many areas where the technology doesn't match your interface requirements or the importance of certain interface behavior is too risky for the Semantic Web core technologies.

For Development Requirements, your results map to these recommendations:

✔ **A score of 13–higher** means that the Semantic Web is probably a Strong Fit for your project. The answers you gave indicated that the Semantic Web would not significantly jeopardize your software development requirements.

✔ **A score of 9–12** means that it's a Possible Fit. You should investigate the Semantic Web a bit more thoroughly for your project. Take time to review the answers you gave that were scored as a 1 or 2 and read the appropriate chapter that discusses that topic more thoroughly.

✔ **A score of 5–8** means that the Semantic Web is probably a Weak Fit for your project. There are too many areas where the tool maturity doesn't match your project requirements or the importance of certain project attributes is too risky for the Semantic Web core tooling and technologies.

After reviewing your Assessment Checklist, see whether you can spot any of these major warning signals that may indicate the Semantic Web is not right for your project:

✔ **Your project needs an unrestricted logical model and a first-order rule-based system for working with complex sets of records.** This is not a fit because the Semantic Web depends on a consistent logical model that does not exceed the model semantics defined in OWL. A Semantic Web system can be built using unrestrained logics, but many of the openness and portability benefits of the Semantic Web disappear in those circumstances. Think twice if your application can't leverage RDF and OWL alone for the data representation.

✔ **Your project depends entirely on linguistic parsing of files.** This doesn't rule out the use of Semantic Web, but it's a clear signal that the hard part of your project will be elsewhere. The use of NLP introduces a significant set of challenges, and the benefits of the Semantic Web in that context need to be extra clear and obvious lest your project take on unnecessary complexity. Consider the heavy use of NLP as a strong warning sign for your project's use of Semantic Web.

✔ **Your project needs huge amounts of data and requires only closed-world query answering.** This warning sign is a clear indicator that a more traditional data warehouse could be a better fit for you. If this is true, you should have other strong and immovable requirements that clearly demand the Semantic Web; otherwise, why add needless complexity to your project?

Making the Decision

Approach your decision cautiously. The Semantic Web technologies will be available for a long time, and there isn't any reason to be an early adopter if you don't absolutely have to be. But if you're clear-headed about the risks of your Semantic Web project, the rewards for your risks could be quite generous.

The checklists provided here are by no means comprehensive; instead, they're intended to get you thinking about how the Semantic Web technologies are different than what you're used to. You have to make early judgments using instinct and informed opinion about which project to authorize, which to cancel, and which ones should try out new technology that is potentially risky.

If you follow a conservative course and apply some of the guided assessments I provide in this chapter, you have a much better chance of avoiding some of the commonplace Semantic Web pitfalls that myself and others have already fallen into!

Chapter 14

Exploring the Limitations of the Semantic Web

*T*his book focuses on providing a straightforward, but optimistic view of the emerging Semantic Web family of technologies. I make every attempt throughout the book to balance the unique power of the new technology against those technologies that are more proven. However, the newness and complexity of the Semantic Web technologies warrants a full chapter dedicated to explaining directly the challenges anyone faces when implementing their new semantic projects.

By most measures, the Semantic Web is a fairly mature set of technologies. Serious work began on RDF as early as 1997. Standardization of RDF and OWL occurred in 2004, and many projects and products have been launched since then. Early-adopter implementations are far enough along that there is a cadre of professionals out there who already have battle scars. But compared to most other technologies, the Semantic Web is clearly still in its incubation period. Relational database technologies, for example, have had more than 30 years of refinement and optimization investments placed into them. Other technologies like Java and XML may only be a few years older on the calendar, but they are significantly more mature because of the sheer number of rapid implementations that have occurred since their inception. In most regards, the Semantic Web has not yet crossed the chasm from early stages to mainstream adoption. Your project should take that situation seriously and adjust accordingly.

The Semantic Web brings many limitations along with its great benefits. As a long-time evangelist for Semantic Web technologies, I thought twice about dedicating an entire chapter in this book to its limitations. I could have easily described the limitations in smaller sections scattered throughout the book. However, I came to the conclusion that newcomers to the technology should have access to a balanced view of the risks and concerns about the Semantic Web. The remainder of this chapter explains how the Semantic Web standards are still evolving to cover language gaps, offer some practical advice about the immaturity of Semantic Web tools, define a few best practices for you to consider, and offer some advice for how to make good choices with your Semantic Web project.

Staying Within the Standards

My emphasis in this book has been primarily on two standards: RDF for graph data and OWL for ontology. These standards are stable, under tight version control, and technically proven in a substantial number of applications. There are patterns to draw from and lessons about them that have already been learned. Most direct discussions about the Semantic Web are implicitly about the use of one of these two standards. RDF and OWL truly are the lynchpin technologies that form the nucleus of the Semantic Web. However, several other standards that I've introduced in this book (see Chapter 4 and Chapter 9) are also very important in the context of building your Semantic Web application:

- ✔ **Gleaning Resource Descriptions from Dialects of Languages (GRDDL):** This standard was recommended by the W3C in 2007 and is used to specify how to extract RDF triples from other types of languages using an XML and XSLT transformation. This is particularly useful if you already have, or plan to have, an XML-centric application that should also be capable of producing RDF triples.

- ✔ **Semantic Annotations for Web Service Description Language (SAWSDL):** This standard was recommended by the W3C during 2007 as a way to specify how Web service data bindings can be mapped to formal models. It isn't tightly coupled to RDF or OWL, but it offers a repeatable way to connect RDF or OWL to Web services with fixed data bindings, thereby making it easier to programmatically find service data that meets the needs of your application.

- ✔ **Semantic Web Rule Language (SWRL):** Not yet approved, this language proposal is part of the Rule Interchange Format Working Group at the Semantic Web. SWRL is a working draft of a rule language that offers more complex and powerful rule extensions to OWL. It's proposed in such a way that it can leverage OWL classes and individuals within rule definitions.

- ✔ **Resource Description Framework in Attributes (RFDa):** Not yet approved, RDFa is squarely aimed at providing an easy way to embed RDF triples within an XHTML-compliant Web page. This format is the W3C's alternative to the more rigidly structured microformats that have developed in an ad hoc manner in several communities.

These six technical standards (RDF, OWL, GRDDL, SAWDL, SWRL, and RDFa) represent the collection of current and potentially near-term languages at the core of the Semantic Web. Many other standards — such as vocabulary standards and application standards — leverage these core technical specifications, but they aren't what I would consider fundamental Semantic Web technical standards.

From a distance, these may seem to be a pretty complete set of languages to build an application from, but you can't actually build a software application from the W3C standards alone. These W3C Semantic Web standards encompass only some very specific technical layers in application architecture focused on data, metadata, and data bindings. They don't directly provide solutions for user interface development, application program executables, or even data management functions that most industrial-strength applications require.

Straying Outside the Standards

Building a complete Semantic Web solution requires you to use non-standard technology. Even if you make every effort to use standards wherever possible, there are many different ways to use the Semantic Web languages that would leave your system incompatible with other Semantic Web applications. For example, your application would still require procedural programs like Java or C++ to make your system executable. The way you choose to implement the logic in your application is precisely the decision that determines how standardized and portable your solution is.

As I discuss in Chapters 7 and 8, many kinds of logic are directly expressible in languages like RDF and OWL. You can use these languages to define fairly complex logic like that which defines a business's Gold Customers, what constitutes an Emergency Evacuation Center, or even a likely Drug Target given a set of manufactured compounds with specific attributes. But you can also, of course, express these logics in conventional software programs. The advantages that the Semantic Web brings in terms of reuse, dynamism, flexibility, and openness also yield to potential inefficiencies such as complexity, performance drags, and even inelegance. The choices that an application architect makes about which logic to place in the Semantic Web data model or in conventional software programs are naturally different than the choices made by other application architects. This is just common sense.

However, the natural diversity of Semantic Web design patterns, how much OWL is used, and where the system logic resides means that many long-standing problems that the Semantic Web aims to address can't be resolved in the very messy real world.

Straying outside the standards is also a natural prerequisite for working with vendor-supplied solutions. Just as the Java and J2EE standards are supposed to resolve application portability problems, the Semantic Web standards are supposed to resolve data portability problems. But just like the reality behind J2EE application servers — that it's quite difficult and rare to swap vendor-supplied servers after a system has been built with it — comprehensive portability of Semantic Web formats is fraught with incompatibility challenges. By all means, use vendor technologies to jump-start your Semantic Web projects, but your architects and developers should choose wisely because your business application is stuck with that choice indefinitely.

Realizing the Implications of a Complete Semantic Web Solution

The implications of choosing to build a complete Semantic Web software application are profound. Unless you're a university researcher or student, I wouldn't recommend it. For all the reasons I mention in previous sections, Semantic Web technologies aren't suited for solving a complete software problem. Instead, the Semantic Web is best suited for solving problems having to do with the reusability, portability, and expressiveness of data languages. But even within the range of the sweet-spot use cases, every Semantic Web buyer and architect should be cautious when implementing it.

Tool immaturity

Semantic Web as an idea and a technical vision has been around since the late 1990s. As technology, the RDF and OWL standards were reasonably complete in 2004. But the tooling required to support these new formats has been frustratingly slow to emerge. In Chapter 9, I introduce you to Stanford University's Protégé tool, Altova's SemanticWorks, and TopQuadrant's TopBraid Composer. However powerful these tools are, and indeed they are quite good at what they do, they aren't known to be mainstream data modeling tools.

In the real-world of industrial software and the multitrillion-dollar markets that it enables, the vast majority of data modelers use tools like Computer Associates ERWIN, Sybase PowerDesigner, and Quest's TOAD database modeler. Software developers writing code in Java most often use standard components for IBM Eclipse or Sun's Java Studio. No matter how you look at it, the mainstream tools for software development are still on the sidelines waiting to see how this whole Semantic Web meme shakes out.

The tools you're left with, the pure-play tools for developing in the Semantic Web formats, can still get the job done, but they're woefully immature compared with the mainstream tools. Feature gaps around team-based configuration management, multi-language development, and interfaces with various platforms and technologies make the Semantic Web tools difficult to fit into existing practices. Likewise, the relative immaturity and lack of global scope for the vendors poses a challenge for procurement officers who typically have specific criteria about who to do business with in order to minimize risk — most newer Semantic Web companies don't fit those profiles.

Scalability limitations

In Chapter 12, I define many facets of scalability to be aware of. When building a Semantic Web application using 2008-era technologies, a system architect should pay very close attention to scalability and performance requirements:

- **How much data?** Semantic Web databases typically allow for a maximum of 300–500 million triples, which for many applications is simply not enough.

- **How much inferencing?** If your application depends heavily on the power of Semantic Web for inferring new data, you can reduce your scalability ceiling by 5–10 times.

- **How close to realtime?** The process of inferring new data is typically a background process that can take minutes or hours to update a fully loaded Semantic Web database; you might be in trouble if your application depends on new facts and implications quickly.

Although these scalability limitations sound quite severe, a large number of software applications fall outside of these scalability boundaries.

Skill shortage

So, say that you've decided to brave immaturity of development tools and that you're convinced that your proposed application won't stress the limits of Semantic Web formats. Now you have to find good people to help you build it!

On any given week, you might be able to find a few hundred open positions in the United States and Canada for Semantic Web skills like RDF, OWL, and graph data modeling, but there aren't enough experienced developers to meet the demand. Your project is competing with many other projects for the developers who already have hands-on experience. Of course, any experienced software developer can *learn* RDF/OWL in a fairly short period, but the experiences of using these languages on a real project are priceless.

Sometimes these skill shortages can be partially or wholly mitigated by partnering wisely with other companies that can cover your skill gaps. Good experience is necessary, in a partner or a new hire, because the new development patterns required by Semantic Web projects is oftentimes more of an art than a science.

New patterns and anti-patterns

Although most of the processes used to create Semantic Web software are just like the processes used to create regular software, new technologies and new skills are required, which naturally leads to new processes and new traps. A *pattern* in software development can be a template for a coded solution (in Java, for example), or it may simply be a repeatable way of doing things in the process. An *anti-pattern* is a solution that seems obvious but usually results in unintended disastrous results.

Here are a few healthy project patterns to pay attention to in a Semantic Web project:

- ✔ **Iterative development:** In Semantic Web application projects, it can be too easy to get caught up in the development of the ontology, the iteration of a perfect model, or planning for innumerable contingencies. Given the inherence complexity of RDF/OWL anyway, it is especially important to keep your development team focused on short delivery cycles with continuous incremental progress. This focus on iterative development is even more important in Semantic Web projects than in conventional software projects.

- ✔ **KISS (Keep it Simple, Stupid):** Think of Occam's Razor (which says that entities must not be multiplied beyond necessity) or Einstein's maxim, "Everything should be made as simple as possible, but no simpler." I can say from experience that you can easily find prima donnas in the realm of Semantic Web who think highly of themselves yet make models and software unnecessarily complex. Use the KISS principle ruthlessly in your project to ensure that you meet milestones and remain focused on outcomes as opposed to the relative beauty of your solution.

- ✔ **Contract-based design:** In the world of Semantic Web, the software contracts are different. In conventional software, the idea of contract-based design is nearly 20 years old and is focused on clearly denoting the signature of each request and the expected format of each reply. Using contracts, different teams can work in parallel to develop complex software instead of having to wait for each step to be completed serially. In the Semantic Web, contracts may take the form of SPARQL query requests (SPARQL is the query language for RDF, described in Chapter 9), RDF result sets, and perhaps even the APIs to an inference engine and the OWL result sets that define the data. Regardless of your particular project's technical choices, stick closely to the contract-based design principles and apply them to Semantic Web formats for your best chance at success.

Here are a few unhealthy project patterns to especially watch for:

✔ **Analysis paralysis:** For some people, the availability of new modeling formats is like giving a kid a new toy. Many people have a tremendous urge to use RDF and OWL to their fullest, to capture all kinds of data, make the model perfect, and anticipate the future. Resist those urges. In all but a few cases, I recommend a tactical approach to RDFS and OWL modeling. Sure, creating data models from scratch is top-down by definition, but it needn't be an exercise of perfection for every model. The tactical approach to RDFS and OWL means to stay focused on just the specified behavior of the application, avoiding modeling any part of the domain not relevant to the application behavior. Without rigorous checks-and-balances, you can easily slip into analysis paralysis on your Semantic Web project.

✔ **Broken triangle:** The iron triangle says that every good quality software project can be changed along three axes of cost, scope, and time, but that changing any one dimension leads to measurable impacts on the others (lest the quality of the project decline). The broken triangle refers to occasions where the developers and managers get out of synch, the triangle is broken, and unrealistic expectations lead to failed projects. In the realm of Semantic Web projects, I especially recommend that you be very conservative on scope and time. Cut your project's scope to the bare minimum and double your first estimates on how long it will take to complete. During the course of your project, use frequent iterations to prevent breaking the triangle and ensure that expectations are always up to date.

Making Good Choices

With a little bit of planning, foresight, and caution, your Semantic Web project can be successful and enjoyable. In software, as in life, making good decisions can lead to an easier path and an enjoyable time.

Partners

Finding good partners to help you is a great way to share the risks and rewards of a tough Semantic Web project. A good partner can come to you as a systems integrator, a software vendor, or an individual. Sometimes you have to pay for your partner's help, but you can also find partners willing to help you for free, or at cost, if you serve as a good reference for them after project is successfully completed.

In the 2009-era, the big systems integrators and software contractors aren't usually going to be your best choice for helping with your Semantic Web projects. Even if they happen to employ a few staff members who know the technology really well, you would be unlikely to have them on your project because they would probably be working on other projects using more mainstream skills. In contrast, if you do your homework about various boutique consulting firms that specialize in the Semantic Web, you may be pleasantly surprised by what you find. I personally know of several who specialize in different domains, a few who would work at cost for the right projects, and even a few who might donate their time and expertise for humanitarian uses of the Semantic Web.

Software vendors can make good partners too. Often, a Semantic Web vendor is looking to showcase a great use of its technology. You can use this desire as a way to ensure that the vendor will help your project be successful, that it will participate actively in your project, and that it will see you through until the end. I identify and recommend a few of these potential partners in Chapters 15 and 17.

Timelines

Working with new technology, new standards, and new resource skills should put any good project manager on his or her toes about project milestones. In this chapter, you've been warned. Most of what you thought you knew about planning, scoping, and estimating software projects has changed. Depending on the architecture choices you've made, you've either pushed some of your object-oriented code into Semantic Web formats, or you've raised data out of the relational database to work with it in the Semantic Web. In either case, you've shifted some fundamental design patterns about how logic and data interact in software. The newer Semantic Web formats have different attributes, different skill requirements, and tooling requirements that you probably haven't had to deal with before. No matter how you decompose your new Semantic Web project, you should be adding multipliers to your timeline estimates to account for all the unknowns you'll surely encounter along the way!

Functional expectations

In the eight years I've been involved with about a dozen substantial Semantic Web projects, I've learned that it's usually best to solve as much of your software problem as possible using conventional technology and to isolate the areas where you need or want to apply Semantic Web technology. By making the bulk of your application based on conventional technology, you both acknowledge that the Semantic Web is limited and guarantee that some substantial part of what you set out to achieve is in fact achievable. The parts of your planned application that can really benefit from the Semantic Web should be partitioned away as much as possible from other core features. And by *partitioned,* I don't mean disconnected, but rather I suggest that you use a common software façade for loosely coupling your software interfaces to the Semantic Web bits of the application. This technical recommendation feeds into the overall project recommendation to keep your functional expectations firmly grounded in reality. Remember, the Semantic Web is not magic.

It's far too easy to get caught up in the power, flexibility, and newness of the Semantic Web. Eventually, every software problem looks like nails to your new-found Semantic Web hammer. But not every software problem is suited for the Semantic Web data formats. A careful examination of your software architecture and functional requirements should yield a reasonably small percentage of requirements that depend directly on the Semantic Web.

One approach that I've used successfully to scope Semantic Web projects is to focus specifically on the data-level queries that you want answered from RDF/OWL. For example, list the application-specific questions and queries that you think would be best answered from a graph database or an inference engine. After you have a good idea of the business benefits of those queries, you can start to decompose them further into queries that are answerable with data you already have, or data that needs to be converted to RDF/OWL. For the data that should come from RDF/OWL, the important business queries can help direct the best way to model your ontologies.

It sounds simple, but it's a good idea nonetheless: Start with the business requirements and then work backwards into the technology choices. Try not to use semantics just for the sake of semantics, and then double or triple your project estimates for the functions that really do need to depend on Semantic Web technologies.

Sticking to Best Practices

The Semantic Web industry is young enough that best practices are still being discovered and rewritten all the time. The Semantic Web of 2008 isn't a fully mature discipline with fully mature practices. However, I can offer at least two kind of best practices: process/project best practices and technical best practices. In the previous sections, I address several components of project/process best practices. Technical best practices are far more relevant to the architects and developers on your Semantic Web project. I name many best practices in Chapters 7 and 8, but here a few more from the W3C to consider:

✔ **Defining Multi-way Relations in Semantic Web:** Detailed ontology pattern guidance for creating and maintaining relationships among individuals and more than one individual or value. See www.w3.org/TR/swbp-n-aryRelations/.

- **Classes as Property Values:** Defines patterns for implementing class names as relationship properties in OWL-DL and OWL-Lite where that explicit behavior isn't allowed. See `www.w3.org/TR/swbp-classes-as-values/`.

- **Specified Values in OWL:** In the OWL 1.0 formats, the developer may need to choose a way to itemize a list of values associated with a property; this best practice describes using class partitions and enumerations of individuals as a way to solve that. See `www.w3.org/TR/swbp-specified-values/`.

- **Semantic Web Best Practices for Object-Oriented Developers:** An introduction to Semantic Web formats as conceptual domain models for OO developers who may have been formally trained in subjects like UML (Unified Modeling Language). See `www.w3.org/TR/sw-oosd-primer/`.

- **Using XML Schema Datatypes in RDF and OWL:** Detailed guidance for how to adopt all XSD Datatype support into your Semantic Web model. See `www.w3.org/TR/swbp-xsch-datatypes`.

- **RDF/OWL WordNet Representation:** This is a reference implementation of the Princeton WordNet into RDF/OWL; it also describes the principles used in conversion. See `www.w3.org/TR/wordnet-rdf/`.

- **Time Ontology in OWL:** Temporal concepts can be difficult to use in a logic system that is not temporally bound; this reference implementation covers a basic implementation for the purposes of creating a scheduling ontology. See `www.w3.org/TR/owl-time`.

- **Whole-part Relationships in OWL Ontologies:** A best practices note to describe how OWL can be used to model the simple cases of whole-part relations, expressing containment, and being able to reason effectively with those assertions. See `www.w3.org/2001/sw/BestPractices/OEP/SimplePartWhole/`.

You can find more technical best practices like these on the W3C Web site at `www.w3.org/2001/sw/BestPractices`.

Technical best practices are a tactical but very good way to protect your project from the pitfalls that others have already experienced. Before starting your project, I strongly encourage you to consider the process, project, and technical best practices presented throughout this book before deciding that the Semantic Web is for you.

Chapter 15

A Guide to Essential Vendor Implementations

In This Chapter

▶ Keeping your eye on key players in the Semantic Web business

▶ Paying attention to important company and product profiles

▶ Identifying consumer and business products that you might be able to use

Sometimes, seeing what others are doing helps spur your own ideas. Or perhaps you just want to jump-start your own project by finding some software that can help you get going. Consumer Semantic Web sites are places you can go to try some of new Semantic Web technology, perhaps as a customer or just a casual surfer. Either way, you might be surprised: Many of these Web sites seem pretty normal on the surface, but as you try some of their cool features, you wonder, "How did they do that?" That's where the Semantic Web magic comes in.

The "Business Software" section of this chapter is more oriented around products you can buy or try for your own project. In some cases, as with the Oracle Database, the product is itself a supplier of Semantic Web technology for you. In other cases, as with the IBM Registry, the product uses Semantic Web technology on the inside as a way to make the product better. In all cases, this chapter can give you a good idea of which companies and products are aggressively moving toward the Semantic Web today!

Consumer Web Sites

Consumer Web sites are applications that you can go ahead and use directly from your everyday Web browser. Typically these consumer Web sites are focused on attracting your attention, and they make money from the advertizing space that they sell. Most of the consumer applications I've profiled for this section use that business model. All of the consumer-facing applications described here are making innovative use of semantic technology to empower their next-generation capabilities.

Twine

URL: www.twine.com

Headquarters: San Francisco, CA, USA

Products (Primary): Twine.com

In a ground-breaking report written in the fall of 2008 by David Provost, Nova Spivack, who is the CEO of Twine, was interviewed about Twine in light of recent developments in the industry. I've worked with David and Nova to provide you some of those facts and insights about Twine and their implementations.

Twine is an interest networking Web site designed to let people share links, comments, files, and more about topics they're interested in. When Twine launched as a beta, it mostly attracted people involved with the Semantic Web. But since then, the diversity of people on Twine has grown rapidly, and now a quick look at the Top 100 Twines (interest categories) show interests as diverse as green business and investing, science discoveries, geopolitics, sustainable living, and thousands more.

Twine is easily one of the best-known Semantic ventures today, but what's truly refreshing about Twine is that it emphasizes what it does (its business mission) and not how it does it (Semantic Web technology). Longstanding members of the Semantic Web community may be left wondering "Where's the beef?" because there aren't any ontology editing screens, model visualizers, or RDF development environments. On the other hand, the general public may come to believe it has finally found the Semantic Web, and it's on Twine.

Twine is built to support regular people who have interests they'd like to share. Because Twine aims be an evolutionary step beyond Facebook or MySpace, with broad interest networking appeal to everybody, don't look for Twine to include any hands-on Semantic Web development features.

If you've started a Twine on cooking, you won't miss the absence of ontology editing tools. In fact, you probably won't care about the Semantic Web technology at all. Instead, you may be far more interested in the bookmark someone just posted to your cooking Twine that leads to a recipe you've never thought of before.

Visible or not, Twine has a lot of semantics at work under the hood in the form of autotagging, Natural Language Processing (NLP), and RDF Semantic Web data. But the technology and the Semantic Web hype surrounding it have been rightfully overshadowed by Twine's business goals and its point for existing in the first place: to be a money-making venture.

Twine's audience demographics and behavior may position the company front and center as a viable media property. For instance, Twine's target demographic is young professionals, an older (which usually means more affluent) demographic than that of Facebook or MySpace, where advertisers have been frustrated in crafting effective campaigns.

Compared with "discovery" sites like Delicious, Digg, or Technorati, where visitors may linger for two minutes, Twiners remain on the site for 15 minutes. In the world of advertising, that's a substantial jump that represents a highly motivating business opportunity, particularly when these visitors are deeply engaged in interests that are important to them and can be identified, quantified, targeted, and served.

Twine is a business that sees an opportunity to use semantic technology in a way that other technologies can't easily replicate, if at all. Semantic Web technology is providing Twine with a competitive advantage in two critical processes: developing a valuable audience, and providing advertisers with a highly targeted, systematic way of reaching this audience.

Entrepreneurs reading this book should be paying attention: You should be looking into any specialty markets where people might benefit from semantics-based social networks, e-commerce sites, or other viable consumer applications.

Harpers Magazine

URL: www.harpers.org

Headquarters: New York, NY, USA

Semantic Technology Products (Primary): Harpers.org (online)

Circulation: 200,000+ (individuals and businesses)

Harper's Magazine is one of the oldest magazines published in the United States, and now it's one of the most technically advanced as well. Beginning in 2003, the magazine began to work with Paul Ford, a Semantic Web visionary, to eke more value out of an initially limited set of content.

Harper's, shown in Figure 15-1, is a popular general-interest magazine with an emphasis on politics, culture, and the arts. It includes content from the *Weekly Review* dating back to 2000, the Harper's Index, a statistical portrait of the world dating back to 1998, and the full text of scanned archives dating back to 1850, when the magazine started.

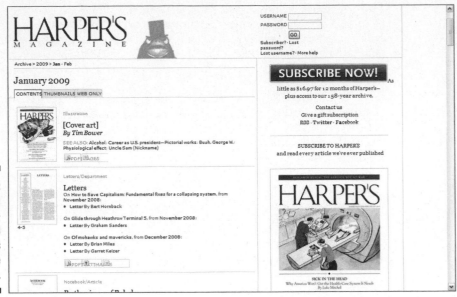

Figure 15-1:
Browsing
the semanti-
cally linked
Harper's
Magazine
archives.

The project to insert some Semantic Web behavior started with segmenting the content into categories and then arranging them into a taxonomy. The technology approach leverages a simple set of ontological relationships, a traditional taxonomy of content, and narrative content that is split into smaller sections and then linked back to the content taxonomy.

Although the net effect of this approach is seemingly complex (to take 300 static pages with fairly static content and enable the Web site to generate more than 1,100 pages of remixed content), the actual usefulness of the Web site improves dramatically. Remixed and repurposed content may appear in many different contexts and in different locations, whereas the underlying data mostly remains stable and easy to manage.

Some of the initial benefits for Harper's, according to Mr. Ford, include an uptick in Web site traffic and higher subscription revenues, lower cost of Web site maintenance, and a growing database of facts and events that benefit online readers in all areas of the Web site.

Albeit a fairly niche implementation, this example from Harper's represents the very best of how even the most simple and elemental use of Semantic Web frameworks can have a huge impact, making static, content-heavy Web sites more dynamic, more open, and better able to respond to reader interests and behaviors.

DBpedia and DBpedia Mobile

URL: http://wiki.dbpedia.org

Headquarters: Berlin, Germany (Primary)

Semantic Technology Products (Primary): Wikipedia Datasets

Facts: 100,000,000+ (converted RDF from Wikipedia)

DBpedia is a somewhat audacious community effort aiming to extract all the information from Wikipedia (the free online encyclopedia) into a structured Semantic Web format. By converting all the Wikipedia unstructured content into structured RDF, as shown by all the different vocabularies named in Figure 15-2, the folks at DBpedia are set to enable users to ask highly targeted questions as queries to a database containing all the Wikipedia data. In contrast to Wikipedia's typical full-text search, the Semantic Web query language can enable much more precise answers and even new applications to be built on top of the Wikipedia data.

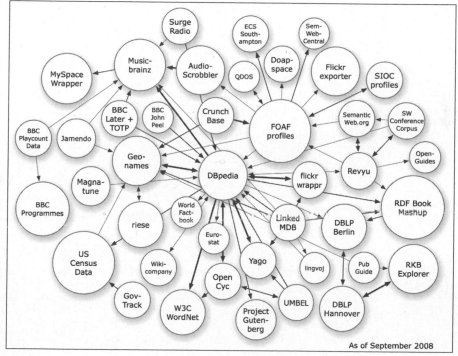

Figure 15-2: The linked data concept: Vocabularies and ontologies from everywhere are connected!

As of September 2008

The DBpedia community, principally located in Europe, has made this information available on the Web using an open-source GNU license. This means that the data can be yours for your application, on a royalty-free basis, using any of the three main interfaces to DBpedia:

- ✔ **SPARQL Endpoint,** which allows standard RDF SPARQL queries into the vast 100m+ triples DBpedia database hosted online

- ✔ **Linked Data Interface,** which allows Semantic Web browsers and crawlers to quickly navigate and drill-around the triples

- ✔ **Database Extract,** which would allow you to import the data into your own RDF database

The Wikipedia source itself consists of more than 7 million articles in 250 languages and a continuous growth rate of more than 3 percent. Wikipedia articles are mostly unstructured content, but they also contain structured content such as information boxes, images with metadata, a categorization scheme, and data tables. This rich data can be easily added to the structured information extracted from the main articles and is included in the overall RDF triples dataset hosted by DBpedia.

Users of DBpedia are usually focused in just a few use case areas. These use cases include improving search engine reliability by merging or referencing DBpedia content in searches, and leveraging the data in new software applications as a way to include royalty-free structured content from the Web. Others on the very cutting edge are leveraging the DBpedia data as the very core of the Linked Data Web project — a global effort to make the Semantic Web pervasive in and of itself.

One particularly compelling software application that is using the DBpedia data is the DBpedia Mobile client for mobile phones. This software client provides a way to see localized data about nearby attractions on a map of where you are now, as shown in Figure 15-3. The Marbles Linked Data Browser is embedded to render views of those attractions and to drill into background information about locations, attractions, restaurant reviews, and any other interlinked dataset.

This DBpedia Mobile application is currently running only on Windows Mobile and a little bit on Apple iPhone at the time of this writing, but it's certainly an application and vision to keep an eye on. I certainly expect more of these kinds of features to make it to phones as a standard service in the years to come.

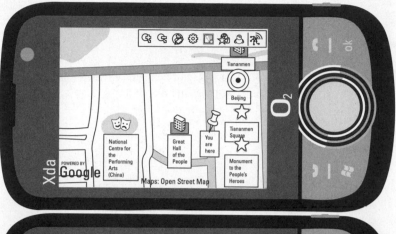

Figure 15-3: Browsing localized Semantic Web data from your phone while in China.

Yahoo!

URL: http://developer.yahoo.com/searchmonkey

Headquarters: Sunnyvale, CA, USA

Products (Primary): SearchMonkey

In his special report written last year, David Provost spoke with Amit Kumar about Yahoo! in light of recent developments in the industry. I've worked with David and other Yahoo! search experts to provide you some of those facts and insights about Yahoo! and their Semantic Web implementations.

The search industry is serious business for marketers, and any new technology or feature that can provide a competitive edge is ruthlessly exploited. SearchMonkey is Yahoo!'s opening shot at using Semantic technology (RDFa, eRDF, and microformats) to produce a search experience that hopes to tilt more eyeballs and market share in Yahoo!'s favor. The use of Semantic Web in search results is an evolving practice, but a simple example is annotating a published Web page so that search software can recognize with certainty that a particular string of numbers is actually a phone number, a date, or perhaps a restaurant ranking.

Another scenario might be the publisher of a Web site that sells concert tickets embedding Semantic Web annotations that deliver telephone numbers and a running count of tickets remaining to a concert. Someone searching for tickets to this concert would see the site's phone number and the remaining ticket count in the search results, thus eliminating the need to navigate to the ticket seller's site to find the same information.

In this concert tickets example, the site owner gets a jump on any competing ticket sellers, and Yahoo! can claim it's offering a better search experience for the user and better services for the advertiser. Consumers of search results win because they stand to get essential information presented on a single page and not distributed across several sites. Even if all ticket sites in the example used Semantic Web annotations to deliver information, all parties would still win because of the quick comparisons this would make possible.

SearchMonkey is a key element in what Yahoo! calls its *Yahoo! Open Strategy* (Y!OS), which is an effort to build a community of developers and publishers for its search platform. Yahoo! hopes that search consumers find the experience compelling enough to start submitting more and more searches through them.

SearchMonkey presently delivers enhanced results for movies, Yelp, LinkedIn, StumbleUpon, and hundreds of other sites found at `http://gallery.search.yahoo.com`.

hakia

URL: www.hakia.com

Headquarters: New York, NY, USA

Semantic Technology Products (Primary): hakia.com Search Engine

Funding: $21,000,000+ (privately held)

hakia is a search engine focused on Web-based semantic searches using graph-based data and ontologies to improve search results. In contrast, most conventional search engines generate results via statistical and popularity-ranking algorithms, but a popular Web site may not always be credible, and a credible Web site may not always be popular. As a result, a search may suffer from wasted search time or drilling around using misleading information.

hakia's semantic technology aims to provide a new search experience that's focused on quality, not popularity. These search results satisfy the following three criteria simultaneously:

✔ Come from credible Web sites recommended by librarians

✔ Represent the most recent information available

✔ Remain absolutely relevant to the query

Users of the Web site find that hakia search results are organized in a tabbed format (see Figure 15-4) that clearly distinguishes results as Web results, hakia Credible Sites, images, and news. This new tabbed format reinforces the delivery of focus, clarity, and credibility in hakia search.

hakia also has a developer community Web site that enables interested people to collaborate on search projects or semantically annotate their own Web pages. A few of the topics being explored in this community are Librarians' Corner; Rate hakia versus Google, Yahoo!, and MSN; Webmasters Tools and Page Submission; Semantic Advertising at hakia.com; and other projects in the Lab.

Semantic search technology like hakia can enable more accurate retrieval of information via concept or meaning match. The technology is effective for many domains and content types, as it is perhaps the only method that can be appropriately applied to credible, dynamic, and structured content. Most of this type of content is statistically flat (infertile) for popularity algorithms (conventional search engines like Google) to work effectively beyond common queries.

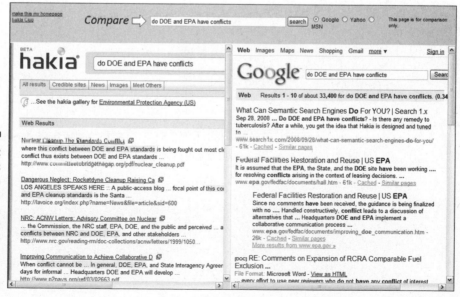

Figure 15-4: hakia is happy to have comparisons versus other popular search engines.

The hakia.com search engine is currently operating in beta mode while the ongoing development and analysis are underway. The folks at hakia are currently indexing credible content in vertical domains such as medicine, finance, law, science, travel, arts, history, as well as other content-rich topics. hakia's language coverage is primarily English. However, coverage of Portuguese, Spanish, Italian, Polish, and Turkish has also been started.

Freebase (by Metaweb)

URL: www.freebase.com

RDF URL: http://rdf.freebase.com

Headquarters: San Francisco, CA, USA

Semantic Technology Products (Primary): freebase.com Open Database

Funding: $50,000,000+ (privately held)

Freebase is a Web site and database created by Metaweb Technologies. It's an open creative commons database that grandly aims to contain all of the world's information. It's a graph database built and populated by a broad community and is free for anyone to query, contribute to, build applications on top of, or integrate into his or her Web site. By structuring the world's data in this manner, using the Semantic Web frameworks, the Freebase community hopes to create and continuously evolve a truly global resource that will one day allow people and machines everywhere to access information far more easily and quickly than they can today.

Freebase covers millions of topic areas in hundreds of knowledge categories. It draws from large, open data sets like Wikipedia, MusicBrainz, and the SEC archives to round out its information. Freebase also contains structured information on popular topics like movies, music, people, and locations. Importantly, this database is well organized and available via open APIs, including an RDF-based linked data API. Any of the Freebase information can be supplemented by a global community of users working together to add structured information on a diverse range of subject areas.

Danny Hillis, the software industry luminary and founder of Freebase, has said that, "All of the information in Freebase will be available under a license that makes it freely shareable." But, in the future, the company hopes to generate business revenue by also organizing and disseminating access to proprietary data that corporations would pay for.

Freebase's ontologies, called Freebase *types,* are themselves user-editable. This way, users and contributors to Freebase can experiment and add their own types, which can become broadly adopted if accepted by the administrator of the information category or domain it applies to.

Technically, the Freebase system runs on a database infrastructure created in-house by Metaweb that utilizes a graph model at its core. Native Freebase queries to the database are made with Metaweb Query Language (MQL), but Freebase also supports an RDF profile built around the linked data principles of the Semantic Web community.

TripIt

URL: www.tripit.com

Headquarters: San Francisco, CA, USA

Semantic Technology Products (Primary): TripIt.com Travel Assistant

Funding: $6,000,000+ (privately held)

Online travel is already more than a decade old, and more than half of U.S. travelers now book their travel online. But as the popularity of airline, hotel, and rental car supplier Web sites has grown, the typical traveler now has to keep track of multiple, potentially confusing, travel reservations to organize their trips. A typical trip today might include a flight booked at United.com, a hotel room booked at Expedia and a rental car booked at Dollar.com.

Organizing these disparate itineraries is where TripIt helps out. To use TripIt, you simply forward all your travel confirmation e-mails to plans@tripit. com. The TripIt Itinerator semantic engine processes and combines all the related bookings into a master itinerary. Then TripIt uses the trip data to automatically pull information from other websites, including

- ✔ Daily weather forecasts from NOAA
- ✔ Local maps and driving directions from Google
- ✔ Unique city guides from Wikipedia, Flickr, and Eventful

TripIt aims to apply the linking power of social networking to improve the travel experience. It will let you share your itinerary and collaborate on planning trips. With TripIt, it's easy to see when your travel plans overlap so people can connect with friends and colleagues while on the road. In fact, a recent collaboration between TripIt and LinkedIn now directly connects you to your LinkedIn connections when you're traveling, so you'll be notified if a LinkedIn connection is in your neighborhood.

The technology at the heart of TripIt is the Itinerator, which is TripIt's patent-pending and proprietary Semantic Web technology for automatically creating itineraries from travel confirmation e-mails. The Itinerator is a technology platform built to work with most major travel Web sites. This engine transforms unstructured e-mails into structured data and is able to intelligently perform tasks for a user, including aggregating related data from other

Web sites and services. Current examples of the data it aggregates include weather, maps, directions, and city guides. Data on the Web is increasingly being geo- and time-indexed, which enables deep personalization.

TripIt is in a unique position to benefit from the coming of the Semantic Web because more and more online data is made machine readable for intelligent agents and services such as TripIt. TripIt has moved beyond the browser to utilize an e-mail interface with support for open standards like iCalendar and microformats. Additionally, the TripIt To Me and TripIt Mobile options enable travelers to access all their travel plans from their mobile devices. The company's goal is to provide travel information when and where users need it, including online, in their calendars, via a mobile device, and of course as a printed itinerary.

TripIt is a classic example of a regular, every-day business model being transformed and empowered by the combination of Semantic Web and Natural Language Processing (NLP) technologies.

ZoomInfo

URL: www.zoominfo.com

Headquarters: Waltham, MA, USA

Semantic Technology Products (Primary): ZoomInfo.com People Finder

Funding: $7,000,000+ (privately held)

People Profiled: 43 million+

Companies Profiled: 3.9 million+

ZoomInfo is a people-finder and business information search engine with information on more than 45 million people and 5 million companies. ZoomInfo's semantic search engine continually crawls the Web, scouring millions of targeted company Web sites, news feeds, and other online sources to identify information on people, companies, products, services, and industries, as shown in Figure 15-5. ZoomInfo organizes this discovered information into easy-to-read profiles that can be queried by anybody.

ZoomInfo technology represents one of the most sophisticated, automatic content-generation systems and has already secured five patents with two more patents pending. The ZoomInfo data is extracted and compiled by NLP, AI algorithms, and data integration programs.

The ZoomInfo semantic search engine analyzes sentences to understand their meanings and to extract relevant information about companies and people, such as the industry a company is in and its products or services, or the company a person works for and her job title. It employs artificial intelligence algorithms to analyze Web site pages and to create a graph model of their contents. With these algorithms, ZoomInfo analyzes the type and content of a Web site based on how it's constructed. ZoomInfo is able to deduce that a specific paragraph is a company description or that a specific address contains the location of a company's headquarters in order to extract the most accurate and relevant information.

After the most relevant data is extracted, information integration logic allows ZoomInfo to sift and to organize data, analyzing the information and determining what's up-to-date and what's not. ZoomInfo then creates or updates company and people profiles to deliver business users fresh, accurate, comprehensive, and objective information. Finally, that content is delivered via a conventional search box, or alternatively as a paid service for third-party businesses to receive the most up-to-date and accurate information inside their own business systems.

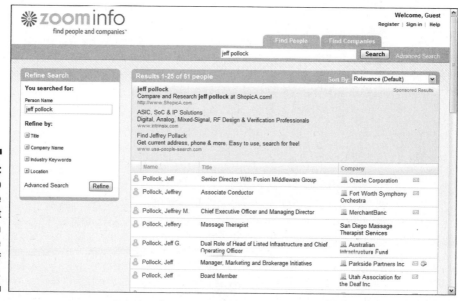

Figure 15-5: ZoomInfo finds me first, but also again at the bottom of the list.

BBC online

URL: www.bbc.co.uk

Headquarters: London, United Kingdom

Semantic Technology Products (Primary): BBC Programmes

Long on the forefront of new technology, the BBC (British Broadcasting Corporation) is no slouch when it comes to using advanced software technologies. The BBC was on the first wave of Web 2.0 technology, and it also is an early adopter of new communication mediums like Twitter. It shouldn't come as any surprise then, that it's also pushing the limits of Semantic Web in the online world of BBC.com.

One of the first forays into the Semantic Web by the BBC was rolled out in order to provide direct access to the actual data backing BBC content and programs. The BBC team designed a Semantic Web ontology covering program data — called the Programmes (using the British English spelling) Ontology. This ontology, as depicted in Figure 15-6, provides Web identifiers for concepts such as brand, series, and episode. The ontology is divided into two main parts. First, it captures categorical information about programs, and the relations between those program categories. For example, it allows the description of a brand, a series constituting it, a subseries, and an episode in it. The second part of the ontology describes episodes and their broadcast content on a particular service.

But the BBC doesn't plan to stop with the Programmes Ontology and simply call it a day with the Semantic Web. Instead, there are a host of initiatives that are in various stages of planning an rollout that cover the use of Semantic Web technology for Linked Data initiatives and the use of NLP to improve the discovery and navigation of content on the BBC Web properties.

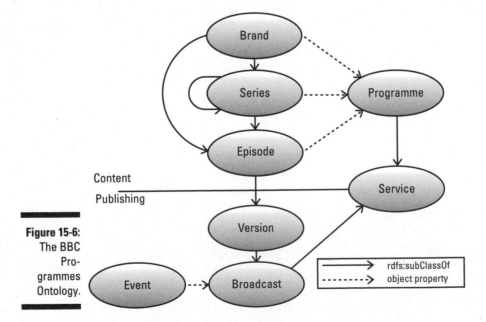

Figure 15-6:
The BBC Programmes Ontology.

The BBC owns and operates many different Web site properties on behalf of the U.K. taxpayers, most of that content and data is public domain, and the properties themselves belong to the people of the U.K. These Web sites might encompass news, music, television and other kinds of media. But how can all the content in the different properties be linked together, or linked with other public domain content? You guessed it: by using the Semantic Web. Working with the Linked Data initiative, the BBC is considering tying into the broader community of free Linked Data by bringing in the BBC Music data, BBC Topics (television), BBC Programmes, BBC News, and other BBC data into the broader community of RDF Linked Data.

Figure 15-7 shows how the BBC Web site content could be transformed by the use of Linked Data and NLP services — giving users of the Web site better content, more accurate linking, and jumping off links (that are automatic and highly reliable) to external content that's relevant to the content that is currently being browsed.

BBC's rich tradition of using cutting-edge technology in media likely portends a long and interesting journey with the Semantic Web. As the next 5–10 years unfold, you'll no doubt see more and more of the BBC content intermingled with public, open-source data from the LinkedIn community, and you'll probably see the BBC leading the way with easy to use Web content with Semantic Web machinery under the hood. A great place to see more of the BBC vision is in this online slide show: `www.slideshare.net/onpause/made-of-links-the-bbc-and-dbpedia-collaboration-at-dublin-core-2008-berlin-presentation`.

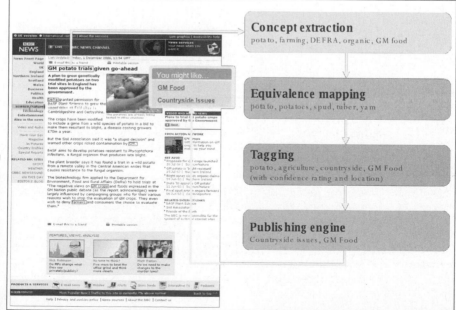

Figure 15-7: BBC vision for automatic annotations and category-based linking.

Business Software

Business software for the Semantic Web is the software that most people may never realize exists. All too often it's only the IT folks who know what software is really powering the enterprise. Nonetheless, even though you may not ever hear about these applications, it's business software that keeps businesses running efficiently and productively. The following Semantic Web business software examples just might change the way your business runs in the future!

Thomson Reuters Calais

URL: www.opencalais.com

Headquarters: New York, NY, USA

Products (Primary): The Calais Initiative

Employees: 50,000

Revenue: $13.94 billion

Installed Base: 5,000 developers, 1.2 million pieces of content processed per day

Again working with David Provost, I've spoken with Krista Thomas from Thomson Reuters to provide you some key facts and insights about its exceptionally cool Semantic Web implementation called Calais.

The Calais Initiative (Calais), wholly owned and operated as a division within Thomson Reuters, comprises several tools for processing text, but the core product is an NLP engine. When presented with a body of text, the Calais Web service returns the *named entities* (the categories to which the document's key terms and concepts are assigned), facts, and events it discovers within the document. The relationships between these items are also identified and embedded in the results. Essentially, the results are the semantic metadata of the document and can be thought of as the document's knowledge content, which can then be published and made available for searching and navigation.

On its own, and applied to one or two small, short documents, this might not seem exceptionally valuable. But deployed on the Web and made available as a free service, Calais is in a position to process massive amounts of data (text, quantitative, graphic, and so on) and extract its knowledge content. After the NLP tasks are complete, the content can then be searched, combined with other content, or remixed and searched along with other data. There are three main types of data that Calais can remix your data with:

> ✔ Any data from the Web
>
> ✔ Proprietary Thomson Reuters content
>
> ✔ Open data from the Linking Open Data project (see Chapter 2)

Further, any combination of the three data sources can be mixed together to address a unique and particular domain of interest.

The Calais team's goal is to provide the world's best tool for extracting structure from any kind of content, recognizing its type, the concepts that are contained, their relationships, and doing so not just within a single file, but across a span of files that could be as large as the Web itself. With recent updates occurring in early 2009 that bring Calais in line with the Linked Data initiative, this vision is well within reach.

The fact that Thomson Reuters, a global publishing giant, is sponsoring Calias suggests that this Semantic Web startup will be around for quite a long time. Furthermore, at this time, Calais is in the final stages of testing its "infinite scalability" initiative, based upon cloud computing principles, which is designed to address growth in demand or spikes in utilization.

Calais has grown very quickly. The effect of this growth has been to discard the original usage projections because demand has so vastly exceeded expectations. Curiously, the vast majority of demand for Calais has existed almost entirely outside of any Thomson Reuters media properties or business units, but according to the company, this is likely to change in 2009.

Deploying Calais over the vast, professionally developed and controlled content in the Thomson Reuters empire would be a remarkable step in the evolution of the Semantic Web. After 150 years as a traditional news wire service and publisher, Thomson Reuters' content in Semantic Web formats could quickly become something not yet fully understood, but quite possibly far more powerful and useful than what any traditional publishers have ever offered their customers.

In addition to the continued internal roll-out of Calais, outside demand is moving beyond experimenters and creative small companies exploring this new service. Demand from large organizations, including well-established publishers, is growing at an unexpectedly high rate. As a result, larger organizations or ventures built around Calais can expect to see availability backed by Service Level Agreements (SLAs). Special situations are also being anticipated where Calais is deployed on an enterprise scale behind a corporate firewall.

Over the past 150 years in the publishing industry, Thomson Reuters has amassed a body of high-quality content that's possibly the largest in the world. This content will continue to grow, but the advent of the Web has unleashed a torrent of new content available to consumers on a global scale.

Because this content is outside Thomson Reuters's editorial and production controls, the company considers it to be "wild" content. This label doesn't mean it's bad — some of it happens to be exceedingly good quality.

Calais puts Thomson Reuters in a unique position to extend its core competencies by including "wild" content alongside content that it controls. This is important to the larger business because:

✔ The fundamental nature of publishing and using content is changing.

✔ Open-source content dwarfs the content Thomson Reuters controls internally.

✔ Professionally produced content will continue to command a premium.

✔ The Open Access movement and similar efforts by academics, researchers, and other content authors seeking to retain control of their work will continue and grow.

✔ Flexible integration/interoperation of different types of content will provide powerful added value to Thomson Reuters customers.

Oracle Database

URL: www.oracle.com

Headquarters: Redwood Shores, CA, USA

Semantic Technology Products (Primary): Oracle Spatial Database

Installed Base: 250,000+ (across all product areas)

Oracle is the world's largest enterprise software company. Oracle sells many products that have some Semantic Web components, but the flagship Oracle Database has the RDF option that is leading the way for commercially successful RDF databases.

As part of Oracle Spatial 11g, an option for Oracle Database 11g Enterprise Edition, Oracle delivers a very advanced overall semantic data management capability. With native support for RDF/RDFS/OWL standards, the Oracle semantic data store enables application developers to benefit from an open, scalable, secure, integrated, efficient platform for RDF- and OWL-based applications. These semantic database features enable storing, loading, and DML access to RDF/OWL data and ontologies, inference using OWL and RDFS semantics and user-defined rules, querying of RDF/OWL data and ontologies, and ontology-assisted querying of enterprise (relational) data.

Oracle Semantic Database features support for storing, loading and DML operations on RDF/OWL models. The database's normalized storage architecture manages the complexity arising from repeated usage of typically long URIs and literal values associated with the subjects, objects, and predicates across triples. This leads to space-efficient storage, and scalable and high-performance loading, querying, and inference of RDF/OWL data.

The Oracle Database features include a native inference engine for efficient and scalable inference using common subsets of OWL semantics. This OWL inference engine makes the existing native inference for RDF, RDFS, and user-defined rules (used for additional specialized inference capabilities) more efficient and scalable. Inference can be done using any combination of these supported entailment regimes.

RDF/OWL data contained in the Oracle Database can be queried using SQL. As with the core Oracle Database Enterprise Edition, the RDF subsystems also incorporate key performance and scalability features that can help address the most demanding enterprise-class semantic Web solutions. Oracle Spatial semantic database features exploit the benefits of Advanced Compression and Partitioning, while fully supporting Real Applications Clusters (RAC). RAC is Oracle's key technology for clustered and grid-enable database systems.

Available since 2004, Oracle has clearly demonstrated a commitment to innovation in the Semantic Web area and is now the leading large vendor supplying foundation technologies for this emerging sector.

IBM Registry

URL: www.ibm.com

Headquarters: Armonk, NY, USA

Semantic Technology Products (Primary): WebSphere Service Registry and Repository

Installed Base: 100,000+ (across all product areas)

IBM is one of the largest overall enterprise software suppliers, covering databases, mainframe software, integration software, and business intelligence systems. It was one of the first to embrace the ideas of the Semantic Web in its research labs and also one of the first vendors to leverage Semantic Web technology in a mainstream way for service-oriented software products.

The IBM WebSphere Service Registry and Repository is principally responsible for the description and discovery of Web Service metadata. Unlike some of the more conventional vendors that stick closely to the troubled UDDI (Universal Description, Discovery, and Integration) standard, IBM chose to forge its own direction with a system that uses RDF and OWL models at the very core of the metadata framework.

In some ways, IBM has only dipped a toe in the water of Semantic Web; most of its investments lay in the more docile IBM Labs environment. But as it releases more mainstream products using RDF, it continues to catch up with Microsoft and Oracle, which each have more and more Semantic Web products already in production.

Garlik Online Identity Protection

URL: www.garlik.com

Headquarters: Esher, Surrey, United Kingdom

Semantic Technology Products (Primary): Data Patrol

Installed Base: Tens of thousands (individuals and businesses)

Responding to the ongoing crisis of identity theft, Garlik aims to give consumers and businesses more power over where and how their information appears on the Web and provides an array of services to protect its customers' information. Garlik was founded by Mike Harris, founding CEO of Egg plc, former Egg CIO Tom Ilube, and former British Computer Society president Professor Nigel Shadbolt. Garlik is one of the first businesses to release a Web-scale commercial application of Semantic Web technology. Garlik's core application Data Patrol enables its customers to find and understand what personal information is in the public domain about them and control their identities on the Web.

Supporting its cutting-edge application of Semantic Web technology, Garlik has notably appointed a panel of world-class ID-protection and Semantic Web technology experts to advise the business including Professor Wendy Hall CBE from the University of Southampton, Sir Tim Berners-Lee, the inventor of the Web and Semantic Web, Simon Davies, director of Privacy International and Daniel Cooper, renowned privacy lawyer with Covington & Burling. Garlik is a privately held, venture-backed firm.

The Garlik technical platform consists of an overall system architecture that depends heavily on the power of RDF, ontologies, and NLP techniques to enable semantically informed search and data harvesting. The RDF triple store is a home-built clustered system that is purported to scale into the tens of billions of statements. Although the inference power of the Garlik system does not include OWL-DL reasoning, the SPARQL query standard is used as a common interface to the repository, and its related application QDOS uses a FOAF-like ontology.

Clearly, the Garlik applications are taking the lead in applied Semantic Web applications. The executives are tireless evangelists for the Semantic Web, not just because they love the technology, but also because they genuinely believe that it offers them and their customers a tangible benefit in the quest to protect identity and prevent identity theft.

Dow Jones Client Solutions

URL: http://solutions.dowjones.com/djcs

Headquarters: New York, NY, USA

Products (Primary): Synaptica

Christine Connors, the global Director of Semantic Technology for Dow Jones, spoke with David Provost for an interview about how Dow Jones is using Semantic Web technology to get ahead in its Client Services division. This section summarizes that interview and describes more about a revolutionary Dow Jones product called Synaptica.

Dow Jones Client Solutions (DJCS) offers a range of software products and consulting services for businesses that depend on publishing content. The Synaptica product marks the company's entry to the Semantic Web space. Synaptica can be used to build and manage vocabularies, taxonomies, thesauruses, and the inherent metadata of these structures. Environments that deploy Synaptica are usually enterprise-oriented and behind a corporate firewall. In these enterprise settings, the customer goals of Dow Jones might be to improve enterprise search results, standardize corporate libraries for compliance purposes, scope out the information that exists within the enterprise, or support the creation of a "single source of truth".

Synaptica has actually been in general release for more than 12 years (but acquired by Dow Jones less than 3 years ago). During that time, increasingly sophisticated and Semantic capabilities have been added, such as support for RDF, OWL, and SKOS, the first two of these being crucial W3C recommendations. Note that Dow Jones's use of the term *taxonomy* may be an expediency to ease the introduction of concepts like ontologies, inferencing, and other "more Semantic" terminology to mainstream audiences.

Dow Jones's (recently acquired by News Corp.) ownership of high-quality, professionally produced content benefits its global install base. Unlike nearly every other entrant in the Semantic industry, Dow Jones could remain quite busy just by introducing Synaptica to each of its existing customers and gradually integrating these capabilities with the vast span content and various media channels owned by News Corp.

The scope of opportunities within News Corp. alone would make most Semantic vendors ecstatic if they occupied a similar almost-preferred-vendor status. If the DJCS team is industrious and inventive, as it certainly appears to be, it may well introduce innovative uses of Semantic technology within its corporate bounds and also among the company's extensive installed base. Managing a vast span of content has given Dow Jones a very clear understanding of metadata and Semantics, and these lessons will be quite valuable to the company's other customers.

What is very clear to even the casual observer is that this is yet another media giant moving forward with an investment in the Semantic Web. Given Dow Jones/News Corp.'s track record of success, the company will quite likely discover interesting and productive uses for Synaptica and everything this product spawns. If your Dow Jones account rep isn't already talking about Synaptica, ask about it — the results could be very interesting.

Microsoft

URL: www.microsoft.com

Headquarters: Redmond, WA, USA

Semantic Technology Products (Primary): Powerset and Connected Services

2008 Revenue: $60 billion (across all products)

Microsoft is no stranger to Semantic Web technology. But rather than seeing a big-bang approach to Semantic Web or selling standalone infrastructure for it, Microsoft instead appears to be dabbling in several different application areas. A diverse range of applications from Microsoft including search, digital asset management, and telecommunications services have all included some degree of RDF/OWL support.

Microsoft Interactive Media manager is a collaborative environment for handling media management tasks for professionals — commonly known as a Media Asset Management system. One common problem area for managing large amounts of digital media is the maintenance of the metadata describing all those assets. Microsoft has invested in an RDF- and OWL-based approach for tagging labels and relationships at the metadata layer; further, a derivative of SPARQL is used for querying the model and finding relations.

Microsoft Connected Services Framework is an application service bundle aimed at telecommunications providers for managing content and networks. One of the core features of this kind of tooling is the maintenance of user profiles. This profile management system for Connected Services Framework uses RDF and SPARQL to ensure flexible and dynamic access to continually changing user profiles.

Finally, one of the high-profile early acquisitions of semantic search technology came when Microsoft acquired Powerset. Powerset's technology is similar to the technology from DBpedia described earlier in this chapter — providing an RDF triples view into Wikipedia data, fully exposed for semantic search, as shown in Figure 15-8. The underlying technology consists of a high-end RDF triples database and a lot of relationship metadata and extraction technology for joining concepts extracted from the unstructured Wikipedia data. At the time of this writing, there's still a lot of speculation about where this technology will end up at Microsoft. One safe guess is that it will be offered as part of the Microsoft Live Search and also for Microsoft Enterprise Search (FAST).

Certain groups at Microsoft are clearly interested in the Semantic Web, but I have yet to see whether the company as a whole will really get behind the trend in a big way.

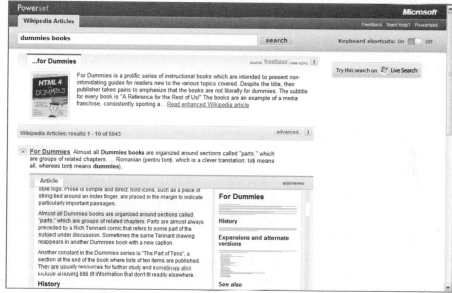

Figure 15-8: Microsoft Powerset searching on RDF-enabled Wikipedia.

Metatomix Semantic Integration

URL: www.metatomix.com

Headquarters: Dedham, MA, USA

Products (Primary): Branded as the "360" family of Applications

Installed Base: 50+

Founded in 2000, Metatomix is a leading semantic integration startup vendor. Metatomix solutions intelligently link data from existing disparate systems to create a common semantic view of information across an enterprise, thereby providing a 360-degree view of business information. As a result, business applications can leverage information that comes from across many data sources. The combined data — including relationships and correlations that were previously undiscovered — can actually create new, insightful information. This information can be added to or modified as needed, without extensive software coding, providing an extremely flexible information foundation for your business applications.

Metatomix has been different from its founding, focusing on the end-to-end business value. As an early adopter of semantic services that have added business rules, workflow, and embraced W3C Semantic Web standards to create an end-to-end development and deployment environment. Metatomix 360 aims to achieve the following:

- ✔ Generate a unified, 360-degree view of data that can extend across enterprise silos, disparate content domains, and unstructured data accessible anywhere on the Web.

- ✔ Automate the enrichment and discovery of previously unobserved relationships.

- ✔ Leverage a rules engine to drive business process based on information discovery.

- ✔ Offer an extensible application layer with dynamic screen generation based upon user role.

Regardless of whether the integration points are traditional databases, Web services, or legacy applications, Metatomix's semantic integration platform can provide a modular framework for solving information-centric business challenges. Leveraging W3C semantic standards such as OWL ontologies for domain descriptions and RDF, for data tagging, the Metatomix platform more tightly links the context of the integrated data to the application for which it is bound. Many conventional middleware approaches are more rigid at the information layer and can't provide the extensibility required to build dynamic applications. This highly flexible, extensible approach allows Metatomix to integrate complex data sources exponentially faster than traditional technologies.

The embedded rules engine then builds on the dynamic data model of the ontology and allows direct action to be taken. Specifically, the customer can select specific entities within the model to iteratively enrich that entity, automating the discovery of previously unobserved relationships. The resulting data is then presented in a single 360-degree perspective via a thin, extensible application layer that offers dynamic screen generation based upon user role.

The distinguishing factor of the Metatomix offering is the complimentary combination of a flexible data integration layer and an intelligent, rules-driven enrichment engine that further discovers related information across the disparate enterprise, all in a single platform. Additionally, data is not moved or replicated; rather, the source data remains where it is, and results are persisted only as needed by the business application.

The net result that Metatomix aims to bring to its customers is the accelerated development and maintenance of real time, dynamic analytical and composite applications, improving corporate insight, decision-making, and operating efficiency.

TopQuadrant TopBraid

URL: www.topquadrant.com

Headquarters: Alexandria, VA, USA

Products (Primary): TopBraid Suite

Installed base: 500+

Both David Provost and myself have worked with TopQuadrant and have used its technologies for years. We spoke with Ralph Hodgson and Dean Allemang about their products, services, and corporate profile.

TopQuadrant's flagship product is TopBraid Suite, an integrated platform comprised of TopBraid Composer, TopBraid Live, and TopBraid Ensemble. Using TopBraid, customers can integrate data, develop and deploy semantic applications and infrastructure, and create applications that process data that have been linked or semantically combined.

TopBraid Composer is a full-strength ontology development tool and supports modeling, application development, data source configuration, and more. As a server platform, TopBraid Live is used to deploy Semantic applications, mashups, and in general, any of the solutions developed with Composer. Ensemble is a collection of out-of-the-box, configurable user interface components. With these components, developers can quickly build semantic applications that end users can use to view and interact with rich, connected collections of information. The net effect is that TopBraid is flexible enough to be used as a content management system and wiki. With add-ins, it can support faceted search, calendaring, maps, timelines, and charts and reports created with BIRT (Business Intelligence and Reporting Tools, a suite of open-source business intelligence tools).

TopBraid Suite has an open architecture and integrates with the best third-party reasoners and Semantic databases such as Oracle 11g and AllegroGraph. This suite is well suited to companies investigating the practicality and value of deploying enterprise applications of Semantic Web technology.

Training on the fundamentals of Semantic technology and its range of products is a key element of TopQuadrant's global reputation. TopQuadrant almost certainly holds more publicly accessible training courses than any other Semantic Web vendor. (See Chapter 18 for more Semantic Web training options.)

In addition to training, TopQuadrant offers unique capabilities in its toolset, such as SPARQLMotion, which is geared toward script developers as a higher-level graphic scripting language. With SPARQLMotion, script writers can connect a series of automated, predefined routines (which can also be user-written) in a way that resembles Yahoo! Pipes or OSX's "Automator" function. As a higher-level language, SPARQLMotion allows a larger team to participate in the development and maintenance of solutions created by the lower-level tools found in TopBraid Suite.

TopQuadrant as a business is purely in execution mode — it has made its plans and now it's focused on linked data exploration (uniquely enabled by SPARQL), semantically enabled content management, and enterprise architecture in a few different industries. The company's solution areas of focus are based on customer demand — TopQuadrant is one of the very few Semantic Web startups with an extensive installed base.

Part V
The Part of Tens

The 5th Wave   By Rich Tennant

"He found a dog site over an hour ago and has been in a staring contest ever since."

In this part . . .

You're near the end of the book, and it's time to debunk those pesky myths you've heard about the Semantic Web and get some useful ideas for where to go next. What's that you say? You haven't read every word in the chapters before this one? That's okay. You can find a ton of useful information in the Part of Tens and have a good idea for the next steps you should take.

Chapter 16

Ten Myths About the Semantic Web

*I*n some circles, it is fashionable to dismiss the Semantic Web. People who fancy themselves more practical or grounded find a million reasons why the status quo will remain the status quo. It is true that there are many futurists promoting the Semantic Web, and there are also many followers who simply have jumped on the bandwagon because the idea sounds cool.

However, it is also true that very smart and practical people have turned to the Semantic Web as a way forward because they've reached the limits of what status quo can solve for them. Practical people who are responsible for finding information in government data, in life sciences drug research data, or in remote corners of the World Wide Web already know the dirty secrets of search engines and have slammed into the limits of SQL. For some folks, the status quo is simply not good enough.

Nonetheless, it will remain trendy to be contrarian long after the Semantic Web is a part of everyday life. Although some contrarians simply can't be convinced to change their minds, others might simply be misinformed — this chapter is for them.

The Semantic Web Is Science Fiction

There has been a groundswell of popular wisdom among techies that the Semantic Web is merely science fiction. Truly, the devil is in the details. If people choose to define the Semantic Web as an all-knowing computer in the sky that can answer your every query and interact with you as if it were a person itself, of course it's science fiction.

But the trouble is that nobody who actually works on the Semantic Web defines it that way. Instead, the definition that most working practitioners ascribe to the Semantic Web is about its ability to link data items, not just pages, into a Web of interconnected models. These linked data items can be narrowly connected for individuals, businesses, and communities, or more widely dispersed to include entire domains of knowledge across the globe. This isn't science fiction at all.

In fact, this book shows you numerous case studies and citations of Semantic Web projects at multibillion dollar companies like Oracle, Eli Lilly, Chevron, IBM, and many more. I can assure you, dear reader, that for-profit businesses do not inject science fiction into their core business operations.

In the end, it may simply be a matter of semantics (pun intended), but the reality of the Semantic Web is definitely not science fiction if you choose to accept the pragmatic working definition of the Semantic Web supplied by the people who actually work on it. From there, you can find irrefutable evidence that the early beginnings of the Semantic Web are upon you already.

The Semantic Web Is for Tagging Web Sites

Still more damaging to the Semantic Web vision is the terribly misleading and mistaken idea that its purpose for existing is to tag Web sites. Somewhere along the way, the Semantic Web got labeled as a way to improve search accuracy. People said that it would do that by embedding hidden tags in Web pages — or, more precisely, that Web developers would have to embed the tags into their Web pages. Perhaps this rumor might seem trivial, but any software developer worth his or her salt would physically recoil at the thought of manually tagging according to some weird "standard."

Luckily, the Semantic Web isn't for that purpose and doesn't have those requirements. Whew! Contrary to popular belief, the Semantic Web . . .

- Is more than just for tagging (although it *can* be used for tagging Web content)
- Is entirely voluntary — not mandatory
- Can be 100-percent automated without developer oversight

Earlier in the book, I talk about microformats and RDFa — both of which are ways to apply Semantic Web–type structured tags within HTML content. Neither microformats nor RDFa are mandatory, and both can be automated. The value of having structure within HTML is that it allows external software systems to more easily load data from the unstructured Web.

But lest you think that this is where the Semantic Web starts and stops, I want to be clear that this whole tagging idea is a very small part of what the Semantic Web can do for you. Several chapters of this book are dedicated to the business value proposition of the Semantic Web, which is completely unrelated to the tagging value of the Semantic Web in the Internet as a whole.

The Semantic Web Will Put Google Out of Business

In April 2008, Google's market capitalization was hovering near $170 billion dollars. Google is among the biggest and most powerful companies in the world. In contrast, the Semantic Web is a small set of data standards that reside with the not-for-profit organization called the World Wide Web Consortium (W3C).

The idea that the Semantic Web could actually displace Google is laughable on many levels. On the one hand, the Semantic Web isn't even a company, or software, or a search engine — how could a nonentity compete with a corporate entity? On the other hand, the Semantic Web isn't even intended to enable better search engines — how could it realistically replace a technology it isn't designed for?

Nonetheless, the media likes hyperbole, tension, and drama. Therefore a sensational article in *The Times* (2008) stated "Google could be superseded, says web inventor!" (the Web inventor being Tim Berners-Lee). But when you read the article itself, it's clear that Tim Berners-Lee said no such thing. He even later admonished *The Times* in his personal blog for misleading readers.

In this case, the facts are that the Semantic Web is still in need of a killer app, and the media wishes this killer app would be in the search engine space. But in spite of several new search engines that do in fact use some Semantic Web standards for encoding metadata and sometimes even for influencing search results, every software engineer knows that search engines are dependent on their text-extraction capabilities, and the Semantic Web has nothing to offer in the text-extraction domain.

Fundamentally the Semantic Web is a great way to encode structured data because it's so flexible, but it has nothing to do with the complex algorithms that create structure from unstructured pages. The search engines that use the Semantic Web languages use them almost exclusively as a post-process to their text-extraction crawlers. Using RDF instead of indices provides some unique benefits that can make semantic search engines valuable for some market areas.

Even if the Semantic Web were an actual entity that could compete with the likes of Google, it by itself would have no hopes for displacing the search juggernaut.

The Semantic Web Is Too Complex to Succeed

Folks are starting to get excited about Web 3.0, and they're digging a little deeper to find out what it's all about and hopefully to start using it. First, they find a cryptic data language called RDF with really obtuse XML syntax. Perhaps that terrible syntax could be forgiven if it all still led to that giant computer in the sky. But next they find three different specifications of OWL based on some kind of math called *description logics*.

Slowly and carefully, they walk away from their computers. That's right about when most people give up. After they start to try and understand how to make their Web page's tagging system compliant with OWL, they decide right then and there that the Semantic Web is too complex to ever succeed.

Even though this book is called *Semantic Web For Dummies,* I'm not here to tell you that it's easy. But it's nowhere near being too complex for success. The main problem is the benchmark to which the Semantic Web is being compared — HTML. HTML is a rendering markup language for documents. It's barely a programming language in the loosest possible sense of the word *programming.*

The more logical benchmark for the Semantic Web specifications is in the area of data and programming languages. For instance, the Semantic Web is a good deal more complex than XML, slightly more complex than database programming, and simpler in many ways than UML and Java. In other words, a moderately competent Java programmer or database developer would have no trouble learning the Semantic Web's core features and be able to program it natively.

Clearly, this is not another HTML parlor trick. Yes, you have to be a software developer to understand how to program in the Semantic Web native languages. But, no, you do not have to be a programmer to *benefit* from the Semantic Web's power and flexibility. Just like you do not have to be a programmer to benefit from a database or from Java, there will be many software applications written with the Semantic Web as a backbone from which you will see benefit — and you will never have to know how to encode RDF as N3 or Turtle via a RESTful Web service. Leave that to the pros.

The Semantic Web Is a Catalog System

Category systems, like the Dewey Decimal System, are manufactured taxonomies that organize content based on some heuristic. In and of themselves, they're valuable for the communities that build themselves up around the system. Some systems, as are popular with Web 2.0 environments, are even self-organizing because the community is constantly adjusting and changing the categories.

But the Semantic Web is not a catalog system. In fact, there isn't even any catalog content in the Semantic Web. The Semantic Web is more like a card catalog drawer full of blank cards and empty indexes. You might rightfully say that the Semantic Web offers a framework for cataloging, but it neither offers the catalog contents nor enforces a particular indexing approach.

Even if you wanted to think narrowly about the Semantic Web as a "catalog framework," you would have to conclude that it was the most powerful catalog framework ever conceived. For example:

- ✔ Any catalog system can be implemented in the Semantic Web languages (community- or authority-based).

- ✔ The Semantic Web languages allow for community-based or librarian-based cataloging (top-down or bottom-up).

- ✔ Graph-type organization can enable easier content discovery. (Search terms can be linked and organized uniquely for whoever is doing the searching.)

- ✔ Cataloging could be achieved at Web-scale (globally upon established protocols like HTTP and URIs).

- ✔ Catalogs that were started by different people at different times using different indexes and systems could still be quickly and easily joined together.

Thus, even though the Semantic Web is not a catalog system, a category system, or even a Dewey Decimal–style index, it could indeed be implemented as a very powerful framework for catalogs. Nonetheless, it is not designed or intended to be a particular occurrence of a catalog system.

The Semantic Web Is an Ivory Tower Design

Long before the international Semantic Web standards were approved in 2004, the Semantic Web had a reputation as an *ivory tower design* flop, meaning that the idea had been created by academics with no basis in the practical world outside of the university. Indeed, it's true that the Semantic Web was largely developed within the university system. However, the Semantic Web's genesis derived from the very pragmatic observation that XML, object-oriented programming languages, and relational databases were insufficient to solve the current data and metadata challenges.

In 1997, an engineer from Apple named Ramanathan Guha and an independent consultant named Tim Bray went to work for Netscape and created a graph-based metadata language called Meta Content Framework (MCF). Eventually, MCF made it into the W3C standards process and was renamed as RDF.

In 1999, the DARPA Agent Markup Language (DAML) and the Ontology Inference Layer (OIL) first received funding to advance software technology that could automatically work with Web data. It sounds funny to say it that way, but software cannot, for the most part, automatically work with data: It needs to be programmed by a human to do so. This fact presents many challenges for working with data at very large scale — automated techniques were needed.

These government researchers had already realized that the model semantics of object-oriented notation, XML, and relational databases were insufficient to program general-purpose algorithms for automating data manipulation. That's why the DAML and OIL languages were created.

After a few years of working out the kinks, the two languages finally merged for good and were ratified as OWL — the Web Ontology Language. Thus, the true history of the Semantic Web comes from commercial businesses (for RDF) and the defense departments of the United States and Europe (for OWL).

Likewise, the Semantic Web is evolving today under much more scrutiny from the commercial world. Companies like Oracle, IBM, Adobe, Sun, Eli Lilly, Citi, and many others have vested interests and committed resources taking part in the formulation and reformulation of the standards.

History and politics aside, the design of the Semantic Web is decidedly neutral. Instead of prescribing a tightly knit framework of specifications, protocols, and other standards, the Semantic Web layers may be adopted one at a time and without any of the others. There is no ivory tower design book that says that RDF must be used in some particular way and only that way will suffice.

Quite the contrary to an ivory tower design, the Semantic Web is a framework that consists of a few data language specifications from which interoperability may be assured. At its most basic level, the Semantic Web prescribes you to encode your data such that it may be easily consumed as an RDF triple. From there, many more levels of adherence exist, but none are mandatory.

The Semantic Web Is Description Logic

If you had already heard the phrase "description logic" before opening this book, you qualify as a true propeller-head. You're either a mathematician or a logician, or you've already been following the Semantic Web standards. There are many kinds of logic, and description logics are one particular family of logics.

Clay Shirky is a regarded author of many forward-thinking technology works, and a vocal skeptic of the Semantic Web. In one particular article he wrote back in 2003, he attempts to trivialize the foundational logic of OWL — description logics. Well, Shirky mistakenly assumes too much of the role for OWL in the Semantic Web.

The first and most important point that you should remember is that the Semantic Web's foundation is RDF — no more and no less. OWL is an extremely useful and much more powerful extension of RDF, but as Jim Hendler says, "a little RDF goes a long way."

Description logics are complex if you try to understand all the math, but if you put that aside and think about why databases matter, you can begin to see why description logics are relevant and important to the Semantic Web discussion.

Databases matter because they provide computational guarantees about interacting with the data that's in them. If I query a database for a record, and that record is in there, the database will find it — guaranteed. This is completely at odds with Google-type search engines. Firstly, they don't even index the whole Web; secondly, they don't provide any computational guarantees about the data they do index. Lastly, they return so many keyword matches that it's frequently impossible to look at all the results. In technospeak, they have weak precision and good recall.

A database has a much smaller set of data to work with, but it has perfect recall and perfect precision. That's what description logics can provide when people use tags that conform to OWL fragments. This is an exceptionally good thing because as the use of these OWL fragments expands over time, the result will be a continually growing, Web-scale database that's even more computationally expressive than a relational database. Unless you're Clay Shirky, databases are good!

The Semantic Web Is Artificial Intelligence (Again)

At the beginning of the 21st century, AI was still a bad word. An AI winter had long iced-over the prospects for artificial intelligence to revolutionize computing. At various points throughout the history of AI research, the media has turned against it, and the funding ran dry. So to call the Semantic Web just another AI technology is to insult the technology and dismiss it as an abject failure.

This particular assertion — that the Semantic Web is artificial intelligence — is true. However, the underlying premise that AI is bad is actually a myth worth debunking. *Artificial intelligence* is a term coined in 1956, and it refers to the creation of intelligent machines. The AI field of research is broad and deep, encompassing areas from speech understanding to the encoding of human knowledge and brain simulation.

Several spectacular failures through the years have contributed to the widely held perception that AI as a whole is a failure, such as in the areas of speech understanding, machine translation, and expert systems. Compounding this perception of failure, the media has widely promoted some few successes that seem trivial in the big picture. IBM's Deep Blue beating Gary Kasparov at chess was a substantial feat, but understandably underwhelming in comparison to all that was promised from AI as a whole.

Nearly all modern software technology like object-oriented systems, business rule engines, relational databases, modern machine code compilers, and countless other algorithms and solution patterns have made their way from the realm of AI science fiction to become workplace science fact. Industries like financial services, life sciences, pharmaceuticals, manufacturing, and retail are all dependent on AI technology for the very core of their operations.

So what if the Semantic Web is AI? Lots of cool stuff was AI, and lots of technology that made people very rich was AI. Maybe when the Semantic Web goes entirely mainstream, everyone will forget this pesky little detail and just wallow in the glory of Web 3.0.

The Semantic Web Is a $20-Billion Industry

Measuring markets is a black art. Analysts get paid huge sums of money and spend months of their time assessing well-defined markets to issue guidance about what they're worth. But the Semantic Web isn't even considered a standalone market in 2008.

Leading software analysts such as Gartner, Forrester, IDC, and Ovum have barely acknowledged the presence of the Semantic Web technology base, much less actually tried to size its value in the marketplace. Some niche analysts, however, have completed substantial research and declared the Semantic Web industry to be a multibillion-dollar industry (Project 10x, 2008, *Semantic Wave 2008 Report: Industry Roadmap to Web 3.0 and Multibillion Dollar Market Opportunities*). To which I say, "Bah!"

Okay, perhaps that's a little harsh. The folks at Project 10x do some wonderful research, but they're also publishing very misleading figures. When a tier-one analyst (like Gartner, IDC, or Forrester) publishes figures about a software marketplace, the analyst publishes figures in terms of annual new license revenue generated in that particular software area. They're usually careful to define just which sorts of products qualify, provide separate figures for services, and exclude loosely related technologies that only partially depend on the main software being considered.

The figures published by Project 10x, on the other hand, are inclusive of Semantic Web software revenues, professional services implementing that software, software revenue of products that embed Semantic Web technology in one way or another, and an aggregate of the venture capital investments occurring in the related fields. Project 10x also openly defines semantic technology as a super-set of Semantic Web technology and lumps in some more traditional AI technologies like business rule engines and text analytics.

Promoting the Semantic Web is admirable, but the implied linkage of these misleading billion-dollar figures to a Semantic Web software marketplace may actually be a disservice to the fledgling industry.

The appropriate way to size a software market is to add up all the new money being spent on licensed software and subscription services to the new technology itself, not including unrelated technology that happens to use some aspect of semantics. A more realistic estimate for 2007–2008 new software revenues in the more narrowly defined Semantic Web area would probably be measured in the tens of millions, not billions.

The Semantic Web Hasn't Changed the World

If the Semantic Web is so great, how come is hasn't changed the world yet? That whole "vision thing" with the Semantic Web is still to blame here. The expectations of the masses upon hearing about the Semantic Web are simply too high to really fulfill — thus, the perception exists that the Semantic Web hasn't really done anything yet.

But what are the facts?

- The Semantic Web has spawned a new way of consuming news from one of the world's largest news organizations — Reuters (CNet News, 2008).

- The Semantic Web is responsible for scientists finding new protein families that might lead to better medicine (Wolstencroft, et al., 2005, *A Little Semantics Goes a Long Way in Biology.* School of Computer Science, University of Manchester, UK).

- Enterprise software companies like Oracle, IBM, SAP, and Microsoft are using Semantic Web technology in their products.

- *The New York Times, Business Week, Information Week,* and *The Economist* have all run stories about how the Semantic Web is changing the technology landscape today.

- Governments across the world are using Semantic Web technology for defense, environmental protection, disaster preparedness, state and local justice, and many other uses.

- The Semantic Web is the backbone for the global cancer research data exchange (National Cancer Institute Thesaurus).

- Universities worldwide have shifted their curriculums to teach the Semantic Web as part of their regular computer science programs.

- European and United States governments alone have invested hundreds of millions of dollars in R&D funding (Davis, Allemang, and Coyne, 2004).

Without a doubt, the Semantic Web has not yet produced the kind of massive societal change that the first Internet revolution did — but don't forget that the Internet "revolution" was quietly happening for several decades before the Internet economic boom, which happened from 1996 to 1999. Sometimes when you're in the middle of massive change, it feels more like evolution than revolution. You may yet look back on the 2000s as the calm before the big Semantic Web boom of the 2010s: *Who knows?*

Chapter 17

Ten Things to Look Forward to Beyond Web 2.0

In This Chapter

▶ Developing better searching, browsing, and social networks

▶ Moving toward less obnoxious advertising

▶ Seeing a giant database in the sky

▶ Explaining the Semantic Web to your grandma

Web 2.0 is still all the rage, and to be fair, there may yet be a few years to go in the love affair happening with the digitally enabled and their social networks. Web sites like Facebook, Twitter, and Digg will continue to bring people together with the Web as a medium. However, with the rise of the Semantic Web, you will certainly witness the next generation of the Web — Web 3.0 if you please — and a new capacity for your machines to become more autonomous and to act on your behalf without any participation of your friends and acquaintances that are part of your online social connections.

This shift to Web 3.0 will be gradual and slow. If you've discovered anything by flipping through this book, it's that the Semantic Web is not for dummies. It takes skilled hands and bright ideas to enable the Semantic Web to seem easy and to simplify your life rather than confuse it. More and more applications that you use on the Web and at work will begin to adopt Semantic Web data. Eventually there will be such a critical mass of software applications producing RDF and OWL that tasks that seem impossible today will be taken for granted in just a few years. In this chapter, I show you what might be on that horizon.

More Cool Features on the Web Sites and Browsers You Already Use

Here are just a few of the compelling new features being brought to you today by the Semantic Web technology:

✔ **Search:** The single most used application in a Web browser is search. Unfortunately, searching can sometimes take a lot of time before you find just the right data you need. But what if you searched and the data you needed came back on the first search results page? That's what Yahoo! SearchMonkey is aiming to do by using Semantic Web metadata with partners and developers. Today, if you search for the name of a restaurant in San Francisco, you see the Yelp rating for that restaurant and a phone number. As time progresses, more and more data may be directly accessible directly from the search results page, which would mean you would spend less time clicking around trying to find stuff.

✔ **News pages:** News pages are another popular destination for most people. Sure, the standard news sites let you customize your news page to create content areas that are filled with content they place there — usually by a category that they pick. Things got a little better with RSS (another RDF Semantic Web application, albeit a simple one) because you can now subscribe to a set of feeds and have them appear in a particular place. But RSS still doesn't let you define content categories that are different than what your news site lets you choose. With more and more news sites shifting to a Semantic Web approach, like what Thomson Calais provides, you may one day be able to fully customize both the layout and category rules of your news homepage.

✔ **Travel:** If you travel a lot, you probably do a majority of your bookings online. Even if you use a travel portal like Expedia or Orbitz, you're very likely to occasionally use the Web site of a particular company. United Airlines, Marriott, and other travel companies usually offer more rewards for booking on their Web sites because they want your business directly. Therefore, you end up with a travel itinerary that has been booked in three or four different systems. New Semantic Web companies like TripIt are aiming to make your life easier by understanding all those different itineraries and merging them into a single, much more useful itinerary that you can travel with.

✔ **Bookmarks:** When I browse the Web, I rarely have the time to bookmark everything that's interesting to me, much less provide a well-organized category system for organizing those bookmarks. The conventional browser system just doesn't cut it for me. Why doesn't somebody make a plug-in that just watches what I browse and automatically organizes old and new content based on what I do and what others like me do? Adaptive Blue does. Its browser plug-in is a semantics-based bookmarking plug-in that injects a bit of intelligence in how the browser maintains your links, actions, and content.

✔ **Social networks:** Taking this idea of interest networking to the next level, a whole range of new social networks based on Semantic Web technologies are emerging. Twine.com is the most popular new interest networking site that looks to move beyond people-to-people connections and onward to people-to-interest connections. The organizing principle on Twine.com is topics that are then connected to other topics and connected to people. These Twines are built using Semantic Web data, which makes them easier to mash-up, remix, and push-out to other people with similar interests that may not have found the content in other areas. In some ways, this is like a popularity contest for content and ideas, not just people and pages.

These are just a few of the compelling new features being brought to you today by the Semantic Web technology. There will be more.

Dramatically More Scalable Digital Knowledge and Machine Intelligence

The Web currently has no intelligence and uses just a tiny fragment of the hypertext ideas promoted more than 70 years ago by Vannevar Bush. But the next generation of the Web, the Semantic Web, will begin to really have intelligence in the structure and format of the data it contains, and more of the kind of rich relationships and linking infrastructure that data on the Web is capable of. Yes, it begins to resemble that giant, distributed database in the sky that the dreamers still envision. But today the Web is still grounded in vast piles of HTML and millions of databases behind HTTP Web servers.

The Semantic Web enables graph data to be connected to other data regardless of distance, at very deep and fine-grained levels, and with the accuracy and correctness that we expect from good databases. These data graphs span many Web servers and usher in an era of open data that is linked together for anybody and everybody to use in the software they need on their own computers. It will literally be the database on the network that everybody can use.

What the Semantic Web provides technically are the protocols and formats for sound data organization. These protocols allow developers to specify object-oriented type inheritance on Web-based data models, sameAs pointers on Web-based data models, transitivity for basic reasoning, and set-based operators like unions and intersections on Web-based data models. Yes, this will evolve into a dramatically more scalable and pervasive form of database and machine intelligence than could have ever come from a single company.

The broader community, the Semantic Web community, is the open, democratic, and self-organizing community that is bringing this new kind of Web database into reality at Web scale on open, standard graph data formats. No, it isn't perfect today and nor will it ever be, but the basic essentials are intact, and there's plenty of evidence that the open global knowledge being placed in RDF and OWL formats will survive and thrive in the royalty-free public domain where they're being placed.

For evidence, you need only look to the Linking Open Data project hosted by the W3C, where hundreds of organizations are placing their RDF and OWL data on the Web and making it interoperable with the basic standards for linking open data. Projects like DBpedia and Freebase look to organize the world's content into RDF browse-able formats and place the data on a cloud of servers (such as Amazon's A9) for you to make your own Semantic Web application.

Widespread Embedding in Enterprise Software

The Semantic Web is all about making data easier to work with, and this fact is not lost on the companies that build business software. Business applications are all about the data, and any competitive edge that a vendor can supply in an application will eventually be added if there's a profit to be had. Businesses like Oracle, SAP, IBM, and Microsoft supply the vast majority of the world's business software systems. These vendors are shipping products today that use RDF or OWL in some way. Some of these vendors have already made architectural commitments to Semantic Web formats that will change the way their applications are built and delivered.

The Semantic Web may not be widely publicized by these major vendors in the short term, but the RDF and OWL technology will be under the hood of most business applications in ten years. The use of the Semantic Web in business systems may not be sexy, and it might be exclusively used as only a metadata language; however, it will be selected because it is a purpose-built metadata language that excels at being flexible and defining very rich relationships between data.

The Web vision for the Semantic Web may always be at odds with business software. Because the ideals of open data, open source, and free software often run counter to a business's needs for security, reliability, and control, don't expect the Semantic Web to change the profit-orientation of businesses or motivate organizations to change course on their business systems. Instead, I'm suggesting that the technical aspects of the Semantic Web stand on their own merits quite separately from the social and global benefits of the Semantic Web vision as a whole.

In ten years, look for more than 50 percent of new business applications to be leveraging RDF or OWL as metadata formats inside the system — "powered by Semantic Web."

New Semantic Web Technical Standards

Semantic Web technologies are still evolving and at a very early stage. As a point of fact, the W3C technology stack is still incomplete, full applications can't be built using the Semantic Web alone, and the standards as they exist today may not fulfill the final Semantic Web vision anyway. The area of knowledge representation (KR) is clearly the core of the Semantic Web, and in that area, there's still a ways to go to reach its fullest potential.

Newer query languages are evolving to extend SPARQL with operators that can take advantage of more reasoning capabilities from the engines that deliver RDF and OWL. Newer business rule standards like SWRL and the outcomes from the W3C RIF (rule interchange format) group will deeply influence how the Semantic Web stores and distributes digital knowledge as part of RDF and OWL formats. Likewise, new extensions will reach into other domains like Web services, databases, UML, and Web languages to include Semantic Web metadata in areas that desperately need a higher level of formality to their metadata uses. If there's one thing you can be sure of, it's that the Semantic Web standards will keep changing and growing.

Greater Expressivity for Core Languages

One area to expect more changes is in the reach of RDF and OWL to take on more conventional software engineering challenges. Because RDF tooling will get simpler and easier to use, there will be ongoing demand for RDF languages to go in new directions. As a data language, OWL will become both simpler and more expressive in ways that makes it easier to use productively on real-world problems. The existing work to specify the OWL 2.0 standard is the first step in this multistep process. Including support for new OWL fragments (described in Chapter 10) will make it easier for data models to be portable and extensible into new logic framework. Other new extensions will make it easier to work with common modeling and inference requirements that arise when building conventional software applications. These expressivity enhancements will be a continuously evolving process during the entire future of the Semantic Web.

Simple-to-Use Tools for Launching Your Own Personal Ontology

There are many possible users of the Semantic Web, each with different needs and desires. Here are a few examples:

✔ Web site developers may want to annotate their Web pages with Semantic Web metadata that improves the usability of their content within search results like Yahoo! SearchMonkey.

✔ Application developers may want to use RDF as a more flexible alternative to XML for their application metadata.

✔ Casual users of social networking sites like Facebook and LinkedIn might want to build a single personal profile that they can use to link and network with people regardless of which social network they belong to.

✔ Casual users of interest networking sites like Twine might want to create a personal ontology of their interests and use that to link with others who share a common profile.

✔ Integration developers and architects could use ontologies as a way of creating hierarchies, vocabularies, and other metadata that is important when linking business applications together.

✔ Corporate librarians at big companies may need to publish business vocabularies that can be consumed by people and applications that streamline business processes.

No matter which community you might envision that needs the ability to make new ontologies, the future will bring ever simpler ways to create and share the richly structured metadata like RDF and OWL that connect things, places, people, interests, and business data.

Developers Scrambling to Take Semantic Web Training

The groundswell since 2004 has been slow but steady: The beginnings of widespread developer adoption are here today. Looking at the job boards, it's easy to see that Semantic Web jobs are already in high demand, well paying, and could be recession-proof because they're inherently spots that are hard to fill. Existing training classes offered for the Semantic Web from several suppliers have been booked to capacity, growing every year since they've launched.

Increasingly, developers are starting to use the Semantic Web as a way to distinguish themselves from the pack. Regardless of the global economy or technology trends, look for the Semantic Web to provide some uniquely distinguishing skills for new software engineers to gravitate toward. The mad rush for training may not be proportional to the rush for HTML training in 1995 and Java training in 1998, but you should definitely expect a spike of developers asking about, "How do I get trained on RDF?"

Semantic Advertising and Marketing Schemes

Because the Semantic Web is all about meaning, it seems obvious to many that it can be a potential boon for advertising companies to get onboard. As it turns out, it's not quite that simple. In fact, there are potentially several ways to make money by injecting Semantic Web technology into the advertising business:

✔ **Targeted ads:** New Semantic Web startups are beginning to use semantic technology to determine the context and placements of ads: Some people are calling this *semantic advertising*. Ad networks such as Peer39 and Ad Pepper Media's iSense stress their use of semantic technology as a competitive advantage in this area of semantic advertising. In general, both companies use semantic technology for natural language processing, entity extraction, and some simple inferencing. Ad Pepper Media iSense goes a bit further with the use of an extensive ontology of terms that help contextualize ad placement.

From one point of view, iSense is quite distinct from the emerging natural language, algorithmic-based semantic classification systems. A team of 40 linguists and lexicographers has spent some four years assigning words from a dictionary to a framework of knowledge categories. The core of the system roughly mirrors some of the ideas inherent in the Semantic Web around word-sense disambiguation. (Is a search for "bug" about cars or insects?) This notion of sense-disambiguation is why simple statistical algorithms used by most add networks, such as looking for high-frequency keywords, don't work very well. The iSense approach is to analyze and understand all the words on a page, not just to identify better or more keywords. By profiling and categorizing the whole page using linguistics, iSense hopes that a more complete picture of the various content themes on a page becomes actionable.

In addition to the linguistic analysis of page content, site publishers may also add metadata to their sites via a bottom-up approach using RDF, RDFa, and eRDF tags and/or microformats. This labor-intensive approach will happen only when the business incentives for doing so are compelling enough. At that point, the metadata could be used to increase the accuracy of ad placements.

✔ **Applied semantic search:** A second big area for advertising with Semantic Web is in the area of applied semantic search. A new cadre of semantic search engines like Hakia, Cognizant, Microsoft Powerset, and others are beginning to use Semantic Web to aid in category and context-based searches. These approaches are gaining some significant traction particularly in vertical domain searches, like law and medicine, where the meaning of words and relationships can be disambiguated relatively easily.

Like most every search engine, the business model for these new semantic search engines ends up being advertising. Companies that advertise in a semantic search engine may ultimately end up bidding on concepts and relationships rather than keywords or phrases. The jury is still out on whether these new vertical search engines can really displace Google or Yahoo!, or instead maybe remain viable in narrower specialty areas. Indeed, perhaps Yahoo! or Google will acquire the technology as Microsoft has done and expand its already massive businesses into the semantic search areas.

✔ **Use of dynamic content:** A third area of interest for advertisers is in the use of dynamic content placed directly from their own IT departments and marketing teams. Unlike the model where an ad company manages the placement of your predefined content, this model lets you change things on the fly. RAMP Digital has applied this concept to dynamically feeding content into interactive Flash ads. The idea is that an advertiser, usually an online a retailer, can expose its latest offers as semantic data, and then the creative person or agency who makes an interactive ad can use the data in real time to dynamically change the context or placement of the ad accordingly.

One key benefit is that as advertisements become more data-rich, or more diverse as part of a larger campaign, this makes the job of maintaining and keeping them fresh much more manageable. This approach could be even more powerful if the data format of these ads were standardized across multiple ad placement companies, perhaps even across multiple industries. Eventually, a marketer could create appealing ads while remaining decoupled from the company that is producing the data. This approach could also enable "mashup ads" that pull data from multiple online sources. Of course, the ownership and intellectual property laws would have to catch up once this started!

✔ **Sponsored placements:** As the Semantic Web data becomes more pervasive, it's inevitable that companies will pay to have their content ranked higher and found easier than other content. Just like linked ads are sorted first on Google and Yahoo!, you may find that querying the Semantic Web yields paid sponsors first. This method hopefully won't bother you too much because the content is much more likely to be useful than current paid spots on the search engines. For instance, if you were to do a search for a restaurant in San Francisco and you got not only reviews from Yelp but also coupons a la the Semantic Web, that'd be pretty neat, wouldn't it?

It's still too early to tell whether anybody's going to get very wealthy on Semantic Web–based advertising, but you can easily see that a lot of people are working hard in the area. A number of potential uses for semantics enhance the existing online advertising business models, but others will require more general uptake of the Semantic Web to really be successful. One thing is for sure: You're very likely to be marketed to online with ever more sophisticated techniques, and the Semantic Web will be a part of that — hopefully for the better!

Technology Managers Planning for New Supporting Workflows

After the rise of the Web 2.0 in the mid-2000s, IT workers rushed to plan activity around the notion of Enterprise 2.0 and how the business organization would change with the impact of new technologies. Similarly, as the ideas of Semantic Web start to take off, we'll see more and more IT managers asking themselves the question, "What do I need to be doing to get ready for the Semantic Web?" Various aspects of the typical IT director responsibilities may be directly influenced by the Semantic Web:

- Intranet
- Portals
- Search engine optimization (SEO)
- Systems integration planning and metadata management
- Collaboration software
- Knowledge worker productivity

You may or may not witness the same levels of urgency that other technologies have spurred, but over the next few years, you will continue to see more and more IT managers looking to plan for the use of semantics in their everyday jobs.

Explaining Web 3.0 to Your Grandmother

Yes, if it takes off the way it might, there's a pretty decent chance that your grandmother may ask you about the Semantic Web during the next few years. The software industry is notoriously faddish, and nowadays the new, hip technology that's popular in software communities has a way of going mainstream.

Already there have been articles in *Business Week, Newsweek, Forbes,* and *The Economist* about the Semantic Web. Although your grandma may not read those magazines, it's not too hard to imagine that the next wave of Semantic Web news coverage may find its way to *People* magazine or your local newspapers. So, how will you answer the question when your grandmother asks you, "Honey, what is all this Semantic Web stuff about?"

Why not try a simple answer like, "The Semantic Web is a new computer language for describing all the knowledge that people could ever save in books or computers. It lets programmers connect facts and ideas that would otherwise be located in all sorts of different places, making it much easier for people to find things they need even though there is so much information in the world"?

That may not be the best definition of the Semantic Web, but it might be one that your grandmother could understand and appreciate. If you have a technologically savvy grandma and she asks you, "Isn't that what Google is for?" you can reply, "Sort of, but Google just helps people find words in documents, whereas the Semantic Web helps people find ideas and concepts in any kind of data." If your grandmother is *very* curious and she asks you what the difference is between finding words and finding ideas, just buy her a copy of this book!

Chapter 18

Ten Next Steps to Take from Here

Say that by now, you're convinced that the Semantic Web is a game-changer. But where do you go from here? This book isn't your final destination for learning the Semantic Web: It's only the first step. This chapter lays out some different paths for bettering your personal understanding of all these new formats, architectures, and ideas that you've grown familiar with.

Try Twine

If you've made it this far into the book and haven't gone out and tried a Semantic Web application, by all means, do so now! Twine is an interest network that continuously catalogs things you might be interested in and connects you to them. Originally conceived by Nova Spivak's Radar Networks, Twine (www.twine.com) aimed to supply a new era of power and features to the social networking Internet craze. However, as the Twine beta progressed and the true potential of the technology became more apparent, it was clear that the underlying technology of Twine could do much more than connect people with tags. Instead, the real genius of Twine is its ability to connect you to people and interests just by watching your behavior on the site. Twine has an uncanny way of knowing what you'll be interested in, and it gets better every time you use it. Go try it now!

Explore Yahoo! SearchMonkey

If you've used Yahoo! Search since the middle of 2008, you're already a user of the Semantic Web — albeit in a small way. Yahoo! has been incorporating the use of SearchMonkey metadata (RDFa, microformats, and so on) to enhance your search results page and make it easier to find what you're looking for.

In fact, the easiest way to see the Semantic Web in action is to try a search on Yahoo! (www.yahoo.com) for a specific restaurant in a city. For example, try searching for one of my favorites by using the search terms *"slanted door san francisco"*). You'll most likely see restaurant ratings, phone numbers, and other interesting data provided by Yelp.com, CitySearch.com, and others in the actual body of your search results — that's a simple example of the Semantic Web mashup in action. The search engine may give you what you need without you having to browse to the page and look for it, saving you effort.

Aside from just using Yahoo! for semantic searches, why not develop your own SearchMonkey extensions? If you already maintain a Web site of any kind, you can create your own extensions that Yahoo! can use during a search. Web sites such as StumbleUpon enable Yahoo! to show Web page ratings in the search result, and other sites such as BlogSpot enable Yahoo! Search to show the Top 10 most recent blog posts for a given search right in the search page. You can do the same with your pages if you want to have people get more when they find you from Yahoo! For more information about developing SearchMonkey extensions, go to http://developer.yahoo.com/searchmonkey/.

Check Out Calais

Calais isn't a consumer Web site that just anybody use, but if you've ever had an urge to build your own mashup and you need to find a service to help you build applications, give Calais a try. In fact, if you're really serious about building cool applications that require data from all sorts of different places, Calais, shown in Figure 18-1, may be your killer app. You can use Calais to grab unstructured data from just about anywhere and turn it into very useful structured data that can be placed on your own application in any way you choose. By now, the value should be obvious; Calais makes unstructured data accessible and usable to anybody who needs it.

Calais uses *linguistic parsing* (also known as *entity extraction*) in a mass-market, service-enabled way to produce RDF triples and Semantic Web data models. The Semantic Web is essential to Calais' value proposition because that's how the data can be so easily repurposed, remixed, and mashed up.

The fourth release of Calais goes beyond the ability to extract semantic data from your content to link that extracted semantic data to datasets from dozens of other information sources such as Wikipedia, Freebase, and the

CIA World Fact Book. Instead of being limited to the linguistic associations found in the content of the document(s) that you're processing, you can develop extensive applications that leverage large and rapidly growing open-source information resources.

Calais is a substantial enabler for the Linking Open Data initiative and is helping to make that "giant database in the sky" vision come to reality.

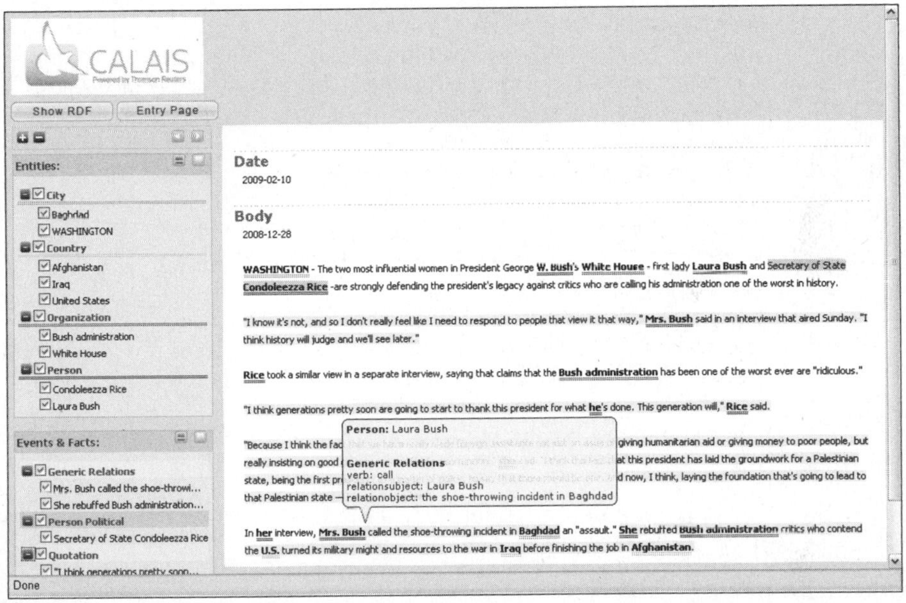

Figure 18-1:
A look at
what Calais
can do
with your
unstruc-
tured text.

Read Up on RDF and OWL Modeling or Attend Training

This book is a broad and comprehensive look at the Semantic Web, but it isn't a deep treatise on how to code with RDF and OWL or how to apply best practices for ontology modeling. A book that I've found quite useful for hands-on projects is *Semantic Web for the Working Ontologist: Effective Modeling in RDFS and OWL* by Dean Allemang and James Hendler (published by Morgan Kaufmann).

A number of good, hands-on Semantic Web courses are offered by reputable consulting firms like TopQuadrant, Semantic Arts, and Zepheira. Here are some example Semantic Web courses offered by Zepheira (http://zepheira.com/solutions/Training/) at the time of this publication:

- **Introduction to Semantic Web Technologies (2 days):** This course is a comprehensive tour of the Semantic Web Technology stack, the vision, and related technologies. The focus is on the individual W3C standards, what they bring to the table, and how to consume and produce them.

- **Applied Semantic Web Technologies (3 days):** This course is designed for students comfortable with the vision of how Semantic Web technologies fit together but who want practice doing so with specific applications.

- **Semantic Technology Bootcamp (5 days):** This course is a fast-paced and comprehensive (but accessible) introduction to semantic technologies and how to apply them in the enterprise. Although it starts with an introduction to the vision, it is appropriate for groups or individuals who know they need to get up to speed quickly and want real examples and strategies for successful adoption in their systems.

- **Data Architect Bootcamp (5 days):** This course is a combination of ideas from the Semantic, Resource-oriented, and XML offerings to provide a comprehensive roadmap for data architects and stewards to successfully and efficiently offer an organization access to its own data. It covers proven strategies for data production, accessibility, transformation, and provenance in the face of ever-changing requirements and business needs. Additionally, this approach includes being able to integrate across data sources including relational databases, RDF graphs, Web pages, Excel spreadsheets, RSS feeds, and so on.

I recommend taking any of these courses before you start on a commercial project aimed at leveraging the Semantic Web.

Read the RDF and OWL Specifications

Yes, I know . . . reading a computer language specification isn't the most exciting thing you're likely to have on your calendar for the weekend. But if you really want to get to the crux of a particular topic and move beyond a given vendor implementation, or simply to have your deepest burning questions answered about the Semantic Web, there's no substitute for reading the source of truth for it all. Here are some of the most important specifications:

- Resource Description Framework (RDF) (www.w3.org/RDF)

- Web Ontology Language (OWL) (www.w3.org/2004/OWL)

- Simple Protocol and RDF Query Language (SPARQL) (www.w3.org/TR/rdf-sparql-query)

- RDF Annotations (RDFa) (www.w3.org/TR/rdfa-syntax)

- ✔ Rule Interchange Format (RIF) (www.w3.org/2005/rules/wiki/RIF_Working_Group)
- ✔ Semantic Annotations for Web Service Description Language (SAWSDL) (www.w3.org/2002/ws/sawsdl)
- ✔ Gleaning Resource Descriptions from Dialects of Language (GRDDL) (www.w3.org/2001/sw/grddl-wg)

These W3C languages form the foundation of the Semantic Web and define its usage across many other areas of interest, such as Web services and XML.

Contact Your Trusted Vendors

If you happen to be a professional who works with software vendors already, your existing software vendors can be a great place to get more information. But usually, you have to find the right people to ask, and you may have to work with several people to find the best Semantic Web contact point to answer your questions. Here are a few vendors and hints to get you started:

- ✔ **Microsoft:** Try asking for the Media Management software group. The group has used an embedded RDF database that runs on Microsoft SQL Server. (www.microsoft.com/)
- ✔ **IBM:** Ask for the Almaden Research Labs, or the WebSphere Registry and Repository software team. Both groups in IBM have substantial experience working with RDF and OWL. (www.ibm.com)
- ✔ **Oracle:** With more than 250,000 customers, Oracle knows a few things about databases. You can visit the Oracle homepage for semantic technology, ask for the Spatial Database software team, or use the e-mail address I give in this book's Introduction and ask me for pointers. (www.oracle.com/technology/tech/semantic_technologies/)

Write Down and Assess New Ideas

One of the single best ways that I can recommend you move forward to make progress is to write down your ideas. Putting thoughts to paper forces you to see their weaknesses and gives you opportunities to improve your ideas. Make some drawings by hand, turn them into PowerPoint, and transfer your notes into a technology vision paper or business plan.

Many Semantic Web businesses started just this way, with a few notes and a picture on the back of a napkin.

Before you talk to your vendors, look for funding, or speak with your boss, you must first think through the business and technical risks. Remember that the Semantic Web is new and scary to many people: The conservative first reaction is to see big risks, big worries, and to move on to safer projects. Work hard to frame your ideas in terms of the benefits you can create, and be very detailed and explicit about how you think the Semantic Web helps you get there.

Most people make a judgment about your idea within the first few seconds of your pitch. If you don't pass this critical "sniff test," you may not get the chance to try again!

Ask Zepheira

You've probably never heard of Zepheira before: It is a niche consultancy with a disproportionately large big brain trust. Its key partners are long-time leaders of the Semantic Web standards and veteran entrepreneurs who have each seen several Semantic Web startup businesses come and go. With the lessons learned from successes and failures, it may provide the critical input you need to succeed the first time around.

The folks at Zepheira are also the minds and hands behind many open-source Semantic Web tools. These newer open-source tools are starting to level the playing field for startups that can't afford expensive software and are looking to use highly advanced free software built on community principles.

Most importantly, the founders of Zepheira are community activists who love to solve big problems with Semantic Web technologies. Usually the folks at Zepheira are willing to listen to new ideas and offer advice for people looking to learn more about the space. When it comes to action, both for-profit and non-profit projects are equally as interesting to Zepheira, and Zepheira is quite willing to help on projects that have big paybacks for the community at large.

Prototype Using Open-Source and Free Software

If you've got a little bit of hacker in you, you no doubt want to jump right in and start trying things now. Earlier in this chapter, I mention the Yahoo! SearchMonkey developer Web site, but going further into the core technology might require that you start looking at Semantic Web infrastructure. Here's a list of some software that you can get a hold of to starting trying things out:

- ✔ **Sesame:** Open-source API for RDF data persistence and more (`www.openrdf.org`)

- ✔ **Oracle:** Most popular commercial database in the world supports RDF/OWL, available freely under the Oracle Technology Network license agreement (`www.oracle.com/technology/tech/semantic_technologies/index.html`)

- ✔ **Jena:** Extremely popular API/Framework for working with RDF, available freely under the Hewlett-Packard license agreement (`http://jena.sourceforge.net`)

- ✔ **Calais:** Thomson Reuters' free entity-extraction service, free for most uses under the Thomson Reuters license agreement (`www.opencalais.com`)

- ✔ **Mulgara:** Open-source RDF database (`www.mulgara.org`)

- ✔ **Pellet:** Open-source OWL reasoner (`http://pellet.owldl.com`)

Hundreds more open-source and free Semantic Web software tools are available: These are just some of the more popular ones that I've had personal, positive experiences with.

Sell Your Boss on the Idea!

Selling your boss on the Semantic Web is probably more difficult than explaining it to your grandmother! (See Chapter 17.) For your grandma, you have to keep things simple, but the challenge with your boss is to simplify it *just* enough while still making clear how your company could really benefit from the Semantic Web.

Chapter 3 is almost entirely focused on making that business case. Try re-reading that for some ideas, and really focus on talking to your boss about the costs of *not* innovating. The best advice I can give you is to find a way for you to start small, show incremental progress, and spend a lot of time listening to your management to understand what their biggest issues really are.

Index

• X •

X12 vocabulary, 147
XACML (eXtensible Access Control Markup
 Language), 56, 145–146
XHTML pages, embedding in. *See* eRDF;
 GRDDL; microformats; RDFa
XHTML pages, extracting from, 175–176
XML (eXtensible Markup Language)
 as governing schema, 121
 inflexibility, enterprise-level, 60
 metadata, 120, 125–126
 misuse and shortcomings, 64–65
 not designed for data, 110–111, 116
 purpose within Semantic Web, 227
 relationship with RDF, 159, 160–163
 typical relationship types, 122
.xml files, 162
XML Schema, 297–298

XML Spy SemanticWorks (Altova), 233–234
xmlns prefix (RDF), 72, 81
XSD data model, 107, 108, 110, 120

• Y •

Yahoo!. *See also* SearchMonkey
 Open Strategy (Y!OS), 346
 Search (search engine), 22, 32, 39
YASNS (Yet Another Social Networking
 Service), 41

• Z •

Zemanta (semantic blog), 36
Zepheira, 389–390, 392
Zitgist (search engine), 39
ZoomInfo (Web site), 33, 350–351

Ready to learn more about Semantic Web?

The Semantic
Technology Conference

SemTech, the Semantic Technology Conference, is the annual conference addressing the commercialization of semantic technologies. Focusing on existing applications and case studies, how-to hands-on tutorials, product reports, and putting you in direct contact with industry thought leaders, SemTech has become THE annual gathering for people interested in Semantic Technologies *since 2004*.

$100
OFF

We are pleased to offer you a special **"Dummies Discount"** of $100 off your registration fee for SemTech.

To claim your discount, visit:
http://semantic-conference.com/SemanticWebForDummies

Want to **EXPLORE** even more?

semantic
universe

Educating the World About Semantic Technologies & Applications

The best online resource for ongoing information and education about Semantic Technologies is the Semantic Universe Network, a vibrant online community and communications hub for the global semantic technology marketplace. The Semantic Universe Network is the professional and educational resource for the people, companies, editorial content, events, products, advertising, research and initiatives within the high-growth semantics sector. The Network was developed and deployed on a sophisticated semantic application platform to facilitate the highest level of user engagement, contextual relevancy and editorial resource matching. At Semantic Universe, you will find:

- Blogs
- Webcasts
- Articles
- Audio & Video archives

- Product Listings
- Community Directories
- Educational Resources
- Live Events and Meetings

FREE MEMBERSHIP

MEMBERSHIP is FREE!
Join today at: http://semanticuniverse.com/SemanticWebForDummies